CORSICA

JEAN-BERNARD CARILLET
MILES RODDIS, NEIL WILSON

CORSICA

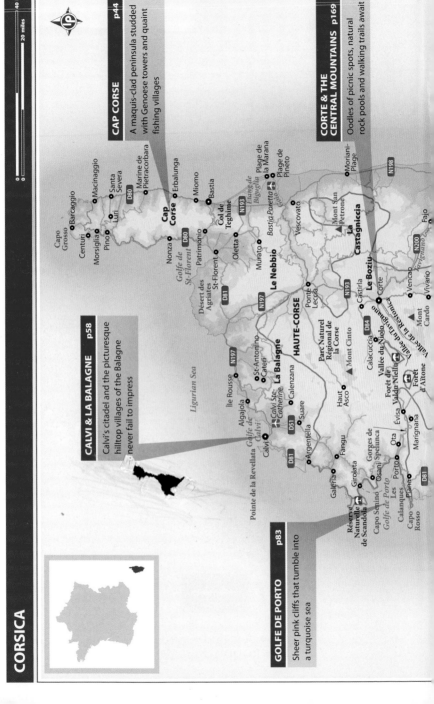

CALVI & LA BALAGNE **p58**

Calvi's citadel and the picturesque hilltop villages of the Balagne never fail to impress

CAP CORSE **p44**

A maquis-clad peninsula studded with Genoese towers and quaint fishing villages

CORTE & THE CENTRAL MOUNTAINS **p169**

Oodles of picnic spots, natural rock pools and walking trails await

GOLFE DE PORTO **p83**

Sheer pink cliffs that tumble into a turquoise sea

40 km
20 miles

Ligurian Sea

Capo Grosso
Barcaggio
Macinaggio
Santa Severa
Centuri
Morsiglia
Pino
Luri
Marine de Pietracorbara
Cap Corse
Erbalunga
Miomo
Bastia
Marina
Nonza
Golfe de St-Florent
Patrimonio
St-Florent
Col de Teghime
Oletta
Murato
Plage de la Marana
Plage de Pineto
Etang de Biguglia
Bastia Poretta
Vescovato
Moriani-Plage
Desert des Agriates
Le Nebbio
Ponte Leccia
Mont San Petrone
La Castagniccia
Le Boziu
Venaco
Vivario
Fajo
N198
N200
île Rousse
Algajola
St-Antonino
Cateri
Calenzana
Calvi
Golfe de Calvi
Calvi Ste-Catherine
Suare
La Balagne
Pointe de la Revellata
HAUTE-CORSE
Parc Naturel Régional de la Corse
Mont Cinto
Haut Asco
Calacuccia
Calvi
Corte
Castirla
Mont Cardo
Vallée du Niolo
Vallée de la Restonica
Vallée du Tavignano
Forêt de Valdu Niellu
Forêt d'Altone
Évisa
Marignana
Ota
Porto
Piana
Capo Rosso
Capo Senino
Golfe de Porto
Les Calanques
Gorges de Spelunca
Osani
Fangu
Girolata
Galéria
Argentella
Réserve Naturelle de Scandola

N197
D80
D81
D51
D84
N193
N197
D81

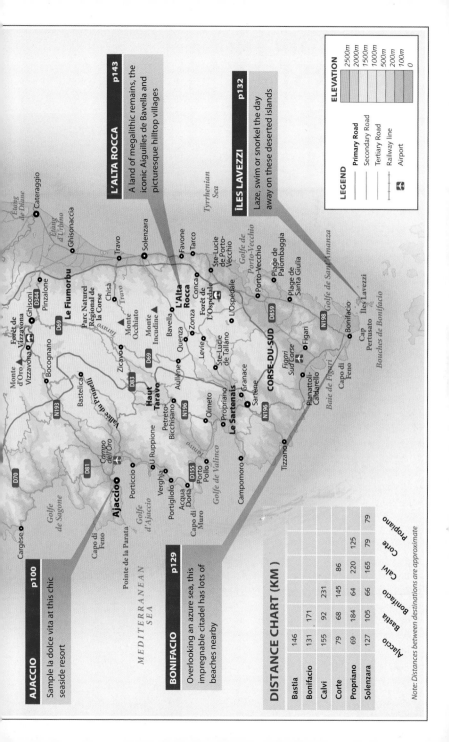

AJACCIO p100

Sample la dolce vita at this chic seaside resort

L'ALTA ROCCA p143

A land of megalithic remains, the iconic Aiguilles de Bavella and picturesque hilltop villages

ÎLES LAVEZZI p132

Laze, swim or snorkel the day away on these deserted islands

BONIFACIO p129

Overlooking an azure sea, this impregnable citadel has lots of beaches nearby

ELEVATION

2500m
2000m
1500m
1000m
500m
200m
100m
0

LEGEND

Primary Road
Secondary Road
Tertiary Road
Railway line
Airport

DISTANCE CHART (KM)

	Ajaccio	Bastia	Bonifacio	Calvi	Corte	Propriano
Bastia	146					
Bonifacio	131	171				
Calvi	155	92	231			
Corte	79	68	145	86		
Propriano	69	184	64	220	125	
Solenzara	127	105	66	165	79	79

Note: Distances between destinations are approximate

INTRODUCING
CORSICA

FROM RURAL RETREATS AND RUSTIC CUISINE TO CHIC COASTAL RESORTS AND STUNNING BEACHES, THE ISLAND OF CORSICA REALLY PACKS A PUNCH.

Take a stunningly contoured coastline, add pleated mountains, and sprinkle in attractive coastal cities and timeless hilltop villages. Next, pepper the island with historical sights, spike it with a taste-bud-teasing culinary scene and there you have Corsica, L'Île de Beauté (the Isle of Beauty).

First and foremost, get your tan. From showy Plage de Palombaggia to multipurpose Plage de Portigliolo, Corsica rolls out one fabulous beach after another. When you've had enough splashy fun, you'll find amazing things to do on dry land as well. Those mountains looming inward hold adventures all of their own, from thrilling canyoning descents to gentle walks in majestic forests. Wherever you go, opportunities for exploration abound. Drive around remote valleys to find that perfect picnic spot, or take a boat trip to discover unspoilt stretches of coastline. Food lovers will revel in trendy *paillottes* (beach restaurants) serving the freshest of fish, and in snug restaurants featuring Corsican staples. For culture buffs, prehistoric sites and heritage buildings await. It's hard to find a better combination of nature, culture and pleasure.

TOP The stunning setting of Bonifacio (p129) BOTTOM LEFT The awesome mountain pass of Scala di Santa Regina (p179), in the central mountains BOTTOM RIGHT The rocky inlets of Les Calanques (p94), Golfe de Porto

BONIFACIO

CORTE & THE CENTRAL MOUNTAINS

GOLFE DE PORTO

AJACCIO

CALVI & LA BALAGNE

ÎLES LAVEZZI

TOP LEFT The vibrant port of Ajaccio (p100) TOP RIGHT Exploring the waters of the Îles Lavezzi (p132) BOTTOM LEFT Calvi's impressive citadel (p59), as seen from the beach BOTTOM CENTRE Coastline along Cap Corse (p44) BOTTOM RIGHT Walking on Col de Bavella (p148), L'Alta Rocca

CAP CORSE

L'ALTA ROCCA

STÉPHANE VICTOR

GETTING STARTED

CORSICA

WHAT'S NEW?

★ A multipurpose cultural centre near Corte (p175)

★ Sea-kayaking trips around Campomoro (p123) and in the Golfe de Pinarello (p141)

★ A *parc aventure* (adventure park) in the Vallée du Cavu (p141)

★ A refurbished museum in the Alta Rocca (p146)

★ Ecofriendly *gîtes ruraux* (self-contained cottages) near Cervione (p253)

★ A botanical park in Île Rousse (p72)

CLIMATE: AJACCIO

Average Max/Min

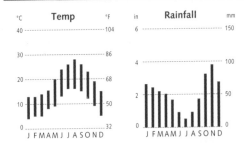

PRICE GUIDE

	BUDGET	MIDRANGE	TOP END
SLEEPING	<€60	€60-140	>€140
EATING	<€15	€15-30	>€30
ACTIVITIES	<€20	€20-50	>€50

MARK WEBSTER

OLIVIER CIRENDINI

TOP Sunrise in the Bavella area (p148) BOTTOM LEFT Large gorgonian, Îles Lavezzi (p132) BOTTOM RIGHT Picturesque Bonifacio (p129) FAR RIGHT Walking the GR20 (p214)

ACCOMMODATION

One of the best features of Corsican tourism is the variety of accommodation options on offer, from rustic *gîtes d'étape* (walkers' lodges) and charming *chambres d'hôtes* (B&Bs) to swish hotels and sophisticated villas. A key factor to consider is the wild difference in price between the high season (July and August) and the rest of the year; during the peak months prices can be jacked up by 100%. Also note that the interior of the island is cheaper than the coast, but options are less varied. For more on accommodation, see p240.

MAIN POINTS OF ENTRY

CAMPO DELL'ORO AIRPORT (AJA; www.ajaccio.aeroport.fr) Ajaccio's airport serves the west. It's 8km from the centre of town.

BASTIA PORETTA AIRPORT (BIA; www.bastia.aeroport.fr) The island's second-most important airport after Ajaccio. Located near Bastia, it's convenient for Cap Corse, St-Florent and eastern Corsica.

FIGARI SUD CORSE AIRPORT (www.figari.aeroport.fr) Located about 20km from Bonifacio and Porto-Vecchio, it's also convenient for Propriano and southern Corsica.

THINGS TO TAKE

* Detailed road maps to tackle those nerve-racking hinterland roads; see p262

* Driving licence, car documents and car insurance

* Lonely Planet's *French* phrasebook

* Walking shoes for the island's oh-so-tempting trails

* A set of smart-casual clothes for that special candlelit dinner

STEPHANE VICTOR

WEBLINKS

L'AGENCE DU TOURISME DE LA CORSE (www.visit-corsica.com) The official tourist-board site.

ALLER EN CORSE (www.allerencorse.com) Accommodation listings and practical information.

PARC NATUREL RÉGIONAL (www.parc-naturel-corse.com) Information on walking.

CORSICA ISULA (www.corsica-isula.com) An exhaustive English-language website.

FESTIVALS & EVENTS

CORSICA

MARCH/APRIL

PROCESSIONS DE LA SEMAINE SAINTE

Easter celebrations include La Cerca (p45) in Erbalunga, U Catenacciu (p125) in Sartène, La Granitola in Calvi and the procession of the Five Orders in Bonifacio.

A MERENDELLA IN CASTAGNICCIA

PIEDICROCE
Festival celebrating regional cuisine; held over the Easter weekend (p159).

MAY/JUNE

FESTIMARE

ÎLE ROUSSE
Celebrates the sea with plenty of fish and seafood specials, plus various amusements. Held late May or early June.

ST-ÉRASME

AJACCIO, BASTIA, CALVI
Nautically themed festivities, boat rides and fishing-boat blessings honour the patron saint of fishermen on 2 June.

FIERA DI U MARE

SOLENZARA
This sea festival held in mid-June features sailing races and seafood-cooking competitions.

CALVI JAZZ FESTIVAL

CALVI
Concerts and jam sessions featuring big names from the international jazz scene take place in late June.

JULY

A NOTTE DI A MEMORIA

BASTIA
A historical re-enactment of the Genoese governor's arrival is held in the citadel; occurs in early July.

NUITS DE LA GUITARE

PATRIMONIO
One of Europe's largest guitar festivals is held in the Nebbio around mid-July (p56).

CALVI ON THE ROCKS

CALVI
Three days of electronic and experimental music; held in mid-July.

TOP Drummers marching through Ajaccio **RIGHT** Procession at the Santa di u Niolo (p180), Casamaccioli

AUGUST

PÈLERINAGE DE NOTRE-DAME-DES-NEIGES

BAVELLA

This pilgrimage to the miracle-working Madonna on Col de Bavella on 5 August draws massive crowds.

FÊTES NAPOLÉONIENNES

AJACCIO

This hugely popular festival celebrating Napoléon's birthday is held in mid-August, and features fireworks, parades and various amusements.

SEPTEMBER

SANTA DI U NIOLO

CASAMACCIOLI

Thousands of pilgrims celebrate the Nativity of the Virgin around 8 September (p180).

RENCONTRES DE CHANTS POLYPHONIQUES

CALVI

Festival of polyphonic singing held at various venues in the citadel. Takes place in mid-September.

TOUR DE CORSE CYCLISTE

A four-day cycling race around the island.

OCTOBER

FESTIVENTU

CALVI

This festival celebrates the role of the wind with hundreds of kites on the beach. It's held in late October.

LES MUSICALES DE BASTIA

BASTIA

Jazz, classical music, dance and theatrical performances.

CULTURE

CORSICA

© BENSLIMAN HASSAN / DREAMSTIME.COM

CHURCHES

CATHÉDRALE ST-ÉRASME
One of Corsica's earliest baroque churches, this has a magnificent organ (p151).

ÉGLISE ST-JEAN BAPTISTE
The most refined example of a baroque church in Corsica (p160).

ÉGLISE STE-MARGUERITE
A landmark in the Castagniccia due to its bell tower and baroque stucco ornamentation (p160).

ÉGLISE ST-DOMINIQUE
A rare example of a Gothic church in Corsica (p131).

CHAPEL OF SAN NICOLAO
In the Boziu, this little Romanesque chapel has magnificent frescos (p181).

ÉGLISE DE SAN MICHELE DE MURATO With its distinctive two-colour banding, this is the most gorgeous Pisan church in Corsica (p57).

ROMANESQUE TO BAROQUE

Possibly the most appealing curiosities on the island's architectural landscape are the delightful 9th- to 11th-century Pisan Romanesque churches of the northwest. Only about 10 survive. Common features are easily discerned: the sober structure of a single nave and no transept; the square-based bell tower; and the typically Tuscan two-tone banding. The most striking Romanesque churches are the Église de San Michele de Murato (p57), and the Cathédrale de la Canonica, south of Bastia. Later came the Genoese, who introduced baroque-style architecture to the island. The most stunning baroque churches can be seen in La Castagniccia; a particularly notable example is in La Porta (p160). The churches all feature splendid church organs and sumptuously decorated interiors, forming a striking contrast to the surrounding landscapes. See p203 for more on religious architecture.

EMILY RIDDELL

TOP Église de San Michele de Murato (p57), near Murato BOTTOM Shopping in Bonifacio (p129) RIGHT Out and about on rue Clemenceau, Calvi (p59) FAR RIGHT Église St-Jean Baptiste (p38), Bastia

TOP MUSEUMS

MUSÉE FESCH France's second-largest collection of Italian paintings. Undergoing renovations at research time (p100).

MAISON BONAPARTE This 19th-century house was Napoléon's birthplace (p102).

MUSÉE DE L'ALTA ROCCA A good introduction to prehistoric Corsica (p146).

MUSÉE DE LA CORSE The most comprehensive museum on the island (p169).

MAISON NATALE DE PASCAL PAOLI Offers an insight into the life of the 'Father of the Land' (p161).

DON'T MISS EXPERIENCES

* Easter celebrations – Corsica's Easter processions are highly colourful (p10)
* Polyphonic chants – The most famous choirs hold performances in churches in summer
* Fresco hunting – Chapels and churches boast some hidden gems
* Buying artisan crafts – The workshops at Pigna are well worth the detour (p78)
* Treasure hunts – Approach locals to solve riddles about Corte's illustrious past (p175)
* Art galleries – Investigate Calvi's showrooms, galleries and workshops (p67)
* Knife making – See master craftspeople fashioning traditional knives (p147)

DOS & DON'TS

* Wear bathing suits on the beach, never in towns or villages
* Don't wear flip-flops or T-shirts in restaurants, cafes or clubs
* Avoid meddling with local politics or criticising the nationalist movements
* Keep your temper – don't use the horn if drivers block the road just to talk
* Be courteous – say *'Bonjour Madame'* or *'Bonjour Monsieur'*

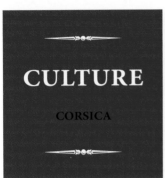

JEFF CANTARUTTI

CULTURE

CORSICA

PREHISTORY

FILITOSA Impressive statues shrouded in mystery (p117).

PIANU DI LEVIE Well-preserved megalithic remains amid an eerie wood (p146).

CAURIA Menhirs and dolmens galore (p126)!

CASTELLU D'ARAGGIO A small complex hidden in the hills (p142).

MUSÉE DE L'ALTA ROCCA Recently upgraded museum that does a good job explaining the island's prehistory and culture (p146).

POLYPHONIC MUSIC

Corsica's unique polyphonic singing is the voice of the island's soul.

A FILETTA (www.afiletta.com) One of Corsica's polyphonic flagships.

JP POLETTI & LES CHOEURS DE SARTÈNE Famous for their gut-wrenching *lamenti* (laments).

JACKY MICAELLI (www.jackymicaelli.com) Considered the best living female vocalist in Corsica.

TAVAGNA (www.tavagna.com) A group that's stayed true to its roots.

I MUVRINI (www.muvrini.com) The stars of Corsican music combine polyphonic vocals with modern instruments.

THE GENOESE LEGACY

Somewhere or other you'll have seen that classic photo of a stately Genoese tower silhouetted on a rocky promontory at sunset. Around 60 of these iconic fortified structures punctuate the coastline, a reminder of centuries of Genoese presence on the island. Dating from the 16th century, they stand today in various states of repair; some of them, such as the Tour de Campomoro (p122), have been wonderfully restored, while others are crumbling away. The most impressive of these stunning structures are to be found around Cap Corse, but southern Corsica and the west coast also boast some superb examples. See p46 for more information.

TOP Menhir statues, Filitosa (p117) RIGHT Corsica contains numerous villages dotted throughout the countryside

SONS OF CORSICA

A great soldier, Sampiero Corso (1498–1567; p191) became known as 'the most Corsican of Corsicans' and fought with French forces against the Genoese occupiers. He secured control of most of the island in 1564, but was finally defeated in a typical Corsican blood feud after he strangled his wife. Pascal Paoli (p193), Corsica's revolutionary leader, headed Corsica during its short period of independence between 1755 and 1769; Corsicans call him the Babbu di a Patria (Father of the Land). He gave Corsica a democratic constitution that inspired that of the United States of America. Though he was Corsica's most famous son, Napoléon (1769–1821; p196) had ambivalent feelings about his homeland and paid scant attention to Corsica during his period of power.

HILLTOP VILLAGES

Traditional Corsican culture can be explored in hamlets scattered through the countless valleys and spurs that slice up the island's dramatic scenery.

* Deep in the Alta Rocca, Zonza is blessed with a fabulous backdrop – the awesome Aiguilles de Bavella (p144).

* Lama is a fairy-tale hamlet with fine mansions and Italianate palazzi (p79).

* Cap Corse's prettiest village, Nonza, clings to the flanks of a rocky pinnacle (p48).

* The splendidly isolated hamlet of Tralonca, in Le Boziu, is served by twisting mountain roads (p181).

OLIVIER CIRENDINI

FOOD & DRINK

CORSICA

JEAN-BERNARD CARILLET

LOCAL PRODUCE

CHARCUTERIE Corsica is famous for its flavoursome cured meats, made from free-range pigs that feed on chestnuts.

CHEESE The island has cheese-making down to a fine art.

OLIVE OIL La Balagne and L'Alta Rocca produce extremely aromatic olive oils.

HONEY Corsican honey is produced from bees that feed exclusively on the wildflowers of the maquis.

WINES & LIQUEURS Corsica has nine Appellation d'Origine Contrôlée (AOC) wines and countless fruit liqueurs.

SEAFOOD Lobster, oysters, squid, sea bass, mussels…Corsica has them all.

CHARCUTERIE

In Corsica, charcuterie has been elevated to an art form. Connoisseurs swear by the *porcu nustrale*, the Corsican pig breed also known as *porcu neru* (black pig); the finest Corsican charcuterie derives its flavour from the pigs' diet of acorns and chestnuts. Wherever you go, you'll find a wide array of cured meats on offer. The most sought-after produce is *prisuttu* (dry ham), which has an unforgettable hazelnut taste. *Lonzu* (tender smoked fillet), cut into thin slices, makes for a wonderful appetiser, while *salamu* (salami-style sausage) is perfect picnic fodder. *Coppa* (shoulder) has a bit more fat than *lonzu* but tastes equally good. In winter, *figatellu* (liver sausage) is eaten grilled. And let's not forget *terrine de sanglier* (wild-boar pâté), usually flavoured with myrtle. Charcuterie can be purchased in speciality shops; see p231 for more information. *Buon appititu!*

OLIVIER CIRENDINI

TOP Meat cooking on an open fire BOTTOM Cured meat RIGHT Corsica supports a thriving fishing industry FAR RIGHT Fresh seafood

TOP INNS

U FRAGNU The specialities at this atmospheric inn couldn't be more Corsican (p181).

A MANDRIA DE SÉBASTIEN Traditional Corsican cuisine in a chic rustic cottage (p167).

LE MOULIN FARELLACCI A gargantuan Corsican menu and fantastic Corsican music (p118).

A PIGNATA A scrumptious seven-course meal and million-dollar views (p147).

U TARAVU Home-cured charcuterie and local cheeses are a taste-bud feast (p110).

OLIVIER CIRENDINI

OLIVIER CIRENDINI

DON'T MISS EXPERIENCES

* Purchasing local products – Stock up on cheese, charcuterie and jams

* Splurging in an *auberge* – Devour traditional dishes at a local inn

* Sampling seafood – Taste a bounteous range of marine offerings at a seafood restaurant

* A meal in a *paillotte* – Lunch at a sand-in-your-toes beach restaurant

* Wine tasting – Tour the best Corsican domaines to find that perfect rosé

* Food fairs – Mingle with local farmers at a country fair

PRODUCE SHOPS

L'ORRIU Porto-Vecchio institution selling top-quality local specialities (p138).

TEMPI FA Jams, wine, cheese and charcuterie in trendy surrounds (p122).

PÂTISSERIE CASANOVA An irresistible selection of Corsican sweets and desserts (p176).

U MUNTAGNOLU Huge range of high-quality Corsican goodies (p43).

TERRA CORSA Fine charcuterie and homemade ewe's-milk cheeses (p98).

JEAN-BERNARD CARILLET

FOOD & DRINK
CORSICA

WEBLINKS

CORSICAN WINES (www .vinsdecorse.com) Comprehensive site on local wines, with full information on wine estates.

CHEESE (www.fromages-corse.org) All about Corsican cheeses and the Fiera di u Casgiu food fair.

TERROIRS DE CORSE (www .corsica-terroirs.com) Information on Corsican specialities, with themed hinterland itineraries.

CORSICAN PRODUCTS (www.casa-corsa.fr) A one-stop shop for Corsican products.

CHARCUTERIE (www.u-porcu -neru.com) Everything about charcuterie, plus pictures.

FOOD FAIRS

Food and wine are celebrated throughout Corsica at rural fairs.

FESTA DI L'OLIU NOVU Ste-Lucie de Tallano's olive-oil festival in mid-March (p148).

FIERA DI A CASTAGNA Honours the chestnut; held in mid-December in Bocognano, near Vizzavona.

FIERA DI U CASGIU Celebrates cheese; takes place in early May in Venaco.

FIERA DI U VINU A wine fair held in early July in Luri (p50).

FOIRE DU COL DE PRATO Lively agricultural fair in July (p161).

CORSICAN WINES: A SUCCESS STORY

How things have changed. Fifteen years ago, Corsican wines did not have a good reputation, but now it's a completely different story. Using modern vinification methods, the younger generation of winemakers have raised the standard of Corsican wine, resulting in a number of domaines, such as Domaine Torraccia (p142) and Domaine Leccia (p56), gaining international recognition. One of the great pleasures of touring the regions of Corsica is tasting your way through them. There are no established wine routes, but there are nine AOC regions you can visit. Most domaines offer wine tasting. See p235 for more information.

TOP The popular meat treat, charcuterie (p231), is found everywhere on the island RIGHT Heaven for food and wine lovers

CHEESE

Gourmands will delight in all the flavours and textures of Corsican cheeses, from hard, tangy *tomme corse* (semihard ewe's-milk cheese) to a soft Niolincu and the star of all Corsican cheeses, the Brocciu (fresh ewe's or goat's cheese). Brocciu is produced from December to June only. It can be eaten fresh or aged; stuffed into eggplants, cannelloni, and omelettes with mint; or baked in a *fiadone* cheesecake. For the bravest connoisseurs or the truly adventurous, the *casgiu merzu* is, quite literally, a 'rotten cheese' alive with maggots! Believe us, it will linger long on the palate.

SWEET TREATS

Ice creams, tarts, cakes and biscuits – Corsica's dessert menu is sure to tempt you.

* *Canistrelli* – Devilish biscuits made with almonds, walnuts, lemon or aniseed

* *Frappe* – Look and taste like little fritters; made from chestnut flour

* Honey – The most fragrant is the *miel de maquis* from the Vallée de l'Asco

* *Falculelli* – Frittered Brocciu cheese served on a chestnut leaf

* *Fiadone* – A light flan made with cheese, lemon and eggs

* Ice cream – Original flavours such as myrtle, Brocciu or chestnut

ANDREW WHEELER / ALAMY

OUTDOORS

CORSICA

BOOKS

À TRAVERS LA MONTAGNE CORSE (FFRP) *The* reference guide for the GR20.

BALADES NATURE EN CORSE (Dakota Editions) Describes 26 short walks. Includes maps and illustrations.

CORSE CANYONS (Franck Jourdan) Has descriptions and reviews of the top canyons.

FALAISES DE CORSE (Thierry Souchard) A reference guide for rock climbing, with information on the best routes.

GR20 – CORSICA: THE HIGH-LEVEL ROUTE (Paddy Dillon) Another reliable guide on the GR20.

LES PLUS BELLES PLONGÉES DE CORSE (Georges Antoni) Good all-round resource for divers. Includes a DVD.

ON LAND

The rugged terrain of this little-populated island really does beg to be hiked, biked, skied, climbed and otherwise actively pursued. The number-one reason to come to Corsica is to get off the roads and into the wild – on foot. Some of the most inspirational hiking trails in Europe are to be found here, from the challenging GR20 to gentle afternoon strolls in the forests and coastal ambles (p214). Canyoning and rock climbing are also well established. But you needn't be limited to your own two feet: try a four-legged creature or see it all from above from a rope slide! These activities have one thing in common: all pass through scenery of bewildering beauty. Good news: you don't need previous experience. Numerous outfits have developed an impressive infrastructure all over Corsica and run programs for beginners. See p206 for more information.

TOP Get a grip while rock climbing (p213) **BOTTOM** Horse riding (p212) on the beach **RIGHT** Your trip to Corsica is incomplete without doing at least one walk (p214) **FAR RIGHT** An inviting spot for a swim

TOP SHORT WALKS

LE TOUR DE SÉNÈQUE Provides a spectacular panorama over Cap Corse (p50).

CAPU ROSSU This slim promontory has stunning views of the Golfe de Porto (p95).

LE SENTIER MULETIER A glorious panorama of Les Calanques from a historic track that few visitors tread (p95).

PLATEAU DU COSCIONE This plateau is reminiscent of Mongolian steppes (p145).

LAC DE MELU & LAC DE CAPITELLU Unforgettable alpine scenery, with two postcard-perfect glacial lakes (p178).

DON'T MISS EXPERIENCES

* Exploring the coastline – Rent a sea kayak or take a guided trip in the Golfe du Valinco (p123)

* Walking – Combine walking, picnicking and taking a dip in the Vallée du Tavignano (p175)

* Taking the plunge – The crystal-clear waters off Îles Lavezzi are an ideal place to learn to dive (p131)

* Playing Tarzan – Glide along cables strung over the Asco river (p180)

* Canyon descents – Plunge down water-polished chutes in the Canyon de la Vacca (p148)

* Horse riding – Gallop along Plage de Cateraggio (p140)

SPECIALISTS

IN TERRA CORSA (www.interracorsa.fr) Covers activities in central Corsica.

CORS'AVENTURE (www.corse-aventure.com) A well-established operator. Offers climbing, walking, sea kayaking, rafting and canyoning.

ALTIPIANI (www.altipiani-corse.com) Mountain biking, canyoning, walking and rock climbing near Corte.

OBJECTIF NATURE (www.objectif-nature-corse.com) Sea and land activities in northern Corsica.

COULEUR CORSE (www.couleur-corse.com) Can organise all types of activities.

OUTDOORS

CORSICA

WEBLINKS

GR20 (www.le-gr20.com/gb) Comprehensive site on the iconic GR20. Includes info on accommodation, wildlife, equipment and the 16 stages.

CANYONING (www.descente-canyon.com) The low-down on the world's best canyons, with a selection of 69 in Corsica.

ROCK CLIMBING (http://escalade.corse.topo.free.fr) Reviews of climbing routes, plus a forum.

VIA FERRATA (www.laviaferrata.net) Has a few pages on Corsica.

SURFING (www.surfing-corsica.fr) All about surfing, including weather forecast and photo galleries.

KAYAKING EXCURSIONS

Guided sea-kayaking trips offer a turtle's-eye view of the coastline.

CORSICAVENTURA (www.ernella.net) Trips on Etang d'Urbino and Tavignano river.

BONIF KAYAK (www.bonifacio-kayak.com) Around Îles Lavezzi and Bonifacio.

SPORTSICA (☎ 06 24 26 51 83) Excursions around the Golfe di Pinarello.

SUD KAYAK (☎ 06 14 11 68 82) Trips on the Baie de Campomoro.

CLUB NAUTIQUE D'ÎLE ROUSSE (www.cnir.org) Around Île de la Pietra and its islets.

DELTA DU FANGU (www.delta-du-fangu.com) Around the Delta du Fangu.

PARCS AVENTURE MADNESS

Fun and accessible to just about anybody, *parcs aventure* are very popular in Corsica. It's an easy way to get a buzz – the only training you need is a 10-minute lesson – and the whole family can take part at the same time. You're still safe though, as the *parcs* are supervised by qualified instructors. There are lots of different fixtures to keep you excited, including zip lines that will make your heart skip a beat – some of them exceed 250m in length! Another draw is the scenery: *parcs aventure* are set up in the most scenic parts of the island. See p212 for more information.

TOP Corsica's windy coastline is popular for windsurfing (p209) RIGHT Canyoning (p210) – the ultimate thrill-seeker activity

AT SEA

With so much water surrounding Corsica, your vacation here is sure to be a dream. Even if you've never dived, snorkelled, sailed, windsurfed or paddled, this is a great place to try these activities: experienced outfitters employ qualified, English-speaking instructors, and cater to all with affordable instruction, convenience and availability. With water temperatures hovering around 24°C in summer and an average of 2800 hours of sunshine each year, you're almost guaranteed the perfect weather for any activity. The western and southern coastlines, especially in the water-sports hubs of Porto, Sagone, Bonifacio, Porto-Vecchio and Propriano, deliver all the goods. To beat the crowds, try kayaking – it's a great way to reach hidden coves and secluded beaches.

SCENIC ROADS

If your legs are twitching, there are kilometres of heart-stopping rides (or drives) along ribbon-thin roads.

* The D80, from Patrimonio to Pino (p48) – In the Cap Corse

* The D81B, from Calvi to Galéria and Porto (p70) – Fantastic views of the sea

* The D268, from Solenzara to Col de Bavella (p166) – Dramatic mountain road

* The D69, from Aullène to Col de la Vaccia (p109)

* The D330, from Cervione to San Nicolao (p156) – Superb views of the coastal plain

JEAN-BERNARD CARILLET

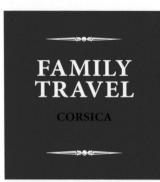

FAMILY TRAVEL

CORSICA

TILL JACKET / PHOTOLIBRARY

TOP BEACHES

PLAGE DE PINARELLO Safe, shallow and reassuring, with numerous restaurants nearby (p141).

PLAGE DE RONDINARA A broad white-sand beach shielded from the winds (p133).

PLAGE D'ARONE Children love this delightful crescent of fine sand – hire a pedal boat for maximum effect (p96).

PLAGE DE PORTIGLIOLO A vast expanse of silky sand, with lots of activities available for kids (p119).

DON'T MISS EXPERIENCES

★ *Parcs aventure* – Swing Tarzan-style through the trees at a 'baby *parc*' (p141)

★ Donkey rides – Feel like an explorer in the maquis (p120)

★ Kayak excursions – Paddle around the Golfe de Pinarello in a 'tri-yak' with Mum and Dad (p141)

★ Introductory dives – Kids aged eight and over can take the plunge (p117)

★ Sailing – Learn the ropes with a qualified instructor (p121)

★ *Calèche* ride – Clip-clop between beaches in a horse-drawn carriage (p54)

TRAVEL WITH CHILDREN

Corsica is an excellent place to explore with kids: there are no major health concerns, the climate is good and the food is easy to navigate (bar some pungent cheeses, perhaps!). There's much to see and do to keep kids happy, from supervised beaches to boat excursions and outdoor adventures. Most outdoor-activity outfits – equestrian centres, dive centres, *parcs aventure,* nautical centres etc – have special gear, pricing and activity options for kids. Except the very urban Bastia area, which lacks family-friendly activities and accommodation, all regions are good bases for families. That said, travelling with kids in Corsica does present a few minor problems; most notably, long rides might bore the little ones. Keep this in mind when planning your itinerary.

TOP Kids of all ages will love Corsica's many *parcs aventure* (p212)

CONTENTS

THE AUTHORS

JEAN-BERNARD CARILLET

Coordinating Author, the South, the Central Mountains
Paris-based journalist and photographer Jean-Bernard
has written extensively about Corsica. An incorrigible
foodie, he confesses a penchant for the robust Corsican cuisine – nothing tastes better than charcuterie
enjoyed riverside in a remote valley. When not looking
for that perfect picnic spot, he tours the hinterland in
search of atmospheric B&Bs, burns off the calories by
meandering along hiking trails or diving the Med, and
attends the island's cultural festivals.

MILES RODDIS

Calvi & La Balagne, the West Coast
Miles lives beside the Mediterranean in Valencia, Spain.
He's hiked the island of Mallorca for Lonely Planet's
Walking in Spain, explored the island of Elba for the *Italy*
guide, and lazed on the beaches of Sardinia for sheer fun.
He's authored more than 30 Lonely Planet titles, includ-
ing *France, Brittany & Normandy, Languedoc-Roussillon*
and *Walking in France.* This is the second time he's mar-
ried these two areas of interest by exploring Corsica –
Mediterranean and French, yet not completely French.

LONELY PLANET AUTHORS

Why is our travel information the best in the world? It's simple: our authors are passionate, dedicated travellers. They don't take freebies in exchange for positive coverage so
you can be sure the advice you're given is impartial. They travel widely to all the popular
spots, and off the beaten track. They don't research using just the internet or phone.
They discover new places not included in any other guidebook. They personally visit
thousands of hotels, restaurants, palaces, trails, galleries, temples and more. They speak
with dozens of locals every day to make sure you get the kind of insider knowledge only
a local could tell you. They take pride in getting all the details right, and in telling it how it
is. Think you can do it? Find out how at lonelyplanet.com.

NEIL WILSON

Bastia & the Far North, the East

After working as a petroleum-industry geologist for several years, Neil gave up the rock business to be a freelance writer and photographer. Since 1988 he has travelled in five continents and written around 55 guidebooks for various publishers. He has travelled extensively in France, visiting annually for the last 15 years, and has worked on Lonely Planet's *France* and *Brittany* guidebooks. Born in Glasgow, Neil defected east at the age of 18 and has lived in Edinburgh ever since.

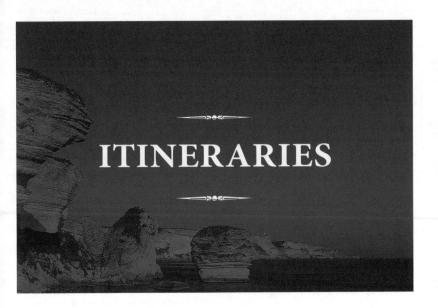

ITINERARIES

THE NORTH'S RICHES

FIVE DAYS // BASTIA TO PATRIMONIO // 130KM

From **Bastia** (p38) motor north to the Cap Corse. After visiting the little harbour at **Erbalunga** (p45), continue to **Macinaggio** (p46), from where you can take a boat trip past the **Îles Finocchiarola** (p46). Next morning, hike along the **Sentier des Douaniers** (p46)

coastal trail as far as **Barcaggio** (p46). Back at the wheel, forge west to **Centuri** (p48) and savour lobster at **Auberge du Pêcheur** (p48). Suitably re-energised, drive the spectacular **D80** (p48) south to **Nonza** (p48), where you can bed down at **Casa Maria** (p242). On day three, enjoy the sophisticated atmosphere of **St-Florent** (p50), then spend the next day working your tan on idyllic **Plage du Loto** (p54). The last day is all about epicurean indulgences – drop into **Patrimonio** (p55) and discover the fine wines of Le Nebbio.

CORSICA'S HEART & SOUL

ONE WEEK // CORTE TO VIZZAVONA // 240KM

Corte (p169) is ideally positioned for exploring the valleys and microregions of central Corsica. Spend your first day taking in Corte's sights. The next day, set the alarm

early because you've got a big day in the little-tramped **Vallée du Niolo** (p179). The **Vallée de la Restonica** (p177) is the place to go on day three. Keep your fourth day for the mysterious **Boziu** (p181) then, on your fifth day, give the car a rest and picnic in the traffic-free **Vallée du Tavignano** (p175). On day six, drag yourself away from Corte and make your way to **Venaco** (p183) – be sure to lunch at a **A Cantina di Matteu** (p184). End the week with a day of gentle walking amid the majestic **Forêt de Vizzavona** (p184).

WESTERN DELIGHTS

TWO WEEKS // CALVI TO AJACCIO // 450KM

Calvi (p59) and the hilltop villages of **La Balagne** (p75) are worth at least three days. Then brace yourself for the hold-on-to-your-hat coastal drive south to **Porto** (p83), via

Galéria (p71). Why not break the journey with a hike to **Girolata** (p91), one of the jewels of this wild coastline? The Porto area has plenty to keep you busy for a good three days. Next, move on to **Ajaccio** (p100) via **Cargèse** (p97) and **Sagone** (p98), allowing three days for Corsica's largest town and its gulf. Finally, duck inland and explore the **Haut Taravo** (p109) and the **Vallée du Prunelli** (p107) – you should plan on three days to do them proper justice.

BEACHSIDE FROLICS

12 DAYS // PORTO-VECCHIO TO PROPRIANO // 280KM

Southern Corsica offers copious versions of the perfect beach. **Porto-Vecchio** (p134) is a good place to start; plan on four days to make the most of the various options in

the area, including **Plage de Palombaggia** (p139) and the **Golfe de Pinarello** (p141). Journey on to **Bonifacio** (p129), which is a great base for exploring the **Îles Lavezzi** (p132) and the **Golfe de Sant' Amanza** (p132) – you'll need three days, minimum. Spare a day for **Tizzano** (p127), where you can rent a boat and find your own pocket of sand. In **Propriano** (p119), allow another four days for the fantastic Golfe du Valinco – be sure to squeeze in the charming seaside towns of **Porto Pollo** (p116) and **Campomoro** (p122).

L'ALTA ROCCA ESCAPE

FIVE DAYS // PORTO-VECCHIO TO LEVIE // 120KM

From Porto-Vecchio, take the twisting D368 to **L'Ospédale** (p143), the gateway to L'Alta Rocca. After soaking up the atmosphere of the **Forêt de L'Ospédale** (p143), head to **Zonza** (p144), which has accommodation options and restaurants. Spend the

next day canyoning (or just marvelling at the fabulous scenery) in the **Bavella area** (p148) and recharge the batteries with a hearty dinner at **Chez Pierrot** (p145) near Quenza. Next morning, explore the Mongolian-like **Plateau du Coscione** (p145) before driving to **Ste-Lucie de Tallano** (p147). On your fourth day, mosey around the village and shop for the perfect olive oil. Keep your fifth day for **Levie** (p146) and the **Cucuruzzu & Capula archaeological sites** (p146). Be sure to pause for lunch or dinner at **A Pignata** (p147) in Levie.

ITINERARIES

HILLTOP VILLAGES ORGY

ONE WEEK // BASTIA TO SOLENZARA // 260KM

Head due south from Bastia (p38), following the N198, before steering inland for a scenic drive around the hilltop villages of the Morianincu (p157). Follow the Corniche de la Castagniccia (p156) to Cervione (p151), where Casa Corsa – Chambres d'Hôtes Doumens (p253) provides a peaceful night's sleep. Meander north through the Castagniccia, stopping at the atmosphere-laden villages of La Porta (p160) and Morosaglia (p161); plan on spending two days here. Back on the coastal road, feast on seafood at Étang de Diane (p163) before exploring the Fiumorbu (p164) – two days in this supremely picturesque microregion should fit the bill. Spend the next day picnicking in the remote Vallée du Travo (p166), before lazing a couple of days away on the beach at Solenzara (p165).

BASTIA & THE FAR NORTH

3 PERFECT DAYS

❧ DAY 1 // TOUR OF CAP CORSE

Take a morning to explore the backstreets of Bastia (p38), making your way up to the citadel for lunch on the terrace at A Casarella (p42) or Chez Vincent (p42). In the afternoon take a drive up the east coast of Cap Corse, pausing for a drink by the harbour at Erbalunga (p45), then continue around the northern tip of the peninsula to keep a date with an early seafood dinner in Centuri (p48). Afterwards, a sunset drive back south along the spectacular D80 coast road (p48).

❧ DAY 2 // VINEYARDS AND VILLAGES

Pick up a guide to the Route des Vins (Wine Road) in the St-Florent tourist office and spend a leisurely morning touring the vineyards of Patrimonio (p55). Linger over a long lunch on the terrace at Osteria di San Martinu (p56), then head off on a driving tour around the villages of the Nebbio (p56). In the evening, take advantage of your new-found knowledge of Corsican wines to sample a range of crus in St-Florent's welcoming Bara Vin (p52).

❧ DAY 3 // BOAT TRIP TO THE BEACH

Wake up over coffee and croissants at any of St-Florent's harbourside cafes, then board the Popeye boat for the half-hour trip along the coast of the Désert des Agriates to beautiful Plage du Loto (p54). Stake your claim to a patch of sand or, better still, hike along the coast to the even more gorgeous Plage de Saleccia (p54). After a hard day of sunbathing and swimming, relax with a gourmet seafood dinner overlooking St-Florent's harbour at La Gaffe (p52) or La Rascasse (p53).

BASTIA & THE FAR NORTH

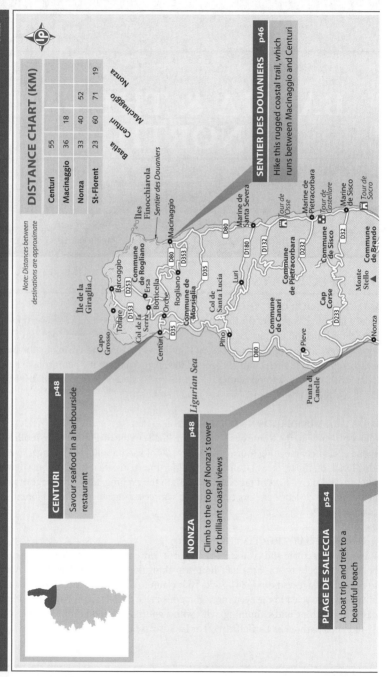

DISTANCE CHART (KM)

	Bastia	Centuri	Macinaggio	Nonza
Centuri	55			
Macinaggio	36	18		
Nonza	33	40	52	
St-Florent	23	60	71	19

Note: Distances between destinations are approximate

CENTURI   p48

Savour seafood in a harbourside restaurant

NONZA   p48

Climb to the top of Nonza's tower for brilliant coastal views

PLAGE DE SALECCIA   p54

A boat trip and trek to a beautiful beach

SENTIER DES DOUANIERS   p46

Hike this rugged coastal trail, which runs between Macinaggio and Centuri

Ligurian Sea

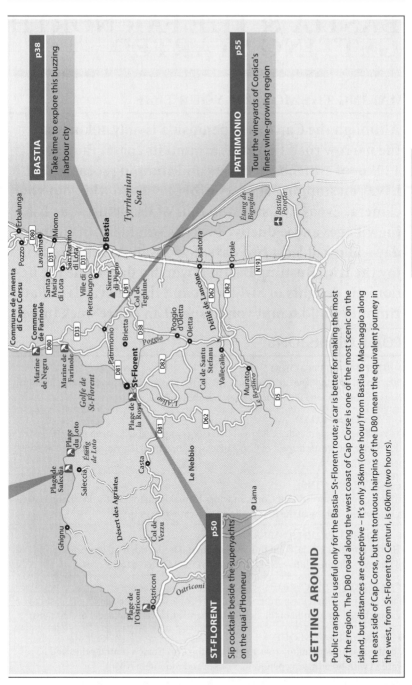

BASTIA p38

Take time to explore this buzzing harbour city

PATRIMONIO p55

Tour the vineyards of Corsica's finest wine-growing region

ST-FLORENT p50

Sip cocktails beside the superyachts on the quai d'Honneur

Tyrrhenian Sea

Erbalunga
Pozzo
Lavasina
Miomo
Santa Maria di Lota
San-Martino di Lota
Ville di Pietrabugno
Bastia
Sierra di Pigno
Col de Teghime
Casatorra
Ortale
Etang de Biguglia
Bastia Poretta

Commune de Amenta di Capu Corsu
Commune de Farinole
Marine de Negru
Marine de Farinole
Patrimonio
Brietta
Poggio
Poggio d'Oletta
Oletta
Défilé de Lancône
St-Florent
Golfe de St-Florent
Col de Santu Stefanu
Vallecalle
Murato
Le Bevinco

Plage de la Roya
L'Aliso
Le Nebbio
Lama

Plage du Loto
Plage de Saleccia
Etang de Loto
Saleccia
Casta
Desert des Agriates
Col de Vezzu
Ghignu
Ostriconi
Plage de l'Ostriconi
Ostriconi

D80 / D31 / D81 / D33 / D38 / D82 / D62 / D5 / N193 / N193

GETTING AROUND

Public transport is useful only for the Bastia–St-Florent route; a car is better for making the most of the region. The D80 road along the west coast of Cap Corse is one of the most scenic on the island, but distances are deceptive – it's only 36km (one hour) from Bastia to Macinaggio along the east side of Cap Corse, but the tortuous hairpins of the D80 mean the equivalent journey in the west, from St-Florent to Centuri, is 60km (two hours).

BASTIA & THE FAR NORTH
GETTING STARTED

BASTIA & THE FAR NORTH

MAKING THE MOST OF YOUR TIME

Although the Cap Corse peninsula is only 40km long, the narrow road that runs around its coast crams in 120km of switchback curves and stunning scenery that'll have you stopping at every other lay-by to whip out your camera. Even a whistle-stop tour of its picturesque fishing villages and seductive beaches would fill an entire day – allow at least two days if you want to relax and enjoy the trip. Bustling Bastia is worth a day, while the hedonistic delights of St-Florent and the vineyards of Patrimonio could tempt you to spend an entire week there.

TOP EXCURSIONS

❦ SENTIER DU LITTORAL
Take a boat trip to Plage du Loto and explore the rocky coastal footpath that leads to Plage de Saleccia, one of Corsica's finest beaches (p54).

❦ THE COAST ROAD
Drive along the spectacular D80 road that clings improbably to steep mountainsides high above the western coast of Cap Corse, with breathtaking views revealed at every bend (p48).

❦ ROUTE DES VINS
Improve your knowledge of Corsican wines by making a tour of the Patrimonio vineyards, home to some of the island's finest muscat vintages (p55).

❦ SENTIER DES DOUANIERS
Hike or horseback-ride along this ancient coastal trail, once used by customs officers, to discover remote white-sand beaches and ruined Genoese towers (p46).

❦ SAN PAULU BOAT TRIP
Take a cruise around the northern tip of Cap Corse aboard the *San Paulu*, past the seabird breeding ground of the Îles Finocchiarola to lovely Barcaggio beach (p46).

❦ LE TOUR DE SÉNÈQUE
Climb to an ancient hilltop tower perched atop Cap Corse's central ridge, and be rewarded with breathtaking panoramas of sea and mountains (p50).

GETTING AWAY FROM IT ALL

Bastia, Nonza and St-Florent are where the crowds gather, so it's not too difficult to find a secluded corner elsewhere in the region.

* **Remote beaches** Pack a picnic and a parasol, and hike along the Sentier des Douaniers or the Sentier du Littoral to find a sunbathing spot all of your own (p46, p54)

* **Inland Cap Corse** Pause to enjoy the Jardins Traditionnels du Cap Corse and the peaceful hamlets along the D180 road, which cuts across the centre of Cap Corse (p49)

* **Nebbio driving tour** Explore the winding back roads and remote villages of inland Nebbio (p56)

ADVANCE PLANNING

There are some events you might want to consider while planning the timing of your trip.

* **A Cerca** Traditional procession that dates back to ancient times; it takes place on Good Friday (p45)

* **Nuits de la Guitare** (www.festival-guitare -patrimonio.com) An eclectic week-long guitar-music festival held in July (p56)

* **Fiera di u Vinu** (www.acunfraternita.com, in French) A celebration of Corsican wines held on the first or second weekend of July (p50)

* **Festival d'Erbalunga** (www.festival -erbalunga.fr) Open-air concerts in Erbalunga's village square; it takes place in August (p45)

TOP SEAFOOD RESTAURANTS

♥ LA RASCASSE
Cutting-edge cuisine (p53)

♥ LE PIRATE
Cap Corse's top table (p47)

♥ LA GAFFE
A local favourite for 30 years (p52)

♥ LA MARINUCCIA
Sunset views while you eat (p53)

♥ AUBERGE DU PÊCHEUR
Dining by the harbour's edge (p48)

♥ LA TABLE DU MARCHÉ
Fresh produce from the local market (p42)

RESOURCES

* **Bastia Tourist Office** (www.bastia -tourisme.com) Information, maps, brochures and listings

* **Cap Corse** (www.destination-cap-corse.com) Useful guide to Cap Corse's villages and walking trails

* **St-Florent Tourist Office** (www.corsica -saintflorent.com, in French) Information on St-Florent and Patrimonio vineyards

* **Haute-Corse** (Charles Pujos) Excellent guide to hiking routes in Haute-Corse, complete with maps and photos (in French, but easy to understand)

BASTIA

· · · · · ·

pop 38,000

Most visitors drive off the teeming ferries from mainland Europe, then head straight out of town for Cap Corse or the beaches around St-Florent. But Bastia warrants more than a fleeting glance. Economically Corsica's most dynamic city, it has a rough-round-the-edges appeal that accepts but doesn't pander to tourism. Linger a little and you won't be disappointed.

The city of Bastia was officially founded in 1372, although there were settlements in the area as far back as Roman times. The Genoese governor of the time, residing in the poorly defended Château de Biguglia in a malaria-infested area several kilometres away, understandably decided to go upmarket and build himself a fortress (*bastiglia,* hence the name Bastia) on the only really significant rocky headland on this stretch of coastline. This fortress – Bastia's citadel – was a strategically important element in protecting the island from seaborne incursions.

But not everyone saw things that way. Many freedom-minded Corsicans saw the fortress as the prime symbol of Genoese oppression. Indeed, on several occasions villagers came down from the mountains and sacked the town in protest over Genoese taxes. But despite the periodic instability, Bastia would continue to expand.

ESSENTIAL INFORMATION

EMERGENCIES // Hospital (☎ 04 95 59 11 11; Furiani; 🕓 24hr) Bus 1, which leaves from opposite the bus station on bd Général Graziani, terminates at the hospital. Police station (☎ 04 95 54 50 22; rue du Commandant Luce de Casabianca; 🕓 24hr)

TOURIST OFFICES // Tourist office (☎ 04 95 54 20 40; www.bastia-tourisme.com; place St-Nicolas; 🕓 8am-8pm Apr-Sep, 9am-noon & 2-5pm Mon-Sat Oct-Mar).

ORIENTATION

Place St-Nicolas, a long, traffic-free rectangle directly opposite the southern ferry terminal, is the heart of Bastia. At the square's northern end, av Maréchal Sébastiani links the southern ferry terminal with the train station. West of the square, parallel bd Paoli and rue César Campinchi, each running north–south, are the main shopping streets.

WALKING TOUR

Map: p40
Distance: 2.75km
Duration: one to 1¼ hours
From the **tourist office** (1; above) on place St-Nicolas, walk south past the **statue of Napoléon** (2; p42). With their steep interior stairs visible from the street, the tall 17th- and 18th-century buildings flanking the square on its southern and western sides could have been transplanted from any provincial Italian city.

From the main square, cours Henri Pierangeli runs into Terra Vecchia, Bastia's oldest quarter; during Genoese rule, Terra Vecchia was occupied by native Corsicans, while the Genoese looked down upon them from Terra Nova. The central square, **Place de l'Hôtel de Ville (3)**, is home to the former town-hall building (now used primarily for weddings); there's a small produce market here in the morning, Tuesday to Friday, and a much larger one on Saturday and Sunday. In the southwest corner is the 17th-century ochre-coloured **Église St-Jean Baptiste** (🕓 8am-noon & 3-7pm Mon-Sat, 8am-noon Sun),

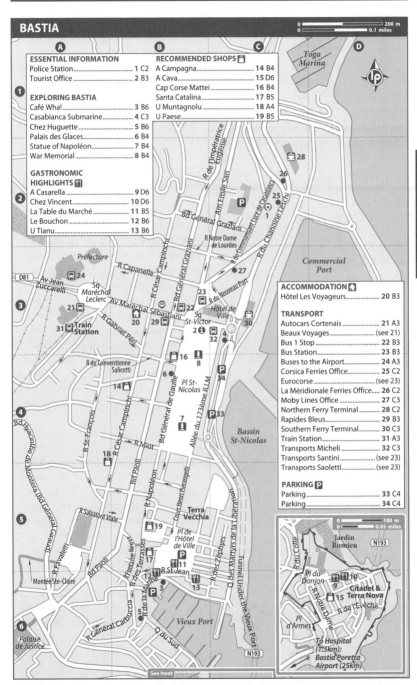

BASTIA

ESSENTIAL INFORMATION	
Police Station	1 C2
Tourist Office	2 B3

EXPLORING BASTIA
Café Wha!	3 B6
Casabianca Submarine	4 C3
Chez Huguette	5 B6
Palais des Glaces	6 B4
Statue of Napoléon	7 B4
War Memorial	8 B4

GASTRONOMIC HIGHLIGHTS
A Casarella	9 D6
Chez Vincent	10 D6
La Table du Marché	11 B5
Le Bouchon	12 B6
U Tianu	13 B6

RECOMMENDED SHOPS
A Campagna	14 B4
A Cava	15 D6
Cap Corse Mattei	16 B4
Santa Catalina	17 B5
U Muntagnolu	18 A4
U Paese	19 B5

ACCOMMODATION
Hôtel Les Voyageurs	20 B3

TRANSPORT
Autocars Cortenais	21 A3
Beaux Voyages	(see 21)
Bus 1 Stop	22 B3
Bus Station	23 B3
Buses to the Airport	24 A3
Corsica Ferries Office	25 C2
Eurocorse	(see 23)
La Méridionale Ferries Office	26 C2
Moby Lines Office	27 C2
Northern Ferry Terminal	28 C2
Rapides Bleus	29 B3
Southern Ferry Terminal	30 C3
Train Station	31 A3
Transports Micheli	32 C3
Transports Santini	(see 23)
Transports Saoletti	(see 23)

PARKING
Parking	33 C4
Parking	34 C4

Corsica's largest church, notable for its twin bell towers and tall classical facade.

From the church, cross rue St-Jean and go down the steps that lead to the **Vieux Port** (4; p42). When Bastia grew into a major port, a new commercial

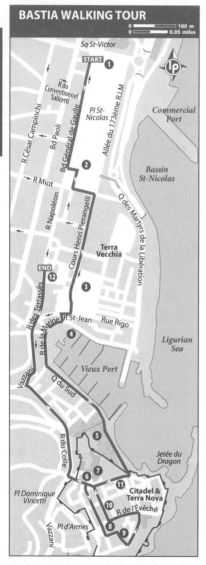

BASTIA WALKING TOUR

harbour was built to the northeast, leaving this sunny strip to pleasure boats, restaurants and cafes.

Hugging the curve of the port, quai du Sud leads to the staircase of rampe St-Charles, which climbs to **Jardin Romieu** (5), a pleasant little garden that seems to cling to the hillside for dear life. At its extremity take the flight of steep stone steps that lead through the citadel's battlements via a tunnel and up to rue St-Michel, where you turn right into **place du Donjon** (6).

Looming over this cobbled square is the **Palais des Gouverneurs** (7; Governors' Palace), a Genoese citadel built in 1530. It was the seat of the Genoese governor of Corsica for more than two centuries; during that time, the Terra Nova quarter, which has recently had many of its buildings refurbished in attractive ochres, reds, yellows and greens, grew up around it. Closed to the public since 1980, the Palais des Gouverneurs will soon be the home of the new Musée d'Ethnographie Corse; at the time of research the museum was due to open in summer 2010.

From the square, head southeast along narrow rue Notre Dame to reach the late-15th-century **Cathédrale Ste-Marie** (8). Inside, drop a €0.20 coin into the box to illuminate the glass-encased silver Virgin Mary. Admire, too, the church's Italian organ, one of the finest on the island, and the finely painted trompe l'œil ceiling. Skirting the side of the church, you come to the rococo **Oratoire Ste-Croix** (9). In one of its side chapels there's a much-venerated black-oak crucifix, reputedly hauled from the sea by fishermen in the 14th century. Above the altar, an unusual sculpture depicting God the Father looks down benevolently.

Drop down a flight of steps and turn left into chemin des Turquines, then left again up the steps of rue de L'Évêché and right into rue de la Paroisse. **A Cava** (**10**; 6 chemin des Turquines) sells traditional Corsican products; try the owner's favourite house liqueur, a 40% eau-de-vie infused with local maquis herbs.

Rue de la Paroisse brings you back to place du Donjon, where you can stop for a drink on the terrace of **Chez Vincent** (**11**; p42). The views over the Old Port from Chez Vincent and its neighbouring terraces are stunning, and especially beautiful at dusk. Exit the citadel and follow rue du Colle northwards, skirting the Vieux Port to join rue des Terrasses, which has several worthwhile craft shops.

Ahead on the right is the imposing facade of the **Oratoire de l'Immaculée Conception** (**12**), with its rich wooden panelling and elaborately painted barrel-vaulted ceiling; it briefly served as the seat of the Anglo-Corsican parliament in 1795. Its throne was meant for King George III, and *God Save The King* was played on the organ at the opening and closing of each session. Head outside; place St-Nicolas is again back in sight.

EXPLORING BASTIA

♥ PLACE ST-NICOLAS //
PEOPLE-WATCH IN BASTIA'S BUZZING FOCAL POINT

This vast square, nearly 300m long and one of France's largest, overlooks the commercial harbour. Shaded by palms and viciously pollarded plane trees, it's bordered by a string of attractive terrace cafes along its western edge. At night rollerbladers race and twirl, taking advantage of this traffic-free space. There's

ACCOMMODATION

Accommodation options in this region range from city hotels in Bastia and sea-front *chambres d'hôtes* (B&Bs) on the Cap Corse coast to rural B&Bs tucked away in the Patrimonio vineyards; read all about them in the Accommodation chapter. The following are some of our favourites:

★ Live it up in style at the boutique **Hôtel Demeure Castel Brando** (p242)

★ Enjoying an idyllic setting among the vines, **Chambres d'Hôtes U Castellu Piattu** (p243) is the perfect rural escape

★ A beautiful farmhouse conversion, **La Dimora** (p243) exemplifies the best in Corsican hospitality

a lively flea market on Sunday mornings and throughout summer it's enlivened by free concerts. On 14 July fireworks spurt and crack overhead to mark Bastille Day.

The prime people-watching spot on the west side of the square is the **Palais des Glaces** (☎ 04 95 31 05 01; place St-Nicolas; mains €10-15; ☽ 7am-2am), a classic cafe with a marble-floored, wood-panelled dining room and attractive terrace tables where you can pick lazily at an ice cream while watching the world go by.

At the square's northern end is Bastia's **War Memorial**, a striking bronze statue of a mother giving her youngest son to the motherland; it's a bombastic theme that's been executed with great sensitivity. Even more evocative for Corsicans is the black conning tower of the **Casabianca submarine**. It's preserved in honour of the captain, Jean L'Herminier, and his crew who, in the months leading up to the recapture of the island from

BASTIA & THE FAR NORTH

Axis forces in 1943, landed agents, arms, radios and supplies in support of the Corsican resistance.

The square also boasts a marble **statue of Napoléon,** his naked torso draped in a camp Roman emperor's tunic as he peers out to sea towards Elba, the place of his first exile.

♥ VIEUX PORT // SIP A COLD ONE BY THE HARBOUR

The most picturesque part of town, Bastia's old port is a crowded harbour ringed by towering 19th-century tenements, some with visibly crumbling walls – the buildings nearest the harbour took a battering during WWII bombing missions designed to drive out Axis occupiers.

The lively waterfront is ringed with tempting terrace restaurants and bars, the ideal spot for an evening refreshment – Mexican-themed **Café Wha!** (☎ 04 95 34 25 79; Vieux Port; ⏲ 10am-2am) is popular with young locals and serves cocktails till 2am, or you could order a bottle of white and half-a-dozen oysters at **Chez Huguette** (☎ 04 95 31 37 60; Vieux Port; mains €18-32, oysters per half-dozen €12-14; ⏲ lunch & dinner Mon-Sat year-round, plus dinner Sun Jul & Aug), whose pavement tables command the best views.

FESTIVALS & EVENTS

See p10 for more festivals and events occurring in Bastia.

Processions de la Semaine Sainte Holy Week is celebrated fervently with colourful processions; they take place in late March or early April.

Feux de la St-Jean A giant bonfire in the Vieux Port celebrates the year's longest day (23 June) and honours Bastia's patron saint.

Festival Arte-Mare A celebration of Mediterranean cinema and cultures for 10 days in mid-November.

GASTRONOMIC HIGHLIGHTS

♥ A CASARELLA €€
☎ 04 95 32 02 32; rue St-Michel; mains €10-23, menus €18-28; ⏲ lunch & dinner Mon-Fri, dinner Sat
Set in the heart of the citadel with a small terrace overlooking the Vieux Port, A Casarella has an interior tastefully decorated with contemporary artefacts and canvases. The innovative cuisine is based on organic Corsican produce, and includes dishes such as millefeuille of swordfish with aubergine and mint, fillet of veal stuffed with herbs from the maquis, and *casciate* (fresh cheese baked in chestnut leaves). Reservations are recommended.

♥ CHEZ VINCENT €€
☎ 04 95 31 62 50; 12 rue St-Michel; mains €11-24; ⏲ lunch & dinner Mon-Fri, dinner Sat
A Casarella's neighbour also has an attractive terrace with great views, and is a friendly, informal spot where you can snack on pizzas (€8 to €10) or select from the dishes chalked up on the blackboard. Go wild and opt for the *assiette du bandit Corse* (Corsican bandit platter; €18.50), a selection of island favourites including stewed veal with chestnuts, ewe's-milk cheese with fig preserve, wild-boar pâté, and roast *figatellu* (liver sausage).

♥ LA TABLE DU MARCHÉ €€
☎ 04 95 31 64 25; place de l'Hôtel de Ville; mains €20-26, menus €25-49; ⏲ lunch & dinner Mon-Sat Jul & Aug, lunch & dinner Wed-Sat Sep-Jun
Tucked away on a peaceful square near the Vieux Port, this smart and elegant brasserie makes full use of the produce market held on the square six mornings a week. It specialises in local seafood – classic dishes include shellfish platters, fried monkfish with tartare sauce,

and grilled sea bass with asparagus and Champagne sauce – but there's also a delicious vegetarian ravioli stuffed with ricotta and white truffle, and topped with a creamy cep-and-rocket sauce.

☙ LE BOUCHON €€

☎ 04 95 58 14 22; 4bis rue St-Jean; mains €12-25; ✎ lunch & dinner Jul & Aug, lunch & dinner Mon, Tue, Thu-Sat Sep-Jun

This quayside restaurant-cum-wine-bar is a great spot for watching the evening promenade along the Vieux Port. The menu is full of tempting dishes such as rich *soupe de poisson* (fish soup), tartare of organic Corsican beef, and grilled tuna with tagliatelle, and there's a good selection of wines by the glass (€3 to €6). Service is affable, if on the slow side.

☙ U TIANU €€

☎ 04 95 31 36 67; 4 rue Rigo; menu €20; ✎ 7pm-1am Mon-Sat Sep-Jul

A local favourite that has hardly changed in a quarter of a century, this informal, family-run place is tucked away down a side street and up a flight of rickety stairs behind the Vieux Port. You'll stagger out after indulging in its superb-value five-course *menu* (set menu) of traditional Corsican favourites, which also includes an aperitif, coffee and a digestif.

RECOMMENDED SHOPS

☙ CAP CORSE MATTEI

☎ 04 95 32 44 38; 15 bd Général de Gaulle

A Bastia institution. The interior of this gloriously retro shop, which has an art deco facade, has hardly changed since the day Louis-Napoléon Mattei first opened for business in 1872. During more than a century of service it has continued to sell not only its celebrated brand-name Cap Corse aperitif, but also various local specialities such as fig jam, olive oil and fruit liqueurs.

There are several other tempting shops selling quality Corsican products such as charcuterie, cheese, honey, wine and liqueur. The following are some of our favourites:

A Campagna (☎ 04 95 34 00 78; 25 rue César Campinchi)

A Cava (6 chemin des Turquines)

Santa Catalina (☎ 04 95 32 30 69; 8 rue des Terrasses)

U Muntagnolu (☎ 04 95 32 78 04; 15 rue César Campinchi)

U Paese (☎ 04 95 32 33 18; 4 rue Napoléon)

TRANSPORT

TO/FROM THE AIRPORT

AIRPORT // Bastia Poretta airport (BIA; ☎ 04 95 54 54 54; www.bastia.aeroport.fr) is 24km south of central Bastia; see p266 for more.

BUS // The bus to Bastia Poretta airport (€8.50, 30 minutes, 10 daily) leaves from in front of the Préfecture building, beside sq Maréchal Leclerc. The tourist office has schedules, and timetables are also posted at the bus stop.

TAXI // Airport taxis (☎ 04 95 36 04 05) cost around €40/55 during the day/night.

GETTING AROUND

BOAT // Bastia has two ferry terminals. The northern one has showers, toilets and an information point (open 7am to 9pm). The main, southern terminal has a ticket office for same-day and advance travel for Société Nationale Corse Méditerranée (SNCM), La Méridionale, Corsica Ferries and Moby Lines. Ferry services head to/from Marseille and Nice on mainland France, and Livorno, Savona, Piombino and Genoa in Italy; see p268 for more. Corsica Ferries, Moby Lines and Le Méridionale also have offices around town (see Map p39).

BUS // The bus station (a grand term for a little parking area with no ticket office) is just north of place St-Nicolas; **Transports Santini** (☎ 04 95 37 04 01) buses leave from the bus station for St-Florent (twice daily). **Autocars Cortenais** (☎ 04 95 46 02 12) buses leave from the train station for Corte (three weekly), while **Beaux Voyages** (☎ 04 95 65 15 02; www .lesbeauxvoyagesencorse.com, in French) buses leave from the same location for Calvi (once or twice daily). **Eurocorse** (☎ 04 95 21 06 31) leaves from route du Nouveau Port for Ajaccio (twice daily), and **Rapides Bleus** (☎ 04 95 31 03 79) buses leave from in front of the post office for Porto-Vecchio (once daily).

CAR // Bastia is a real traffic bottleneck, so try to avoid driving into the town centre during rush hour, and leave plenty of time to check in for ferry departures – the last few miles into town can take half an hour or more during busy times.

PARKING // On-street parking can be a problem in the town centre, though you can usually find a space in the dark and cramped underground car park beneath place St-Nicolas.

TAXI // **Taxis Oranges Bastiais** (☎ 04 95 32 24 24) and **Taxis Bleus** (☎ 04 95 32 70 70) provide taxi services.

TRAIN // The **train station** (☎ 04 95 32 80 61) is at the western end of av Maréchal Sébastiani, beside sq Maréchal Leclerc. There are several trains daily to Ajaccio (four hours) and Corte (two hours), and two daily to Calvi (three hours) via Île Rousse (2½ hours); the latter two destinations require a change at Ponte Leccia.

CAP CORSE

· · · · · ·

The maquis-covered Cap Corse peninsula, 40km long and around 10km wide, stands out from the rest of Corsica, flicking a giant geographical finger at the French Riviera. A wild and rugged region, it's often described as 'an island within an island'.

This northern tip of Corsica, the nearest to mainland Europe, was an important centre for merchants and trading. For many years the peninsula was ruled by im-

portant noble families from Genoa, who prospered from trading wine and oil, and regarded Cap Corse as an ally. It has a long maritime tradition and was, apart from Bonifacio, the only area within Corsica whose people made a living from fishing.

Indeed, the inhabitants of Cap Corse were the first islanders to broaden their horizons overseas, emigrating to the French colonies in North Africa and the Americas. Once they had made their fortune, however, many returned home, with the most successful commissioning a colonial-style house, known as a *maison des américains* (see the boxed text, p47).

Today, punctuated by watchtowers built by the Genoese, the cape is dotted with charming coastal fishing villages and small communities perched precariously up in the hills.

The west coast, with wilder scenery and narrow switchback roads, contrasts with the gentler eastern coastal strip. It's possible to dash around the cape's perimeter in one day of driving, but it's better to make trips radiating out from Bastia or St-Florent over two or more days.

ESSENTIAL INFORMATION

TOURIST OFFICES // **Macinaggio Tourist Office** (☎ 04 95 35 40 34; www.ot-rogliano -macinaggio.com, in French; port de plaisance de Macinaggio; ⊙ 9am-noon & 2.30-6pm Mon-Sat, 9am-noon Sun Jun-Sep, 9am-noon & 2-5pm Mon-Fri Oct-May) The only tourist office on Cap Corse.

TRANSPORT

CAR // The D80 snakes its way all around Cap Corse, in the main clinging close to the spectacular coastline. Allow plenty of extra time; progress, especially on the west coast, will be slow as you negotiate the tight bends and pass oncoming traffic warily – the 60km from St-Florent to Centuri will take at least 1½ hours.

BUS // **Transports Micheli** (☎ 04 95 35 14 64) runs from the Bastia tourist office to Erbalunga and Macinaggio (three daily Monday to Friday, one Saturday), while **Transports Saoletti** (☎ 04 95 37 84 23) has a service every Wednesday from the bus station to Nonza and Patrimonio.

EASTERN CAP CORSE

EXPLORING EASTERN CAP CORSE

♥ LA CORNICHE // DRIVING HIGH ABOVE CITY AND SEA

This spectacular road, which begins in central Bastia at the north end of rue César Campinchi, makes a wonderful drive that's easily accomplished in a couple of hours. The D31 snakes its way around the steep mountain slopes looming to the north of the city – where you'll be tempted to pause and explore the little villages of **Ville di Pietrabugno**, **San Martino di Lota** and **Santa Maria di Lota** – before dropping to **Miomo** and, once more, the coast. Again and again, you'll enjoy stunning views of the shore and, far out to sea, the islands of the Tuscan archipelago.

Consider stopping in the peaceful hamlet of San Martino di Lota, 6km from Bastia, to enjoy lunch at the **Hôtel-Restaurant La Corniche** (☎ 04 95 31 40 98; www.hotel-la corniche.com; mains €12-24; ☽ lunch & dinner Feb-Dec). Its gourmet restaurant has a magnificent panoramic terrace and is strong on local produce; the slow-roasted lamb with wild thyme is superb.

♥ ERBALUNGA // EXPLORE AN ANCIENT FISHING VILLAGE

It would be a shame not to make a brief stop to visit Erbalunga's little harbour, one of the cape's prettiest. It's difficult to imagine the time when the port, where today only a handful of boats bob along-side a crumbling Genoese tower, was a thriving entrepôt. Then more important than either Ajaccio or Bastia, the port exported wine and olive oil to Genoa.

Leave your car in the free car park beside Hôtel Demeure Castel Brando and wander down to the tiny village square and quayside, which has a cluster of cute cafes and restaurants. Narrow alleys lead through shady courtyards to the tower, home to an informal art gallery in summer. In the 1930s and '40s the village became an artists colony – it was nicknamed the Collioure du Cap after the famous art colony in southwest France – and many artists are still based here today.

Each August, the **Festival d'Erbalunga** (☎ 04 95 33 20 84; www.festival-erbalunga.fr) promotes open-air concerts in the village's central square.

Delightfully placed on Erbalunga's small, shady square, with the harbour just in view, **A Piazzetta** (☎ 04 95 33 28 69; pizzas around €8, mains €12-16; ☽ lunch & dinner) offers pizzas and a regularly changing menu, with most choices pulled from the sea. For something special head for Le Pirate (p47).

♥ A CERCA // AN ANCIENT PROCESSION FROM ERBALUNGA

On Good Friday, the people of Erbalunga, Pozzo and a couple of nearby hamlets take part in A Cerca (literally 'the Search'), a procession said to reflect an ancient fertility rite that goes back to pagan times. At dawn, men, women and children set out from their villages on a 14km circular pilgrimage walk along the paths that link their communities. Each procession is often within sight of the other three, yet they never intersect or overlap.

Once back in the village, Erbalunga's pilgrims wind into a spiral, called the Granitola (Snail), that gradually unfolds

GENOESE TOWERS

Around 60 of the 85 towers that the Genoese built in Corsica in the 16th century remain standing today in various states of preservation. Mostly round but occasionally square, these fortified structures are about 15m high and are particularly common around Cap Corse.

The avowed motive for constructing the towers was to protect the island from Berber raiders, but you can't help thinking that in building them Genoa also sought to protect its strategic and commercial interests in Corsica from European challengers. Sited around the coastline so that each was visible from the next, the towers formed a vast surveillance network. A system of signals enabled a message to circle the island in one hour.

There are several fine examples of these structures around Cap Corse, including the Tour de l'Osse (south of Porticciolo), and those at Erbalunga (p45), Marine d'Albo, and along the Sentier des Douaniers (below).

as the participants continue on their way, while another element of the procession forms itself into the four arms of the cross.

❦ SAN PAULU BOAT TRIPS // BIRDWATCH, SUNBATHE AND HIKE THE COAST

The hub of the eastern cape, **Macinaggio** has a pleasant little harbour that offers the island's best moorings; everything from small sailing boats to sleek luxury yachts are berthed here. With a range of activities, the town makes a good base for exploring the northern reaches of the promontory.

In July and August the **San Paulu** (☎ 04 95 35 07 09; www.sanpaulu.com; port de plaisance), which docks opposite the Macinaggio tourist office, cruises along the stunning coastline to **Barcaggio** and back (round trip adult/child €22/11, two hours). The return trip takes a turn around the nature reserve of the **Îles Finocchiarola**, an important breeding site for seabirds – take your binoculars. Sailings are at 11am and 3.30pm from Macinaggio, leaving Barcaggio at noon and 4.30pm.

If you prefer sunbathing to birdwatching, you can take the morning boat and spend the afternoon at Barcaggio's remote and beautiful white-sand beach, returning on the 4.30pm boat (round trip adult/child €24/12). The boat can also be used to allow a one-way hike along the Sentier des Douaniers coastal trail from Macinaggio to Barcaggio (see below).

❦ SENTIER DES DOUANIERS // EXPLORE THE RUGGED CAP CORSE COAST

Hikers will love the Sentier des Douaniers (Customs Officers' Trail), a rugged coastal path that leads away from the beach at Macinaggio and, winding its way through fragrant maquis, hugs the protected shoreline. Views are spectacular, with various sections grazing the coastline, looking out to the Îles Finocchiarola, and passing the Genoese **Tour de Santa Maria** and **Tour d'Agnello**.

The trail leads on to Barcaggio; for this first stage, allow up to three hours. From here continue for another 45 minutes to **Tollare**, from where it's a hefty but spectacular four-hour trek to the harbour at Centuri. It's not a particularly strenuous walk, but be sure to take a hat and plenty of water; there are no springs en route. Avoid the midday sun, which can be especially ruthless along this strip of coast.

In July and August it's possible to do only the first section between Macinaggio and Barcaggio, returning on the *San Paulu*; see opposite for details.

♥ CENTRE ÉQUESTRE U STAZZU // RIDE HORSEBACK ALONG AN ANCIENT TRAIL

Hiking isn't the only way to explore the Sentier des Douaniers, the ancient footpath that winds around the rugged northern tip of Cap Corse. The **Centre Équestre** (☎ 04 95 35 43 76; 🕑 9am-6pm May-Sep) based at Camping U Stazzu, 2km north of Macinagio, offers guided horseback rides along the coastal trail (€20 per hour), as well as pony-trekking on the beach for kids from five years of age (€12 per half-hour).

GASTRONOMIC HIGHLIGHTS

♥ LE PIRATE // ERBALUNGA €€€

☎ 04 95 33 24 20; www.restaurantlepirate.com; port d'Erbalunga; mains €20-40, menus €29-90; 🕑 lunch & dinner Jul & Aug, lunch & dinner Wed-Sun Mar-Jun & Sep-Dec

Renowned beyond Corsica for its cuisine and service, Le Pirate is one of Cap Corse's most distinguished gourmet restaurants. Sit in the elegant vaulted dining room or on a terrace right next to the harbour, and peruse a menu that features foodie delights such as red mullet scented with verbena oil and lavender, octopus risotto with cuttlefish ink, and langoustine tortellini with roast-hazelnut infusion.

♥ OSTERIA DI U PORTU // MACINAGGIO €€

☎ 04 95 35 40 49; port de Macinaggio; mains €15-22, menus €16-25; 🕑 lunch & dinner Feb-Nov

Enjoying a superb location opposite the marina, this friendly restaurant with appealing red-and-yellow decor is run by a dynamic young team. It serves the freshest of fish and seafood, and it's a minor agony deciding between the five-course *menu découverte* (€22) of Corsican dishes and the seafood *menu de la mer* (€25).

♥ U SANT'AGNELLU // ROGLIANO €€

☎ 04 95 35 40 59; mains €10-18, menu €20; 🕑 lunch & dinner mid-Apr–mid-Oct

A mere 5km west of Macinaggio yet a world away from the crowded coast, the

MAISONS DES AMÉRICAINS

In the 19th century, many Corsicans emigrated to mainland France or to her colonies to escape poverty. Others headed to the Americas, especially the USA, Venezuela, Puerto Rico and Peru, to seek their fortune. In many hamlets of Cap Corse, only the eldest son of his generation remained behind. Some, having made their pile, returned to the villages of their birth and built themselves a fine residence, known as a *maison des américains*. In striking contrast to the more-modest local rural architecture, these proud structures, often with a nod towards Italian palazzi or colonial architecture, proudly asserted 'I have made it. Look at me and mine.'

Around Cap Corse, you can identify these extravagances by their sheer size, their generally rectangular shape and their steep four-sided roofs. Adornment often includes a monumental staircase, a pillared balcony above the main entrance and gardens planted with palms and exotic trees.

area's cosiest and most welcoming choice sits up in the hills, with a panoramic terrace that commands stunning views. The menu features mainly local products, from grilled veal to roast kid to vegetable tart, and varies according to what's available at the market that morning; the signature dessert, *mousse de brousse au miel* (local cream cheese whipped to a mousse with honey), is delightful. From Macinaggio, take the D80 westward and turn left onto the D53, signed Rogliano.

WESTERN CAP CORSE

❦ CENTURI // SAVOUR SEAFOOD AT A HARBOURSIDE RESTAURANT

The tiny, boat-crammed harbour of Centuri is not only the prettiest and most picturesque in Cap Corse, it's also home to the most important crayfish fleet on the island, landing 3 tonnes of the beasties each year. Many of them travel only as far as the *viviers* (live tanks) of the dozen or so seafood restaurants that cluster tightly round the harbour.

There are few more-pleasant spots to savour a seafood feast than in one of these eateries, though you should expect to pay around €150 per kilo for the privilege of dining on crayfish. Stroll around and take your pick – we enjoyed an excellent lunch at the **Auberge du Pêcheur** (☎ 04 95 35 60 14; mains €12-22, menu €25; ☺ lunch & dinner Apr-Oct) on a shady terrace overlooking the harbour. Our charcuterie and fish soup was followed by a *fritto misto de poissons du Cap* (mixed fry of Cap Corse fish), all washed down with a delicious San Quilico rosé from Patrimonio.

❦ THE COAST ROAD // DRIVE THE SPECTACULAR D80

The D80 road along the west coast of Cap Corse is one of the most spectacular

on the island, a long, looping rollercoaster of a ride with stunning views and breathtaking drops into the sea. It's best taken north to south, as part of an anticlockwise tour of the peninsula – the views are best with the mountains of central Corsica in the background – and at a leisurely pace. Despite recent improvements, many stretches are still only wide enough for one vehicle, so take care.

The road passes by several ruined Genoese towers, and in several places minor roads lead off the D80 and corkscrew down to little beaches, called 'marines'. These include Marine de Negru, a shingle beach backed by cliffs and overlooked by a Genoese tower, and the sandy beach of Marine de Farinole, famed for its challenging surfing.

By the way, the ugly industrial scar just north of Nonza – where the road looks like it might crumble into the sea – is a former asbestos quarry that was abandoned in the 1960s. The stone waste from the quarry was dumped into the sea, but washed up again to form the massive shingle beach below Nonza.

❦ NONZA // EXPLORE CAP CORSE'S MOST ENCHANTING VILLAGE

Clinging to the flanks of a rocky pinnacle topped with a stone tower, the village of Nonza is easily the most attractive on the cape's western coast. Its jumble of schist-roofed stone houses looks ready to tumble down the steep hillside, seemingly anchored only by faith and a tangle of pine trees and pink oleander blossoms. Take some time for yourself to wander among its steep and meandering alleys – so tight and precipitous that no vehicle will ever negotiate them – before stopping for a drink at the delightful open-air **Café de**

CORSICA'S PATRON SAINT

Just north of the church in Nonza, a path descends steeply from the road to the Fontaine Ste-Julie, a spring dedicated to Corsica's patron saint. A memorial plaque on the small shrine describes how, in AD 303, 'St Julie was martyred and crucified for her Christian beliefs. After her death, her breasts were cut off and hurled against the rock, whence this miraculous spring arose'. From its twin outlets, the water flows cool on even the hottest day.

Below the fountain, the path drops sharply down to the long strip of grey shingle beach, little frequented at this end and great for Robinson Crusoe–like solitude. To reach it by car, head 2km northward along the D80, then cut left along a narrow paved road that leads to the shore. Take a sun umbrella, as there's no shade.

la Tour, its tables clustered around the village fountain in the shade of a trio of plane trees.

Next door to the cafe, which sits beside the main road in the heart of the village, is the red-and-yellow 16th-century Église Ste-Julie, with a polychrome marble altar created in Florence in 1693. Opposite the church, a steep, stepped lane leads up to the 18th-century Tour de Nonza (admission free; 8am-sunset). In contrast to the circular towers build by the Genoese, this one – built during the era of Pascal Paoli – is square; in summer there's an exhibition of local arts and crafts inside, and the views from the top are superb.

Nestled among the rock outcrops below the tower is La Sassa (06 11 99 49 93; mains €10-25; lunch & dinner May-Oct), a scatter of rickety tables and benches on a clifftop terrace. Serving snacks, salads and ice creams through the day, it turns out steaks, beef ribs, and lamb and prawn kebabs in the evening. There's live music from 7pm on weekends, and on Thursdays in July and August.

INLAND CAP CORSE

The D180 crosses the Cap Corse peninsula between Pino and Marine de Santa Severa, giving access to the peaceful little village of Luri and the expansive views from the Col de Santa Lucia.

🌱 LES JARDINS TRADITIONNELS DU CAP CORSE // TASTE LURI'S LOCAL FRUIT AND VEG

☎ 04 95 35 05 07; www.lesjardinstraditionnelsducap corse.org; admission €4; 9-11.30am Mon-Fri May-Oct

This experimental organic garden has been developed to preserve and display the indigenous strains of plants that have been cultivated in Cap Corse in centuries past, including olive, fig, cherry, plum and peach trees; vegetables such as zucchinis, tomatoes, aubergines, and sweet and flavoursome *oignons de Sisco* (Sisco onions); as well as native wild plants such as maritime pines, green oaks, chestnut trees and arbutus bushes.

Pick up a leaflet and wander through the gardens, then return to the *maison du goût* (tasting house), where you can sample and buy a range of fresh local products such as *cipullina* (onion preserve) and *fiurone* (fig jam), all made by the voluntary association that runs the gardens.

The gardens are 800m east of Luri, on the south side of the road – look for the parking area just before the road crosses the river. It's not signposted.

TOP **FIVE**

SCENIC VIEWPOINTS

★ **Bastia's Citadel** (p40) – Great views over the Vieux Port

★ **Tour de Sénèque** (below) – The crest of Cap Corse

★ **D80 Coast Road** (p48) – An ever-changing panorama of coast and mountain

★ **Tour de Nonza** (p49) – A dizzying outpost perched high above the sea

★ **Sierra di Pigno** (p57) – A supreme vantage point above the Golfe de St-Florent

❦ A MIMORIA DI U VINU // LEARN ABOUT THE WINES OF CORSICA IN LURI

☎ 04 95 35 06 44; adult/child €3/free; ⏲ 10am-noon & 4-7pm Tue-Sat Jun-Sep

Luri's little wine museum presents the history of Corsica's wine industry through displays of winemaking equipment and interviews with traditional winemakers. Best of all, it offers an amusing and interesting introduction to wine tasting by firstly challenging you to describe various scents and flavours before moving on to the local wines themselves.

Each year, on the first or second weekend of July, Luri hosts the **Fiera di u Vinu** (www.acunfraternita.com, in French), a wine festival with market stalls, barbecues, musical events and, of course, lots of wine tasting.

❦ LE TOUR DE SÉNÈQUE // HIKE TO AN ANCIENT LOOKOUT TOWER

From the Col de Santa Lucia (381m), the highest point of the D180, some vigorous walking, mostly through mixed woodland, will bring you to the Tour de Sénèque and perhaps the finest of the cape's many superlative-inspiring panoramas.

Leave your car beside the dilapidated chapel at the *col* (pass) and follow the red flashes as far as a complex of abandoned buildings. Here the gradient becomes stiffer and you'll be using all four limbs to negotiate one brief stretch. But what a vista! From the crumbling Genoese tower, the view embraces both Cap Corse's eastern and western shorelines, as well as the Monte Stello range, the cape's north–south dorsal spine. Allow one hour for this fairly strenuous, hugely rewarding walk.

LE NEBBIO

· · · · · ·

The Nebbio, relatively lightly travelled, is something of a buffer zone, squeezed between Bastia and Cap Corse to the north and La Balagne, with its coastal fleshpots and rugged interior beauty, to the southwest.

West of the fashionable St-Florent stretches the little-visited expanses of the Désert des Agriates, fringed by some of Corsica's most beautiful beaches. The Nebbio is also one of the island's prime wine-producing areas: there are more than 30 vineyards in and around Patrimonio, still in the hands of small-scale producers. The first Corsican region to be granted Appellation d'Origine Contrôlée (AOC) status, Patrimonio produces some of the island's finest vintages.

ST-FLORENT (SAN FIURENZU)

pop 1500

If you believe the locals, the chic resort of St-Florent, the Nebbio's main town (in fact its only place of any size), is a kind of St Tropez in miniature – and indeed, if you stroll alongside the marina where luxury yachts the size of your house are moored, you'll see what they're driving at. The town compensates for the absence of major monuments with a welcoming, laid-back atmosphere and some delightful nearby beaches. And, for a place of its size, it has some first-class restaurants.

ORIENTATION

St-Florent is little more than a village, and is easily explored on foot. The main D81 road from Bastia and Patrimonio skirts the eastern side of the town and leads into place des Portes, the main square and a major traffic bottleneck. The narrow streets of the old town stretch northward towards place Doria. Crossing the river Poggio, the D81 continues south towards Oletta, while sandy Plage de la Roya stretches westward.

ESSENTIAL INFORMATION

TOURIST INFORMATION // St Florent
tourist office (☎ 04 95 37 06 04; ☺ 9am-noon & 2-5pm Mon-Fri, 9am-noon Sat)

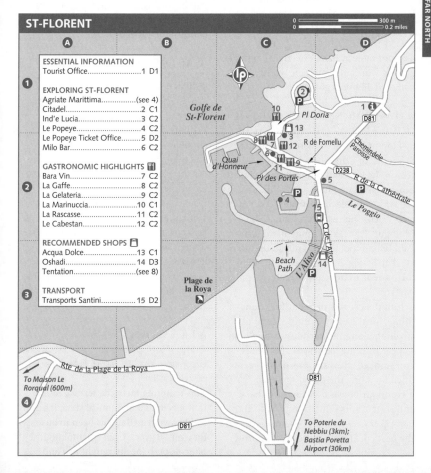

ST-FLORENT

| 0 | 300 m |
| 0 | 0.2 miles |

ESSENTIAL INFORMATION
Tourist Office.........................1 D1

EXPLORING ST-FLORENT
Agriate Marittima................(see 4)
Citadel....................................2 C1
Ind'e Lucia.............................3 C2
Le Popeye..............................4 C2
Le Popeye Ticket Office.........5 D2
Milo Bar.................................6 C2

GASTRONOMIC HIGHLIGHTS 🍴
Bara Vin.................................7 C2
La Gaffe.................................8 C2
La Gelateria...........................9 C2
La Marinuccia.....................10 C1
La Rascasse.........................11 C2
Le Cabestan.......................12 C2

RECOMMENDED SHOPS 🛍
Acqua Dolce........................13 C1
Oshadi................................14 D3
Tentation............................(see 8)

TRANSPORT
Transports Santini...............15 D2

Golfe de St-Florent

Pl Doria

R de Fornellu

Chemindele Paroisse

Quai d'Honneur

Pl des Portes

D238

R de la Cathédrale

Le Poggio

O de l'Aliso

L'Aliso

Beach Path

Plage de la Roya

Rte de la Plage de la Roya

To Maison Le Rorqual (600m)

D81

To Poterie du Nebbiu (3km); Bastia Poretta Airport (30km)

EXPLORING ST-FLORENT

☗ PLACE DORIA // RELAX AND WATCH THE WORLD GO BY

Centred on a cute little fountain lined with bronze frogs, place Doria is the cool and shady heart of old St-Florent. Though only a few steps away from the bustling harbour, the old square seems to move at a slower pace. Cafe tables are scattered beneath a spreading plane tree, and there are a couple of benches in the far corner that enjoy superb sunset views.

Both locals and tourists meet here for a drink and a chat, or to buy an ice cream from Ind'ê Lucia. The atmosphere is at its best in early evening – grab an outdoor table at Bara Vin (right), order a glass of wine and watch the world (well, half of St-Florent) go by.

☗ QUAI D'HONNEUR // COCKTAIL HOUR AMONG THE SUPERYACHTS

St-Florent likes to think of itself as the St Tropez of Corsica, and not without reason. Its gourmet restaurants, secluded beaches and good harbour within easy cruising distance of the Côte d'Azur attract celebs such as Elton John, Kylie Minogue, Jean-Paul Gaultier and Jean-Paul Belmondo, whose gin palaces moor at what 'St-Flo' has christened the quai d'Honneur to match its counterpart in 'St Trop'.

Join the crowds of beautiful young things for the early-evening ritual of strolling along the harbour, trying not to peer into the luxurious afterdecks and smoked-glass saloons of the yachts lined up along the quay. The quai d'Honneur boasts a dozen or so bars and restaurants – the trendy Milo Bar (☎ 04 95 37 19 19; rte Neuve; ☽ 10am-2am) has the best cocktails, served with appro-

priate hauteur, and its terrace provides a grandstand view of the goings-on in the harbour. Afterwards, head for a seafood dinner at La Gaffe (below) or La Rascasse (opposite).

☗ CITADEL // STRETCH YOUR LEGS, SOAK UP THE VIEW

An easy not-even-10-minute ascent from the harbour brings you to the rather forlorn and tumbledown outer bulwarks of St-Florent's citadel. Built under the Genoese, its much-restored interior is closed to the public. What makes the climb worthwhile is the eagle's-eye panorama from the ample terrace that extends beneath the fortification.

GASTRONOMIC HIGHLIGHTS

☗ BARA VIN €

☎ 04 95 37 04 48; place Doria; mains €6-16; ☽ 4pm-late May-Sep

With its impressive range of AOC Patrimonio wines by the glass (€3.50 to €7) and tables spilling onto place Doria, this is a top place for an early-evening drink – recommended crus include the white from Clos Teddi, and the muscat from Domaine de Catarelli. You can snack on tapas or turn the experience into a full dinner; the menu runs from an excellent *assiette de charcuterie* (charcuterie platter) or a Spanish tortilla to a sizeable platter of mixed dishes or even steak and chips.

☗ LA GAFFE €€

☎ 04 95 37 0012; quai d'Honneur; mains €12-59, menu €28; ☽ dinner Mon & Tue, lunch & dinner Wed-Sun mid-Feb–mid-Nov

This tempting quayside terrace restaurant, decorated in nautical style, is a St-Flo favourite that has been in business for over 30 years. Chef Chantal Bourneuf offers superb locally caught fish and seafood – such as *araignée de mer* (spider crab) with tagliatelle, *daube de lotte* (monkfish stewed with wine and vegetables), *sautée de St-Jacques* (fried scallops in a rich seafood reduction) – that's cooked simply and with care.

❦ LA GELATERIA €
rue de Fornellu; per scoop €1.50; ◷ 1.30-7pm May-Oct, 1.30-10pm Jul & Aug

You'll probably have to wait a while in line at this popular spot, which offers more than 50 different flavours of home-made ice cream. All the usual favourites are there, plus some more-original ones, such as maquis herbs, Murato chestnut and (oh, yes!) Nebbio olive oil.

❦ LA MARINUCCIA €€
☎ 04 95 37 04 36; place Doria; mains €25-45, menu €23; ◷ dinner Tue, lunch & dinner Wed-Sun May-Oct

Perched on a terrace built out over the sea in a hidden corner of the town, La Marinuccia offers a choice of seafood or beef, both beautifully prepared. The house speciality is *sardines au Brocciu* (sardines stuffed with goat's- or ewe's-milk cheese and mint), while daily specials such as *fricassée de langouste et St-Jacques* (fricassee of crayfish and scallops) are scrawled on the blackboard. Book a table for an hour before sunset, and enjoy the sound of waves lapping on the rocks as you watch the sun descend into the gulf in a blaze of glory.

❦ LA RASCASSE €€
☎ 04 95 37 06 99; quai d'Honneur; mains €16-48, menu €38; ◷ lunch & dinner mid-Mar–Oct

Arguably the finest of St-Florent's gourmet restaurants, La Rascasse combines elegance and attentive service with imaginative and flavoursome seafood. House specialities include salt-baked sea bass with fennel (€70 for two), and

fresh crayfish (€14 per 100g), as well as inventive dishes such as ravioli of mussels flavoured with leek. You can dine in the brick-arched interior or on the harbourside terrace, next to the giant yachts.

❦ LE CABESTAN €€
☎ 04 95 37 05 70; rue de Fornellu; mains €13-30, menu €17; ◷ lunch & dinner mid-Apr–Oct

This barrel-vaulted tunnel of a place with a small mezzanine floor is very much of the island – there's polyphonic singing in the background, and it does a great-value *menu Corse*. The *soupe de poissons* is huge and hearty, and the *daurade* (sea bream), stuffed with tomato, lemon and herbs from the maquis, is grilled to perfection.

RECOMMENDED SHOPS

❦ ACQUA DOLCE
place Doria

This tiny shop-cum-workshop tucked in a corner of place Doria sells a range of handmade gold and silver jewellery set with semiprecious stones including turquoise, jet and coral. Prices are reasonable, beginning at €20 for earrings, €40 for necklaces and €25 for bracelets.

❦ OSHADI
☎ 04 95 37 00 21; www.oshadimassages.com; quai de l'Aliso

One of the few such places on the island, Oshadi is a shop and cafe that offers organic produce, natural cosmetics, essential oils and healthy eating supplements; it also has a Turkish bath (€12 for 30 minutes) and offers massages.

❦ TENTATION
☎ 04 95 37 06 21; Strada Nova

Set on the quayside opposite the super-yacht berths, this place specialises in women's fashion, with a range of elegant dresses, skirts, trousers, shorts and shirts, mainly made from white or black linen.

❦ POTERIE DU NEBBIU

☎ 06 18 52 79 51; D82, plaine d'Oletta

Located 3km southeast of St-Florent on the road to Oletta, this unassuming little roadside pottery turns out beautiful glazed stoneware in a range of traditional and modern designs. It's a one-man operation, and you can watch the potter at work; he speaks a little bit of English.

TRANSPORT

BUS // The bus stop is just south of the main square. **Transports Santini** (☎ 04 95 37 04 01) buses depart for Bastia (twice daily).

CAR // St-Florent is a traffic bottleneck – driving across the main square in the morning or late afternoon will involve a long wait. Bastia airport is a 30km drive southeast from St-Florent via the winding D82; allow at least 40 minutes.

PARKING // On-street parking is tight in the town centre – it's best to park on the outskirts and walk in.

AROUND ST-FLORENT

❦ PLAGE DU LOTO // TAKE A BOAT TRIP TO THE BEACH

The picture-postcard Plage du Loto (also called Plage du Lodo, du Lodu and, to complete the confusion, du Lotu), on the edge of the Désert des Agriates, is a superb 400m stretch of fine white sand fringing a shallow bay of brilliant turquoise water. It's a beautiful spot for swimming and sunbathing, and the shallow water is safe for children to play in. Apart from a small wooden jetty, the beach is completely undeveloped – no hotels, no snack bars, no deckchairs – so bring a picnic and plenty of water, and some form of shade.

Plage du Loto is hard to get to by land – it's either a long, hot hike along the coastal path from St-Florent, or a slow and bumpy 4WD ride from the D81 at Casta. But the easiest way to get to the beach – a 30-minute boat trip from St-Florent harbour – is also the most enjoyable; it's a classic St-Flo experience. Two companies run boat trips to the beach. From mid-June to September **Le Popeye** (☎ 04 95 37 19 07; www.lepopeye.com; round trip adult/child €14/8) departs St-Florent at least hourly from 8.30am to 3.30pm, and departs from the beach from 11.20am to 7.30pm; in May and early June there are five boats a day each way (10am to 1.45pm outward, noon to 4.30pm return). You can buy tickets on the pier, or book in advance at Le Popeye ticket office on the town square.

Agriate Marittima (☎ 06 17 50 65 58; www.agriate-marittima.com; round trip adult/child €14/8) departs from the same pier, and has similar timings. It also offers the option of continuing from Plage du Loto to Plage de Saleccia by *calèche* (horse-drawn carriage; round trip adult/child €29/20).

❦ PLAGE DE SALECCIA // HIKE ALONG THE AGRIATES COAST

Just a few kilometres west of Plage du Loto lies the bigger and even more beautiful Plage de Saleccia, a 1000m-long strand of dazzling white sand backed by scented groves of Corsican pine, where chestnut-coloured cattle often snooze alongside the sunbathers. You can get here from Plage du Loto by *calèche,* but it's far more rewarding to walk. A coastal path known as the **Sentier du Littoral** runs all the way from St-Florent to Ostriconi (45km), but the stretch linking Loto and Saleccia is just under 4km, and can be linked with the inland trail used by the *calèches* to make an excellent circular walk.

From the jetty at Plage du Loto go left then right up a steep trail to the *calèche* stand, and follow the dusty 4WD track into the maquis. Enjoy the view of the central mountains ahead as you breathe in the scent of pine needles baking in the sun and listen to the chirr of cicadas. Go right at a junction with some ruined stone sheds and, at the fork where you can see a campsite ahead, go right again to reach the western end of the beach; the walk takes around 45 minutes. To return, head for the far end of the beach (20 minutes), then follow the path along the coast (55 minutes). The total distance for the walk is 8km; allow around two hours of walking.

There are no facilities on the beach, but there's a little shop and a bar at the nearby **Camping U Paradisu** (☎ 04 95 37 82 51; www.camping-uparadisu.com; ☺ bar 9am-midnight), which serves snacks from noon.

♥ PATRIMONIO // DISCOVER THE FINE WINES OF THE NEBBIO

Located 6km from St-Florent, Patrimonio has two principal claims to fame: its vineyards and its annual guitar festival. You'll recognise the village from a distance by its 16th-century **Église St-Martin**, a stout stone construction of granite and brown schist that's become an informal icon for the Corsican wine industry.

Patrimonio sits in the centre of a natural amphitheatre of limestone crags known as the **Conca d'Oro** (Golden

BASTIA & THE FAR NORTH

∼ WORTH A TRIP ∼

Between St-Florent and the mouth of the Ostriconi river lies an arid landscape known as the **Désert des Agriates**, an area of low chalky mountains and a maquis so sun scorched that even the plants seem rocklike.

It's hard to believe this area was once Genoa's breadbasket. Indeed, right up until the 20th century, life in the area was governed by the rhythms of seasonal livestock grazing and sowing. In October shepherds from the Nebbio highlands and the Vallée d'Asco would bring their goats and sheep down for the winter, and in June farmers arriving by boat from Cap Corse would take over the area. At one time, the region was as famous for its olive groves as those of the Balagne villages. But the widespread use of *écobuage* (cultivation on burnt stubble) and the devastation wrought by fires fanned by the prevailing winds transformed the once-fertile soil into a stony, barren desert.

The 35km of coastline, by contrast, offer spectacular back-to-nature scenery. The Plage de Saleccia (opposite) – setting for the film *The Longest Day* (1960) – stretches for nearly 1km, its shimmering white sand and turquoise waters comparing favourably with any tropical-island paradise. The smaller but equally as stunning Plage du Loto (p54) and **Plage de l'Ostriconi**, at the eastern and western edges of the Agriates region respectively, are also superb. Some claim the latter has the finest-grained sand in all of Europe.

In the 1970s, various hare-brained schemes were proposed to transform the area, including building a Club Med–style holiday complex. All were resisted and nowadays the full 5000-odd hectares of the Désert des Agriates enjoy protected status.

Shell), where the chalk and clay soil has been used for growing vines since Roman times. The Patrimonio area was the first in Corsica to be granted an AOC seal of quality; the region's vineyards are small, the vines are pruned and picked by hand, and most adhere to organic principles of agriculture. The signed Route des Vins leads from St-Florent around nearly 500 hectares of land cultivated by around 30 small growers; ask at the St-Florent tourist office (p51) for its slender *AOC Patrimonio: La Route des Vins* brochure. Most of the wineries welcome visitors for tastings without appointment.

The wines themselves – crisp dry whites, rosés more golden than pink, and robust reds – well merit your attention. The sweet and fruity muscat dessert wine, once exported in quantity by the Genoese, now rarely gets beyond the island.

The following are among the recommended *caves* (cellars):

Clos de Bernardi (☎ 04 95 37 01 09) Top-notch reds from a certified organic producer.

Domaine de Catarelli (☎ 04 95 37 02 84) Superb muscat.

Domaine Gentile (☎ 04 95 37 01 54; www .domaine-gentile.com) Perhaps the most exclusive cru.

Domaine Leccia (☎ 04 95 37 11 35; www .domaine-leccia.com) Excellent reds that regularly win awards.

Domaine Orenga de Gaffory (☎ 04 95 37 45 00) The pick of the full-bodied reds.

♥ NUITS DE LA GUITARE // LISTEN TO LIVE MUSIC UNDER THE STARS

For a week each year in July, Guitar Nights, one of the highlights of Corsica's summer calendar, puts the tiny Nebbio village of Patrimonio on the map for something other than its excellent wines. The **Association Les Nuits de la Guitare** (☎ 04 95 37 12 15; www.festival-guitare-patrimonio.

com) organises an eclectic program that in any one year might include Corsican, classical and flamenco guitar, and styles as diverse as rock, salsa, blues and jazz. The 2009 line-up, for example, included singer-songwriter Tracy Chapman, Ten Years After guitar legend Alvin Lee, flamenco maestro Vicente Amigo and Irish rock-guitarist Pat MacManus.

Events take place on an outdoor stage flanked by a couple of menhir statues. Tickets (€30 to €40 per night) are available from the festival office in Patrimonio, selected music and bookshops across Corsica, and online.

♥ OSTERIA DI SAN MARTINU // TUCK INTO BARBECUED LAMB ON AN OPEN-AIR TERRACE

This attractive **restaurant** (☎ 04 95 37 11 93; Patrimonio; mains €13-17, menu €22; ☽ lunch & dinner Jun-Sep) with views over the vineyards specialises in hearty meat dishes grilled over vine twigs on an open-air barbecue; we savoured the lamb chops, juicy, tender and still pink in the middle. It also does a magnificent four-course *menu Corse*, which includes a giant platter of local charcuterie. The house wines are supplied by Domaine Lazzarini, located just up the road and run by the owner's brother.

DRIVING TOUR

Distance: 70km
Duration: four hours

From St-Florent, take the D81 northward and drop into **Patrimonio** (p55) if you haven't already visited it; should you be off to a late start, Osteria di San Martinu (above) makes a great lunch stop.

Otherwise, continue to the **Col de Teghime** (536m), high up on the island's spine and straddling the mountains between Bastia and St-Florent. Less than a kilometre beyond the pass, take a narrow tarred road left for the steep 4.5km ascent to the summit of the **Sierra di Pigno** (961m), bristling with radio and telephone antennae. From its windy top, there are soul-stirring views in all directions: eastward as far as the Italian island of Elba on a clear day, west to the Golfe de St-Florent and the Désert des Agriates, and north over the snaggle-toothed peaks of Cap Corse. Below you sprawls Bastia, extending almost to the shimmering waters of the Étang de Biguglia.

Return to the *col* and take the signed D38 to pass through the straggling hamlets of **Poggio d'Oletta** and **Oletta**, the latter dominated by its 18th-century Église de San Cervone. At the northern entrance to Oletta, just off the D38,

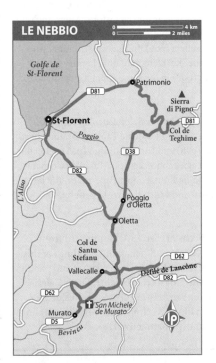

LE NEBBIO

Golfe de St-Florent

Patrimonio

D81

Sierra di Pigno

St-Florent

D81

Poggio

Col de Teghime

D38

L'Aliso

D82

Poggio d'Oletta

Oletta

Col de Santu Stefanu

D62

Vallecalle

Défilé de Lancône

D82

D62

San Michele de Murato

Murato

D5

Bevincu

L'Auberge A Magina (☎ 04 95 39 01 01; menu €15, mains €15-20; ☯ lunch & dinner Tue-Sun Apr-Oct) has great views across the Nebbio from its terrace.

At the roundabout marking the **Col de Santu Stefanu**, 4km beyond Oletta, there is a possible detour. But first pause at the second of two monuments honouring the Moroccan troops and their French officers who, at this strategic spot and at the Col de Teghime, fought to take Bastia in 1943, the first French town to be liberated from Axis rule. From the roundabout, two roads, the D62 and the D82, snake around the deep gash of the **Défilé de Lancône**, then drop to the N193 and the coast; for a switchback thrill, follow the more-spectacular D62 for a kilometre or two as it creeps along the contours of this narrow gorge, then return to the roundabout to take the exit signed Murato.

You can't miss the gorgeous Pisan Romanesque **Église de San Michele de Murato**, with its distinctive green-and-white stripes and checkerboard patterning. The white blocks (chalk) came from St-Florent, while the green (ophite) was quarried from the bed of the nearby Bevincu river. Naive figurines carved in the stone peer down from the upper reaches. The church dates from around 1140, and local legend has it that the structure was built in just one night by angels. During Corsica's brief independence in the 18th century, the village of **Murato**, a kilometre or so further along the road, was the seat of the new state's mint.

If night's approaching by now, Chambres d'Hôtes Gaucher (p243) is a warmly recommended *chambres d'hôtes* (B&B) just a short drive away in the hamlet of Vallecalle. From here, head east to the D82 and follow this road north to return to St-Florent.

CALVI & LA BALAGNE

3 PERFECT DAYS

☙ DAY 1 // EXPLORING CALVI

Get your beach work in early, before the sun gets too intense. Then explore Calvi's citadel (opposite) for stunning seascapes and views as well as for the history. After lunching lightly, drive to the chapel of Notre Dame de la Serra (p66) for a magnificent bird's-eye view of Calvi or walk out along Pointe de la Revellata (p66). In the early evening, window-shop in the old quarter, then stroll along the short length of quai Landry (p65) at sunset. End the day with dinner in a restaurant (p68) in the same small historical area.

☙ DAY 2 // ÎLE ROUSSE & AROUND

Spend the cooler part of the morning exploring the Parc de Saleccia (p72). Enjoy an early lunch at the splendid Michelin-starred Restaurant Pasquale Paoli (p75), then head inland to explore the Balagne villages of Pigna (p78) and Sant'Antonino (p81), allowing at least an hour for each. Returning, take in the agreeably eccentric Musée de Corbara (p78; note those restricted entry hours!). Back in Île Rousse, sip an aperitif on the terrace of venerable Café des Platanes (p73), wind down and watch the world drift by.

☙ DAY 3 // A COASTAL ESCAPE

Follow the spectacular, lightly travelled D81B coastal road (p70) southward from Calvi. At Argentella (p71) explore the furnaces, dam and remaining buildings of this abandoned silver mine. In the small seaside resort of Galéria, hire a kayak and paddle the waters of the Delta du Fango (p71), renowned for its rich birdlife. From Galéria, take the D351 as it follows the valley of the river Fango (p72) upstream. Beside the river are several choice spots for a picnic and a dip in its clear waters. Backtrack almost to Galéria and return to Calvi by the faster, almost-as-attractive D81.

CALVI

· · · · ·

pop 5500

Calvi, 'capital' of the Balagne region, is the closest Corsican town to France's Mediterranean coast; indeed, with its thriving cafe culture and restaurants ringing the port, it might have been transplanted from the Côte d'Azur. Explore the lanes and alleys of the citadel, dine at a restaurant near quai Landry, and loll on the town's long strand of beach. Make sure, too, that you jump aboard the rickety Tramway de la Balagne as it trundles to Île Rousse and back.

It was the Romans who first established a settlement here. Frequently exposed to raids by Barbary pirates, Calvi fell under the fairly loose control of Pisa from the 11th to 13th centuries. In the late 13th century, rivalries between local lords caused Calvi's inhabitants to turn to the republic of Genoa for protection. Using Calvi and the southern town of Bonifacio as bases, Genoa soon took control of all Corsica.

The city's most famous hour came in 1553, when France dispatched its troops to invade Corsica. Joined by Turkish forces under the command of the Turkish privateer Dragut, this motley fleet captured Bastia, St-Florent and Bonifacio but failed to take Calvi. In recognition of the town's resistance, Genoa gave the town its motto: *Civitas Calvi semper fidelis* (City of Calvi forever faithful).

ESSENTIAL INFORMATION

TOURIST OFFICES // Tourist office (☎ 04 95 65 16 67; www.balagne-corsica.com; port de plaisance; ☺ 9am-noon & 2-6pm Mon-Sat, 9am-1pm Sun May-Oct, 9am-noon & 2-6pm Mon-Fri Nov-Apr) Covers Calvi and La Balagne. Produces an audioguide to the citadel (€7). Tourist office annexe (☺ 10am-12.30pm & 3-6pm Tue-Sat, 3-6pm Sun mid-Jun–Aug, 11am-6pm Tue-Sat early Jun & Sep) A seasonal annexe just inside the citadel.

EXPLORING CALVI

♥ TRAMWAY DE LA BALAGNE // CLASSIC RAIL JOURNEY BESIDE GETAWAY BEACHES

Every year the beaches and hidden coves of the Balagne coastline come to life with the first beach towel of summer. The lifeline that connects these isolated coves is the Tramway de la Balagne (☎ 04 95 65 00 61; www.ter-sncf.com, in French; single/return €5.40/8).

This bone-shaking little train trundles between Calvi and Île Rousse up to eight times daily between Easter and September, calling at 15 stations en route, all of which are request only. Hop off at an intermediate halt for a quiet rocky cove or, for sand, leave the train at Algajola or Plage de Bodri, the last stop before Île Rousse.

There has been talk for years of improving the rolling stock but so far little has changed. All to the good – the train's lo-fi quality adds to its charm. Indeed, rail enthusiasts from all over the world now converge on Calvi to ride what's affectionately known as *u trinighellu* (the trembler) before it's finally put out to pasture. Bag a seat on the seaward side.

♥ CITADEL // CALVI'S DEFENSIVE BASTION: HISTORY AND SPECTACULAR VIEWS

No entry tickets, no visiting hours, no compulsory guided tour – you're free to explore the citadel's heterogeneous cluster of buildings as the mood takes you,

(Continued on page 64)

CALVI & LA BALAGNE

CALVI & LA BALAGNE

CALVI & LA BALAGNE

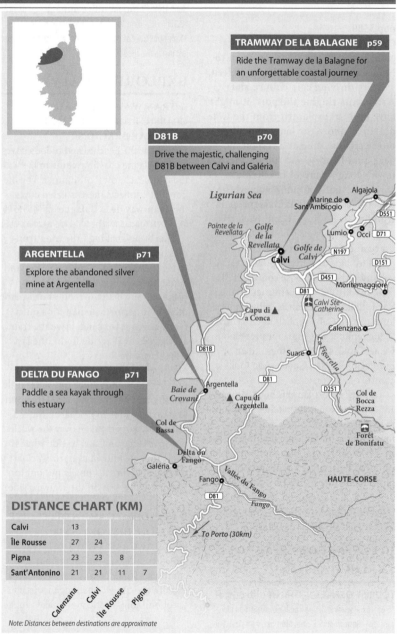

TRAMWAY DE LA BALAGNE   p59

Ride the Tramway de la Balagne for an unforgettable coastal journey

D81B   p70

Drive the majestic, challenging D81B between Calvi and Galéria

Ligurian Sea

ARGENTELLA   p71

Explore the abandoned silver mine at Argentella

Algajola

Marine de Sant'Ambrogio

D551

Pointe de la Revellata   *Golfe de la Revellata*

Lumio   Occi   D71

Golfe de Calvi

N197

Calvi

D151

D451

Montemaggiore

D81

Calvi Ste-Catherine

Capu di a Conca

Calenzana

Suare

D81B

Figarella

D81

DELTA DU FANGO   p71

Paddle a sea kayak through this estuary

Baie de Crovani   Argentella

Capu di Argentella

D251   Col de Bocca Rezza

Col de Bassa

Forêt de Bonifatu

Delta du Fango

Galéria

Fango   *Vallée du Fango*

HAUTE-CORSE

D81

Fango

To Porto (30km)

DISTANCE CHART (KM)

	Calenzana	Calvi	Île Rousse	Pigna
Calvi	13			
Île Rousse	27	24		
Pigna	23	23	8	
Sant'Antonino	21	21	11	7

Note: Distances between destinations are approximate

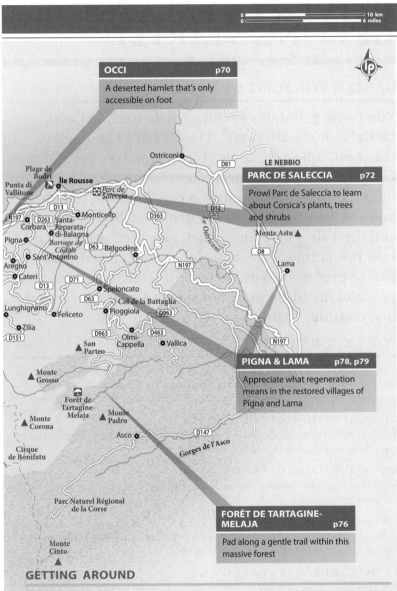

OCCI   p70

A deserted hamlet that's only
accessible on foot

LE NEBBIO

PARC DE SALECCIA   p72

Prowl Parc de Saleccia to learn
about Corsica's plants, trees
and shrubs

PIGNA & LAMA   p78, p79

Appreciate what regeneration
means in the restored villages of
Pigna and Lama

**FORÊT DE TARTAGINE-
MELAJA**   p76

Pad along a gentle trail within this
massive forest

CALVI & LA BALAGNE

GETTING AROUND

You can comfortably survive on the coast without a vehicle, taking the Tramway de la Balagne
between Calvi, Île Rousse and intermediate stations. But to head southward or to experience the
seductive inland delights of La Balagne, a vehicle of your own is the only way. In this chapter, we
detail two full-day driving routes that explore inland (p76 and p80), plus a circular day outing south
of Calvi (p70).

CALVI & LA BALAGNE
GETTING STARTED

MAKING THE MOST OF YOUR TIME

You could profitably spend a whole week in Calvi, La Balagne's main resort. Don't restrict yourself to the coast, however; allow at least two days to explore Calvi's delights, then grab the steering wheel to explore inland Balagne for a couple more. Build in, too, the hold-on-to-your-hat coastal drive southward to Galéria and the Vallée du Fango. Then give the car a rest and take the Tramway de la Balagne, the dinkiest train you've ever swayed on, to visit Île Rousse, Calvi's more peaceful northern neighbour; if you're after tranquillity, consider basing yourself here.

TOP EXCURSIONS

☙ BOAT TRIPS TO THE RÉSERVE NATURELLE DE SCANDOLA
Take a boat trip with Colombo Line – the journey is a thrill in itself – to this spectacular marine and terrestrial nature reserve with its rich birdlife and stunning cliffs (p66).

☙ INLAND TO THE FORÊT DE BONIFATU
A varied day's driving that embraces a couple of vineyards, a venerated chapel and the opportunity to walk deep into silent forest (p76).

☙ INLAND VILLAGES OF LA BALAGNE
A scenic driving tour that also takes in the main villages of the interior, including the craft settlement of Pigna (p80).

☙ BIANCONI SCUPERTA
Sit back in air-conditioned luxury as you enjoy a guided visit, planned by a local historian and executed by his enthusiastic young team (p64).

☙ CIRCULAR DRIVE SOUTH OF CALVI
A full day of stunning panoramas with the chance to prowl an abandoned silver mine, sea kayak and swim in freshwater pools (p71).

☙ TRAMWAY DE LA BALAGNE
Clunk and sway on this classic rail route as it snakes along the coast between Calvi and Île Rousse (p59).

CALVI & LA BALAGNE

GETTING AWAY FROM IT ALL

You'll rarely find yourself truly alone on the coast in summer. If you head upward and inland, however, you'll find near-empty roads and a wealth of walking opportunities among small hamlets.

* **Delta du Fango** Silent paddling along a bird-rich estuary (p71)

* **Small coves below the Tramway de la Balagne** It *is* still possible to find a less frequented beach (p59)

* **Occi** You may well have company on the walk up to this deserted village, but if you continue onward you'll find satisfying all-alone striding (p70)

* **Forêt de Tartagine-Melaja** A deep, silent inland forest (p76)

TOP WALKS

♣ POINTE DE LA REVELLATA
Walk the promontory that extends south of Calvi for great views of the town and its backdrop of mountains (p66)

♣ NOTRE DAME DE LA SERRA
A huffing, puffing ascent from Calvi to a haunting shrine and vista followed by a hands-in-pocket descent (p56)

♣ OCCI
An easy ascent to a haunting deserted hamlet, then onwards to enjoy the changing panorama of coastal seascapes (p70)

♣ FORÊT DE TARTAGINE-MELAJA
Quiet padding through dense woodland, as long or short as you care to make it (p76)

TOP EATING EXPERIENCES

♣ EAT
Epicurean delight at the foot of the citadel (p68)

♣ LE JARDIN
Delightful dining in a lovely leafy garden (p68)

♣ RESTAURANT PASQUALE PAOLI
Michelin-starred newcomer that's Corsican to the core (p75)

♣ L'ESCALE
Popular dining in Île Rousse's old quarter (p74)

♣ CASA MUSICALE
Dine on the terrace or in the barrel-vaulted interior (p79)

♣ U CALLELU
Serves the freshest of produce (p69)

RESOURCES

* **La Balagne** (www.balagne-corsica.com) Site of Calvi and Île Rousse tourist offices; also covers the Balagne in general

* **Ma Balagne** (www.mabalagne.com) Multilingual message board with links to Balagne-related blogs

* **Parc Naturel Régional de la Corse (PNRC)** (www.parc-naturel-corse.com, in French) The body that administers much of inland Corsica

CALVI & LA BALAGNE

(Continued from page 59)

enjoying superb wraparound views of Calvi and its bay at almost every turn.

Built in the late 15th century by the Genoese, it has seen off several major assaults down the centuries, fending off everyone from Franco-Turkish raiders to Anglo-Corsican armies – notably during the siege of 1794, when the citadel was attacked by the forces of the revolutionary leader Pascal Paoli (see the boxed text, p193), supported by the British. During the ensuing battle, a young captain by the name of Horatio Nelson lost his right eye.

Just above place Christophe Colomb, pass through the **citadel entrance** (an arch with the town's motto inscribed above it), and take one of the alleys that lead steeply upward to **place d'Armes** and the former Palais des Gouverneurs Génois. Built in the 13th century and extended during the 16th, it was once the palace of the Genoese governors of La Balagne. Now renamed **Caserne Sampiero**, it serves as the officers' mess hall for the French Foreign Legion, who are billeted just outside town (you'll probably come across soldiers wearing the regiment's distinctive white hats, which are known as *képis*).

The **Cathédrale St-Jean Baptiste** (☾ 9am-6pm) overlooks place d'Armes. To the right of the high altar and protected behind glass, the ebony *Christ des Miracles* is credited with having saved the town from Franco-Turkish invasion in 1553; legend has it that the besieging fleet turned tail after the citizens paraded the statue through their streets.

Popular belief also has it that the (now missing) central panel of the 15th-century triptych on the wall behind the altar was destroyed by an English cannonball during Nelson's siege. Others sources aver that it was simply filched. What's indisputable is that it was replaced by a particularly kitsch statuette of the cathedral's patron, John the Baptist.

Retrace your steps to the place d'Armes. The little street on the left leads to the **Oratoire de la Confrérie St-Antoine** (Oratory of the St Antoine Brotherhood; ☾ 10am-6pm), whose facade features a primitive slate lintel depicting the abbot St Antoine. The interior walls are decorated with 15th- and 16th-century frescos (some, alas, severely timeworn) and, on the north wall, there's an imposing ivory Christ figure. Opening hours can be irregular.

The citadel has five bastions, each offering wonderful seascapes. Near Bastion Celle in the northwest corner a marble plaque marks the alleged **birthplace of Christopher Columbus**.

❦ BIANCONI SCUPERTA //
GUIDED TOURS LED BY A LOCAL HISTORIAN
The enthusiastic young team of **Bianconi Scuperta** (☎ 06 30 78 94 93, in French; per person half-day €40, full day €45-55; ☾ Apr–mid-Nov) offers original tours of La Balagne based upon themes such as 'saints and bandits', 'the Corsican soul' and 'feudal lords and feudal arts'. Tours are generally in French, but are also regularly in English in the high season, and prices include travel by air-conditioned vehicle.

❦ VAGABOND'ARTE // **WALK AND CREATE IN THE BALAGNE COUNTRYSIDE**
Join artist Cathy Astolfi (Corsican as they come, despite her first name), creator of **Vagabond'Arte** (☎ 04 95 34 21 82, 06 46 21 84 66; www.cathy-astolfi.com, in French; workshop incl materials €20; ☾ Apr-Oct), as she leads a rural

walk and open-air guided workshop (2½ hours). Based on their day's experience, participants can sketch or paint, create a video or photographic record, or assemble a work of installation art. Reserve in advance. No prior knowledge is necessary.

🍴 **QUAI LANDRY // A QUAYSIDE STROLL**

With pleasure craft bobbing to starboard, bars and restaurants beckoning to port, a short sunset stroll along the quay brings you to the **Tour de Sel**, built for defence and later serving as the town's

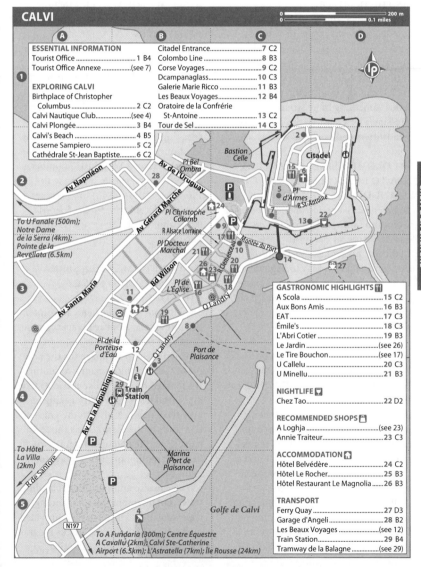

CALVI

ESSENTIAL INFORMATION	Citadel Entrance 7 C2
Tourist Office 1 B4	Colombo Line 8 B3
Tourist Office Annexe .... (see 7)	Corse Voyages 9 C2
	Dcampanaglass 10 C3
EXPLORING CALVI	Galerie Marie Ricco 11 B3
Birthplace of Christopher	Les Beaux Voyages 12 B4
Columbus 2 C2	Oratoire de la Confrérie
Calvi Nautique Club .... (see 4)	St-Antoine 13 C2
Calvi Plongée 3 B4	Tour de Sel 14 C3
Calvi's Beach 4 B5	
Caserne Sampiero 5 C2	
Cathédrale St-Jean Baptiste.. 6 C2	

GASTRONOMIC HIGHLIGHTS 🍴
A Scola 15 C2
Aux Bons Amis 16 B3
EAT 17 C3
Émile's 18 C3
L'Abri Cotier 19 B3
Le Jardin .... (see 26)
Le Tire Bouchon .... (see 17)
U Callelu 20 C3
U Minellu 21 B3

NIGHTLIFE 🍷
Chez Tao 22 D2

RECOMMENDED SHOPS 🛍
A Loghja .... (see 23)
Annie Traiteur 23 C3

ACCOMMODATION 🛏
Hôtel Belvédère 24 C2
Hôtel Le Rocher 25 B3
Hôtel Restaurant Le Magnolia ... 26 B3

TRANSPORT
Ferry Quay 27 D3
Garage d'Angeli 28 B2
Les Beaux Voyages .... (see 12)
Train Station 29 B4
Tramway de la Balagne .... (see 29)

CALVI & LA BALAGNE

salt store. The quay can be elbow-to-el-bow strollers at aperitif time, a veritable Italian *passeggiata*; wait until sunset, when many have retired to dine and the light is at its mellow best.

❦ CALVI'S BEACH // SAND AS FAR AS THE HORIZON

Stand beside **Calvi Nautique Club** (☎ 04 95 65 10 65; www.calvinc.org, in French; ☺ daily Apr–Oct) and sweep your eye around the shoreline of the Golfe de Calvi to its furthest limit. Except for a single short rocky strip, it's sand all the way. If you fancy something more strenuous than pressing a beach towel, the club rents windsurfers and sea kayaks.

❦ COLOMBO LINE // TRAVEL BY SEA TO RÉSERVE NATURELLE DE SCANDOLA

Between April and October, the boats of **Colombo Line** (☎ 04 95 65 32 10; www .colombo-line.com, in French, ☺ daily Apr–Oct) sail to the magnificent Réserve Naturelle de Scandola. From May to September, you can make the same journey more intimately on its catamaran, which also does a full-day excursion to the Désert des Agriates.

❦ POINTE DE LA REVELLATA // APPROACHING MAINLAND FRANCE GIVES BEST VIEWS OF LA BALAGNE

A two-hour (round trip) walk along a well-defined track brings you to the nearest Corsican point to the French mainland, home to a lighthouse and a gorgeous view of Calvi and the sheer, spiky mountains of La Balagne, still coiffed with snow until early June. Look-ing southward, a wilder, even more beautiful coastline recedes. To get to Pointe de la Revellata, drive 3.5km west

of place Christophe Colomb along the D81B, and park at the bend in the road. The route's clear; look for the blue paint blobs if in doubt. When the lighthouse is well in sight, bear right at the sign stating *200m demi tour officiel*.

❦ BELOW THE WATER LINE // SNORKELLING AT A COUPLE OF PRIME SITES

Snorkellers can flap their flippers around the limits of the Réserve Naturelle de la Pointe de la Revellata. Here fish, no respecters of boundaries, swim in abundance, and you stand a reasonable chance of an encounter with dolphins sneaking over the border of the reserve for dinner. Qualified divers can descend to the wreck of a WWII B-17 bomber, barely 200m off shore; sign on with **Calvi Plongée** (☎ 04 95 65 33 67; www.calviplongee2b .com, in French; quai Landry; ☺ Mon-Sat Apr–mid-Oct) or another of Calvi's several dive operators.

❦ NOTRE DAME DE LA SERRA // THE FINEST BIRD'S-EYE VIEW OF CALVI

Signed from the same bend as Pointe de la Revellata, a pocked blacktop road runs for 1.5km up to this windswept spot, a place of pilgrimage for the peo-ple of Calvi for more than five centuries. It's marked by a tiny chapel and a statue of a shrouded Virgin Mary gazing out over the Golfe de Calvi. In the guise of Our Lady of the Sierra, she's the town patron; see the plaques of thanks for her intervention on the wall beside the main gate.

You can also approach this splendid viewpoint by a none-too-demanding afternoon hike. The town map provided by the tourist office (p59) marks the trail, which starts beside Hôtel La Villa.

ARTS & CRAFTS // GLASS, POP ART AND KNIVES

At **Dcampanaglass** (☎ 04 95 47 81 60; www
.dcampanaglass.com; cnr Montée du Port & rue Clemenceau; ☺ 10am-noon & 3-7pm Mon-Sat, 3-7pm Sun),
glass-blower Dominique Campana and
his American wife, Carol, display and
sell his sensuous, flowing pieces of art.
Each Tuesday and Thursday, you can
see him at work beside his kiln. In case
you're seduced by some fragile creation,
they ship worldwide.

Granted, most of the canvases Marie
Ricco displays are way too large to tuck
into your cabin baggage but, for the
experience, do drop by the splendid
Galerie Marie Ricco (☎ 04 95 39 48 18;
www.galeriemariericco.com; 3 bd Wilson; ☺ 10am-
12.30pm & 4-8pm Mon-Sat Apr-Oct), a sparkling
ultracontemporary touch in an otherwise traditional town.

At **A Fundaria** (the Forge; ☎ 06 79 17 09 96;
http://monsite.wanadoo.fr/afunderia; av Christoph
Colomb; ☺ 9am-noon & 3-6pm Mon-Sat Mar-Jan),
Patrick Martin fires and fashions traditional knives for hunters and fellow
craftfolk, plus daggers, axes and more-
creative works in steel and bronze.

L'ASTRATELLA // DISTILLING WILD HERBS FOR NATURAL MEDICINES

Pleasantly cluttered and with a pair of
amiable, panting dogs, **L'Astratella** (☎ 04
95 60 62 94; www.astratella.com, in French; ☺ 2-6pm
or 7pm Mon-Sat) has at its heart a distillery
that's like a bootlegger's, but on a grand-
er scale. The team, committed to aroma-
therapy, collects wild herbs and flowers
such as myrtle, rosemary and juniper,
and you can buy the distilled essences in
phials and bottles from the shop. To get
here, drive along the N179, turn right
3.75km after the airport turning and follow signs for 1.4km.

COACH TOURS // LET SOMEONE ELSE DO THE DRIVING

Corse Voyages (☎ 04 95 65 00 47; www
.corsevoyages.com, in French; bd Wilson; ☺ Mon-Sat
year-round) and **Les Beaux Voyages** (☎ 04
95 65 11 35; www.lesbeauxvoyagesencorse.com, in
French; place de la Porteuse d'Eau; ☺ Mon-Sat year-
round) do half- and full-day tours to destinations such as the Forêt de Bonifatu,
Cap Corse and the inland villages of the
Balagne.

CENTRE ÉQUESTRE A CAVALLU // ON HORSEBACK THROUGH THE PINES

This **horse-riding centre** (☎ 04 95 65 22
22; www.a-cavallu.com, in French; ☺ Mon-Sat Jul &
Aug, Wed, Sat & Sun Sep-Jun) offers guided trail
rides (€20 per hour) and, for experienced

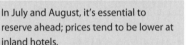

ACCOMMODATION

In July and August, it's essential to
reserve ahead; prices tend to be lower at
inland hotels.

For our picks, see the separate
Accommodation chapter. Our special
favourites include the following:

★ **Chambres d'Hôtes A Flatta** (p245) is
the ultimate road's-end getaway

★ Wonderful, welcoming **Chambres
d'Hôtes U Chyosu di a Petra** (p246)
has bags of character

★ Family-run and friendly **Hôtel Cala di
l'Oru** (p244) is in a quiet part of Île
Rousse

★ **Hôtel U Palazzu** (p245) is a
magnificent restored 18th-century
mansion

★ **Hôtel Restaurant Le Magnolia**
(p244) is a recently renovated belle
époque mansion with a great garden
restaurant

CALVI & LA BALAGNE

riders, the chance to canter through the surf. To get here, drive along the N197 in the direction of the airport, turn left around 2km from the centre of town and head 500m down a dusty track.

GASTRONOMIC HIGHLIGHTS

❦ A SCOLA €

☎ 04 95 65 07 09; mains around €15; ☺ 10am-7pm Mar-Oct

It may be difficult to imagine, but this tiny place opposite the cathedral door was once a primary school for girls. Nowadays, Annie Consorti runs a pleasant little tea house that's ideal for a refreshing cup, restorative snack or scrumptious pastry as you explore the citadel. Grab the table nearest to the picture window, which has a stunning view of the bay, and make sure you browse the collection of antiques and bric-a-brac.

❦ AUX BONS AMIS €€

☎ 04 95 65 05 01; rue Clemenceau; mains €20-27, menus €18-35; ☺ Apr-Sep, closed Wed except Jul & Aug

Aux Bons Amis has a short, select à la carte choice, and serves up the best of fresh fish and seafood amid nautically themed decor. Its recommended *menu saveur terroir* (€18) is a wonderful sample of island specialities.

❦ EAT €€

☎ 04 95 38 21 87; cnr Montée du Port & rue Clemenceau; mains around €18, menu €29; ☺ closed Wed year-round

No, not an Anglicism to enrage the conservatives of the Académie Française; rather, EAT is the acronym of *épicurien avant tout* (above all, epicurean). And indeed dishes are a gastronomic delight – indulge in a

dreamy dessert of mango ice cream on a pistachio-cream bed stabbed with a crisp almond biscuit. What is lost in translation is the size of a dish, which is indicated by L (in fact, a half-portion) or XL (full portion). Eat in the all-maroon interior, on the terrace, or in the shade of a lone olive tree.

❦ ÉMILE'S €€€

☎ 04 95 65 09 60; quai Landry; mains €32-50, menus €50-120; ☺ daily mid-Mar–mid-Oct

You'll need to keep your eyes open to find Émile's, which is up an easily overlooked flight of steps that leads from the quay to the restaurant's scenic 1st-floor terrace. Calvi's choicest restaurant has been awarded one Michelin star, and you'll certainly enjoy a sophisticated dining experience here – why, even the menu reads like a book of poetry.

❦ L'ABRI COTIER €€

☎ 04 95 65 12 76; rue Joffre; mains €16-25, menus €23-33; ☺ daily mid–Mar-Oct

With its pastas and risottos, saltimbocca and tiramisu, this popular spot has a decidedly Italian flavour. Ask for one of the coveted tables beside the panoramic window, one floor up and lording it over the restaurant terraces below. The cuisine is creative; try, for example, the sea bass accompanied by a basil flan.

❦ LE JARDIN €€

☎ 04 95 65 08 02; rue Alsace Lorraine; mains €18-24, menus €21-27; ☺ lunch & dinner Tue-Sun, dinner Mon

The courtyard restaurant of Hôtel Restaurant Le Magnolia (p244) is a wonderfully relaxing option. Enjoy generous portions beneath the vine-twined branches of the eponymous magnolia tree; the mussels, steamed in a sauce of cream, vermentinu wine (an aromatic

Corsican white) and wild fennel, are as you've never tasted them before.

❦ LE TIRE BOUCHON €€

☎ 04 95 65 24 41; rue Clemenceau; mains €14-24.50, menu €18; ✆ Jun-Sep, closed Wed Apr, May & Oct

This cheerful option, as much wine bar as restaurant, is a delight. Perch yourself on the balcony overlooking the crowds milling on rue Clemenceau, then order from the dishes of the day, posted on a chalkboard. Treat yourself to a taste of the finest Calvi or Patrimonio Appellation d'Origine Contrôlee (AOC) wine (listed on *four* blackboards – you sense the staff's priorities), available by the glass or bottle.

❦ U CALLELU €€

☎ 04 95 65 22 18; quai Landry; mains €25-30, menu €23; ✆ Mar-Oct, closed Mon except Jul-Sep

Updated four times annually, the *menu* at this informal, laid-back eatery chases the changing seasons. Its exuberant owner proudly tracks down the best in the area's local produce: meat and veg from the market, wine direct from the vineyards and fish straight off the boats. This place is hugely popular with Calvais – read the eulogies in the visitors book.

❦ U FANALE €€

☎ 04 95 65 18 82; www.ufanale.com, in French; rte de Porto; mains €18.50-31, menus €18-24; ✆ lunch & dinner Wed-Mon, lunch Tue Mar-Dec

The young brother and sister who run the lighthouse offer affable service as they bustle about the busy terrace, popular with locals and visitors alike. Dishes are delightfully presented, though you may find the fresh flowers stuck onto most mains unnecessarily gimmicky. Make sure you save a corner for the *coupe glacée U Fanale*, a measure of eau-

de-vie drizzled over scoops of chestnut ice cream.

❦ U MINELLU €€

☎ 04 95 65 05 52; traverse de l'Église; mains €14-19.50, menu €19; ✆ Wed-Mon Apr-Jun & Sep–mid-Oct, dinner daily Jul & Aug

The leafy terrace and vaulted interior of U Minellu are justifiably packed and popular. Run by a youthful, smiling team, the restaurant offers an excellent-value *menu* that's authentically Corsican from starter to dessert; try, in particular, the peppery stewed wild boar with polenta. It doesn't accept credit cards.

NIGHTLIFE

❦ CHEZ TAO

☎ 04 95 65 00 73; rue St-Antoine; ✆ 9pm-5am Jun-Sep

Within the citadel and occupying what was once an episcopal palace, this hip bar is a Corsican institution. Before WWII, White Russian émigré Tao Kanbey de Kerekoff designed the terraces and the lavishly decorated vaulted interior. Nowadays it's run in the same flamboyant style by his son, Tao-By, who tinkles the ivories from 11.30pm. Earlier, it's live music on the terrace, and after 2am a DJ takes you through the night.

RECOMMENDED SHOPS

❦ ANNIE TRAITEUR

☎ 04 95 65 49 67; www.annietraiteur.com, in French; 5 rue Clemenceau; ✆ 7am-7pm

The shelves of this large emporium creak with jars and tins, pickles and jams – all that's best of Corsican goodies. Cooling in the fridges is a superb range of cheeses and fresh charcuterie, while hams and sausages hang in festoons from the ceiling. Once you're back home you can buy a delicacy or two from the website to recall your Corsican holiday.

♥ A LOGHJA
☎ 04 95 65 39 93; 3 rue Clemenceau; ⏱ 9.30am-8pm Mar-Oct

On a smaller scale than Annie Traiteur and precisely two doors away, this appealing barrel-vaulted specialist shop deals only with small, independent Corsican suppliers. Wines are from smaller vineyards, and the cheeses come direct from the farm – see if you can resist indulging in a slice, cut fresh from the large wheels on the counter. You'll pay a little more for the produce but every mouthful merits the extra cost.

TRANSPORT

AIR // Calvi's Ste-Catherine Airport (☎ 04 95 65 88 88; www.calvi.aeroport.fr) is 7km southeast of town. There are daily flights to mainland France, notably Marseille and Paris (Orly). Thomson (www.flights.thomson.co.uk) has weekly flights to and from London (Gatwick) and Manchester, May to September. A taxi (☎ 04 95 65 03 10) to and from town costs €20.

BOAT // Ferries run to/from Nice (France) and Savona (Italy) from the ferry quay; see p268 for details.

BUS // Les Beaux Voyages (☎ 04 95 65 11 35; www.lesbeauxvoyagesencorse.com, in French; place de la Porteuse d'Eau) runs one bus, Monday to Saturday year-round, from Calvi to Bastia via Île Rousse.

TRAIN // There are at least two departures daily to Bastia and Ajaccio, each requiring a change in Ponte Leccia. For Île Rousse, take the Tramway de la Balagne (p59).

BICYCLE // Garage d'Angeli (☎ 04 95 65 02 13; www.garagedangeli.com, in French; place Christophe Colomb) rents bikes.

PARKING // Calvi has a number of car parks dotted around town.

AROUND CALVI
······

♥ OCCI // A ROMANTIC LONG-ABANDONED MOUNTAIN HAMLET

The only way to visit the deserted settlement of Occi is on foot – and that's what's helped to preserve it. To enjoy the emptiness and a fabulous panorama of the Golfe de Calvi you must make a steepish, exhilarating ascent from Lumio, 10km east of Calvi.

DRIVING FROM CALVI TO PORTO

You *could* play safe and take the main D81 that runs between Calvi and Porto. Consider taking the D81B, however: slower yet more satisfying, it snakes along the coast from Calvi nearly as far as Galéria, traversing awesome coastal scenery before turning inland, where dun-coloured meadows nestle against sheer granite cliffs.

The tight switchback bends will have you wrestling with the steering wheel, and the sheer drops to the waves will send butterflies fluttering around the stomach. The narrowness of the road also means that passing other vehicles – not those in your own lane but those coming *at* you – becomes a nerve-racking game of chicken. There are no guard rails, rock falls are frequent and the road surface is riddled with potholes. Oh, and watch out for stray mountain goats!

It's not a road trip for the faint-hearted, but if you're prudent and take your time you'll enjoy one of Corsica's most spectacular drives.

CALVI & LA BALAGNE

Leave your vehicle in the car park opposite Hôtel Restaurant Chez Charles, beside the N197 at Lumio's northern limit. Beyond the sign for Occi, tarmac gives way to track, then path, well waymarked with dark blue blobs and arrows. After 25 to 35 minutes, this ancient mule track brings you to your goal.

Occi's renovated chapel, with plaster and cement slapped on indiscriminately, contrasts with the dignity of the dwellings' skilfully crafted drystone walls, inexorably tumbling back to the earth. The coastal settlements of Marine de Sant'Ambrogio and Algajola stand out clearly below and from the highest point you can make out the stabbing finger of Île Rousse.

Exploring over, you can head back to the car park, or carry on to enjoy a circular walk back to Lumio. Continuing on, follow the red dots up a zigzagging path to enjoy easy, mostly level walking beneath the crest. Keep well to the right of a small chapel, then turn right at a T-junction to follow a steeply descending path to Lumio. Walk through the village to your car; the total walking time should be 1¾ to two hours.

🐾 ALGAJOLA (ALGAGHJOLA) // A QUIET SANDY BEACH

A splendid crescent of sandy beach, loved by surfers for its waves, curves northward from tiny Algajola, located 15km from Calvi and 7km west of Île Rousse. Normally quieter than its larger neighbours, the beach makes for a fun day trip from either Calvi or Île Rousse by the clanking Tramway de la Balagne (p59).

There's an appropriately minuscule **tourist office** (☎ 04 95 62 78 32; 🕙 9am-noon) in a room at the back of the station.

If you're looking for somewhere to eat, you really ought to indulge in a *pierrade* (meat, fish or seafood sizzled on a hot stone) on the broad terrace of friendly **La Veille Cave** (☎ 04 95 60 70 09; place de l'Olmo; mains €14-17, menus €17.50-22; 🕙 lunch & dinner Tue-Sun, dinner Mon Apr-Oct). Alternatively, opt for the *agneau Corse de lait,* local baby lamb, roasted to perfection.

🐾 ARGENTELLA // EXPLORE AN ABANDONED SILVER MINE

If you've a penchant for industrial archaeology, follow the D81B southward from Calvi for around 20km to Camping Morsetta. The track opposite its bar leads to this deserted silver-mine complex.

Several companies have extracted silver from the lead-bearing rock, including a British company that installed steam engines and constructed a dam to collect water for cooling in the 19th century.

Root around the furnaces (taking care – the structures really are tottering) and crumbling administrative quarters. Then walk up to the old dam where frogs croak and plop, and baby turtles bask. Looking back, the complex resembles an abandoned monastic settlement. If you have the energy and time, you can continue up the track for around 45 minutes to the mine itself, where there are more abandoned buildings.

🐾 DELTA DU FANGO // SILENT PADDLING THROUGH A QUIET ESTUARY

At the small seaside resort of **Galéria**, rent a sea kayak from **Delta du Fangu** (☎ 06 22 01 71 89; www.delta-du-fangu.com, in French; per hr €5; 🕙 10am-6pm Jun-Sep), based beneath the Genoese tower. As you paddle you'll see a wealth of aquatic birds and, if you're lucky, tiny freshwater turtles.

♥ **VALLÉE DU FANGO // DEEP ROCK POOLS UP A LITTLE-TRAVELLED VALLEY**

For a riverside picnic and a refreshing dip, take the D351 eastward from Galéria along the valley of the river Fango. Precisely 1.4km beyond the village of Fango, clear pools glisten beneath Ponte Vecchiu, a steeply arched Genoese bridge. If the best spots have been taken, there are several other opportunities upstream beside steep yet shallow gorges.

ÎLE ROUSSE (ISULA ROSSA)

· · · · · ·

pop 2750

With its turquoise and lapis lazuli waters a striking contrast against the porphyry-coloured rocks from which it takes its name, Île Rousse (the Pink Island) makes an excellent base both for exploring the rich hinterland of La Balagne and for indulging in seaside pleasures.

Ironically, this appealing holiday resort, the entry point for tens of thousands of holidaymakers from mainland Europe, was originally founded as a Corsican political statement. In 1758 the nationalist leader Pascal Paoli (see the boxed text, p193) thumbed his nose at Genoa-controlled Calvi, barely 25km along the coast, by establishing the town; soon, what was a quiet fishing hamlet became a serious commercial rival to its larger neighbour.

ESSENTIAL INFORMATION

TOURIST OFFICES // Tourist office (☎ 04 95 60 04 35; www.balagne-corsica.com; av Joseph Calizi; ⏰ 9am-7pm Mon-Sat, 10am-1pm Sun mid-Jun—mid-Sep, 9am-noon & 2-6pm Mon-Fri mid-Sep—mid-Jun)

EXPLORING ÎLE ROUSSE

♥ **VISIOGUIDE // A NOVEL WAY TO EXPLORE THE TOWN**

These days, many major sites offer an audioguide to help you around. But the cheerful team at Île Rousse's tourist office (☎ 04 95 60 04 35; www.balagne-corsica.com; av Joseph Calizi; ⏰ 9am-7pm Mon-Sat, 10am-1pm Sun mid-Jun—mid-Sep, 9am-noon & 2-6pm Mon-Fri mid-Sep—mid-Jun) has gone one better with the Visioguide (€7), where photos accompany the audioguide, the first of its kind in France. Let yourself be led around town and onto Île de la Pietra.

♥ **PARC DE SALECCIA // LOVELY GARDEN SHOWCASING THE PLANTS AND FLOWERS OF CORSICA**

Wander the 7 hectares of these landscaped gardens (☎ 04 95 36 88 83; www.parc-saleccia.fr, in French; rte de Bastia; admission €7.50; ⏰ 10am-8pm Jul & Aug, 9.30am-7pm Tue-Fri & Sun, 2-7pm Mon & Sat Apr-Jun, Sep—mid-Oct) to explore the flora of the island – the tough plants of the maquis, pines, myrtles, fig trees, over 100 varieties of olive tree and, in season, bank upon bank of azaleas and oleanders bursting with colour. The gardens are 4.5km from town on the Bastia road.

♥ **GALERIE SAETTA // PHOTOGRAPHS OF CORSICA AND THE WORLD BEYOND**

Antoine Périgot, Corsican and world traveller, displays stunning photos of Corsica and his African travels in his gallery (☎ 06 12 73 83 29; www.miccanomi.fr, in French; rue d'Agila; admission free; ⏰ 10am-2pm & 6pm-midnight May-Oct), located in a former wine cellar. *Corsica Muntagna,* his magnificent coffee-table album of Corsica's mountains through the seasons, took two full years to compile. For those holi-

CALVI & LA BALAGNE

day postcards home, purchase some of his original shots (€0.70 each, €9 for a pack of 16).

♥ PLACE PAOLI // COFFEE AND HISTORY IN ÎLE ROUSSE'S CENTRAL SQUARE

At the heart of this square, the **statue of Pascal Paoli**, 'Babbu di a Patria' (Father of the Land), keeps a weather eye on the state of the nation. It's a place to relax, sit back and enjoy a drink beneath mature plane trees to the click and thud of lobbed *pétanque* balls. Choose the

terrace of venerable **Café des Platanes** (⏱ 7am-midnight daily), in business since 1928, or retreat from the heat inside the cafe, where it's all varnished woodwork and brass rails.

♥ COVERED FOOD MARKET // A TINY TEMPLE TO FRESH PRODUCE

It's small and everything's over by 1pm. But it's not often that you get the chance to buy your picnic fare in a classified historical monument. Constructed around 1850, the open-sided **market building**

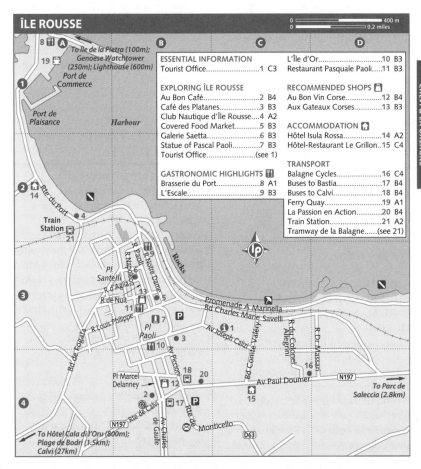

ÎLE ROUSSE

0 — 400 m
0 — 0.2 miles

To Île de la Pietra (100m); Genoese Watchtower (250m); Lighthouse (600m)
Port de Commerce
Port de Plaisance   Harbour
Rte du Port
Train Station

Pl Santelli
R. Paoli
R. Napoléon
R. Notre Dame
R. d'Agila
R. de Nuit
R. Louis-Philippe
Rocks
Bd du Fogata
Pl Paoli
Pl Marcel Delanney
Rte de Calvi
Av Piccioni
Promenade A Marinella
Bd Charles Marie Savelli
Av Joseph Calizi
Bd Comte Valéry
R. du Colonel Allegrini
R. Dr Massari
Av Paul Doumer
N197
To Parc de Saleccia (2.8km)
Av Charles de Gaulle
Monticello
D63
To Hôtel Cala di l'Oru (800m); Plage de Bodri (1.5km); Calvi (27km)

ESSENTIAL INFORMATION
Tourist Office........................1 C3

EXPLORING ÎLE ROUSSE
Au Bon Café..........................2 B4
Café des Platanes..................3 B3
Club Nautique d'Île Rousse....4 A2
Covered Food Market...........5 B3
Galerie Saetta.......................6 B3
Statue of Pascal Paoli............7 B3
Tourist Office.....................(see 1)

GASTRONOMIC HIGHLIGHTS
Brasserie du Port...................8 A1
L'Escale...............................9 B3

L'Île d'Or............................10 B3
Restaurant Pasquale Paoli.....11 B3

RECOMMENDED SHOPS
Au Bon Vin Corse................12 B4
Aux Gateaux Corses............13 B3

ACCOMMODATION
Hôtel Isula Rossa................14 A2
Hôtel-Restaurant Le Grillon..15 C4

TRANSPORT
Balagne Cycles....................16 C4
Buses to Bastia....................17 B4
Buses to Calvi.....................18 B4
Ferry Quay.........................19 A1
La Passion en Action...........20 B4
Train Station........................21 A2
Tramway de la Balagne......(see 21)

(place Paoli; ☽ 8am-1pm) with 21 classical columns (thickly disproportionate, it must be said) resembles a Greek temple to food.

☙ AU BON CAFÉ // A CLASSIC COFFEE HOUSE

You'll smell the aroma of freshly roasted beans wafting from **Au Bon Café** (☎ 04 95 60 02 40; place Marcel Delanney; ☽ 8.30am-12.30pm & 3-7.30pm Mon-Sat) well before you reach this small celebration of the divine brew. Run by the same family since 1932, it has beans from around the world, jute sacks piled high, coffee makers of all shapes and complexities, and a slowly turning giant roasting pan that's close to celebrating its first century of action.

☙ A BEACH AWAY // A SEASIDE WALK TO A QUIETER BEACH

To escape the crowds that throng Île Rousse's three sandy beaches, take the **Sentier des Douaniers**, a path once patrolled by vigilant customs officers, which leads south of the train station and along the coast to the even sandier, even longer **Plage de Bodri**. Alternatively, hop on the Tramway de la Balagne for just one station or, if you're driving, take the N197 westward and turn right after Camping Bodri.

☙ PADDLING AROUND THE PROMONTORY // AN UNDEMANDING SEA-KAYAK OUTING

Club Nautique d'Île Rousse (☎ 04 95 60 22 55; www.cnir.org, in French; rte du Port; ☽ Mar-Christmas) organises gentle two-hour sea-kayak trips (€30 including kayak hire) around Île de la Pietra and its offshore islets, with a built-in sea dip en route. Rental alone costs €11/17 per hour for a single/double.

☙ ÎLE DE LA PIETRA // WALKING TO THE TIP OF ÎLE ROUSSE

For an easy stroll, head over the short umbilical causeway that links rocky Île de la Pietra to the mainland, past a small **Genoese watchtower** and up to the **lighthouse**, from where there's a spectacular seascape. Allow 20 to 30 minutes for the round trip from the port.

☙ STRETCHING THE LEGS A LITTLE MORE // A GREAT RESOURCE FOR WALKERS

The **tourist office** (☎ 04 95 60 04 35; www .balagne-corsica.com; av Joseph Calizi; ☽ 9am-7pm Mon-Sat, 10am-1pm Sun mid-Jun–mid-Sep, 9am-noon & 2-6pm Mon-Fri mid-Sep–mid-Jun) sells a wallet file (€12) that details four easy, signed country walks in the immediate vicinity of the town. They vary in length between 6km and 20km, and you can always simply nibble off a section of the longer ones.

GASTRONOMIC HIGHLIGHTS

☙ BRASSERIE DU PORT €€

☎ 04 95 60 10 66; www.brasserie-du-port.com, in French; Port de Commerce; mains €15-22, menus €15.50-17.50; ☽ Mon-Sat

Three brothers run this busy brasserie, a favourite with both locals and the passing trade. Located right beside the ferry jetty, the restaurant has large picture windows providing optimum views of mountain and bay (less so when a giant ferry blocks the sight lines). Enjoy large leafy salads, and the freshest of fish and seafood, all washed down with wine by the jug.

☙ L'ESCALE €€

☎ 04 95 60 10 53; rue Notre Dame; mains €12-24; ☽ 7am-2am daily

You'd be well advised to reserve at this big, bustling place; request a table on

CALVI & LA BALAGNE

the terrace overlooking the bay. Content yourself with a pizza (€11 to €12.50), take it relatively light with one of the vast, frondy salads, or perhaps go for a plate of steaming mussels, prepared in six different ways. Whatever you do, save an extra-large cranny for one of the giant desserts, eased down with a nip of the 65-proof firewater that's proffered free with the bill.

☙ L'ÎLE D'OR €€

☎ 04 95 60 12 05; place Paoli; mains €15-22, menus €15-21; ☽ daily

At this spot beside the main square, you can eat inside or in the shade of the awnings that protect the restaurant's vast terrace. The choice of dishes is wide: the menu is especially strong on fish and seafood, and there are options for all budgets, from a simple salad or pizza to a full-blown dinner.

☙ RESTAURANT PASQUALE PAOLI €€€

☎ 04 95 47 67 70; www.pasquale-paoli.com; 2 place Paoli; mains €20-35; ☽ dinner Thu-Tue Jul & Aug, lunch & dinner Mon, Tue, Thu-Sat, lunch Sun Sep-Jun

Awarded a Michelin star when it had been barely two years in business, the whitewashed, vaulted Pasquale Paoli belongs to a pair of passionate gastronomes, both Corsican to their boots. As a bust of the great liberator watches over the tables, the maître d' describes with infectious enthusiasm the chalked-up dishes of the day; there's no printed menu, but an Anglophone assistant is on hand if something gets lost in translation.

RECOMMENDED SHOPS

☙ AU BON VIN CORSE
place Marcel Delanney

Head here to stock up on Patrimonio wines – red, rosé, white and muscat –

drained directly from the shop's gleaming aluminium tanks, or sip on the spot from the greater range of local crus. For supplementary vitamin C, choose the *vin aux fruits* (fruit wine; €2.20).

☙ AUX GATEAUX CORSES
rue de Nuit

Get your fingers sticky at this simple – spartan even – boutique with its freshly baked Corsican specialities such as *canistrelli* (biscuits confected from lemons, aniseed, flecks of chocolate and raisins) and sweetmeats based on chestnuts.

TRANSPORT

BOAT // Ferries run to Nice, Marseille and Toulon (France) and Savona (Italy) from the ferry quay; see p267.
TRAIN // There are two departures daily to Bastia and Ajaccio, each requiring a change in Ponte Leccia. Tramway de la Balagne links Île Rousse and Calvi; see p59 for details.
BUS // Beaux Voyages (☎ 04 95 65 11 35; www.lesbeauxvoyagesencorse.com, in French) buses between Calvi and Bastia pass through Île Rousse; the tourist office has schedules. Bus stops are unmarked.
BICYCLE // Balagne Cycles (☎ 04 95 38 12 99; www.balagne-cycles.com, in French; av Paul Doumer) and La Passion en Action (☎ 04 95 60 15 76; av Paul Doumer) rent out bikes.

LA BALAGNE INTERIOR

· · · · · ·

What beckons here is the dramatic landscape. Granite outcrops, their colours changing by the hour, are sliced by ravines and sheer gullies, while the scattered hilltop villages – a church, town hall, cafe and that's it – are a world away from the coastal fleshpots. Around the villages, once-prolific olive groves compete with

CALVI & LA BALAGNE

cherry, walnut and chestnut trees as they struggle to survive the twin onslaughts of human neglect and forest fire.

You'll need a vehicle and a minimum of two days to savour the charms of inland La Balagne. There's a lot to pack in, and you won't be averaging more than 50km per hour. Clunk your safety belt and brave the twisting minor roads that thread these inland treasures.

Should you want to break the journey, see p245 for a selection of attractive rural sleeping choices, each full of character and providing a more economical alternative to coastal hotels.

INLAND FROM CALVI

♥ FORÊT DE TARTAGINE-MELAJA // A MAGNIFICENT DRIVE AND GENTLE FOREST WALKING
From Calenzana, drive along the D963 until it peters out after 18km beside a forestry lodge (p245). The drive is a stunning one – but isn't for those who fear heights. Tame at first, it then snakes along a narrow, lightly trafficked corniche where even a cow is an event.

The forest – oak and chestnut in the tight gorges, primarily pine on the upper slopes – occupies a massive 2700 hectares. For an idyllic picnic spot, cross the bridge beyond the lodge and head upstream to a tiny silted-up dam. Easiest among several walking options is a marked trail that follows the valley downstream.

DRIVING TOUR

Distance: 67km
Duration: one day
Head southeast from Calvi along the N197. After 4.5km, turn right onto the D151, then left at the first roundabout

to take the D451. From way below, you'll soon see the peeling facade of the 17th-century baroque Église de St-Augustin in **Montemaggiore**. Perched 400m above the plain, the village was once a major centre for olive oil production before fires devastated the area in the 1940s. From the church terrace there's a splendid panorama of Calvi and the coast.

In **Lunghignano**, 1.5km further on, the old olive press of **U Fragnu** (☎ 04 95 62 75 51; www.ufragnu.com; ☯ 9am-noon & 2-6pm Apr-Oct) still squeezes its own oil, despite a fire that destroyed around 80% of the trees when it swept through the valley in 2005. A four-minute DVD (ask for the English version) explains the oil-production process. In addition to olive products in many guises, U Fragnu sells delicious homemade cakes. As you leave, spare a pat for Georges, the ever-patient donkey who turns the grindstone.

The tiny village of **Zilia**, 3km beyond, gives its name to a popular Corsican mineral water; the spring lies just off route. For something stronger, turn off after a further 3.75km for a *dégustation* (tasting session) at the reputed vineyard of **Domaine d'Alzi Pratu** (☎ 04 95 62 75 47; ☯ 9am-noon & 1.30-7pm Mon-Sat, closed Sat Sep-Jun).

Two kilometres beyond this small winery is the Romanesque **Chapelle de Santa Restituta**, dedicated to the martyred patron saint of nearby Calenzana, beheaded in the village square in the early 4th century. The townspeople originally planned for the chapel to be elsewhere but all changed when, so goes the story, their building materials were mysteriously and repeatedly moved at dead of night. The spirit of Restituta, they concluded, was telling them where she wanted her chapel. The adjacent olive grove and its picnic tables make a delightful, shaded spot for an alfresco lunch.

You can expect to see plenty of walkers in **Calenzana**, 1.5km beyond the chapel. La Balagne's most populous town prior to the development of seaside tourism, it's the trailhead for both the GR20 (p214) and Mare e Monti (p217) long-distance walking routes. Park your car in the square beside Église St-Blaise, which has a splendid free-standing neobaroque bell tower. Inside, the simple wooden pews con-

trast with the church's high-baroque decor, including the vast marble altar. Beneath and around the tower are buried the remains of some 500 Austrian mercenaries who were killed here in battle in 1732, when the village was a major pocket of opposition to Genoese occupation.

If you're in need of something to snack on, pass by friendly **E Fritelle** (Tiassu Longu; 7am-5pm), which has been making crunchy biscuits of all kinds for more than 25 years. See them slowly gyrating by the trayful as they bake in the

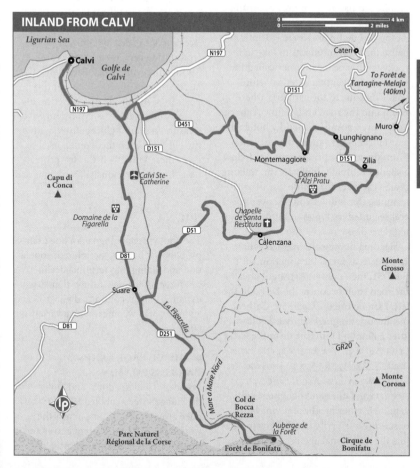

INLAND FROM CALVI

Ligurian Sea

Calvi
Golfe de Calvi
N197
N197
D451
D151
Calvi Ste-Catherine
Capu di a Conca
Domaine de la Figarella
D81
Suare
D81
La Figarella
D251

Cateri
To Forêt de Tartagine-Melaja (40km)
D151
Muro
Lunghignano
Montemaggiore
D151
Zilia
Domaine d'Alzi Pratu
Chapelle de Santa Restituta
Calenzana
Monte Grosso

GR20
Monte Corona

Mare a Mare Nord
Col de Bocca Rezza
Auberge de la Forêt
Parc Naturel Régional de la Corse
Forêt de Bonifatu
Cirque de Bonifatu

CALVI & LA BALAGNE

oven at the rear, and leave with a packet of *cujuelle*, the crunchy biscuits made with white wine that are found only in Calenzana.

On the Calvi side of town, take a left turn onto the D51 to descend to the first flat plain of the day, where you may hit dizzying speeds in excess of 60km/h. After you've gone 9km, take a left turn onto the D251 at a T-junction and head towards the **Forêt de Bonifatu**, a dense and all-but-impenetrable mix of maritime and laricio pines, holm oaks and other broad-leafed trees. Outcrops of granite – pink, beige or grey according to the light – stain the upper reaches. At the **Col de Bocca Rezza** (510m), pause for a few moments to take in the rocky landscape, sometimes called the Chaos de Rezza, that extends before you. Continue to the car park, where you'll find the road ends below **Auberge de la Forêt**, a walker-friendly hotel with a restaurant that's more than decent. From the nearby bridge, you can follow a shaded footpath downstream, walking beside the river for a little less than 15 minutes; this will let you discover several secluded rock pools that invite you to take a dip.

Heading homeward, retrace your tyre tracks as far as the junction with the D51, then continue straight ahead; the road soon becomes the D81. On the left, 2km before the Calvi Ste-Catherine airport, a signed sandy track leads, after 600m, to **Domaine de la Figarella** (☎ 04 95 61 06 69; www.domaine-figarella.com, in French; ☷ 11am-1pm & 4-8pm Jun-Sep, 3-6pm Wed & Sat Oct-May), where Achille and Marina Acquaviva, father and daughter, cultivate their vines in adjacent vineyards, observing a friendly familial rivalry that pits the traditional against the ultra-

modern. Taste for yourself and decide where you stand.

Continue to the roundabout at the junction with the N197 and turn left to return to Calvi.

INLAND FROM ÎLE ROUSSE

❦ MUSÉE DE CORBARA // A VERY PERSONAL COLLECTION

☎ 04 95 60 06 65; place de l'Église, Corbara; admission free; ☷ 3-6pm Jun–mid-Oct)

Art historian Guy Savelli has single-handedly assembled this fantastic treasure trove of Corsican historical artefacts, which includes an original *Account of Corsica* by James Boswell (recounting his Corsica travels and his meeting with Pascal Paoli) and a fascinating set of early-20th-century postcards. Alongside his collection of pistols and small arms, Monsieur Savelli treasures a set of fighting knives. 'In the old days, even the women used to carry these knives – it was for protection,' he says ominously. Donations are welcome.

PIGNA

The craft village of Pigna is a fine example of how a hamlet, victim of depopulation and falling into terminal decline, can forge itself a new future, thanks to a dynamic mayor, committed villagers and an influx of newcomers with a variety of talents.

❦ THE VILLAGE LANES // CAR-LESS ROAMING

Wander at will up, down and along the village's steep cobbled alleys. If you poke around, you'll come across the workshops of a potter, an engraver and a painter, plus fashioners of musical boxes, lutes, flutes and more. If you need more structure, you'll find a stylised map pinned to the noticeboard opposite the village church.

❤ CASA SAVELLI // THE FINEST CORSICAN PRODUCE, SOURCED FROM SMALL-SCALE PRODUCERS

Dominique Giantini, the creator of **Casa Savelli** (☎ 04 95 61 80 49; ⏲ 10.30am-1pm & 3-7.30pm Mon-Sat Apr-Oct), produces her own olive oil and boils up her own jams. The rest of the gastronomic riches to be found in her tasteful boutique come directly from small-scale Corsican farmers, each of whom she knows personally.

❤ A QUIET TERRACE // A TINY RETREAT FROM THE MADDING CROWD

Few of Pigna's daily throng of visitors get as far as **A Casarella** (⏲ daily mid-Apr–mid-Oct), at the village's southwestern limit, even though it's well signed from the church square. On this lovely little vine-shrouded terrace you can nibble on a tapa or two, sip fresh organic fruit juices and spoon down homemade ice cream.

❤ MUSICAL EVENTS // MUSIC IN THE MOST INTIMATE OF SETTINGS

Year-round musical events are organised by **Festivoce** (☎ 04 95 61 73 13; www.casa-musicale .org/festivoce, in French). The major annual happening is a series of recitals in early July in the village's bijou auditorium (maximum capacity: 120).

❤ CASA MUSICALE // FINE DINING WITH A MUSICAL THEME

Located in the sterling hotel of the same name (p245), this equally individual **restaurant** (☎ 04 95 61 76 57; www .casa-musicale.org, in French; mains €16-21, menu €19; ⏲ daily Feb-Dec) is a delightful place to dine, whether you're out on the terrace overlooking the plain or down in the barrel-vaulted interior, whose walls are hung with musical instruments of all kinds and shapes. Advance reservations are essential in summer.

CALVI & LA BALAGNE

∽ WORTH A TRIP ∽

If you're travelling the N1197 between Île Rousse and Ponte Leccia, build in a detour to browse the cutesy hamlet of **Lama**. Clinging to a rocky spur, with Monte Astu (1535m) rearing above, it's an impressive example of how a village on the skids can redefine and revitalise itself. Nowadays it's confident and prosperous looking, and almost every building, from humble cottages to fine bourgeois mansions and Italianate palazzi, seems to have been painted. Bright flowers are everywhere, and the town receives essential services: the post office again functions, a van provides a mobile grocery service, the baker calls by every day except Monday, and the greengrocer and butcher drop in on Friday. There's even an open-air swimming pool.

For further details and for information on walks in the area, visit the **tourist office** (☎ 04 95 48 23 90; www.vacancesalama.com; ⏲ 9am-1pm & 2-6pm Jun-Sep, 9am-noon & 2-5pm Mon-Fri Oct-May), which also has a long list of attractive *gîtes* that can be reserved via its website.

♣ U PALAZZU // EXQUISITE GOURMET DINING IN A RUSTIC SETTING

Set in a converted olive mill, this independently run **restaurant** (☎ 04 95 35 16 47; mains €30, menu €52; ☺ Apr–Oct, closed Wed except Jul & Aug) is affiliated to the magnificent top-end hotel of the same name (p245). Savour the staggering view from its terrace, or enjoy the stone paving and heavy wooden beams of the interior. For something lighter at lunchtime, select from the range of salads and cold cuts (€14 to €25).

DRIVING TOUR

Distance: 90km
Duration: one day

Head eastward from Île Rousse along the N197 and, after 7km, turn right for **Belgodère**. Its square – fulcrum of the village with its fountain, war memorial, a couple of cafes and a church – could stand in for many a Balagne village. For a wonderful panorama of the olive groves and meadows of the Vallée du Prato and the coast beyond, go through an arch between the two cafes and walk

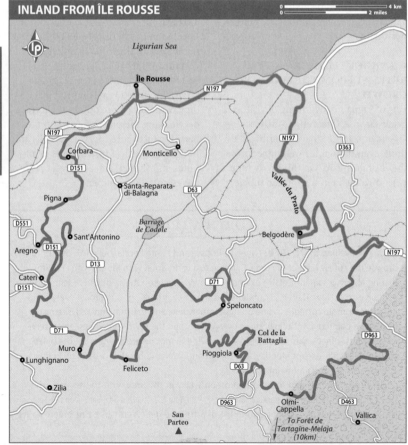

INLAND FROM ÎLE ROUSSE

steeply uphill to the scant remains of an old fort.

Continuing along the N197, turn right after another 7km onto the D963. As it traverses the lonely heights, you stand a good chance of spotting bearded vultures, golden eagles and red kites planing above.

In **Olmi-Cappella**, scarcely bigger than its name, La Balagne's first secondary-school building now serves as town hall, post office and – an essential stop for walkers – **tourist office** (☎ 04 95 47 22 06; ✆ 9-11.45am & 1.30-4.30pm Mon-Fri Apr-Jun, Sep & Oct, 9-11.45am & 1.30-4.30pm Mon-Fri, 10am-1pm Sat Jul & Aug). It carries seven sheets (€1 each) that describe in detail walks of 3km to 11km; each sheet has an explicit 1:25,000 map. For nibbles en route, call by **Biscuiterie Casanova** (☎ 04 95 61 91 76), 200m below the church. In existence for over a century, it turns out 13 varieties of biscuit using traditional Corsican recipes.

Around 3km beyond the village, turn sharp right onto the D63, signed Pioggiola. (Alternatively, if time allows, you can continue to the end of the D63, deep in the dramatic Forêt de Tartagine-Melaja.) At the **Col de la Battaglia** (1099m), pause for a drink on the terrace of **La Merendella**. Few *buvettes* (drink stands) can boast such a view, looking down upon Speloncato, the reservoir behind Barrage de Codole and the long sweep of coastline beyond. Savour it from the terrace, or drop down to the orientation table just below to pick out the features and, if the wind's in the right direction, spot a hang-glider or two riding the thermals above the coastal plain.

A steep, twisting 7km descent brings you to **Speloncato** (Spiluncatu; 600m), which owes its name to the nearby caves (*e spelunche* in Corsican), and its charm to the little streets densely packed with stone houses. Continue through the village towards Île Rousse and turn left at a T-junc-

tion onto the D71 to reach **Feliceto** and the cellars of **Domaine Renucci** (☎ 04 95 61 71 08; www.domaine-renucci.com, in French; ✆ 10am-noon & 3-6.30pm Mon-Sat mid-Apr–Sep), which produces a range of great AOC wines from its vineyards in the valley below.

Continuing along the D71, fork right after 8km onto the D151 for the hilltop village of **Sant'Antonino** (490m). One of the prettiest villages in the Balagne, it's also one of the most visited and can be hideously crowded in high summer. You can avoid the steep ascent to the top of the village by hiring a donkey (€10; every 30 minutes from 3.30pm June to August). Climb to the top of the cobbled streets, bordered by shops selling everything from quality goods to gewgaws (it's not only the tourists who get milked – you can even buy asses'-milk soap), for ever-more impressive views. Back at the car park, stop by the vaulted cellar of **Clos Antonini** (✆ Apr-Oct), noted as much for its citrus juices as its wines, and relish a refreshing glass of freshly squeezed lemon juice trickled over ice. Alternatively, try the astringent cocktail of Olivier Antonini's own white wine mixed with a dash of lemon juice.

Returning to the D151, turn right. In the village of **Aregno**, you'll spot Église de la Trinité, standing out within the village cemetery. Built in the two-tone Pisan Romanesque style, it's a reminder of the distant days when Pisa, not Genoa or Paris, controlled the island's destiny. Among the engaging basalt figurines adorning the facade, note the little fellow beneath the pediment, picking a thorn from his foot.

From Aregno, continue along the D151 to the junction with the N197, and turn right to return to Île Rousse. En route, if you still have time in hand, you could drop into Corbara or Pigna; the latter is best seen towards the end of the day, once the summer crowds have left.

THE WEST COAST

3 PERFECT DAYS

🌴 DAY 1 // TWO WORLD HERITAGE SITES
In Porto, rise early to savour a heart-stopping panorama of Les Calanques (p94) before the crowds arrive. Back in town, sip your morning coffee on the terrace of Le Palmier (p89) for a fine view of the next venue, the little harbour's Genoese tower (p89). Lunch light, then take an afternoon boat trip to the Réserve Naturelle de Scandola (opposite). Back at base, drive to Hôtel Les Roches Rouges (p96) for a magnificent sunset view of Les Calanques from its terrace, then retreat to the restaurant for a gourmet dinner.

🌴 DAY 2 // IN NAPOLÉON'S BOOTSTEPS
Memories of Napoléon abound in Ajaccio, his birthplace. Spend the morning visiting Maison Bonaparte (p102), Musée A Bandera (p102) and the resplendent Salon Napoléonien (p102). Lunch has to be in the belle époque dining room of Le Grand Café Napoléon (p104); to walk it off, drive out to Pointe de la Parata (p106) for an easy, breezy stroll along the headland. After dark, head for Le Spago (p104) for a light dinner in a contemporary setting.

🌴 DAY 3 // INLAND EXERCISE
Head up and inland, where it's greener and cooler. Take the shaded, signed path into the spectacular Gorges de Spelunca (p92), which leads, via a Genoese bridge, to the village of Évisa (p91). Lunch on exclusively local produce at A Tràmula (p93) and pick up some calorie-rich snack food at the delicatessen next door. Then take the easy walking route that leads from Évisa to the Cascades d'Aïtone (p92), where you can take an invigorating plunge into a freshwater pool.

TRANSPORT

See p105 for transport links from Ajaccio.

BUS // **Autocars Ceccaldi** (☎ 04 95 22 41 99; www.autocars-ceccaldi.com, in French) runs two buses daily between Porto and Ajaccio, calling by Piana, Cargèse and Sagone. It also connects Ajaccio with Évisa one to three times daily, and runs between Porto and Calvi daily between mid-May and September. Between July and mid-September, **Autocars Mordiconi** (☎ 04 95 48 00 04) runs one bus per day Monday to Saturday on the route between Porto and Corte via Évisa and Calacuccia.

GOLFE DE PORTO

· · · · · ·

Defined by the Réserve Naturelle de Scandola at the tip of its northern arm and the slender finger of Capu Rossu at its southern limit, the coastline of the Golfe de Porto is a tumble of steep cliffs that shelter small, enchanting coves.

PORTO

pop 400

Backed by sheer pink cliffs tumbling into a turquoise sea, Porto has a setting that's simply superb. This little holiday town makes a great base for exploring the mountainous interior, plus the two Unesco World Heritage Sites of Les Calanques and the Réserve Naturelle de Scandola.

There's no town hall, no church, none of the usual trappings and symbols of a town. Only the stout Genoese tower recalls the days when Porto was a harbour for today's sleepy inland village of Ota.

ESSENTIAL INFORMATION

TOURIST OFFICES // **Tourist office** (☎ 04 95 26 10 55; www.porto-tourisme.com; place de la Marine; ⏰ 9am-6pm Mon-Sat Apr & May, 9am-7pm Mon-Sat, 9am-1pm Sun Jun-Sep, 9am-7pm Mon-Sat Oct-Mar) Sells the excellent *Hikes & Walks in the Area of Porto* (€2.50).

EXPLORING PORTO

❦ **BOAT TRIP TO THE RÉSERVE NATURELLE DE SCANDOLA //** **SPECTACULAR SEA-LEVEL PERSPECTIVES OF A WORLD HERITAGE SITE**

There's no vehicle access or footpath that leads into the magnificent, protected Scandola nature reserve, so the only way to get up close is by sea. Boats visit from other west-coast ports (see below)

(Continued on page p88)

THE WEST COAST

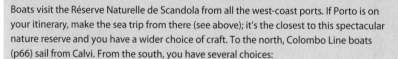

BY BOAT TO THE RÉSERVE NATURELLE DE SCANDOLA

Boats visit the Réserve Naturelle de Scandola from all the west-coast ports. If Porto is on your itinerary, make the sea trip from there (see above); it's the closest to this spectacular nature reserve and you have a wider choice of craft. To the north, Colombo Line boats (p66) sail from Calvi. From the south, you have several choices:

★ **Croisières Grand Bleu** (☎ 04 95 26 40 24; www.croisieresgrandbleu.com, in French; rue Marbeuf) A local company operating from Cargèse.

★ **Découvertes Naturelles** (☎ 04 95 73 12 66; www.decouvertes-naturelles.net, in French) Sailings from Ajaccio, Porticcio and Propriano.

★ **Nave Va** (☎ 04 95 28 02 66; www.naveva.com). The biggest player. Operates from Cargèse, Sagone, Ajaccio and Porticcio.

THE WEST COAST

THE WEST COAST

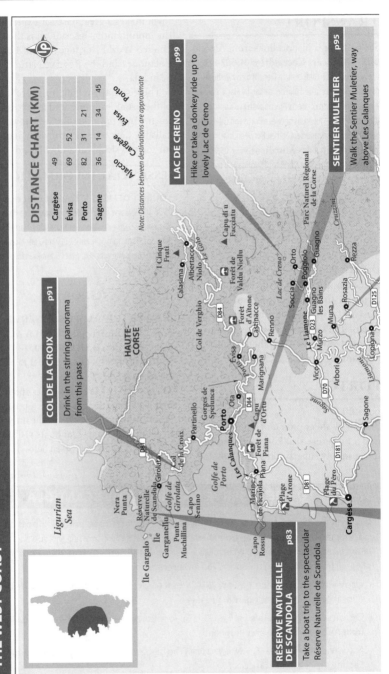

DISTANCE CHART (KM)

	Ajaccio	Cargèse	Évisa	Porto
Cargèse	49			
Évisa	69	52		
Porto	82	31	21	
Sagone	36	14	34	45

Note: Distances between destinations are approximate

LAC DE CRENO   p99

Hike or take a donkey ride up to lovely Lac de Creno

SENTIER MULETIER   p95

Walk the Sentier Muletier, way above Les Calanques

COL DE LA CROIX   p91

Drink in the stirring panorama from this pass

RÉSERVE NATURELLE DE SCANDOLA   p83

Take a boat trip to the spectacular Réserve Naturelle de Scandola

Ligurian Sea

Nera Punta

Réserve Naturelle de Scandola

Île Gargalo

Garganellu

Punta Muchillina

Île

Golfe de Girolata

Capo Senino

Girolata

Golfe de Porto

Capo Rossu

Les Calanques

Martinu de Ficajola

Piana

Plage d'Arone

Plage du Péro

Cargèse

Partinello

Col de la Croix

Gorges de Spelunca

Porto

Ota

Forêt de Aïtone

Évisa

Capu d'Ortu

HAUTE-CORSE

Col de Verghio

Marignana

Castirlacce

Renno

Calasima

I Cinque Frati

Albertacce

Niolo

Le Golo

Forêt de Valdu Niellu

Capu di u Facciatu

Lac de Creno

Orto

Poggiolo

Soccia

Guagno

Guagno les Bains

Parc Naturel Régional de la Corse

Cruzzini

Rezza

Rosazia

Muna

Le Liamone

Vico

Murzo

Arbori

Sagone

Liamone

Sagone

Lopigna

Cognacce

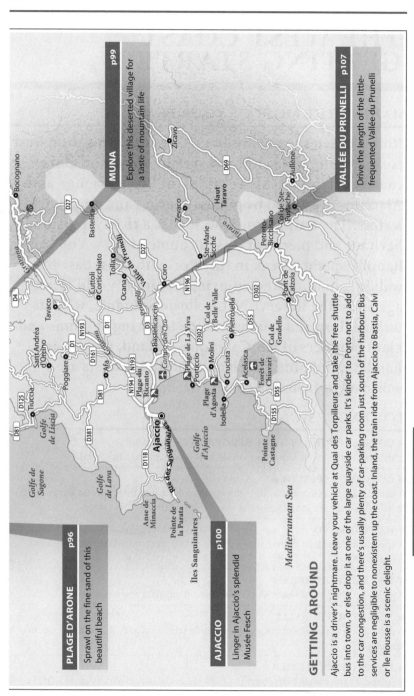

MUNA   p99

Explore this deserted village for a taste of mountain life

VALLÉE DU PRUNELLI   p107

Drive the length of the little-frequented Vallée du Prunelli

PLAGE D'ARONE   p96

Sprawl on the fine sand of this beautiful beach

AJACCIO   p100

Linger in Ajaccio's splendid Musée Fesch

GETTING AROUND

Ajaccio is a driver's nightmare. Leave your vehicle at Quai des Torpilleurs and take the free shuttle bus into town, or else drop it at one of the large quayside car parks. It's kinder to Porto not to add to the car congestion, and there's usually plenty of car-parking room just south of the harbour. Bus services are negligible to nonexistent up the coast. Inland, the train ride from Ajaccio to Bastia, Calvi or Île Rousse is a scenic delight.

Mediterranean Sea

THE WEST COAST
GETTING STARTED

MAKING THE MOST OF YOUR TIME

Roller-coaster your way along Corsica's straggling west coast for plunging cliffs, staggering views and glorious coastal driving. Its three gulfs – of Porto, Sagone and Ajaccio – are edged by golden beaches and aquamarine waters. The only town, Ajaccio, has a rich Napoléonic heritage and merits at least a couple of days. You can happily spend a week in tiny Porto, the best base for walking, boating and enjoying a pair of World Heritage Sites: the Réserve Naturelle de Scandola, with its unique flora and fauna, and the teetering columns and giant boulders of Les Calanques. Inland, mountain hamlets, and pine, beech and chestnut forests are a world away from the coastal fleshpots.

TOP EXCURSIONS

♥ COL DE VERGHIO TO THE BERGERIES DE RADULE
A shortish upland walk from a mountain pass to a shepherd's hut (p93).

- -

♥ GORGES DE SPELUNCA
A gentle walk to a Genoese bridge allows you to delve into these spectacular gorges; there's also a chance for a freshwater swim en route (p92).

- -

♥ HAUT TARAVO
A spectacular hinterland drive with a choice of two great mountain restaurants for lunch (p109).

- -

♥ ÎLES SANGUINAIRES
A gentle boat trip to offshore islets, complete with aperitif and swim (p102).

- -

♥ VALLÉE DU PRUNELLI
A drive along a spectacular gorge, plus lakeside relaxation and heart-stopping panoramas (p107).

- -

♥ LE SENTIER MULETIER
A splendid breezy walk high above the cliffs of Les Calanques and its crowds (p95).

- -

GETTING AWAY FROM IT ALL

You *can* be alone on the coast in summer if you're prepared to seek out one of the multitude of small coves, which may require a scramble. For better chances of solitude, simply head inland, up and into the woods.

* **Hire a boat or paddle your own canoe** Porto, in particular, offers plenty of scope for independent nosing along the coast (p89)

* **Sentier des Muletiers** Gaze down upon Les Calanques from this little-hiked former mule track (p95)

* **Lac de Creno** Hike or bounce on the back of a donkey to this hidden mountain lake (p99)

TOP INLAND EXPERIENCES

♣ FORÊT D'AÏTONE
Cool, green, tranquil CO2-sucking, woodland where laricio pine and beech shield you from the summer sun (p91)

♣ A DRIVE TO THE ABANDONED TOWN OF MUNA
A spectacular, thrilling ascent and a roam around a deserted village (p99)

♣ LAC DE CRENO
A lovely upland lake, only accessible on foot or, in season, by pony (p99)

♣ LAC DE TOLLA IN THE VALLÉE DU PRUNELLI
Paradise for a picnic, followed by a swim or kayak paddle through the lake's still waters (p107)

TOP EATING EXPERIENCES

♣ LE MAQUIS
Delightful food and a cheeseboard that spills over (p90)

♣ LE GRAND CAFÉ NAPOLÉON
Refined dining in a belle époque ballroom (p104)

♣ U TARAVU
Home-cured charcuterie and cheeses, plus farm-raised lamb (p110)

♣ L'ANCURA
Smart harbourside dining (p98)

♣ HÔTEL LES ROCHES ROUGES
Gourmet dishes and a panoramic view (p96)

♣ A TRÀMULA
Meals made from home-grown and local produce (p93)

RESOURCES

* **Destination Ouest-Corse** (www .destination-ouest-corse.net) Tourist information for the west coast

* **Ota Porto** (www.porto-tourisme.com) Tourist office site covering the Golfe de Porto and inland

* **Pays d'Ajaccio Tourist Office** (www .ajaccio-tourisme.com) Official site for visitors to the Golfe d'Ajaccio and inland

* **Parc Naturel Régional de la Corse** (PNRC; www.parc-naturel-corse.com, in French) Website of the body that administers much of inland Corsica

THE WEST COAST

(Continued from page 83)

but leaving from Porto offers the shortest journey. Between April and October, four companies sail to the base of its cliffs, often taking in Les Calanques and Girolata. Birdwatching (look out for puffins, cormorants and a colony of breeding ospreys) is at its richest until late June. And your captain's sure to point out the strange seaweed that forms a thin grey crust around the water's edge.

Smaller boats, such as the *Mare Nostrum* I and II of **Porto Linea** (☎ 06 08 16 89 71; www.portolinea.com, in French; tickets Hôtel Monte Rosso), can nudge into coves and caves that are denied to weightier craft. Other operators include **Nave Va** (☎ 04 95 26 15 16; www.naveva.com; tickets Hôtel le Cyrnée), the biggest of the companies with the largest boat, and **Pass'Partout** (☎ 06 75 99 13 15; tickets Restaurant La Tour Génoise), a newish player with an attractive small boat. **Via Mare** (☎ 06 07 28 72 72; www.viamare-promenades.com; tickets Hôtel du Golfe) along with Porto Linea, is one of the most experienced of the operators.

Commentaries are only in French so do pass by the tourist office in advance

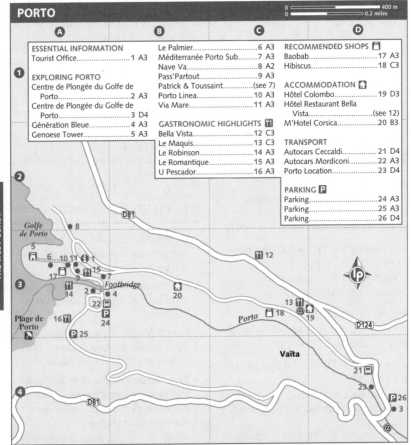

PORTO				0 ——— 400 m / 0 ——— 0.2 miles

A **B** **C** **D**

1

ESSENTIAL INFORMATION
Tourist Office........................1 A3

EXPLORING PORTO
Centre de Plongée du Golfe de
   Porto................................2 A3
Centre de Plongée du Golfe de
   Porto................................3 D4
Génération Bleue..................4 A3
Genoese Tower.....................5 A3

Le Palmier.............................6 A3
Méditerranée Porto Sub.........7 A3
Nave Va................................8 A2
Pass'Partout.........................9 A3
Patrick & Toussaint.............(see 7)
Porto Linea.........................10 A3
Via Mare.............................11 A3

GASTRONOMIC HIGHLIGHTS 🍴
Bella Vista...........................12 C3
Le Maquis...........................13 C3
Le Robinson.........................14 A3
Le Romantique.....................15 A3
U Pescador..........................16 A3

RECOMMENDED SHOPS 🛍
Baobab................................17 A3
Hibiscus..............................18 C3

ACCOMMODATION 🏠
Hôtel Colombo.....................19 D3
Hôtel Restaurant Bella
   Vista...............................(see 12)
M'Hotel Corsica...................20 B3

TRANSPORT
Autocars Ceccaldi................21 D4
Autocars Mordiconi.............22 A3
Porto Location....................23 D4

PARKING 🅿
Parking...............................24 A3
Parking...............................25 A3
Parking...............................26 D4

2

Golfe de Porto

D81

3

5
🏠 6 10 11 1ℹ
17 9 15
14 2 4
22 🅿
Footbridge
20

Plage de Porto
16 🍴 24 🅿 25

🍴 12

13 🍴
@ 19
18

Porto
D124

Vaïta

21

23

🅿 26
3

@

D81

for a copy of its free pamphlet, *Visit of the Natural Reserve of Scandola by Sea*.

♥ PORTO'S BEST PANORAMAS //
A TYPICAL CORSICAN WATCHTOWER AND A SUPERB SUNSET PANORAMA

For the best view in Porto, climb precisely 176 steps to the high point of the little town's renovated 16th-century **Genoese tower** (admission €2.50; ☺ 9am-7pm Apr-Jun & Sep, 9am-9pm Jul & Aug). Inside, interpretive panels tell of the financing, construction and functioning of these watchtowers, and of the tough existence of the *torregiano*, the tower watchman; arm yourself at the reception kiosk with the English brochure, which gives a full translation. Seawards the views are magnificent; looking back you'll appreciate how tiny Porto really is.

For a sterling sunset view of the harbour and tower, install yourself on the tight little terrace of **Le Palmier** and sip a pastis or enjoy an ice cream as the daylight fades.

♥ HIRING A BOAT OR CANOE //
DOING IT YOUR WAY ON THE WATER

For exploration at your own pace, paddle your own canoe (from €10/20 per hour/three hours) to Les Calanques or put-put to Scandola in a motor boat (from €75/115 per half-/full day). **Patrick & Toussaint** (☎ 06 81 41 70 03; www.patrickettoussaint.com), among others, rents motor boats, canoes and sea kayaks too.

♥ WALKING // A GOOD GUIDE TO HIKING AROUND PORTO

The *Hikes & Walks in the Area of Porto* brochure (€2.50) from the tourist office (p83) details 28 signed walks at all levels

---

ACCOMMODATION

It's essential to reserve both coastal and inland hotels in July and August.

For our picks, see the separate Accommodation chapter. Our favourites among the favoured include the following:

* ★ For the last word in caring luxury, head to **Hôtel les Mouettes** (p248)

* ★ **Hôtel Marengop248** is a one-off – quirky, truly individual and completely charming

* ★ For fresh air and organic country cuisine, book into **Maison d'Hôte Giargalo** (p247)

* ★ High in the hills, **Maison d'Hôte Châtelet de Campo** (p248) is a delightful *chambres d'hôtes* (B&B)

* ★ **Hôtel Colombo** (p246) is a bright boutique-style hotel

---

of difficulty. For longer treks, supplement this with the IGN Top 25 sheet *Porto & Calanche de Piana*.

♥ SNORKELLING // JOIN THE DIVERS TO EXPLORE UNDERWATER PORTO

Porto's three diving outfits, all based at the quay, offer snorkelling trips (€15 including equipment) to choice spots including the fringe of the Scandola reserve. All offer introductory dives and courses for beginners, too. **Centre de Plongée du Golfe de Porto** (☎ 04 95 26 10 29, 06 84 24 49 20; www.plongeeporto .com, in French; ☺ Easter-Oct) **Génération Bleue** (☎ 04 95 26 24 88, 06 07 43 21 28; www.generation-bleue.com; ☺ May-Oct) **Méditerranée Porto Sub** (☎ 04 95 26 10 27, 06 14 94 08 94; www.plongeecorse.fr; ☺ mid-Apr–Sep)

THE WEST COAST

GASTRONOMIC HIGHLIGHTS

❦ BELLA VISTA €€

☎ 04 95 26 11 08; www.hotel-corse.com, in French; rte de Calvi; mains around €25, menu €26; ☯ dinner Apr–mid-Oct

You may get better views with your dinner elsewhere in this tiny town but nowhere will you find better fare. The *menu gourmand* is creative and offers plenty of choice. For something even more original, order the house speciality, *cabri* (grilled and lightly roasted suckling goat; €46 to €70), which serves two to three people. You'll need to ask for it when you reserve – it takes a full 45 minutes to prepare.

❦ LE MAQUIS €€

☎ 04 95 26 12 19; www.hotel-lemaquis.com; mains €20-29, menus €20-54; ☯ lunch & dinner mid-Feb–mid-Nov

There's a cosy all-wood interior but, for preference, reserve a table on the balcony, which has great views and candles flickering all around. Service is friendly and the food's a delight. Save a cranny for the cheeseboard, which has around a dozen different varieties, mostly nameless and all bought directly from Corsican dairies. For a special treat, opt for the *menu de la mer* (€54), which includes ravioli stuffed with scallops and topped with a sea-urchin sauce; grilled lobster; and *that* cheeseboard.

❦ LE ROMANTIQUE €€

☎ 04 95 26 10 85; mains €16-24, menus €18-20; ☯ lunch & dinner mid-Apr–Sep

With a terrace directly overlooking the port, and tablecloths of soft Provençal ochre and orange, it's as romantic as the name proclaims. Portions are ample and the *menu Corsica* (€20) is much more varied than the usual restaurant set menus. Choose, for example, the *tourte à la mode Corse*, slices of pie stuffed with *lonzu* (tender smoked pork fillet), white cheese and herbs.

❦ U PESCADOR €

☎ 04 95 26 15 19; mains €10-15, menus €13.50-18; ☯ lunch & dinner May-Sep

Near the beach (with the sea just out of sight, alas), the Fisherman does a quite magnificent fish soup. Both the fish and seafood (ah, the fresh lobster!) will have been recently pulled from the Mediterranean by Porto fisherman Antoine Fieschi. If the restaurant is full (as it tends to be), walk over to **Le Robinson** (☎ 04 95 26 17 60; ☯ lunch & dinner), equally simple and also offering Monsieur Fieschi's fresh fish, at comparable prices.

RECOMMENDED SHOPS

❦ BAOBAB

The jazzy hats, bags, T-shirts and beach mats at this colourful boutique are commissioned directly from local producers in Madagascar.

❦ HIBISCUS

rte de La Marine

This great little delicatessen specialises in richly scented sausages, charcuterie and other Corsican gastronomic delights. Its taster plate makes for a great snack.

TRANSPORT

CAR & SCOOTER // Porto Location (☎ 04 95 26 10 13) hires out cars (from €58 per day) and scooters (from €46).

PARKING // Driving through Porto can be a slow shuffle. It's better to leave your car in the parking area behind the beach and walk over the footbridge.

BICYCLE // Porto Location (☎ 04 95 26 10 13) also rents mountain bikes (from €15 per day).

THE WEST COAST

NORTH OF PORTO

♥ COL DE LA CROIX (BOCCA A CROCE) // SPLENDID VIEWS AND AN OPTIONAL HIKE

At this *col* (pass), 22km north of Porto on the D81, there's a perfectly placed *buvette* (drinks stand), and a stirring panorama southward to the Golfe de Porto – Piana perched high on its far shore, Porto's fort just poking out – and northward to the rosy crags of the Réserve Naturelle de Scandola. See below for details of a hike from the pass to Girolata.

♥ GIROLATA (GHJIRULATU) // POSTCARD-PRETTY HAMLET REACHED ONLY BY BOAT OR ON FOOT

It's the journey that counts – whether it's by boat from Porto and other coastal resorts or on foot from the Col de la Croix. From a distance, Girolata, set within a horseshoe-shaped bay and guarded by a well-preserved Genoese fort, is stunning. Close up, it can be overcrowded in July and August, with an armada of sightseeing boats, on their way to or from the Réserve Naturelle de Scandola disgorging their passengers.

To walk here from Col de la Croix (above), follow the orange blazes of the **Sentier du Facteur** (Postman's Path)

FORÊT D'AÏTONE

In the 17th century, the Genoese forged a path through this thick, tangled woodland to Sagone, from where the forest timber was transported to the shipyards of Genoa. There, the tall, straight laricio-pine trunks, some 60m in height, were fashioned into beams, masts and cross-pieces for the powerful Genoese navy, long the masters of the Mediterranean.

downhill through dense maquis. After about 15 minutes, there's a welcome spring and trough, ideal for dunking your head. Twenty minutes or so later, the path curls around pebbly **Tuara cove**. From here, two paths thread through the maquis; take the one signed Ghjirulatu. There's a stunning view over the village and its bay as the trail meets the Mare e Monti Nord route after some 30 minutes. Descending to Girolata, which has plenty of choices for lunch or a drink, takes a further 30 minutes.

To return, cross back over Girolata's beach, then take the signed Sentier du Facteur option, which follows the line of the coast (with its share of rocky ups and downs) as far as the Tuara cove. Allow 3½ to four hours for the round trip.

INLAND FROM PORTO

The D84 snakes above the plunging Gorges de Spelunca to take in Évisa and pass through the Forêt d'Aïtone, a 1670 hectare woodland. Greener and cooler than the coast, it's predominantly composed of laricio pines and beech trees, as well as Mediterranean pines, firs and larches. Beyond the Col de Verghio, 34km from Porto, stretches the Vallée du Niolo.

EXPLORING INLAND FROM PORTO

♥ ÉVISA // THE CHESTNUT VILLAGE

The lively little village of Évisa, between the Gorges de Spelunca and the Forêt d'Aïtone, is popular with walkers due its location at the junction of the Mare a Mare Nord and Mare e Monti Nord trails.

Its more-general fame arises from its annual chestnut harvests. Although the harvests are now mere gleanings

GUY LE FACTEUR

The Sentier du Facteur (Postman's Path) is named after the postman Guy Ceccaldi, a strapping ex-legionnaire with a flowing white beard who recently retired. In his prime, Guy the Postman would regularly walk to Girolata and back, bringing not only the mail but news of the outside world as well.

compared with the bumper years of the 19th century, they still pull in more than 1000 tonnes of chestnuts each year, most of which is ground into chestnut flour. Évisa chestnuts even have their own appellation, and the village holds **La Fête du Marron**, a chestnut festival that's celebrated every November.

❦ WALKING INTO THE GORGES DE SPELUNCA // A TASTE OF A SPECTACULAR CANYON

Until the D84 was hacked from the mountain, this former mule track, partly cobbled, was the only link between the villages of Ota and Évisa. It runs along the steep sides of the Spelunca canyon beneath huge, humbling cliffs.

To get to the trailhead, leave Porto by the D84 (direction Évisa). After about 10km, turn left onto the D124 and, 2.2km from the junction, park your vehicle by a double-arched road bridge; the trail, blazed in orange and punctuated by interpretive panels in French, is signed Spelunca beside the bridge. The rocky path soon begins to climb fairly steeply up the western flank of the valley, but oak, ash and boxwood provide plenty of shade. After around 30 minutes, you reach **Ponte Zaglia**, a Genoese-style bridge slung across a tributary of the river Porto in 1798. Nearby, you can refresh yourself in the inviting rock pools.

Allow between an hour and 1½ hours to complete this easy there-and-back walk.

For a more stretching hike, you can continue beyond Ponte Zaglia as far as Évisa. The shaded path ascends the steep hillside by a series of switchbacks, emerging onto the D84 beside the village cemetery. For this variant, count on around four hours for the round trip from the road bridge.

Upon your return, a three-minute walk up the D124 brings you to **Ponte Pianella** (marked Ponte Vecchju on some maps), another Genoese bridge.

❦ MEETING THE COCHON COUREUR // ENCOUNTER THE ROAMING CORSICAN PIG

It can happen in many places around the island. But you stand a particularly good chance of a close encounter of the porcine kind at any of the hundred and one bends in the D84 as it mounts from Évisa to Col de Verghio. On this trip we happened across a big black sow with her 11 scurrying piglets, plus an aunt of theirs who tried her best to scrabble into the back seat of the car.

❦ CASCADES D'AÏTONE // WALK TO WATERFALLS AND NATURAL POOLS

As you rise higher from Évisa on the D84, look out after 3km for a sign for this tumble of waterfalls and naturally scooped-out basins that serve as miniature swimming pools; they're only about 10 minutes off the road along a pleasant footpath. In high summer, arrive early or late in the day, since they can be very crowded.

Or you can also walk up to the falls from Évisa, following a section of the Mare a Mare Nord long-distance trail, the **Chemin des Châtaigniers** (Chestnut Grove Route). This easy two- to 2½-hour

THE WEST COAST

(7km) out-and-back walk is marked in orange, with 13 interpretive panels (in French) that explain chestnut farming, once a mainstay of the local economy.

This walk begins beside Modern Bar, near Évisa's eastern end. For the first 45 minutes it follows a sandy lane between chestnut groves, where Mediterranean and laricio pine are gradually reasserting themselves. After the trail intersects with the D84, take the wide path that drops gently to the Cascades d'Aïtone, and paddle or plunge into their cooling waters.

❦ WALKING FROM THE COL DE VERGHIO (BOCCA DI VERGHJU) TO THE BERGERIES DE RADULE // UNDEMANDING MOUNTAIN WALK TO A SHEPHERD'S HUT

Corsica's highest drivable pass, the **Col de Verghio** (1467m) marks the boundary between Haute-Corse and Corse-du-Sud. A giant statue of Jesus in a long cloak stands guard and, in summer, a vendor of Corsican produce and drinks is his constant companion.

This out-and-back walk, waymarked in orange, takes off from behind the statue of Jesus. Easy on both the eye and body (allow about 1½ hours for the round trip), it threads at first through a forest of chestnut and laricio pine, offering glorious views of the Vallée du Niolo and the dark stain of Calacuccia's lake.

With the *bergeries* (shepherds' huts) already in sight, turn left at a T-junction where the track meets the red and white blazes of the GR20. In summer, a shepherd lives in this cluster of huts and sheep pens. Arrive before 2pm and you can enjoy his cheeses and a snack or drink. It's well worth pushing onwards for around 15 minutes to get to a shady spot where a natural stone basin catches water tumbling over a ladder of small falls.

GASTRONOMIC HIGHLIGHTS

❦ A TRÀMULA // ÉVISA €
☎ 04 95 26 24 39; mains €14; ☺ lunch & dinner

So many Corsican eateries proclaim their use of local products, but few name their providers on the menu. Mathieu and Patricia Ceccaldi list all their small-scale Corsican producers, whose goods supplement their own home-grown fruit and vegetables, potted meats, charcuterie and chestnut flour. It's small, so you'll need to reserve – ask for a table on the tiny balcony overlooking the valley. Afterwards, you can pick up some prime produce from their delicatessen, right next door.

❦ LA CHÂTAIGNERAIE // ÉVISA €€
☎ 04 95 26 24 47; www.hotel-la-chataigneraie .com, in French; mains €12-19; ☺ lunch & dinner mid-Apr–mid-Oct

The restaurant of this appealing hotel (p247) deserves a visit for its own sake. For a not-so-light lunch, opt for its

PIGS ON THE RUN

The only wild pigs now left in Corsica are wild boar; the porkers you see beside – or serenely squatting in the middle of – mountain roads are domestic animals known as *cochons coureurs* (free-ranging pigs). It is estimated that there are 15,000 free-ranging pigs in Haute-Corse and 30,000 in Corse-du-Sud – and every last animal belongs to someone.

The finest Corsican pork derives its flavour from the pigs' diet of acorns and chestnuts. The charcuterie produced in Corsica is excellent, though you should be aware that some of the specialities sold on the island with a Made in Corsica tag are in fact made from imported pork meat. See p231 for more on Corsican charcuterie.

THE WEST COAST

mixed platter of Corsican meats (€12). For something even more substantial, try the chef's version of saltimbocca, made with chunks of tender veal and Brocciu (goat's- or ewe's-milk cheese), or the *filet de porc aux cèpes et châtaignes* (fillet of pork with chestnuts and cèpe mushrooms). The homemade desserts too are winners, all.

RECOMMENDED SHOPS

❦ **NICOLE & PASCAL SANTUCCI**
☎ 04 95 26 25 32; Castinacce; ✸ lunch & dinner
The Santuccis sell their home produce at country fairs and from their tiny, tasteful shop, set beside the D70, just beyond Castinacce. Everything on sale comes from their farm; Nicole bakes the cakes and biscuits and bottles the fruit, while Pascal cures the charcuterie and mills the chestnut flour. Stop by for a drink on the terrace and see if you can resist…

LES CALANQUES (LES CALANCHES)

Les Calanques, almost sheer and more than 400m high, rear up above the sea in teetering columns, towers and irregularly shaped boulders of pink, ochre and ginger. As you sway around switchback after switchback on the D81 between Porto and Piana, one breathtaking vista follows another.

The writer Guy de Maupassant, who visited Corsica in 1880, likened these strange geological formations to 'some monstrous race, a nightmare menagerie, petrified by some profligate god'. More prosaically, this giant granite jumble, a World Heritage Site, was formed by the erosion of wind and sea.

For the full technicolour experience, Les Calanques need to be savoured on foot – ideally in the relative coolness of

DEVIL'S WORK

Les Calanques are the stuff of legend. Way before Guy de Maupassant's flight of fancy, local folklore had it that they were fashioned in a tantrum by the devil himself, who was enraged by a shepherdess who had spurned him. If you squint and apply a little imagination of your own, you can make out her petrified form, her husband, their dog and other fantastic forms – a giant's head, eagle, dromedary and even a mitred bishop.

early morning, before the crowds arrive, or at sunset, when the rocks almost glow with muted copper tones. The tourist office in Piana (opposite) has a useful leaflet, *Piana: Sentiers de Randonnées* (€1), which details six walks within the area.

If you're driving, there's very limited roadside parking; the early car gets the space. Les Calanques are an easy walk from Piana, which has more-ample parking facilities, but do be wary of traffic on the tight bends.

For a unique sea-level perspective, take a boat tour (p83) or hire your own craft (p89).

❦ **WALKING TO THE CHÂTEAU FORT // AN OUT-AND-BACK STROLL TO A STAGGERING PANORAMA**
Park near the Tête de Chien (Dog's Head), a distinctively shaped rock that's signposted on a large bend in the D81, 3.5km east of Piana. Set out early to avoid the crowds that throng this accessible trail, and avoid wearing sandals; the route is rocky and steep in places. Your goal, reached after 20 to 30 minutes, is a broad natural platform known as the Château Fort (Fortress),

from where the view over the Golfe de Porto and the inlets of Les Calanques is stunning.

❦ LE SENTIER MULETIER // A WALK THAT OVERLOOKS LES CALANQUES

To reach the start of this walk, whose length you can vary at will (even half an hour will leave you with glorious images burned on the retinas), leave the D81 at the sign *Stade and Sentier de Randonnée*, 1.6km east of Piana, and drop your vehicle in the car park beside a dusty football pitch.

At a second sign, *Ancien Chemin de Piana à Ota*, follow this former mule trail, which was the only link between Piana and Ota until the D81 was built in 1850. After about 15 minutes, it emerges onto a glorious flat corniche, constructed with the sweat of human labour, that snakes around the hillside, giving glorious views of Les Calanques.

If you're up here for the views, continue until the trail starts to descend steeply, then retrace your steps. For more of a workout, drop with the track until it meets the D81 beside a small shrine to the Virgin Mary, then head back.

The full out-and-back walk takes around 1¼ hours.

PIANA & AROUND

pop 450
Peering down over the Golfe de Porto from its small plateau, Piana makes a seductive alternative to Porto, especially if you're after quietness (guaranteed, even in high summer, once the day's through-traffic has rumbled on) and a little beach inactivity (Plage d'Arone, the area's finest, is a spectacular 12km drive away).

Piana has a history of silence. In the 15th century Piana was ruled by the hot-headed *seigneurs de Leca*, who governed a vast area on the west coast of the island. Rebelling against Genoa, they – and the entire male population – were massacred. The Genoese then banned anyone from living in Piana, which only came to life again in the 18th century, once Genoese influence on the island was on the wane.

ESSENTIAL INFORMATION

TOURIST OFFICES // Tourist office (☎ 04 95 27 84 42; www.sipiana.com; ☉ 9am-5pm Mon-Fri, 9am-noon Sat & Sun Jun-Sep, 8.30-11.30am & 1.30-4pm Mon-Fri Oct-May) Set back from the main road, beside the post office.

EXPLORING PIANA & AROUND

❦ PIANA'S OLD QUARTER // A LOOK AROUND THE VILLAGE

To enjoy old Piana, explore the streets behind Église Ste-Marie, which are all bordered by attractive renovated stone houses. On the facades of too many dwellings, however, the lovely original stonework is masked by a patina of cement.

❦ WALKING CAPU ROSSU (CAPO ROSSO) // HIKING A SLIM PROMONTORY WITH CONSISTENTLY MAGNIFICENT SEASCAPES

To get to the start of the trail along Capu Rossu, take the D824 (signed Plage d'Arone) out of Piana, follow it for 6km and park below a snack bar at a bend where the road begins to dip. From here, you can clearly make out the silhouette of your goal, the Tour de Turghiu.

THE WEST COAST

The path descends steadily through scrub to pass the first of several ruined *bergeries,* set on the left after around 20 minutes. About an hour out, it meets a restored *bergerie* with a pink-tiled roof and traces of a circular threshing floor. Here, turn right (northward) to tackle the steep climb to the tower, which at first takes a tightly zigzagging path, then follows cairns. After some 30 minutes of ascent, flop down at the base of the Tour de Turghiu, where there's a sheer 300m drop to the sea and heart-stopping views of the Golfe de Porto and Golfe de Sagone.

Make sure you set out early, take plenty of water and wear a hat, since there's scarcely a square centimetre of shade. Allow three to 3½ hours for the round trip.

❦ MARINE DE FICAJOLA // HYPERSTEEP DESCENT PROVIDING TERRIFIC VIEWS OF LES CALANQUES

From the church in Piana, follow the D824 towards the Plage d'Arone for 1km, then turn right onto the narrow D624 for a white-knuckle 4km descent through rocky red mountains with stunning views over Les Calanques. Leave your vehicle at the end of the road and follow the path for about 10 minutes to this tiny cove, where lobster-fishing boats once used to take shelter. You're here for the splendour of the ride down, though – the pocket of beach can get very crowded in high summer.

❦ PLAGE D'ARONE // GORGEOUS CRESCENT-SHAPED STRAND OF FINE SAND

Plage d'Arone, as a small monument will tell you, has a special place in Corsican history; it was here in 1943 that the first weapons for the Corsican resistance arrived aboard the submarine *Casabianca.* The water's limpid, the sand will trickle through your toes and the beach is a good deal less crowded than those of most west-coast resorts.

To get here, follow the D824 for 12km until it peters out at the beach. The ridge drive itself is well worth the journey: it cuts through wild mountain scenery offering splendid views over the Golfe de Porto.

GASTRONOMIC HIGHLIGHTS

❦ CAFÉ DE LA PLAGE // PLAGE D'ARONE €€

☎ 04 95 20 17 27; pizzas €9-13.50, mains €20-25; ☽ lunch & dinner Apr-Sep

This cafe has a delightful vine-shaded terrace that's just a pebble's throw from the beach. For the freshest of fish, check out that day's catch, chalked up on the blackboard – there were eight varieties on the day we passed and all were sourced from a local fisherman. If you need to work off lunch, it conveniently hires out sea kayaks and pedalos.

❦ HÔTEL LES ROCHES ROUGES // PIANA €€

☎ 04 95 27 81 81; mains €22-25, menus €32-40; ☎ lunch & dinner

At the restaurant of this splendid hotel (p247), settle into a comfortable cane armchair, and savour gourmet nouvelle cuisine, magnificent decor (the frescos are a Unesco-recognised monument) and exceptional views of the gulf through vast picture windows. Dishes are inventive, if small, and there's a good selection of local wines, which are also available by the half-bottle. The terrace, looking over Les Calanques at sunset, must offer one of the finest views on earth. Even if you aren't dining, do pause there for a drink.

♣ LE CASANOVA // PIANA €
☎ 04 95 27 84 20; mains €9-20, menu €16.50; ☻ lunch & dinner Apr-Oct

No, not a philandering patron – rather, it's the name of the friendly family (Mum, Dad and two sons) who run this bustling restaurant. Located in an attractive stone house whose terrace occupies most of the square, Le Casanova serves a *menu Corse* (€16.50) that includes specialities prepared, like all its charcuterie, by the village butcher. Alternatively, go à la carte and indulge in large wood-fired pizzas (€8.50 to €11.50) or the house speciality, *coquille St-Jacques au myrte* (scallops cooked in myrtle liqueur).

GOLFE DE SAGONE

······

The Golfe de Sagone, where the hills descend more gently to longer shallower beaches, is altogether softer than the Golfe de Porto, its more rugged northern neighbour.

CARGÈSE (CARGHJESE)

pop 1100
This sleepy little town owes its origin to a community of 730 Greeks, granted exile here by Genoa in 1676 as they fled the Ottoman Turks. Nowadays, the town's charm lies in its quiet streets and the gleaming white facades of its houses. The best of its five beaches is Plage du Péro, a long strand of pure-white sand located 1.5km north of town.

ESSENTIAL INFORMATION

TOURIST OFFICES // Tourist office (☎ 04 95 26 41 31; www.cargese.net, in French; ☻ 9am-1pm & 2-6pm Mon-Sat mid-Jun–mid-Sep, 9am-noon & 1-6pm Mon-Sat mid-Sep–mid-Jun)

EXPLORING CARGÈSE

♣ GREEK & LATIN CHURCHES // MEMORIES OF GREEK IMMIGRATION
Although Cargèse is more renowned for its beaches, the town's two decorative churches provide a pleasant cultural interlude and an insight into the town's Greek past. Some of the icons in Èglise Catholique de Rite Grec (☻ 9am-6pm) were brought to the town by the original refugees and are fine examples of the art. The present building dates from 1852, when it replaced the original place of worship, which was no longer large enough to accommodate the expanding congregation. Like all Greek churches, its main features are the richness of its ornamentation and the delicacy of the portraits of the iconostasis, the traditional painted wooden partition separating altar from nave. More modern is the mural at the western end depicting the fate of this tiny Greek community.

No doubt a trifle envious of the Greek community's extravagant church, the town's non-Greek community decided to erect a rival Roman Catholic church, the Èglise Latine Ste-Marie (☻ 9am-6pm). It was completed in 1828, although seven years later God let them down and wind blew the roof off. There's an intriguing trompe l'œil ceiling but, at the end of the day, the church's best feature is the view over the gulf from the square at its west end.

GASTRONOMIC HIGHLIGHTS

♣ A VOLTA €€
☎ 06 19 55 11 84; mains around €15; ☻ 10am-11pm May–mid-Sep

At the end of rue du Docteur Petrolacci in the old town, A Volta will delight you. The menu changes as the day progresses, but the sweeping panorama from its broad terrace remains constantly splendid. Decorated in soothing grey and silver, it offers breakfasts, a copious and creative brunch, and great à la carte fare, including nine inventive pastas, mains such as beef, fish and scallop tartare, and a long, lip-smacking list of ice creams and sorbets.

☙ LE CABANON DE CHARLOTTE €€
☎ 06 81 23 66 93; mains €13-26, menus €16-21;
🕑 lunch & dinner Apr-Oct

This appealing choice offers sophisticated dining in an intimate environment at the end of the main jetty. Seating is made from solid teak, and fish dishes, subtly prepared, are the very freshest. Service is with a smile.

☙ U RASAGHIU €€
☎ 04 95 26 48 60; mains €16-22, menus €15-23;
🕑 lunch & dinner Mar-Oct

You'll love it or hate it. The white-suited crooner with slicked-back hair entertains diners three times weekly; choose Monday, Wednesday or Friday dinner for an authentic French seaside experience, or one of the other nights for quieter dining. You'll eat well on this vast quayside terrace; fresh fish dishes are particularly well prepared and come with tempting garnishing.

RECOMMENDED SHOPS

☙ A CAVAGNOLA
rue du Docteur Dragacci; 🕑 9am-7.30pm May-Sep

A stone's throw from the tourist office, A Cavagnola carries a great range of Corsican delicacies. It also has a small terrace where you can tuck into pizzas, salads, sandwiches and paninis.

☙ TERRA CORSA
☎ 04 95 22 40 21; av Colonel Fieschi

Corsica abounds in shops selling local specialities. But how many can claim that the rich variety of cheeses, displayed pell-mell in the window, are all from the milk of the owners' ewes? In the hills behind Cargèse, Jean-Xavier Capodimacci tends his flocks while Ruiz, his wife, runs their delicatessen, a richly scented emporium with festoons of sausages, hams, local wines and liqueurs, jams, herbs and conserves.

SAGONE (SAONE)

pop 250

Driving southward to Sagone, the coast becomes less craggy and the hills more rounded and desiccated. The chief attraction of this thin strip of a town is its beautiful, steeply shelving beach.

☙ L'ANCURA // DELIGHTFUL DINING BESIDE THE MARINA
Fresh fish, hauled in by a local fisherman, arrives daily at L'Ancura (☎ 04 95 28 04 93; mains €20-30; 🕑 lunch & dinner May-Sep), and the restaurant's delightful desserts are all made on the spot. Despite the rough-and-ready appearance of the exterior, it's a stylish little place with linen napkins, pleasing modern tableware and a little nook of a bar for sipping an aperitif. Dinner reservations are essential. The downside on our last visit: offhand, unsmiling service.

☙ DOLCI GERONIMI // OVER 50 VARIETIES OF ICE CREAMS AND SORBETS
Mmm, and *what* ice creams and fresh-fruit sorbets! Behind Dolci Geronimi (☎ 04 95 28 04 13; 🕑 Apr–mid-Oct), an airy cafe where you can eat in or take out by the tubful, the Geronimis confect a wondrous variety of ices. Try the *framboise* (raspberry) and you'll imagine you're eating the pulped fruit on a cold day; alterna-

tively, indulge in the *tutti frutti,* a synthesis of fresh juices. Many are more creative and some flavours, such as Brocciu, carrot or chestnut flour, require a measure of daring on the part of the purchaser.

INLAND FROM SAGONE

Extending between Sagone and Col de Verghio, this mountainous microregion makes for a great day of inland driving. It also offers ample scope for walkers.

♥ MUNA // A DESERTED VILLAGE AND A SUPERLATIVE DRIVE

Muna is a ghost village. Still gripping the mountainside, its only evident life are a few quicksilver lizards and a family of feral cats that nuzzle your ankles. Its setting, backed by sheer crags and with views extending to the Mediterranean, is as spectacular as the exhilarating road that brings you here.

As you pick your way up the hillside, you get a feel for how life was lived in this typical mountain village. The spring still flows, a twisted vine still shades an abandoned porch and the huge grindstone of the village mill totters on its axle. The chapel remains locked and intact and, if you open the communal oven, the aroma of wood smoke wafts out. The war memorial still honours the one Rossi and eight Niviaggiolis who gave their lives in WWI.

To get here from Murzo, follow the D4 for 7.7km, then park opposite a yellow postbox, 400m beyond a sign for the village. A steep, mostly cobbled track leads to the village in less than 10 minutes.

♥ WALKING FROM SOCCIA TO LAC DE CRENO (LAVU DI CRENU) // HIKE OR HORSE RIDE?

From the village of Soccia, follow signs for the lake for 3km, then leave your vehicle beside the small summertime cafe at the end of the road. In July and August you can **hire a donkey or pony** (per hr/half-day €10/25) to clip-clop up the rocky trail that clings to the southern flank of the valley. If you're hiking, you can't go wrong – just look out for the yellow and orange blazes, and donkey droppings. There's no shade until, after around 45 minutes, you enter a pine wood where a welcome spring flows. Around five minutes beyond the spring, **Lac de Creno** (1310m) is a lovely green oasis. Fringed by spongy sphagnum moss and encircled by laricio pines, it's the perfect picnic spot. In spring, you'll have the added delight of water lilies in flower. Since it's a particularly sensitive protected area (one of the rarities here is the *drosera,* a carnivorous plant, so keep your boots on!), there's no swimming. Allow around 2½ hours for the round-trip.

♥ A MERENDELLA // SEASONAL FARE STRAIGHT FROM THE GARDEN IN SOCCIA

☎ 04 95 28 34 91; rte de l'Église; mains €19, menus €25-35; ⏲ lunch & dinner Thu-Tue Apr-Oct

At this mountain restaurant, dishes vary according to the season – and according to what's in the restaurant's kitchen garden. The engaging young owners have created flexible *menus* (set menus) that allow you to pick anything from a simple dish to a full four-course meal. Alternatively, go for the restaurant's speciality, a generous sampling plate (€23). The whole experience is a delight: beneath you is the soft lawn; above, trees of cherry, apple and peach; and stretching before you is the green of oak and chestnut forest. Credit cards aren't accepted.

THE WEST COAST

♣ COUVENT DE ST FRANÇOIS //
A CHURCH SERVING A STILL-
ACTIVE MONASTIC COMMUNITY
Looking over a tight valley to the village of Vico, this elaborately decorated 17th-century church has a fine wooden crucifixion in the south aisle, which predates the monastery and is reputed to be Corsica's oldest. In the sacristy, behind the altar, there's a wonderful carved chestnut cope chest. In the 18th century, the church served as a communal burial ground and, after the funeral service, bodies were dropped through a trapdoor and covered with quicklime.

Afterwards, pass by Vico, with its narrow, tree-lined streets and tall town houses. Although it's peaceful after dark, during the day it's busy with local trade, ramblers stocking up on fresh produce, and men playing boules on place Padrona.

GOLFE D'AJACCIO & AROUND

· · · · · ·

Two contrasting towns sit in the crook of the arm of the Golfe d'Ajaccio: eponymous Ajaccio, smart, commercial and Corsica's largest town; and Porticcio, its seaside playground across the bay. Inland, by contrast, lies some of the island's wildest, least spoilt countryside.

AJACCIO (AJACCIU)

pop 63,700
Ajaccio owes its status to its most famous son, Napoléon Bonaparte, born here in 1769. Commanding a lovely sweep of bay, the city breathes confidence. Yes, tourism matters to its economy, but this major commercial and passenger port goes about its business almost oblivious to the stream of summertime visitors. With its mellow-toned buildings, large marina and cafe terraces, it has more than a whiff of the Côte d'Azur.

Legend attributes Ajaccio's origins to the mythical Greek hero Ajax. In fact, modern Ajaccio probably dates from no earlier than 1492, when Genoese families first began moving here. Indigenous Corsicans were banned from living in the town until 1553, when it was seized by Sampiero Corso (see the boxed text, p191) and his French allies, assisted by the Turkish privateer Dragut. Recaptured in 1559 by the army of the Republic of Genoa, the town was not truly open to Corsicans until 1592.

ESSENTIAL INFORMATION

TOURIST OFFICES // Parc Naturel Régional de la Corse information office (PNRC; ☎ 04 95 51 79 00; www.parc-naturel-corse.com, in French; 2 rue Sergent Casalonga; ⏰ 8am-5pm Mon-Fri) Information on the park, its hiking trails and open-air activities. Tourist office (☎ 04 95 51 53 03; www.ajaccio-tourisme.com; 3 bd du Roi Jérôme; ⏰ 8am-7pm Mon-Sat, 9am-1pm Sun Apr-Jun, Sep & Oct, 8am-8pm Mon-Sat, 9am-1pm & 4-7pm Sun Jul & Aug, 8am-12.30pm Mon-Fri, 8.30am-12.30pm & 2-5pm Sat Nov-Mar)

EXPLORING AJACCIO

♣ MUSÉE FESCH // FRANCE'S LARGEST COLLECTION OF ITALIAN PAINTINGS OUTSIDE THE LOUVRE
At the time of writing, the splendid Musée Fesch and the adjacent Chapelle Impériale were both closed for renovations, and were expected to reopen in late 2010. Consult the tourist office for the latest information.

THE WEST COAST

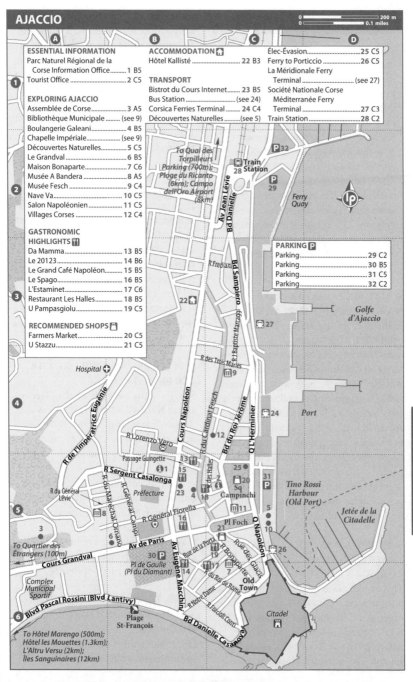

AJACCIO

Train Station

To Quai des Torpilleurs Parking (700m); Plage du Ricanto (6km); Campo dell'Oro Airport (8km)

Av Jean Lévie

Bd Danielle

Ferry Quay

Golfe d'Ajaccio

R Frediani

Bd Sampiero

J Baptiste Marcaggi

Hospital

R des Trois Maries

Cours Napoléon

R du Cardinal Fesch

Bd du Roi Jérôme

Q l'Herminier

Port

R Lorenzo Vero

Passage Guingette

R Sergent Casalonga

R des Halles

Sq Campinchi

Tino Rossi Harbour (Old Port)

R du Général Lévie

R du Maréchal Ornano

R du Général Campi

Préfecture

R Général Fiorella

Pl Foch

Q Napoléon

Jetée de la Citadelle

To Quartier des Étrangers (100m)

Av de Paris

Rue de la Porta

Rue des Glacis

Old Town

Cours Grandval

Pl de Gaulle (Pl du Diamant)

Av Eugène Macchini

Rue Bonaparte

R du Roi de Rome

Complex Municipal Sportif

Blvd Pascal Rossini (Blvd Lantivy)

Plage St-François

R Notre Dame

R Forcioli Conti

Bd Danielle Casanova

Citadel

To Hôtel Marengo (500m); Hôtel les Mouettes (1.3km); L'Altru Versu (2km); Îles Sanguinaires (12km)

THE WEST COAST

NEW CAPITAL

Corsica's largest town and nowadays the site of the Assemblée de Corse, Ajaccio rose to fame under Napoléon Bonaparte, its most illustrious native son. In 1811 he decreed that Corsica should be a single *département,* with Ajaccio as its capital. Bastia, which lost its status as the island's main town, was enraged, but Napoléon justified his decision by asserting that Ajaccio 'should be the capital…since it is a natural harbour that lies across the water from Toulon and is thus the closest to France after St-Florent'. In accordance with the emperor's wishes, Ajaccio went on to spearhead the campaign to Gallicise the island.

♥ MAISON BONAPARTE // NAPOLÉON'S BIRTHPLACE

In the 19th century **Maison Bonaparte** (☎ 04 95 21 43 89; rue St-Charles; admission €5; ☺ 9amnoon & 2-6pm Tue-Sun Apr-Sep, 10am-noon & 2-4.45pm Tue-Sun Oct-Mar) almost became a place of cult worship, where the more-ardent devotees would tear off a strip of wallpaper or prise away a tile as a relic. Even today visitors are asked to dress in a respectful manner, as though entering a hallowed place. The house where Napoléon lived until he was packed off to school on the mainland, aged only nine, houses memorabilia of the emperor and his siblings, whom he planted on the thrones of Europe.

♥ MUSÉE A BANDERA // QUAINT TRADITIONAL MUSEUM OF CORSICAN CULTURE

This quirky place will appeal to lovers of unreconstructed, touch-screen-tabooing museums. The **Musée A Bandera** (☎ 04 95 51 07 34; 1 rue du Général Lévie; admission €4; ☺ 9am-7pm Mon-Sat, 9am-noon Sun Jul–mid-Sep, 9am-noon & 2-6pm Mon-Sat mid-Sep–Jun) is itself

something of a museum piece – and is all the more lovable for it. Among our favourite exhibits are a giant model of the 1769 battle of Ponte Novo that confirmed French conquest of the island; a proclamation by one Gilbert Elliot, viceroy of the short-lived Anglo-Corsican kingdom (1794–96); and some yellowing 19th-century magazine pages recounting the arrest of infamous Corsican bandits.

♥ SALON NAPOLÉONIEN // ANOTHER NAPOLÉONIC SHRINE

High on the ceiling fresco of this **ceremonial room** (☎ 04 95 51 52 62; town hall; place Foch; admission €2.30; ☺ 9-11.45am & 2-4.45pm or 5.45pm mid-Jun–mid-Sep, 9-11.45am & 2-4.45pm or 5.45pm Mon-Fri mid-Sep–mid-Jun) sits the emperor, enthroned in majesty and surrounded by soldiers, clergy and courtiers. Here too are sculptures and paintings of the imperial family, and a veritable mint of medals and coins struck in Napoléon's honour.

♥ BOAT TRIPS // EXPLORE THE GOLFE D'AJACCIO

Sign on at the quayside kiosk of **Découvertes Naturelles** (☎ 04 95 73 12 66; www .decouvertes-naturelles.net, in French; ☺ May-Sep) to enjoy a half-day sailing trip to the Îles Sanguinaires. To see these tiny islands in their very best light, choose the romantic sunset trip, complete with aperitif and underwater lighting. For day outings to the Réserve Naturelle de Scandola and Les Calanques, see p83.

Alternatively, for a brief taste of the gulf, simply hop on the passenger ferry to Porticcio; see p105 for details.

♥ RUE DU CARDINAL FESCH // A STREET FOR HOLIDAY SHOPPING

Linger along this carefree, car-free street and its lateral offshoots. Push beyond the fairly tacky touristware and fare at its southern end to find a range of fun boutiques, plus a couple of long-established Corsican favourites.

Oh, the aroma of fresh crusty bread as you walk into **Boulangerie Galeani** (3 rue du Cardinal Fesch)! Anaïs, who serves you, is the fourth generation of a family that's been baking bread and pastries for more than 150 years. Everything, including the bakery's own-recipe *beignets de Brocciu* (Brocciu fritters) and *canistrelli* (biscuits made with almonds, walnuts, lemon or aniseed), is confected on the premises.

Villages Corses (44 rue du Cardinal Fesch) is a specialist delicatessen packed with Corsican delicacies.

♥ LE GRANDVAL // HAVE A DRINK AND TAKE IN THE OLD-CORSICA ATMOSPHERE

Opened in 1892, this friendly little **bar** (☎ 04 95 21 13 15; 2 cours Grandval; ⊗ 6.30am-9pm Mon-Sat), owned by Jean-Claude Fieschi (see p105), has changed little, except for the addition of a formica counter 30 years ago and the passing away of its 70-year-old parakeet in 2008. Haunting photos of the Ajaccio of yesteryear plaster the walls and outside you can sit under the palm tree, planted by the owner's grandfather on the 100th anniversary of Napoléon's death.

♥ BIBLIOTHÈQUE MUNICIPALE // A RETREAT FROM THE STREET

If the hubbub and heat of rue du Cardinal Fesch becomes trying, just step into the 30m-long **reading room** (admission free; ⊗ 9am-noon & 2-5pm Mon-Fri) of Ajaccio's municipal library to savour its coolness, silence, floor-to-ceiling leather-bound volumes, wooden ladders and 18m-long central table, the whole speaking of serious-minded research.

♥ QUARTIERS DES ÉTRANGERS // FORMER ENCLAVE FOR NORTHERN EUROPEAN WINTER VISITORS

Clues still remain to the elegant lifestyle of wealthy British and German residents of Ajaccio, early snow birds who chased the winter sunshine. Above cours Grandval, today's **Assemblée de Corse** building was formerly the Grand Hôtel d'Ajaccio et Continental. Beside cours Général Leclerc (cours Grandval's continuation), the **former Anglican church** is now a dance school, while at No 13 the **Cyrnos Palace hotel** lives on as a private house. On parallel bd Marcaggi and its continuation, bd Scamarron, a few **villas** with sad, unkempt gardens still stand.

♥ PLAGE DU RICANTO // THE BEST OF AJACCIO'S BEACHES

Spread your towel on this long strand of golden sand, 6km northeast of town, and feel especially sybaritic as you watch the joggers puff along its popular exercise trail.

GASTRONOMIC HIGHLIGHTS

♥ DA MAMMA €

☎ 04 95 21 39 44; passage Guingette; mains €12-20, menus €12-23; ⊗ lunch & dinner Tue-Sat, dinner Sun & Mon

Tucked away down a steep alley and shaded by a magnificent rubber tree, Mama's Place offers very reasonably priced fare and a variety of *menus*. The one costing €23 includes cannelloni with Brocciu, and roast goat.

♥ L'ALTRU VERSU €€

☎ 04 95 50 05 22; www.laltruversu.com; Les Sep Chapelles, bd Commêne; mains €22-28, menus €32-39; ⊗ lunch & dinner Apr-Sep, lunch & dinner Tue-Sun Oct-May)

'The Other Side', freshly installed in new premises, remains one of the island's top destinations for creative Corsican cuisine; try, for example, the sorbet tinged with Pietra beer. Your hosts, the Mezzacqui brothers (Jean-Pierre front of house, Pierre powering the kitchen) hitch on their guitars and serenade guests each Friday and Saturday night.

🍴 LE 20123 €€

☎ 04 95 21 50 05; www.20123.fr, in French; 2 rue Roi de Rome; menu €32; 🕑 dinner Tue-Sun

This Corsican bistro started life in the village of Pila Canale (postcode 20123 – hence the name). When the Habani family came to the big city, they recreated their old restaurant – village pump, a washing line sagging with pantaloons, a classic Vespa, life-sized dolls in traditional dress and a hotchpotch of grandad's country paraphernalia. It all sounds a bit tacky, yet diners flock here for its well-prepared country cooking. There's no à la carte –just a single *menu,* presented orally. Reservations are essential.

🍴 LE GRAND CAFÉ NAPOLÉON €€

☎ 04 95 21 42 54; www.grandcafenapoleon.com, in French; 10-12 cours Napoléon; mains €24-30, menus €30-45; 🕑 lunch & dinner Mon-Sat

The cuisine's a dream and the three-course weekday lunchtime *menu du marché* (€17) represents quite exceptional value. Push beyond the streetside terrace (itself an Ajaccio institution) to the august belle époque former ballroom, with its tall mirrors, high ceilings, soaring cream arches – and a portrait of *l'empereur* himself, pointing towards the reception desk. The clientele is mostly mature local regulars. If the dessert selection features the fruit tart – a crispy, rich delight with a base of ground-almond pastry – ask

no further. Lunchtime reservations are essential.

🍴 LE SPAGO €€

☎ 04 95 21 15 71; rue du Roi de Rome; mains €11.50-19.50, menu €20; 🕑 lunch & dinner Mon-Fri, dinner Sat

At this cool designer restaurant decked out in lime green, the oil and vinegar dispensers squirt just the right amount, and the men's and women's toilets are designated by the creative use of a pair of green apples – we'll leave you to discover exactly how. You won't find a single Corsican speciality on the menu, just great salads and tasty, inventive dishes such as fillet of cod in a mango sauce. There's wi-fi, too, if you care to linger over coffee.

🍴 L'ESTAMINET €€

☎ 04 95 50 10 42; 5-7 rue du Roi de Rome; mains €17.50-20, menus €18.50-25; 🕑 dinner Jun-Sep, dinner Mon, Sat & Sun, lunch Tue, lunch & dinner Thu & Fri Oct-May

The glorious bar of dark stained wood could almost be a pulpit, and you could practically play chess on the jazzy black-and-white floor tiles. The food is delightful, there's a well-chosen wine list and the cheeses are organic.

🍴 RESTAURANT LES HALLES €€

☎ 04 95 21 42 68; 4 rue des Halles; mains €11-28, menus €15-29; 🕑 lunch & dinner Mon-Sat

The welcome's warm and informal at this friendly, family-run place, where granddad and grandson rule in the kitchen, and grandma and granddaughter run the front of house. *Menus* mainly feature fresh fish that's come only as far as the fishmonger opposite. Eat beneath the giant awning or, if it's cool, under the vaults of this former wine cellar. There's live music to accompany Friday and Saturday dinners.

INTERVIEW: JEAN-CLAUDE FIESCHI *Miles Roddis*

Jean-Claude Fieschi, passionate photographer, collector of old cameras and unofficial recorder of Ajaccio, runs his little bar, Le Grandval (see p103) with his wife, Marie-Jeanne, just as his mother and grandfather did before him. It's still much the same as when it opened and the bar is plastered with images of old Ajaccio that represent only a fraction of his collection. He walks me from image to image.

What's changed? And for better or for worse? This convent, bulldozed. The military hospital, demolished for that monster over there. Here's how the square looked nearly a century ago. And *of course* things were better when we were young. They've cut down so many of the trees that graced the town, and the traffic's a nightmare. People [I take a quick, quizzical gaze at his terrace, packed with locals] don't live outside as they used to before TV.

Where do you take your own vacations? My wife sometimes slips up to Paris to stay with her daughter. Me, I usually stay right here on the island, driving around, getting to know it more. Just occasionally, I'll visit the mainland, if there's a meeting of camera collectors or old photograph aficionados. [As we speak a friend drops in with an early print of a Corsican soldier in return for a modest banknote.]

And eating out, when you can? Nothing better than a meal with our friends who run L'Altru Versu [p103].

☙ U PAMPASGIOLU €€

☎ 04 95 50 71 52; 15 rue de la Porta; mains €14-28; ⏱ dinner Mon-Sat

The Poppy has been garlanded by just about every French gastronomic guide, and you'll dine very well indeed on the small terrace or within the cool brick-vaulted interior. Go à la carte, or choose the *planche spuntinu* (snack selection) or *planche de la mer* (fish and seafood selection) for a great selection of Corsican specialities served on wooden platters.

RECOMMENDED SHOPS

On Fridays in July and August, shops stay open until midnight, and there's live music and street entertainment.

☙ FARMERS MARKET

sq Campinchi; ⏱ 8am-noon Tue-Sun

For fish, flowers, fruit and vegetables, Corsican cheeses and meat products, browse this large open-air market, located right in front of the tourist office.

☙ U STAZZU

1 rue Bonaparte

For five generations, the owners of this shop have been rearing pigs in the high mountains, feeding them on acorns and chestnuts, and dispatching them when they're still tender and barely two years old. In addition to its superb charcuterie, U Stazzu also sells the usual range of Corsican specialities from other small producers.

TRANSPORT

TO/FROM THE AIRPORT

AIR // Campo dell'Oro airport (AJA; ☎ 04 95 23 56 56; www.ajaccio.aeroport.fr) is 8km east of town; see p266 for more.

BUS // Town bus 8 (€4.50, 20 minutes) runs frequently between the airport and Ajaccio's bus station.

TAXI // A taxi costs around €25.

THE WEST COAST

GETTING AROUND

BOAT // Société Nationale Corse Méditerranée (SNCM; www.sncm.fr) runs ferries to/from Nice and Marseille, while Corsica Ferries (☎ 08 25 09 50 95; www.corsicaferries.com) serves both Nice and Toulon; see p268 for more. Découvertes Naturelles (☎ 04 95 73 12 66; www.decouvertes-naturelles.net, in French) runs a ferry to Porticcio (one way/return €5/8, 20 minutes, three to six daily). La Méridionale (☎ 08 10 20 13 20; www.lameridionale.fr) has overnight sailings from Marseille.

TRAIN // At least two trains run daily to/from Bastia via Vizzavona and Corte. A minimum of two serve Calvi via Île Rousse, both destinations requiring a change in Ponte Leccia.

PARKING // Parking in the centre of Ajaccio is a nightmare. From the free parking area at Quai des Torpilleurs, an equally free shuttle bus runs every 15 minutes. There are large paying car parks beside the entrance to the ferry terminal and beneath place de Gaulle.

BICYCLE // Bistrot du Cours Internet (☎ 04 95 21 44 75; 10 cours Napoléon; per 6/12hr €10/13) rents bikes; it also offers internet access, wi-fi and free book exchange. Élec-Évasion (☎ 06 23 66 64 79; place du Marché; per 1/3hr €7/18) hires out electric bikes.

BUS // Major bus companies have offices in the Corsica Ferries terminal. The companies provide service from Ajaccio to most parts of the island.

AROUND AJACCIO

❦ **POINTE DE LA PARATA & ÎLES SANGUINAIRES // A WILD HEADLAND AND SCATTER OF OFFSHORE ISLANDS**

From the car park at Pointe de la Parata, you'll find a short, much-trodden walking trail that leads around the promontory. A stroll along here rewards you with great sea views and tantalising close-ups of the four islets of the Îles Sanguinaires, thus called (their name means 'Bloody') in honour of their distinctive red rock.

Tiny as they are, the islands support over 150 different plant species and, since there are no terrestrial predators, they're a haven for seabirds.

❦ **A CUPULATTA TORTOISE CENTRE // EUROPE'S LARGEST TORTOISE SANCTUARY**

Located 21km from Ajaccio towards Corte on the N193, A Cupulatta (☎ 04 95 52 82 34; www.acupulatta.com, in French; admission €9.50; ☉ 9am-6pm or 7pm May-Oct) shelters approximately 3000 hardbacks, representing more than 150 species from all over the world. It's well documented in multiple languages. Interesting tortoise fact: if the ground temperature when a mother lays her eggs is above 28°C, there's a greater probability of the young ones being female. Under 28°C, they're more likely to hatch out male. (It's strictly tortoise lore, though, so don't worry about any side effects of the air-con!)

PORTICCIO (PURTICHJU)

pop 2300

Extending thinly along the length of its sandy beach, Porticcio suffers from its proximity to Ajaccio, 18km away by road and much nearer if you take the ferry across the bay; in summer it's bumper to bumper with holiday traffic. But let's not be too churlish: there's a great beach and a jolly seaside atmosphere, and a visit will give you a good sense of a typical French holiday resort.

ESSENTIAL INFORMATION

TOURIST OFFICES // Tourist office (☎ 04 95 25 01 09; www.porticcio-corsica.com; ☉ 8.30am-6pm Mon-Sat Apr-Sep, 8.30am-4pm Mon-Fri Oct-Mar) A kiosk beside the landing stage.

EXPLORING PORTICCIO

❦ PLAGE DE LA VIVA // ONE OF CORSICA'S FINEST BEACHES

This lovely crescent of sandy beach, undeniably Porticcio's best asset, curls northward. Above it are enough bars, restaurants and water-sports centres to keep the most demanding holidaymaker happy.

❦ WATER SPORTS // GOING BEYOND THE BEACH

To put the crowds on the beach behind you, hire a windsurfer, sea kayak or catamaran from **Centre Nautique de Porticcio** (☎ 04 95 21 40 43; ☺ Apr-Sep) or, for less effort, rent a zodiac from **Loca-Nautic** (☎ 04 95 25 17 85; www.loca-nautic.com, in French; ☺ Jul & Aug).

GASTRONOMIC HIGHLIGHTS

Nearly all restaurants have wide terraces overlooking Plage de la Viva; they offer a feast for the eyes, perhaps less so for the stomach.

❦ LA SALADERIE €€

☎ 04 95 25 08 77; salads €8-29, menus €18-21; ☺ lunch & dinner Apr-Oct, lunch & dinner Fri-Wed Nov-Mar

The view of the beach from here is only oblique, but you do dine on a pleasant vine-shaded terrace with a wooden deck. As you'd anticipate from its name, La Saladerie serves lavish, creative salads. It also offers avocados prepared in 10 different ways, fresh pasta dishes (€10 to €22.50), and meats grilled over a wood fire.

❦ LE CLUB €€

☎ 04 95 25 00 42; mains €21-29, menu €32; ☺ lunch & dinner mid-Dec–mid-Nov

For fine dining, Le Club stands head and shoulders above the competing beach-side restaurants. There's a comfortable, pleasing dining room decked out in shades of ochre – if you can tear yourself away from the lovely terrace. The fish is determined by what's in the fishermen's nets, and the desserts by the in-house pastry chef are works of art. For a snack, call by the adjacent Délices Club, its bakery, which turns out tasty sandwiches, quiches, pizzas, and meringues the size of giant snowballs.

TRANSPORT

PARKING // There are two central free car parks, one in front of the post office and the other beside the Carrefour supermarket.

BOAT // Découvertes Naturelles (☎ 04 95 73 12 66; www.decouvertes-naturelles.net, in French) runs a ferry to Ajaccio (one way/return €5/8, 20 minutes, three to six daily)

DRIVING TOURS

VALLÉE DU PRUNELLI

Distance: 85km
Duration: one day

If you've had a temporary surfeit of mountain vistas and superb seascapes, take a day to explore the gentle lower Vallée du Prunelli and its wilder upstream gorges.

Leave Ajaccio by the Bonifacio highway and, after 10km, take a slip road, signed D3 Bastelicaccia. The valley, wide, lush and cultivated in its lower reaches, is green and gentle on the eye. Some 5km after Bastelicaccia, at **Le Jardin des Abeilles** (☎ 04 95 23 83 88; www.lejardindesabeilles.com, in French; ☺ year round), bee-keeper Denis Casalta explains in English how he moves his 600 hives up the valley, month by month, following the flowering, to create his six varieties of honey, all of which are for sale.

THE WEST COAST

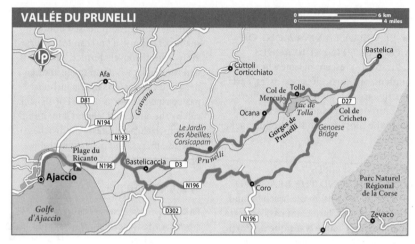

VALLÉE DU PRUNELLI

Call too by **Corsicapam** (☎ 04 95 23 81 88; ☾ 8.30am-noon & 2-6pm Mar-Nov), just across the road. Here, Jean-Pierre and Paul Caux distil organic essential oils and create cosmetics from the myriad powerfully scented herbs and shrubs of the maquis. You can buy their products from their small showroom.

At **Col de Mercujo**, 12km higher up the valley, drink in a pair of superb panoramas. Look back from the pass to the village of Ocana in the middle distance and the sea beyond. Then take a 10- to 15-minute walk along a sandy track for a plunging view of the Gorges du Prunelli and **Lac de Tolla**, artificially constructed but no less attractive for that.

One kilometre beyond the *col,* turn right to descend to the lakeside, where a couple of cabins offer snacks and drinks. It's also a glorious spot for a dip in the clear waters. Alternatively, stay dry and hire a kayak, canoe or pedalo.

The road runs above the **Gorges du Prunelli**, always present but more-rarely visible, as it snakes its way through mixed wood. Turn left for a 10km out-and-back signed diversion to **Bastelica**, a mountain village that's famous for char-

cuterie made from local *cochons coureurs* (free-ranging pigs; see the boxed text, p93). It's also the birthplace of Sampiero Corso (see the boxed text, p191), whose flamboyant statue stands proud here. If you've postponed lunch, **Restaurant Chez Paul** (☎ 04 95 28 71 59; menus €17-26; ☾ lunch & dinner), in the upper part of the village, has a wonderful terrace and picture window overlooking the valley. You'll receive a warm welcome from your bluff host, with his foghorn voice and waggish chat.

Heading back along the D27, you reach **Col de Cricheto**, and the opportunity for a train ride or a country walk. We don't normally recommend those little trains but this one's special: Christian and Jean-Marie Lorenzon have carved out a one-hour route through the maquis and chestnut forest of their family land for the **Petit Train du Maquis** (☎ 04 95 28 41 36; www.cricheto.com, in French; tickets €12.80; ☾ departures 10.30am, 11.45am, 1.30pm & 3pm mid-Apr–mid-Oct). If you're after something more active, walk their 3.5km **Sentier Découverte** (Discovery Trail; admission €5.60), which has interpretive panels in French.

Back at the wheel, drive another 1.5km, then take a 10-minute round-trip stroll to a bijou **Genoese bridge** that's a shady spot for a swim or paddle. Continuing, it's downhill nearly all the way until the intersection with the N193. Turn right to return to Ajaccio.

HAUT TARAVO

Distance: 152km
Duration: one day
In the furthest reaches of the Vallée du Taravo, at the very heart of the island, are a cluster of tiny, austere one-bus-a-day hamlets. Nowhere guards the secrets of traditional Corsica better than this remote valley, clad in beech, chestnut and holm oak.

Leave Ajaccio by the Bonifacio highway, scud along the N196 and, after 32km, turn left onto the D83. The village of Ste-Marie Sicché, the first encountered, could stand for many in the Haut Taravo. It's a trim community of solid stone homes, many recently painted and clearly cared for. The same can't be said, alas, for the neglected fortified tower built in 1553 by resistance hero Sampiero Corso (see the boxed text, p191) – even its plaque is scarcely visible. Nor can the same be said for the sad, crumbling 10th-century Romanesque chapel, with its caved-in roof and trees thrusting up through the aisle. To reach the chapel, go right off the D83 at the Chapelle Romane sign. For the tower, turn left beside the current (intact) church and travel as far as a T-junction. An easy 20-minute walk from the junction takes in both the chapel and the tower.

The Haut Taravo has two exceptional choices for authentic Corsican cuisine, so it's worth building your day around

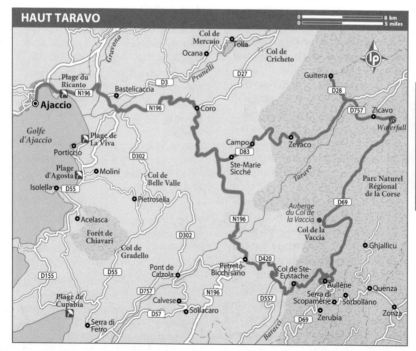

THE WEST COAST

lunch; whichever you choose, do phone to reserve. At the far side of **Zevaco**, you'll find the splendid **U Taravu** (☎ 04 95 24 46 06; menus €19-28; ☽ lunch & dinner May-Sep, dinner Fri, lunch & dinner Sat, lunch Sun Dec-Apr), an affable roadside place run by the Andreucci family. Portions are lavish (the €28 *menu* includes the family's farm-raised lamb), and *menus* include both wine and coffee. Lunch over, drop down to the cellar below the restaurant, duck below the festoons of sausage, and pick up a hank or two of charcuterie from the Andreuccis' farm, a couple of their cheeses or a bag of their own chestnut flour as a reminder of a great country meal.

If it's still too early for lunch, continue for a further 6km beyond Zevaco, then take the D28 left for barely five minutes to **Guitera**, home of **Chez Paul-Antoine** (☎ 04 95 24 44 40; www.chez-paul-antoine.com, in French; menus €15-25; ☎ lunch & dinner). Here you can enjoy home-cured meats, pâtés, sausages – basically, everything that can be salvaged, scented and spiced from domestic pigs and wild boars (see also the boxed text, p234).

Back on the D83, turn left onto the D757 and follow signs to the mountain hamlet of **Zicavo**. Popular with walkers down from the heights, Zicavo lazily spreads itself along the flank of the mountain, its main street an avenue of pollarded lime trees bordered by sturdy grey-granite houses.

At a T-junction just beyond Zicavo, turn right onto the D69. Park at a bridge 1.3km later and take a not-even-two-minute walk upstream, where you can paddle or swim at the base of a **waterfall**.

The forest drive gives flickering glimpses of the spectacular valley below, and of folds of hills rolling to the horizon in lighter and lighter shades of grey. At a fork, take the right-hand option, signed Aullène. From here, the road narrows appreciably and views become wider, more open and more awesome. Drivers should postpone their sightseeing, however, since there are sheer drops over many of the barrierless bends. At the **Col de la Vaccia**, sit back on the terrace of the Auberge du Col de la Vaccia, and drink in the magnificent panorama before and behind you. Once over the *col,* the most spectacular driving of the day begins.

Aullène merits a short stop. In the village, turn right onto the D420 for a more-gentle drive, the darker forests of laricio pine on your left contrasting with the lighter green of chestnut and oak. After 22.5km, turn right to rejoin the N196 and return to Ajaccio, but not before saying a final farewell to the river Taravo – 5km beyond the junction, look right as you cross the modern road bridge to see the river way below, spanned by a handsome Genoese bridge.

THE SOUTH

3 PERFECT DAYS

☙ DAY 1 // PREHISTORIC SURPRISES
Who were the mysterious 'people of the sea' who appeared on Corsican shores around 1100 BC? Chances are we'll never know all of their secrets, but a visit to the menhir statues at Filitosa (p117) sure can make the head spin with ideas. From there, it's an easy drive to the megaliths of Cauria (p126). A visit to the Bronze Age vestiges of Cucuruzzu and Capula (p146), in the heart of L'Alta Rocca, completes the trip.

☙ DAY 2 // BEACHSIDE HEDONISM
Start your day with a mooch around Porto-Vecchio's *haute ville* (upper town), then head to Plage de Palombaggia (p139) before the crowds do. From here, don your best bikini and leg it south to Plage de la Folacca (p139) in time for lunch at Tamaricciu (p140). Spend the afternoon flopped out on a decadently thick mattress, or work your suntan far from the crowds at little-known Plage de Cateraggio (p140). Come dusk, feast on seafood at Le Gregale (p134).

☙ DAY 3 // THE ACTIVE LIFE
Your biggest decision for today: on land or at sea? If it's at sea, head to Baie de Piantarella (p133) for a gentle kayaking excursion, then spend the afternoon diving with groupers at Mérouville (p131). If it's on land, the *parc aventure* (adventure park; p144) in the Fôret de L'Ospédale beckons. Enjoy lunch at U Funtanonu (p144), then push on to Col de Bavella, where you can burn off the calories with a canyon descent (p148). Finish the day at A Pignata (p147) with an energy-replenishing Corsican meal.

THE SOUTH

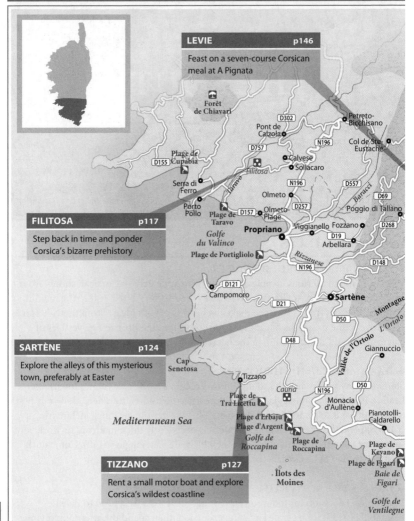

LEVIE p146
Feast on a seven-course Corsican meal at A Pignata

FILITOSA p117
Step back in time and ponder Corsica's bizarre prehistory

SARTÈNE p124
Explore the alleys of this mysterious town, preferably at Easter

TIZZANO p127
Rent a small motor boat and explore Corsica's wildest coastline

Forêt de Chiavari
Pont de Calzola
Petreto-Bicchisano
Col de Ste-Eustache
Plage de Cupabia
Calvese
Sollacaro
Serra di Ferro
Olmeto
Porto Pollo
Plage de Taravo
Olmeto-Plage
Propriano
Viggianello
Fozzano
Póggio di Tallano
Arbellara
Plage de Portigliolo
Campomoro
Sartène
Giannuccio
Cap Senetosa
Tizzano
Cauria
Monacia d'Aullène
Pianotolli-Caldarello
Plage de Tra Licettu
Mediterranean Sea
Plage d'Erbaju
Plage d'Argent
Golfe de Roccapina
Plage de Roccapina
Plage de Keyano
Plage de Figari
Îlots des Moines
Baie de Figari
Golfe de Ventilegne
Golfe du Valinco

GETTING AROUND

In the most touristy urban areas, especially Bonifacio, Porto-Vecchio and Propriano, as well as along the most popular beaches, finding a parking spot in summer is maddening. The trick is to arrive early in the morning. In the villages, you'll have less trouble finding parking spaces. On the whole, southern Corsica is fairly easy to navigate, and you can expect numerous gorgeous runs and dramatic scenery (especially in the Alta Rocca); be prepared, however, for lots of hairpin bends and narrow roads. Distances are usually expressed in hours, rather than in kilometres.

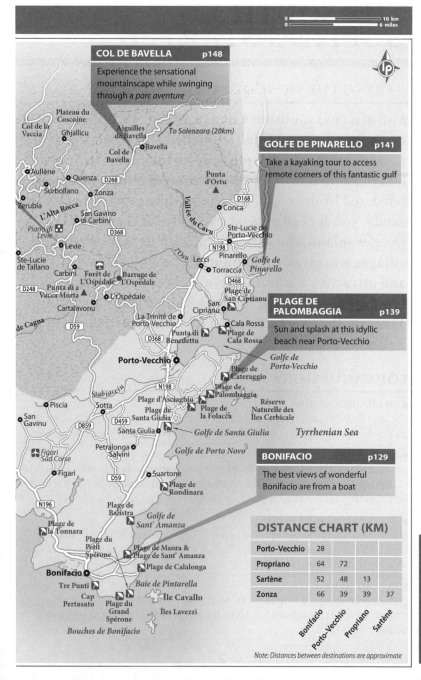

0 ———— 10 km
0 ———— 6 miles

COL DE BAVELLA   p148

Experience the sensational mountainscape while swinging through a *parc aventure*

To Solenzara (20km)

GOLFE DE PINARELLO   p141

Take a kayaking tour to access remote corners of this fantastic gulf

Plateau du Coscione
Col de la Vaccia
Ghjallicu
Aiguilles de Bavella
Col de Bavella
Bavella
Aullène
Quenza   D268
Sorbollano
Zonza
Zerubia
L'Alta Rocca
San Gavino di Carbini
Piano di Levie   D368
Levie
Punta d'Ortu
D168
Conca
Vallée du Cavu
Ste-Lucie de Porto-Vecchio
Ste-Lucie de Tallano
Carbini
Forêt de L'Ospédale
Barrage de L'Ospédale
D248
Punta di a Vucca Morta
L'Ospédale
N198
Lecci
Pinarello
Torraccia
Golfe de Pinarello
D468
Cartalavonu
de Cagna
D59
La Trinité de Porto-Vecchio
D368
Punta di Benedettu
San Cipriano
Plage de San Cipriano
Cala Rossa
Plage de Cala Rossa

PLAGE DE PALOMBAGGIA   p139

Sun and splash at this idyllic beach near Porto-Vecchio

Porto-Vecchio
Golfe de Porto-Vecchio
Plage de Cateraggio
Plage de Palombaggia
Plage d'Asciaghiu
Plage de la Folacca
Réserve Naturelle des Îles Cerbicale
N198
Stabiacciu
Piscia
Sotta
Plage de Santa Giulia
D459
Santa Giulia
Golfe de Santa Giulia
San Gavinu
D859
Petralonga
Salvini
Golfe de Porto Novo
Tyrrhenian Sea

BONIFACIO   p129

The best views of wonderful Bonifacio are from a boat

Figari Sud Corse
Figari
D59
Suartone
Plage de Rondinara
N196
Plage de Balistra
Golfe de Sant' Amanza
Plage de la Tonnara
Plage du Petit Spérone
Plage de Maora & Plage de Sant' Amanza
Plage de Calalonga
Bonifacio
Tre Punti
Baie de Pintarella
Cap Pertusato
Plage du Grand Spérone
Île Cavallo
Îles Lavezzi
Bouches de Bonifacio

DISTANCE CHART (KM)

	Bonifacio	Porto-Vecchio	Propriano	Sartène
Porto-Vecchio	28			
Propriano	64	72		
Sartène	52	48	13	
Zonza	66	39	39	37

Note: Distances between destinations are approximate

THE SOUTH

THE SOUTH
GETTING STARTED

MAKING THE MOST OF YOUR TIME

Multifaceted southern Corsica offers a mix of hedonistic, cultural and adrenaline-fuelled experiences. There's nowhere better to sample la dolce vita than in the alleys of Bonifacio or Porto-Vecchio, and the coastline is bordered by dozens of Seychelles-like expanses of white sand – you'll need at least a week to do them justice. Deeper inland, the Alta Rocca, with its stalwart hilltop villages and awesome mountainscapes, prehistoric sites and attractive B&Bs, merits another five days. Keep a few days spare for the region's hidden gems, including Tizzano, the enigmatic town of Sartène and the wild Vallée de l'Ortolo.

TOP EXCURSIONS

💀 HELICOPTER RIDES
The sky's deep blue and there's no haze? Book a helicopter ride and see the coastline, the beaches and mountains from the air – you'll never forget the experience (p135).

💀 FILITOSA
Southern Corsica is better known for its splendid beaches and chic coastal cities than its prehistoric remains, but you'll be amazed by the mysterious megaliths at Filitosa. Get an audioguide and ponder Corsica's 'Stonehenge' (p117).

💀 BOAT TRIPS FROM BONIFACIO
Admire Bonifacio's awesome position on top of magnificent chalky cliffs and deep inlets with transparent blue water from out at sea. You can also take a longer itinerary taking in the Îles Lavezzi (p131).

💀 SUNSET CRUISE
Embark on a sunset cruise in the Golfe du Valinco – the colours that ranges from ochre to golden as the sun sets will ignite the imagination of photographers and romantic souls (p120).

THE SOUTH

GETTING AWAY FROM IT ALL

Southern Corsica may be very touristy in the high season, but it's possible to escape the crowds and find your own slice of paradise.

* **Vallée de l'Ortolo** Retreat from the N196 to this timeless valley, which feels like it's at the end of the world (p126)

* **Tizzano** This coastal village appears at the end of the D48 like a mirage (p127)

* **Quenza** Set in the Alta Rocca, this gem of a village is the perfect place to rejuvenate mind and body (p145)

* **Pays de Colomba** To glimpse *Corse profonde* (deep Corsica), take a trip into Propriano's hinterland for perched villages and wonderful panoramas (p120)

TOP ACTIVITIES

If you want to try something you've never done before, southern Corsica is the place.

* **Parcs aventure** Ready for a thrilling, yet undemanding, ride along a zip line? Bookmark the Bavella area (p148), which is an atmospheric playground. The sensational Aiguilles de Bavella as a backdrop are an added bonus.

* **Diving** Get up close and personal with *big* groupers at Mérouville (p131), an iconic, easy dive site in the Lavezzi archipelago. Sightings are guaranteed, in less than 20m.

* **Canyoning** Learn the ropes (literally) of canyoning in the gentle Canyon du Baracci (p121), an easy canyon descent featuring various leaps in natural pools. Beginners are welcome – no previous experience is necessary.

TOP BEACHES

PALOMBAGGIA
Photogenic and deservedly popular (p139)

CUPABIA
Intimate paradise, killer sunsets (p116)

PORTIGLIOLO
Excellent for sunbathing and water sports (p119)

RONDINARA
A horseshoe-shaped beach lapped by clear waters (p133)

ÎLES LAVEZZI
A clutch of uninhabited islets (p132)

PETIT SPÉRONE
The south's most elegant beach (p132)

PINARELLO
Sweeping blond sand backed by pine trees and restaurants (p141)

ROCCAPINA
Fantastic setting under Dalí-esque rock formations (p128)

RESOURCES

* **Corse Sud** (www.corse-sud.net) A comprehensive link to all things south Corsican

* **Corsica Isula** (www.corsica-isula.com) An exhaustive website with useful links

* **Corsica Travel Guide** (www.corsica travelguide.com) A commercial website with useful tourist information

* **Stone Pages Corsica** (www.stonepages .com/corsica) A terrific online tour of Corsica's prehistoric sites

THE SOUTH

GOLFE DU VALINCO

· · · · · ·

Shaped like a huge bite chomped out of the fretted coastline of Corsica's west coast, the Golfe du Valinco offers some of the wildest and most rugged coastal scenery of the island. At the eastern end of the bay is Propriano, a buzzing holiday centre in summer. There are also two smaller coastal pleasures on each side of the bay's open mouth: on the north side is Porto Pollo, and on the south is Campomoro, both blessed with magnetic beaches lapped by lapis lazuli waters. The Golfe du Valinco even shines under the water, with a collection of truly fantastic dive sites that are suitable for all levels of proficiency.

TRANSPORT

BUS // From mid-September to June, **Alta Rocca Voyages – Ricci** (☎ 04 95 51 08 19; www.alta-rocca-voyages.com) runs a daily bus service, except Sunday, between Ajaccio and Zonza via Porto Pollo, Olmeto-Plage, Propriano and Sartène. **Eurocorse** (☎ 04 95 76 13 50) has two daily services (one on Sunday) between Ajaccio and Bonifacio via Olmeto, Propriano, Sartène and Porto-Vecchio in July and August. From September to June it runs one daily service Monday to Saturday.

BOAT // Ferries link Propriano with Toulon, Marseille and Porto Torres (Sardinia); see p268 for details. You can buy tickets at **Sorba** (☎ 04 95 76 04 36; quai L'Herminier, Propriano), a shipping agency representing all the ferry lines.

PARKING // Keep in mind that there's very limited roadside parking in Porto Pollo and Campomoro; the early car gets the space. Propriano has more-ample parking facilities.

PORTO POLLO & AROUND

Porto Pollo has great water sports, superb beaches and good accommodation, not to mention a wonderfully unfussy ambience and a location close to the archaeological site of Filitosa. And all this is set in an area of rolling hills and fragrant maquis pushed up against the Mediterranean. Despite its popularity with young people and families, who flock to the town in high season, Porto Pollo retains the atmosphere of a small fishing village and is a great base from which to explore the surrounding countryside.

EXPLORING PORTO POLLO & AROUND

❦ BEACHES // FEEL THE SAND IN YOUR TOES

East of Porto Pollo, **Plage de Taravo** is a choice stretch of sand for families and kitesurfers. The more-secluded **Plage de Cupabia**, with its long, wide expanse of brilliant-white sand and azure waters, is much more appealing. It's accessible from the tiny hilltop village of Serra di Ferro, perched 4km above Porto Pollo; take the sealed road off the D155.

❦ HORSE RIDING // CLIP-CLOP THROUGH THE COUNTRYSIDE

The countryside around Porto Pollo is a top spot for horse riding, with a good network of riding tracks criss-crossing the maquis. On the road to Serra di Ferro (take the D155), the reputable riding centre **Fil di Rosa** (☎ 04 95 74 08 08; 1-/3hr ride €20/45; ☽ Mon-Sat by reservation) is ready to take you on guided rides ranging from one-hour jaunts (€20) to day-long excursions. The three-hour ride is recommended, especially if you relish the idea of experiencing the fantastic Plage de Cupabia from a saddle. Children aged over 10 are welcome.

❦ NAUTICAL SENSATIONS // COMBINE ACTION AND EXPLORATION

If you're new to windsurfing and sailing, the calm waters off Porto Pollo are a good place to be initiated. **Centre Nautique de Porto Pollo** (☎ 06 09 40 37 65; ☙ daily May-Sep), near the harbour, handles rentals (from €16/35 per hour for a surfboard/catamaran) and also lessons. Sea kayaking is also available (from €10/35 per hour/day); it takes about two hours to get to Plage de Cupabia. Centre Nautique also hires

ACCOMMODATION

Accommodation options in this region range from ultraluxurious hotels and upmarket villas to atmospheric B&Bs and affordable midrange ventures in the hinterland. Bookings are essential in July and August. For a complete list of recommendations, see the Accommodation chapter. These are some of our favourites:

★ **Les Bergeries de Palombaggia** (p251) is a place of easy bliss, with stunning views of Plage de Palombaggia

★ There's only one word to describe **A Pignata** (p253): heaven!

★ Secluded and congenial, **Chambres d'Hôtes Bergeries de Piscia** (p250) has killer views from the swimming pool

★ Run by charismatic Pierrot, **Chez Pierrot** (p252) is an authentic B&B

★ **Hôtel Alivi** (p251) is sleek, intimate and well designed

out small 6HP motor boats (no licence required) for €30/55 per half-/full day. They're the perfect way to explore the secret inlets west of Porto Pollo, or to get to magnetic Plage de Cupabia in less than an hour.

Diving's more your thing? Porto Pollo is an ideal launching pad if you want to check out the best dive sites of the gulf. Terrific spots include Les Aiguilles, Les Cathédrales and Le Jardin, all within easy reach from the harbour. For beginners there are sheltered inlets within the gulf, which offer safe conditions for an introductory dive. **Porto Pollo Plongée** (☎ 06 85 41 93 94; www.portopollo-plongee.fr; ☙ daily May-Oct by reservation) is one of the best diving operations in the area and employs English-speaking staff; it also offers twice-weekly snorkelling trips near Les Cathédrales (€20). A single dive costs from €35.

❦ CORSICAN NIGHT // LISTEN TO HAUNTING REFRAINS WHILE DEVOURING GRILLED MEATS

Don't miss the *soirée corse* (Corsican night) on Wednesday and Friday in summer at the restaurant **U San Petru** (☎ 06 19 94 79 95; Serra di Ferro; mains €9-17; ☙ lunch & dinner daily May-Sep, lunch Mon-Sat & dinner by reservation Oct-Apr). It's in the centre of the spectacular perched village of **Serra di Ferro**. Sink your teeth into a *côte de porc* (pork chop) or *côte de veau* (veal chop), served indoors or alfresco on the shady terrace, while listening to live Corsican music.

❦ FILITOSA // EXPLORE THE VESTIGES OF THE MYSTERIOUS SHARDANES

The archaeological site of **Filitosa** (☎ 04 95 74 00 91; www.filitosa.fr; admission €6; ☙ 8am-8pm Apr-Oct) is sure to pique your curiosity.

THE SOUTH

SEA PEOPLE

Who were the Torréens, the people who appeared on Corsican shores around 1100 BC, drove out the settled inhabitants of Filitosa, destroyed many of their statues and built the *torri* (circular monuments) in their place? The traces they left are very faint indeed.

According to Roger Grosjean, the archaeological authority on Filitosa, they could actually have been Shardanes, the people enigmatically known to historians as 'sea people', who battled the pharaoh Ramses III. They probably originated from Anatolia, Crete or along the coast of the Aegean Sea. It's said that, after having been defeated by Ramses III, the Shardanes made their way to Corsica and Sardinia before slipping back into obscurity.

There are still many unsolved mysteries connected with this famous site, which was discovered in 1946 by the owner of the land on which it's situated.

The oldest findings on the site suggest a cave-dwelling population. There are remnants of pottery, arrow heads and farming tools that point to fixed settlements beginning as early as 3300 BC.

The menhir statues of the megalithic period are even more impressive; the fact that they were erected at all marks a major advance in skill. The purpose of these granite monoliths, 2m to 3m high and carved to represent human faces or entire human figures armed with weapons, is not entirely clear. You'll first come to the menhir statue known as Filitosa V. This one has a distinctive, rectangular head, and is the largest and best-armed statue in Corsica; a sword and a dagger are both clearly visible. If you continue along the path you'll come to some caves and the foundations of several huts before you get to the central *torre* (circular monument), which has six little statues. One of these statues is known as Filitosa IX, and its face is considered to be one of the masterpieces of megalithic art. Another highlight is a group of five menhir statues lined up in an arc around the foot of a 1200-year-old olive tree.

At the entrance there's a small museum with information about the Torréens-Shardanes (see the boxed text, left).

From Filitosa, you can drive a few kilometres east to **Calvese** and **Sollacaro**, two untouristed hamlets blessed with lovely surroundings.

GASTRONOMIC HIGHLIGHTS

LA CANTINE DU GOLFE €€

☎ 04 95 74 01 66; Porto Pollo; mains €9-26, menus €12-26; lunch & dinner May-Oct

This clean-cut eatery boasts contemporary furnishings, a sexy atmosphere and elegantly presented dishes that might include pasta, bruschette, fish or lamb. The lovely terrace overlooking the marina is another drawcard.

LE MOULIN FARELLACCI €€

☎ 04 95 74 62 28; http://lemoulinfarellacci.free.fr; Calvese; mains €10-17, menu €35; dinner mid-Jun–mid-Sep

The full monty! A brilliantly converted olive mill, an impossibly copious six-course dinner, lovely views from the terrace and the cheeriest *soirées chants et guitares* (song-and-guitar evenings) for miles around – if you're after a typical Corsican experience, this place is hard to beat. We guarantee it's authentic, and the lads who sing and play the guitar know their stuff. Bookings are essential.

PROPRIANO (PRUPRIÀ)

pop 3500

At the eastern end of the Golfe du Valinco, Propriano draws water-sports enthusiasts, beach bums, fish lovers and sweet tooths. Architecturally speaking, the town feels modernish and a bit sterile – if it's robust charm you're after, head to Sartène, which is a mere 15-minute drive away – but the bustling waterfront is full of atmosphere in summer, and a few beaches have managed to retain their beauty despite the tourist development.

ESSENTIAL INFORMATION

TOURIST OFFICES // Tourist office (☎04 95 76 01 49; www.oti-sartenaisvalinco.com; ☀8am-8pm Mon-Sat, 9am-1pm & 4-8pm Sun Jul & Aug, 8am-12.30pm & 2.30-7pm Mon-Sat May, Jun, Sep & Oct, 9am-noon & 2-6pm Mon-Fri Nov-Apr) At the marina.

EXPLORING PROPRIANO

Propriano's prime attraction is its water-based activities, but there are also plenty of options for landlubbers.

❧ BEACHES // SOAK UP RAYS ON PRETTY BEACHES

The best of the little beaches in town are **Plage du Lido**, west of the lighthouse, and its neighbour, the appealing **Plage du Corsaire**. Both are suitable for kids, and have crystal-clear water that just begs to be swum in.

You can also head to the fantastic **Plage de Portigliolo**, 7km south of town on the road to Campomoro. What a beach! It's an incredible 4km long and, with its fine, white sand and lack of development, is by far the nicest in the area. There's little or no shade, so bring your own, as well as plenty of water.

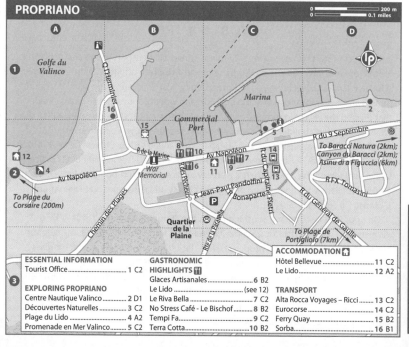

THE SOUTH

♥ BOAT EXCURSIONS // SAIL ALONG PRISTINE COASTLINES
The best way to explore the Golfe du Valinco and the lovely bays that grace the coast further south is to take a boat trip.

Promenade en Mer Valinco (☎ 06 12 54 99 28; www.promenade-en-mer-a-propriano .com; ☼ daily May–mid-Oct) offers perhaps the most original and ecofriendly cruise. The *'pique-nique convivial'* is a delightful 3½-hour excursion on a catamaran (adult/child €38/19, maximum 12 people), which includes a swimming stop in an idyllic cove. Bring a picnic. It also runs regular tours with an outboard-powered 12-seater (adult/child €16/11, 1½ hours). Romantic souls and photographers will opt for the sunrise or sunset cruise (adult/child €24/12, 1¼ hours).

Découvertes Naturelles (☎ 06 03 77 42 56; www.decouvertes-naturelles.net; ☼ daily May–mid-Oct) has a day trip that embraces all the coves and inlets down to Tizzano. There's a three-hour swimming stop at the wonderfully intimate cove of Tivella, which isn't accessible from the road. From Tivella, you can take a guided walk with a conservationist to the Senetosa lighthouse – an enlightening experience that's a fun way to learn about the area's unique environment. The trip costs €45.

♥ DONKEY RAMBLING // EXPLORE THE MAQUIS WITH A FOUR-LEGGED FRIEND
If you want a gentle approach to exploring the area, nothing can beat a donkey ride high in the hills overlooking the Golfe du Valinco, on the mule paths through the maquis, or down to the Rizzanese river for an oh-so-refreshing dip in a secluded natural pool. The children ride the donkey while the parents walk; a guide leads the animal. It's fun, safe and easy. Contact

---

∽ WORTH A TRIP ∽

If the beaches start to overwhelm, a 30-minute drive will transport you to another world. From Propriano, take the D19 to **Viggianello** and **Arbellara**, about 10km from the coast. A further 4km or so will bring you to **Fozzano**, a typical Corsican village with lofty granite houses and sweeping views over the gulf. Fozzano was notorious for the bloody feuds that divided the village in the 19th century, but it's now a peaceful settlement with a couple of eye-catching buildings, including the 14th-century **Torra Vecchia** and the 16th-century **Torra Nova**. Feeling peckish? Head to Viggianello's **Chez Charlot** (☎ 04 95 76 00 06; mains €10-15, menu €19; ☼ lunch & dinner mid-Apr–Sep), which specialises in traditional Corsican fare at very reasonable prices. There's a breezy terrace with mind-boggling views over the gulf. In Arbellara, you can stock up on organic cheese and cured meats at **Fromagerie L'Eternu** (☎ 04 95 73 46 79).

On your way back, take a soothing dip in the **Bains de Caldane** (☎ 04 95 77 00 34; admission €4; ☼ 9.30am-11pm Sat & Sun mid-Jun–mid-Sep, 9.30am-8pm mid-Sep–mid-Jun), sulphur hot springs with therapeutic properties. For the ultimate indulgence, order a glass of Champagne and drink it while lounging in the pool (€12). The springs are in the Fiumicicoli valley; to get here from Arbellara, follow the D119 until the junction with the D268, turn left until the junction with D148, and follow the signs.

Heading back to Propriano along the D268, you'll go past the **Spin'a Cavallu Genoese bridge**, hidden down the road.

Asinu di a Figuccia (☎ 06 03 28 92 00, 06 03 28 81 85; per donkey €60; ☺ Apr, Jul & Aug), signposted on the D257, between Propriano and Olmeto. The owners also sell high-quality olive oil from their own olive trees.

❦ PARC AVENTURE & CANYONING // SWING THROUGH THE FOREST À LA GEORGE OF THE JUNGLE

About 3km from Propriano, off the D257, there's an excellent *parc aventure* set up by **Baracci Natura** (☎ 06 20 95 45 34; www.baraccinatura.fr; rte de Baracci; admission €15-20; ☺ daily Jul & Aug) in a forest of cork oak trees. Two circuits are available. The *découverte* is suitable for children over five years, and the 'sensation' is equipped with zip lines, Nepalese bridges, swings, platforms and other fixtures that will make your heart race.

Further along the valley, canyoning is available in the **Canyon du Baracci**. It's an enjoyable circuit, with one 25m zip line, various jumps into natural pools and three toboggans that plunge down water-polished chutes. A half-day will set you back €35; contact Baracci Natura for information. Staff speak English.

❦ THE SEAFRONT // SOAK UP THE GOOD VIBES ALONG THE MAIN STRIP

A gentle wander along the seafront makes a pleasant prelude to a seaside aperitif or a fine meal at one of the town's good restaurants. You can start from the marina, opposite the tourist office, and walk towards the west, up to Plage du Lido. It's a short walk but allow plenty of time as there are lots of temptations along the way, from a glass of wine at trendy Tempi Fa (p122) to a scrummy ice-cream concoction at Glaces Artisanales (right).

❦ WATER SPORTS // GLIDE ON TRANSLUCENT WATERS

Why not try windsurfing, kayaking or sailing? The waters off Propriano are usually mirror calm – ideal for beginners and children. The **Centre Nautique Valinco** (☎ 06 12 54 99 28; www.centre-nautique-valinco.com; ☺ daily mid-May–Sep) is on the beach, about 250m beyond the tourist office. It rents out windsurfers (€16 per hour), sailboats (from €16 per hour) and kayaks (from €12 per hour), and organises private and group lessons for people aged 'from seven to 77'. English is spoken.

GASTRONOMIC HIGHLIGHTS

The main drag, av Napoléon, is almost wall-to-wall with restaurants. Most eateries boast a terrace overlooking the sea.

❦ GLACES ARTISANALES €

☎ 06 74 52 79 26; av Napoléon; ice creams from €1.50; ☺ 9am-6pm Mon-Sat Mar-Jun & Sep, daily 9am-8pm Jul-Aug

It's hard to resist the generous scoops and creamy delights at this little ice-cream parlour on the main strip. Eschew predictable favourites and indulge in a new taste sensation: the Brocciu (ice-cream flavoured with goat's- or ewe's-milk cheese) and *châtaigne* (chestnut) are outstanding. So is the *myrte* (myrtle).

❦ LE LIDO €€

☎ 04 95 76 06 37; av Napoléon; mains €18-30; ☺ lunch & dinner Tue-Sun May-Sep

A relatively young chef who's built a fine reputation, Romuald cooks dishes that are local, fresh and, most importantly, a feast for the taste buds. The *langouste au four* (lobster; €22 per 100g) is his signature dish, but his regularly changing menu is always imaginative. Dinner is best enjoyed on the oh-so-romantic

THE SOUTH

little terrace behind the verandah, with the waves almost lapping your toes. You'll be in seventh heaven.

☙ LE RIVA BELLA €€

☎ 04 95 76 24 69; av Napoléon; mains €9-25, menus €12-20; ☺ lunch & dinner Mon-Sat Apr-Jun & Sep-Oct, lunch & dinner daily Jul-Aug

This snazzy spot with elegant furniture strives to take customers on a culinary journey. Its savoury Mediterranean dishes are given a creative twist, then are presented with gusto on amusing plates; try the linguine and prawns flambéed with Grand Marnier. Pounce on the brilliant-value *menus* (set menus), and wash it all down with a glass of Appellation d'Origine Contrôlée (AOC) Sartène.

☙ NO STRESS CAFÉ – LE BISCHOF €€

☎ 04 95 76 30 00; av Napoléon; mains €9-25, menus €16-25; ☺ lunch & dinner May-Sep

The ambitious Bischofs have moved from their former den in a backstreet into sexier surrounds on the seafront. Diners continue to be delighted, however, by the eclectic menu, which favours fresh ingredients. The *brochettes* (meat skewers) are grilled to perfection, and the 550g rib steak has attained cult status. Generous wood-fired pizzas are also available.

☙ TEMPI FA €

☎ 04 95 06 16 52; av Napoléon; tapas €6, platters from €8; ☺ 9am-late Apr-Sep

Don't miss this supercool tapas and wine bar on the seafront. It serves amazingly delicious *piattini* (tapas-style cheese and charcuterie assortments), as well as more-substantial platters. Wooden barrels on the small street terrace are ideal for watching the world go by. It also doubles as a produce shop. A winning formula.

☙ TERRA COTTA €€

☎ 04 95 74 23 80; av Napoléon; mains €17-27, menu €32; ☺ lunch & dinner Mon-Sat Apr–mid-Nov

A sterling reputation precedes this ode to innovative Mediterranean dishes. Both the colourful indoor dining room and the agreeable terrace within grasp of the bobbing boats provide the perfect setting in which to sample, say, a *croquant de denti à la citronnelle* (dentex bream cooked with citronella). The *ananas rôti au safran et romarin* (roasted pineapple with saffron and rosemary) is a perfect coda to a delightful meal.

CAMPOMORO

pop 150

Picturesquely surrounded by undulating maquis-carpeted mountains, and blessed with idyllic beaches, the seaside resort of Campomoro is a gem. At the southern tip of the gulf, it really feels like the end of the line. Though there is only a handful of accommodation options and restaurants dotted around its large sandy beach, its low-key atmosphere makes it an attractive holiday destination. If you fancy something more strenuous than unrolling a beach towel, there's also plenty to do in the gulf, from diving to hiking to kayaking. Be warned, however: the place becomes packed in high season. During this period it's difficult to find both a bed for the night and a parking space in town.

☙ TOUR DE CAMPOMORO //
A TYPICAL CORSICAN GENOESE TOWER

A major landmark in the gulf, the stately Tour de Campomoro is at the end of the beach, crowning a promontory. Built in the 16th century by the Genoese, the tower is one of Corsica's largest, and is the only one on the island to have been fortified with a star-shaped surrounding wall. A fantastic lookout point, it was lovingly restored in 1986.

♥ COASTAL WALKS // LEAVE THE CROWDS BEHIND

The coastline between Tizzano and Campomoro is extremely alluring: a string of hard-to-reach inlets lapped by crystalline waters, the mandatory idyllic beaches, and vast expanses of chaotic granite boulders. Running between Tour de Campomoro and Cap Senetosa, the **Sentier Littoral Campomoro** takes in some of the most scenic spots in the area. It takes roughly five hours to complete (one way), but you can also choose to walk smaller sections; the easiest one is the loop known as **Boucle des Pozzi** (1½ hours). In theory you can continue as far as Tizzano but the section between Cap Senetosa and Tizzano is poorly marked.

The walks are detailed in the *De Campomoro à Senetosa* leaflet, available at the tourist office (p119) in Propriano.

♥ PLAGE DE CAMPOMORO // A GORGEOUS STRAND OF FINE SAND

Campomoro's turquoise waters and luscious ribbon of white-sand beach, backed by the Tour de Campomoro, are a major attraction for visitors, but come early if you want to secure the best patch in summer. Calm waters make it ideal for swimming. The rocky shorelines at each end are also prime spots for snorkelling.

♥ WATER SPORTS // GOING BEYOND THE BEACH

When it comes to fun in, on and under the water, Campomoro is an excellent base. The topography of the gulf perfectly lends itself to a sea-kayaking tour – it's the only way to access some of the most

---

TOP FIVE

SCENIC WALKS

Whether you're travelling along the stunning coastline or through the hinterland, there's a profusion of scenic walks in southern Corsica. Best of all, they're gentle and easy, and allow you to explore some truly amazing spots:

★ **Sentier Fazzio** (p132) – On the outskirts of Bonifacio, yet a world away from the city's hullabaloo; tantalising inlets, fantastic views and heavy-scented maquis

★ **Cap Pertusato** (p131) – Admire Sardinia and the Bouches de Bonifacio from up high

★ **Piscia di Gallo** (p144) – A gentle stroll to a dramatic waterfall

★ **Sentier Littoral Campomoro** (left) – Explore Corsica's wildest stretch of coastline, with not a house in sight

★ **Plateau du Coscione** (p145) – Just you, an undulating plateau and semiwild horses

---

pristine and beautiful coves and *cala* (inlets) along the coast (and, incidentally, escape the crowds). **Sud Kayak** (☎ 06 14 11 68 82; kayaksud@aol.com; 3hr tour €30), based right on the beach next to U Spuntinu restaurant, offers guided tours around the gulf, with a focus on marine life, history and geology. The three-hour excursion is totally undemanding, and includes swimming stops and a *spuntinu* (snack). You might even come across dolphins frolicking around your kayak; they are lured to the area by an aqua farm that lies just offshore.

Campomoro is also an obvious launching pad for the superb dive sites located at the entrance of the gulf. Sign

THE SOUTH

on with **Campomoro Plongée** (☎ 06 09 95 44 43; www.campomoro-plongee.com) or **Torra Plongée** (☎ 06 83 58 81 81; www.torra-plongee .com). Both welcome beginners and experienced divers, and can arrange *baptêmes* (introductory dives) in secluded coves.

😋 U SPUNTINU // FINE DINING RIGHT ON THE BEACH

This well-regarded **eatery** (☎ 04 95 74 21 99; mains €9-24, menu €19; ☺ lunch & dinner Apr-Oct) boasts a spiffing location, with a veranda overlooking the beach. It's not all about the location, however; the restaurant produces Corsican food with modern flair, including beautifully presented salads, tasty pasta, fresh fish (at €6.50 per 100g, it's a snip) and meat dishes cooked *brasero*-style (on a small tabletop grill).

LE SARTENAIS

· · · · · ·

So traditional. So proud. So Corsican. While only 13km separate Propriano from Sartène (the 'most Corsican of all Corsican towns' according to French novelist Prosper Mérimée), a gulf divides them. The Sartenais is different to the rest of the island – more inward looking, more secretive, adamantly steeped in tradition. The fast-paced coastal life seems light years away. Tourism has had little impact; the area is a reminder of what the whole of Corsica used to be like. Don't miss it.

TRANSPORT
- -

BUS // From July to mid-September, **Alta Rocca Voyages – Ricci** (☎ 04 95 51 08 19; www.alta -rocca-voyages.com) runs a daily bus service between Ajaccio and Zonza via Porto Pollo, Olmeto-Plage, Propriano and Sartène. **Eurocorse** (☎ 04 95 76 13 50) has two daily services (one on Sunday) between Ajaccio and

Bonifacio via Olmeto, Propriano, Sartène and Porto-Vecchio in July and August (one daily service from Monday to Saturday from September to June).

PARKING // There's a couple of parking facilities outside the old town.

SARTÈNE (SARTÈ)

pop 2500

If you want to see a slice of real Corsica, be sure to squeeze Sartène into your sojourn. With high granite walls, tall town houses, and narrow alleys that twirl you unexpectedly into quaint nooks and crannies, the town's austere yet eye-catching architecture combines with the natural setting – Sartène is perched high over the Vallée du Rizzanese – to create an unrivalled ambience. If you plan a visit in spring, try to coincide it with the Catenacciu procession, a tradition dating from the Middle Ages that's a definite must see.

ESSENTIAL INFORMATION
- -

TOURIST OFFICES // Tourist office (☎ 04 95 77 15 40; www.oti-sartenaisvalinco.com; cours Soeur Amélie; ☺ 9am-7pm Jun-Sep, 9am-noon & 2-6pm Mon-Fri Oct-May)

EXPLORING SARTÈNE
- -

More than specific sights, it's the experience of ambling around the town centre, with its cafe-lined square and fortress-like houses that will live long in your memory.

😋 OLD TOWN // FEEL THE BEAT OF SARTÈNE'S HISTORIC HEART

The old town is an atmospheric labyrinth of stone stairways and little streets, some of them so narrow that two people can barely pass through. On place Porta, you can't miss the bell tower of **Église Ste-Marie** (1766). Next to the church is the building that was the palace of the Genoese lieutenants in the 16th century; it now houses the **hôtel de ville** (town hall). If you go through the gateway below the former palace, you will come out on the narrow streets of the **Santa Anna district**, which is the real jewel of the old town. Explore it at your leisure, then head back to place Porta for a well-deserved glass of *pastis Dami en terrasse* (Corsican pastis served on a terrace).

❦ U CATENACCIU // IMMERSE YOURSELF IN SARTÈNE'S UNIQUE TAKE ON EASTER

On the eve of Good Friday, Sartène is the setting for one of the most fascinating religious ceremonies on the island – the Procession du Catenacciu. In a colourful re-enactment of the Passion, the *catenacciu* (literally, 'the chained one'), an anonymous, barefoot penitent covered from head to foot in a red robe and cowl, carries a huge cross through the old town, dragging heavy chains at his feet. The *catenacciu* is followed by a procession of other penitents (eight dressed in black, one in white), who are members of the clergy and local notables.

When they are not in use, the chains and cross of the *catenacciu* can be seen in the Église Ste-Marie.

GASTRONOMIC HIGHLIGHTS

❦ BERGERIE D'ACCIOLA €
☎ 04 95 77 14 00; rte de Bonifacio, Acciola; mains €8-15; ☽ lunch & dinner Jun-Sep
A mandatory stop for gourmands, this produce shop set in a lovely granite house on the Bonifacio road doubles as a restaurant, using a charming terrace at the back. How does *galette à la farine de châtaigne* (chestnut-flour pancake), followed by cheesecake with orange sound? Don't leave without buying a pungent

casgiu casanu (farm cheese) at the shop. Local wines are available too. It's 8km from Sartène.

❦ AUBERGE SANTA BARBARA €€
☎ 04 95 77 09 06; www.santabarbara.fr; mains €22-36, menu €34; ☽ lunch Tue-Sun Jul-Aug, lunch & dinner Jul-Aug, lunch & dinner Tue-Sun Apr-Jun & Sep–early Oct
Send your taste buds into a tailspin at this iconic restaurant serving authentic dishes with a creative twist. Award-winning chef Gisèle Lovichi is a true alchemist, with such delectable concoctions as *daube de manzu tagliatelle* (veal stew with tagliatelle) or *côte de veau châtaignes confites* (veal chop with preserved chestnuts). A respectable wine list and exemplary service complete the picture. It's about 1.3km from the centre on the road to Propriano; follow the signs. Book ahead.

RECOMMENDED SHOPS

❦ LA CAVE SARTENAISE
☎ 04 95 77 10 08; place Porta; ☽ Apr-Oct
Its exceptional selection of local wine makes La Cave Sartenaise an excellent stop for tipplers. If it's not crowded, the staff will be happy to give advice (in French) on the best Sartène wines to add to your cellar. There's plenty of other Corsican goodies (charcuterie, olive oil, cheese) too. It's right below the town hall.

❦ U MAGGIU
☎ 04 95 77 21 36; Vieille Ville; ☽ Apr–mid-Oct
The wonderful stalls positioned in front of the cute granite facade are designed to tempt the devil (and the photographer) in you. And they do. Especially if you add the shelves displaying rows of lovingly homemade jams. And honey. And charcuterie. And liqueurs.

THE SOUTH

AROUND SARTÈNE

❦ PREHISTORIC SITES OF THE SARTENAIS // WANDER AMID MYSTERIOUS DOLMENS AND MENHIRS

About 15km south of Sartène, the desolate and beautiful Cauria plateau is home to three megalithic curiosities that rank among the most interesting on the island: the *alignements* (lines) of menhirs of Stantari and Renaju, and the Fontanaccia dolmen. The Alignement de Stantari consists of nine stones: the fourth from the left represents a sword, and its next two neighbours represent faces with their mouths open in muted cry. The Alignement de Renaju is larger, slightly less orderly and 300m further on, at the edge of a little wood. From there, find the path to the Fontanaccia dolmen, about 400m away. This megalithic monument is the largest of its type in Corsica. Archaeologists and historians seem to agree at least that the dolmens mark burial sites. But what of the menhirs? Whatever their origins, they form a mystical backdrop to a one-hour walk through the area.

From Sartène, follow the road to Bonifacio for 2km before turning off onto the winding D48, on the right. The megalithic site at Cauria is signposted to the left after another 8km; take the D48a.

❦ DOMAINE MOSCONI // BUY A BOTTLE OF ROSÉ IN A FAMILY-RUN WINERY

After exploring the megaliths of Cauria, you can stop at Domaine de Mosconi (☎ 04 95 70 49 42; www.domainemosconi.com; rte de Tizzano), further down on the road to Tizzano. This reputable winery produces an excellent AOC Sartène, and has a large tasting room where you can sample its rosés and reds; we love its Cuvée Ariale. Perfect for a picnic on a secluded beach.

❦ HORSE RIDING // TROT ALONG THE BEACH OR THROUGH THE MAQUIS

For horseback trail rides in unspoilt scenery, you can't do better than the well-regarded equestrian centre Cavadda di Santu Pultru (☎ 06 88 70 42 05; www .randochevalcorse.fr; rte de Tizzano; 2hr/full day from €40/95). Emmanuel Lucchini leads excellent excursions into the maquis that take

---

∼ WORTH A TRIP ∼

Vallée de l'Ortolo… Promise you won't tell *too* many people about this timeless valley? From Sartène, take the D50 to the southeast, in the direction of Mola. The narrow road plunges downhill amid spectacular scenery – mountains, vineyards, forests and fields. In the middle of nowhere, the farm **U Cavaddu Senza Nome** (☎ 04 95 77 18 47, 06 10 39 14 29; www.ucavaddu.fr; Ranfonu, Ortolo; ⌾ Feb-Nov) welcomes visitors to a heavenly property. Your hosts, a German–Austrian couple (fluent in English), sell *légumes de saison* (seasonal vegetables) and delicious Alta Rocca honey (€11 per 1kg pot), and children will enjoy the farm animals pottering about. Bikes are available for hire (a perfect way to explore the valley) and you can splash in the nearby Ortolo river. Campsites (from €17 for two people) are available.

Afterwards, you could head to the reputable **Domaine Saparale** (☎ 04 95 77 15 52; www.saparale.com; ⌾ by appointment) for a wine tasting. Ah, the Cuvée Casteddu…

THE SOUTH

in the prehistoric site of Cauria, as well as beach rides, during which you and your horse splash straight into the turquoise sea. The stables are on the D48, near the junction with the road that leads to Cauria.

TIZZANO & AROUND

At the end of the D48, which peels off the N196 about 17km to the north, another world awaits. You'll be smitten by the mellow tranquillity of Tizzano's charming little cove, which has thankfully escaped massive tourist development due its relative isolation. It's also an ideal springboard for excursions to a string of staggeringly beautiful beaches and coves that are inaccessible by land – they beg exploration, Robinson Crusoe style.

❤ BEACHES // SWIM IN CRYSTAL-CLEAR WATERS

Tizzano has a picturesque beach with tantalising azure waters – **Cala di l'Avena** – but the 2km-long golden-sand **Plage de Tra Licettu**, 6km to the southeast and accessible via a dirt track (or in your own boat), is even more impressive. Most importantly, it's much less crowded in summer, making it well worth the bumpy ride. But for total tranquillity, consider renting a boat or a kayak to get to even more secluded beaches.

❤ KAYAKING & BOATING // SAVOUR SECLUDED BAYS AND BEACHES

Sea kayaking is a heavenly way to explore coves and inlets inaccessible from land, including **Cala di Conca** and **Cala di Tivella** (to the west), or **Plage d'Erbaju** and **Plage d'Argent** (to the east), where you can laze in idyllic surrounds, far from the crowds – bliss! **Stintu Marinu**

TOP **FIVE**

CULTURAL SIGHTS

- ★ **Pianu di Levie** (p146) – Well-preserved megaliths near Levie
- ★ **Filitosa** (p117) – Prehistoric vestiges shrouded with mystery
- ★ **Église Ste-Marie Majeure** (p129) – Elaborate church in Bonifacio
- ★ **Cauria** (opposite) – Menhirs galore
- ★ **Porte Génoise & Bastion de France** (p135) – Ruins of an old Genoese citadel in Porto-Vecchio

(☎ 06 10 61 35 10; www.stintu-marinu.com; ☻ May-Sep), based at the harbour, rents two- and three-seater kayaks for €35 per half-day. Another outfit is **Aqua Mondo – Location de Kayak** (☎ 06 14 23 50 93; ☻ July–mid-Sep), on Plage de l'Avena.

Renting a small motor boat is the next best way to experience the pristine coastline and beaches. Stintu Marinu has small five-seater motor boats for €60/90 per half-/full day; no licence is required. These boats can nudge into tiny inlets that are denied to larger models. A map of the coast is provided, as well as life jackets; bring snorkelling gear and a picnic.

❤ CHEZ ANTOINE – THE BEACH // REVEL IN THE FRESHEST OF SUCCULENT SEAFOOD

An immutable seafood favourite that's been around since 1960, **Chez Antoine** (☎ 04 95 77 07 25; Tizzano; mains €12-22; ☻ lunch & dinner May-Sep) is beloved by all who come here. Brothers Julien and Flo know their stuff when it comes to serving lobster or grilled fish (sea bass, red mullet or weever, depending on the daily catch; from €7 per 100g). The decor has been recently upgraded, and it's now a snazzy spot

THE SOUTH

with elegant furnishings and a breezy terrace overlooking the harbour. There's a sushi bar downstairs.

LE SARTENAIS TO BONIFACIO

· · · · · ·

From Sartène, the N196 wriggles south to the Col de Roccapina, and then veers due east to Bonifacio. This is Corsica's far southwestern corner, and the island's most sparsely populated area. Rather than dashing straight to Bonifacio, it's well worth making a few detours from the main road to explore this quirky region. The rewards? Splendid views, dazzling turquoise bays, hidden beaches and bizarre rock formations, all backed by rolling hills carpeted with fragrant maquis and vineyards. Looming majestically on the horizon, the Uomo di Cagna (1215m) – a peculiarly-shaped giant boulder eroded by sea winds – is a major landmark.

❦ BEACHES // ON THE BEACH OR IN THE WATER? YOU DECIDE

About 20km from Sartène and 30km from Bonifacio, there's a lay-by on the roadside, from where you can admire the Roccapina site, a Dalí-esque rock formation that is (vaguely) reminiscent of a lion. There's a photogenic Genoese tower on the hilltop above. The view down to the shimmering waters of Plage de Roccapina from the lookout is seductive. The invitation to swim in crystal-clear waters being irresistible, take the potholed track, leading off the main road next to Auberge Coralli, and follow it downhill for 3km. The beach is fine and sandy, making it particularly suitable for children.

Some 20km from Bonifacio on the N196, a secondary road leads from the village of Pianottoli-Caldarello down to the tranquil Plage de Kevano, which tends to be less crowded in summer.

If you're action hungry or in search of good photo ops, head to Plage de la Tonnara, about halfway between Pianottoli-Caldarello and Bonifacio. This windswept beach makes windsurfing and kitesurfing hounds go gaga. Even if you're not a water-sport aficionado, it's hard to tear yourself away from the aerials performed by windsurfers and kitesurfers here. Another up-and-coming kitesurfing and windsurfing spot is Plage de Figari, in Baie de Figari, a few kilometres to the northwest. Want to give it a try? Contact one of the outfits based on the beach.

❦ DOMAINE DE MURTA // SHOP FOR AN ORGANIC AOC FIGARI

It's a simple affair, but Domaine de Murta (☎ 04 95 71 00 34; ☽ year-round), whose shop is right in the centre of the village of Figari, has made a name of itself with quality organic wines. A bottle costs from €7.

❦ POGGIO DI MASTRI // HEARTY MEALS IN RUSTIC SURROUNDS

Bring an empty tum: the five-course *menu* served at Poggio di Mastri (☎ 04 95 71 02 65; Figari; menu €40; ☽ May-Oct) is a culinary feast based on choice pieces of meat the size of doorstops, organic vegetables and prepared-to-perfection desserts. The dining room impresses, with a huge fireplace, hefty beams and wooden furniture, but the location close to the main road is a disadvantage.

❦ CHEZ MARCO // THE BEST FISH RESTAURANT FOR MILES AROUND

Lobster is king of the castle at Chez Marco (☎ 04 95 73 02 24; Baie de Figari; menus €55-99; ☽ Apr-Oct). This is the place towards which all heads turn when it comes to tasting a bounteous range of marine offerings. The location is ace, and there's a large dining area with exposed wooden beams, stone walls and lobster pots hanging from the ceiling, plus a terrace overlooking the sea.

BONIFACIO (BUNIFAZIU) & AROUND

· · · · · ·

pop 2700

With its stunning setting, breathtaking layout and distinctly Italian flavour, Bonifacio is indisputably southern Corsica's star attraction. The *haute ville*, which is a compact mesh of twisting streets hemmed in by ancient buildings, is dramatically perched on a thin peninsula. Down below, a fjord, about 100m wide, plunges in behind the great cliffs to form the town's fine natural harbour. And the shimmering blue seas of the Îles Lavezzi are a short boat ride away.

The flip side to all this beauty is that Bonifacio is fiendishly crowded in July and August.

The town as we know it today was probably founded by the Marquis de Toscane Boniface in AD 828, and was taken by Genoa in 1187.

Genoese Bonifacio had to fight for its life twice. The first occasion was in 1420, when Alphonse V of Aragon laid siege to the town for five months, on the grounds that Pope Boniface VIII had given Corsica to Spain; according to legend, the Escalier du Roi d'Aragon (King of Aragon's Stairway) was carved at this point.

The second siege took place in 1553. This time it was an alliance between French troops, followers of Sampiero Corso and the Turkish pirate Dragut, who aimed to liberate the town. Bonifacio resisted the attack for 18 days. Together with the rest of the island, it was returned to the Genoese in 1559.

ESSENTIAL INFORMATION

TOURIST OFFICES // Tourist office (☎ 04 95 73 11 88; www.bonifacio.fr; rue Fred Scamaroni; ◷ 9am-8pm May–mid-Oct, 9am-noon & 2-6pm Mon-Fri mid-Oct–Apr)

EXPLORING BONIFACIO & AROUND

❦ **THE HAUTE VILLE // LOADS OF ATMOSPHERE AS WELL AS MESMERISING PANORAMAS**
Bonifacio boasts numerous historical buildings – testimony to its rich past – that are best discovered wandering amid the narrow streets of the *haute ville*.

From the marina, the paved Montée Rastello and Montée St-Roch lead to the *haute ville*'s **citadel** via Porte de Gênes (Genoa Gate; pedestrian access only). To the north is the **Bastion de l'Étendard** (admission €2.50; ◷ 9am-7pm Apr-Oct), a remnant of the fortifications built in the aftermath of the siege in 1553. It is home to the **Mémorial du Passé Bonifacien** (Memorial to Bonifacio's Past; admission €2.50 ◷ 9am-7pm Apr-Oct), where various episodes in the town's history have been recreated. To the south of the bastion are **place du Marché** and **place de la Manichella**, with their jaw-dropping views over the limestone cliffs to the east.

Dating from the 14th century, the unmissable **Église Ste-Marie Majeure** is famous for its loggia, under the arches of which the notables of the town used to gather. Opposite it is the old **cistern**, in which the town formerly collected rainwater from the many aqueducts

BONIFACIO

THE SOUTH

ESSENTIAL INFORMATION
Tourist Office......................1 B3

EXPLORING BONIFACIO
Bastion de l'Étendard..........2 C3
Boat-Trip Booths...............3 E3
Cistern.........................(see 7)
Corsica Diving.................4 E2
Église St-Dominique...........5 A4
Église St-Erasme..............6 D3

Église Ste-Marie Majeure.....7 C4
Mémorial du Passé Bonifacien...(see 2)

GASTRONOMIC HIGHLIGHTS
Cantina Doria.................8 C4
Kissing Pigs..................9 C3
L'Archivolto..................10 C4
Stella d'Oro - Chez Jules....11 C4

ACCOMMODATION
Hôtel des Étrangers..........12 E1

Hôtel Genovese...............13 B4
Hôtel Le Colomba.............14 B4

TRANSPORT
Eurocorse....................15 E3
Ferry Terminal...............16 B3
Scoot Rent...................17 C3

PARKING
Parking......................18 E3
Parking......................19 E2
Parking......................20 F3
Parking......................21 A4
Parking......................22 B3
Parking......................23 B3

To Barakouda (1km);
Golfe de Sant'Amanza (6km);
Le Gregale (6km); Plage de
Rodinara (20km); Figari
Sud Corse Airport (21km)

To Domaine de Licetto (2km);
Tre Punti (2km); Cap
Pertusato (4km); Baie de
Piantarella (6km); Plage
de Calalonga (6km); Plage du
Grand Spérone (6km); Plage du
Petit Spérone (6km)

To Cap Pertusato (3.5km)

Av Sylvère Bohn

Giovasole

Marina

Q Jérôme Comparetti

Av Charles de Gaulle

Quai Sennola

Sentier Fazzio

Goulet de
Bonifacio

To Anse de Fazzio;
Cala Paraguan

To Madonetta
Lighthouse (800m);
Grotte du Sdragonato (1km);
Îles Lavezzi (11km)

To Église St-François (300m);
Gouvernail de la Corse (300m);
Marine Cemetery (300m)

Haute
Ville

To La Poudrière (200m)

Barracks

Citadel

Montée St-Roch

Q Banda del Ferro

Arcade de la
Carrotola

Jardin de la
Carrotola

R St-Dominique

Pl St-
François

Pl Carrega - Montepagano

R F Scamaroni

R St-Jean Baptiste

Montée
6
Montée
St-Roch

R St-Erasme

Montée Rastello

Porte de
Gênes

Pl du
Marché

Pl
d'Armes

R Archivolto

R Doria

Pl de la
Manichella

R Longue

R du Palais
de Garde

Pl Fondago

running above the streets of the *haute ville*.

Keep an eye on your feet as you climb down the **Escalier du Roi d'Aragon** (admission €2.50). Legend has it that the 187 steps running down from the southwestern corner of the citadel to the sea, 60m below, were carved in a single night by the king of Aragon's troops during a siege in 1420. It is more likely that this impressive scar down the side of the cliff was carved to allow access to a spring discovered by monks.

To the west of the citadel is the **Église St-Dominique** (admission €2.50), one of the few Gothic churches in Corsica. It houses reliquaries carried in processions through the town during a number of religious festivals.

Further to the west, you'll pass by a few windmills before reaching the eerily quiet **marine cemetery**, with its immaculate lines of tombs and imposing mausoleums, and the adjoining **Église St-François**. At the western tip of the peninsula, an underground passage dug by hand during WWII leads to the **Gouvernail de la Corse** (Rudder of Corsica; admission €2.50), a rock about a dozen metres from the shore with a shape reminiscent of the rudder of a ship.

The tourist office (p129) offers a pass that allows entry to four of the city's attractions for €6.

☙ BOAT TRIPS // VIEW BONIFACIO FROM THE SEA

The best way to marvel at the town's precarious position on top of magnificent chalky cliffs is to take a boat trip. The one-hour itinerary (€18) includes the Goulet di Bonifacio, several *calanques* (deep rocky inlets) with clear aquamarine waters, the **Madonetta lighthouse**, the Escalier du Roi d'Aragon (above) and

the mysterious **Grotte du Sdragonato** (Little Dragon Cave), with its multicoloured seabed and shafts of light.

Numerous companies vie for customers in summer; ticket booths are located on the marina. The companies also offer longer itineraries focusing on the Îles Lavezzi.

☙ DIVING // NOSE TO SNOUT WITH A CORPS DE BALLET OF GROUPERS

You don't need to be a strong diver to enjoy Bonifacio's underwater riches. The Îles Lavezzi – the most popular diving area – feature a variety of sites suitable for all levels, including beginners. At Mérouville, divers are guaranteed to get up close and personal with big groupers. **Barakouda** (☎ 04 95 73 13 02; www.barakouda .com; rte de Porto-Vecchio), about 2km from the centre on the road to Porto-Vecchio, and **Corsica Diving** (☎ 06 15 05 20 61; www .corsicadiving.fr; quai Sennola) are two well-established dive operators. A single dive starts at €35.

☙ CAP PERTUSATO // WALK OR DRIVE, BUT DON'T MISS THAT PERFECT PICTURE

The seamless view of the cliffs, the Îles Lavezzi, Bonifacio and Sardinia from Cap Pertusato is absolutely memorable. It's a fantastic, easy walk along the cliffs; from the signposted starting point, which is just to the left of the sharp bend on the hill up to Bonifacio's *haute ville,* turn left and a ramp of paving stones climbs to the top of the cliffs. When you get there, follow the path along the cliffs to the southeast. There is low-growing maquis on your left; to the right, a sheer drop down to the sea. After about 30 minutes, the path joins the D260, which leads to the signal station and **lighthouse**, from where the views are phenomenal. Allow three hours for the return walk. There's no shade. By car, take the D58, which runs by the hospital; it's signposted.

❦ SENTIER FAZZIO // A WALKING TRAIL WITH KILLER VISTAS

This is a much less hyped trail than the one that goes to Cap Pertusato, which is reason enough to do it. Beginning near Hôtel des Étrangers, it takes in the **Cala Paraguan** and the delightful **Anse de Fazzio**, accessible only on foot, before winding along the cliffs back to Bonifacio. It affords views of the Madonetta lighthouse and the citadel from the west; most pictures of the citadel are taken from the east, from the path leading to Cap Pertusato. It's an easy 2½-hour walk along a well-marked path, but there's no shade. Pick up the *Sentier Fazzio* leaflet at the tourist office (p129).

❦ ÎLES LAVEZZI // SWIM THE DAY AWAY IN A NATURE RESERVE

Part of a protected area known as the **Réserve Naturelle des Bouches de Bonifacio**, the Îles Lavezzi, or the Archipel des Lavezzi (Lavezzi archipelago), is a clutch of uninhabited islets made for those who love nothing better than splashing in tranquil lapis lazuli waters or strolling across powder-soft beaches.

In summer, various companies organise **boat excursions** (adult around €33) to the island; you can book at the ticket booths located on Bonifacio's marina. Boats are operated in shuttle fashion, which allows you to linger on the islands. On the way back, the boats pass close to Île Cavallo. You will need to bring your own lunch and drinks, as you cannot buy anything on the islands. There are also trips to the islands from Porto-Vecchio (p135).

❦ BEACHES // SEYCHELLES-LIKE STRETCHES OF SAND

Bonifaciens' favourite sunbathing place (and the town's best-kept secret) is **Tre Punti** (Three Points), a few kilometres to the east, down the road leading to Cap Pertusato. Reached after a 10-minute walk from the road, these lovely coves at the base of chalky cliffs offer excellent snorkelling and swimming in jade waters, as well as stunning views of Bonifacio in the distance. There's no sand or shade, however.

Further to the northeast, between Baie de Piantarella and Porto-Vecchio, the jagged coastline is regularly punctuated by stretches of gorgeous white-sand beach. From Baie de Piantarella, it's an easy 10-minute walk to the **Plage du Petit Spérone**, a tiny turquoise bay with tourist-brochure-esque appeal. Continue walking along the coast until you reach **Plage du Grand Spérone**, where you might spot a celeb or two, given the vicinity of the ultraexclusive Golf de Spérone hotel.

Plage de Calalonga is a bit harder to find, but it doesn't get too crowded. To get there, follow the D58 east of Bonifacio for 6km, from where you'll need to walk a further 200m down a sandy track to the beach.

About 7km east of Bonifacio, the **Golfe de Sant' Amanza** is a hot windsurfing and kitesurfing spot and draws a crowd when the wind is right. It also offers excellent sunbathing opportunities, with a good range of beaches that includes **Plage de Maora, Plage de Balistra** and **Plage de Sant' Amanza**. All around the gulf, there are lots of coves and beaches that aren't accessible by car (no crowds!); **Pouss Vagues** (☎ 06 74 41 36 62, 06 07 94 25 82; www.poussevague.com; Golfe de Sant' Amanza; ☯ mid-Apr–mid-Oct) rents six-seater 6HP motor boats. It will cost you €85/115 per half-/full day, petrol included; no licence is necessary. It also rents kayaks from €10 per hour. To get to the Golfe de Sant' Amanza, follow the D60, just off the main Bonifacio–Porto-Vecchio road.

The phenomenal horseshoe-shaped Baie de Rondinara is home to the beautiful, sandy **Plage de Rondinara**, a salt-white strip of sand lapped by turquoise waters. As it's backed by pines, you'll find it a gorgeous place to sun yourself. To get to it from Bonifacio, take the Porto-Vecchio road for about 16km, at which point you'll see a small turn to the right.

☙ KAYAKING // SEE THE BAIE DE PIANTARELLA FROM A DIFFERENT PERSPECTIVE

The lovely **Baie de Piantarella** ranks among the best spots in southern Corsica for water sports, including windsurfing, kitesurfing and kayaking. With a kayak, you can effortlessly reach nearby Plage du Petit Spérone or **Île de Piana**, which are both blessed with white-sand beaches. **Bonif Kayak** (☎ 06 27 11 30 73; www.bonifacio-kayak.com; ☽ May–Sep) rents kayaks from €14 per hour, and runs guided kayak trips around the bay, with a focus on flora, fauna and geology (adult €35). Find Bonif Kayak at the eastern tip of the beach, towards Plage du Petit Spérone.

GASTRONOMIC HIGHLIGHTS

☙ CANTINA DORIA €
☎ 04 95 73 50 49; rue Doria; mains €8-12, menus €13-17; ☽ lunch & dinner Mon-Sat Apr-Sep
Success has done nothing to dull the buzz at Cantina, an unpretentious, cav-

ernous little joint in the *haute ville*. The menu contains invigorating dishes such as *porc à la Pietra et châtaignes* (pork with Pietra beer and chestnuts) and *lasagnes au fromage Corse* (lasagne with Corsican cheese). There's outdoor seating, but get here fast to score a table.

☙ DOMAINE DE LICETTO €€
☎ 04 95 73 03 59; www.licetto.com; rte du Phare; menu €35; ☽ dinner Mon-Sat Apr-Jul & Sep–mid-Oct, dinner daily Aug
Right in the maquis, Domaine de Licetto has won plaudits for its gargantuan *menu*: aperitif, Corsican soup or charcuterie, two main courses, cheese platter (gastronomic adventurers will want to try the *casgiu merzu*, which is crawling with little white maggots), dessert, digestif and wine. Menu stalwarts include *agneau de lait* (suckling lamb) and *aubergines à la bonifacienne*. The food is fresh and delicious, and the restaurant strives to use only local ingredients.

☙ KISSING PIGS €€
☎ 04 95 73 56 09; quai Banda del Ferro; mains €10-18, menus €12-20; ☽ closed Wed & Sun in low season
By the harbour, this trendy restaurant and wine bar offers some of the best charcuterie and cheese platters in town. For the indecisive, the *moitié-moitié* (half and half), which is a combination of the two, is the prefect answer. Since Corsican tipples also feature highly here, let things rip with a glass of local rosé (from €4).

☙ L'ARCHIVOLTO €€
☎ 04 95 73 17 58; rue Archivolto; mains €13-20; ☽ lunch Mon-Sat Apr-Jun & Sep, dinner Jul-Aug
This Bonifacio institution feels like an antique shop, with an onslaught of quirky collectables from floor to ceiling. Foodwise, it's no less impressive, with *salade de poulpe à la coriandre* (octopus

THE SOUTH

salad with coriander), *lasagnes chèvre aubergines* (lasagne with goat cheese and eggplants) and a dozen other mouth-watering concoctions. In summer the tables spill out onto the piazza outside.

♥ LA POUDRIÈRE €

☎ 04 95 73 53 63; mains €9-15; ☺ lunch & dinner May-Sep

Although it's in the *haute ville*, the oh-so-cute La Poudrière remains a find – the crowds tend to flock to the eateries that lie within the citadel. Located in a former *poudrière* (powder store) near the marine cemetery, it specialises in super-fresh dishes made from ingredients that come directly from small-scale Corsican farmers. The tart with tomato and goat's cheese, the cheese platter, the *tartine* (slice of bread) with goat's cheese, fruits and honey – they all sing in the mouth. And the views from the terrace are gorgeous.

♥ LE GREGALE

☎ 04 95 73 51 46; Plage de Maora; fish €6 per 100g, lobster €13 per 100g; ☺ dinner Jun-Sep

Fish lovers will be in seventh heaven – this well-regarded spot serves the freshest of fish in rustic-chic surrounds. Depending on the daily catch, the menu may feature John Dory, sea bream, sea bass…and lobster. It's a family affair, with Mum, Dad (the cooks) and two sons (fishermen and waiters). So cute. It's slightly set back from Plage de Maora, so there are no views.

♥ STELLA D'ORO – CHEZ JULES €€

☎ 04 95 73 03 63; rue Doria; mains €15-26, menu €23; ☺ Apr-Sep

Ask a Bonifacien for their favourite restaurant in town and there's a fair chance that they will nominate Chez Jules. Set in a former oil mill, it serves local specialities cooked to perfection; try the *aubergines à la bonifacienne* (eggplants

cooked with cheese). Leave room for the *dessert du chef* (homemade dessert of the day) – the *délice au Brocciu frais* (a pastry with Brocciu cheese) melts in the mouth.

TRANSPORT

TO/FROM THE AIRPORT

AIR // Figari Sud Corse airport (FSC; www .figari.aeroport.fr) is 21km north of Bonifacio, near Figari. See p266 for further infomation. There's no public transport to/from the airport. A taxi costs about €40.

GETTING AROUND

BUS // Eurocorse (☎ 04 95 70 13 83) has two daily services (one on Sunday) between Bonifacio and Porto-Vecchio, Sartène, Propriano and Ajaccio in July and August. From September to June, it runs one daily service from Monday to Saturday. For Bastia, you'll have to change in Porto-Vecchio.

CAR // Come prepared: in summer, Bonifacio is such a popular destination that it does to cars what a spider's web does to flies.

PARKING // Use one of the few car parks dotted around town (from €2 per hour) or find a hotel that provides a parking space.

BOAT // Bonifacio is the main jumping-off point for Santa Teresa di Gallura (Sardinia); see p269 for details.

SCOOTER // Scoot Rent (☎ 06 25 44 22 82; quai Banda del Ferro) rents scooters for €40 per day – a good way to avoid traffic-gridlock purgatory in summer.

PORTO-VECCHIO (PORTI-VECCHJU)

. . . . . .

pop 10,600

Shamelessly seductive and fashionable, Porto-Vecchio is often dubbed the Corsican St Tropez – and it's no wonder. Sitting in a marvellous

bay, it's the kind of place that lures French A-listers and wealthy tourists. If you're looking to seriously indulge, Porto-Vecchio has lots of chic hotels and exclusive *résidences de tourisme* (condominium-style accommodation), plus a well-established party reputation during the high season. Although there is no beach by the town proper, some of the island's best, and most famous, beaches are close by.

Try to come during shoulder seasons if you can, when Porto-Vecchio reverts to a charming, relatively low-key coastal town. And if all that bling and bustle overwhelms, the rustic Alta Rocca is never far away.

ESSENTIAL INFORMATION

TOURIST OFFICE // Tourist office (☎ 04 95 70 09 58; www.destination-sudcorse.com; rue Camille de Rocca Serra; ☺ 9am-8pm Mon-Sat, 9am-1pm Sun May-Sep, 9am-12.30pm & 2-6.30pm Mon-Fri, 9am-12.30pm Sat Oct-Apr) Provides handy audioguides in English.

EXPLORING PORTO-VECCHIO

☙ THE HAUTE VILLE // MOOCH AROUND PORTO-VECCHIO'S HEART AND SOUL

Porto-Vecchio is fairly short on sights, but the *haute ville*, with its picturesque backstreets lined with restaurant terraces and designer shops, has charm in spades. The atmospheric rue Borgo gives a glimpse of what the city was like in earlier days. The ruins of the old Genoese citadel are well worth a peek – you can't miss the **Porte Génoise** and the **Bastion de France** (closed to the public).

☙ BOAT TRIPS // ADMIRE THE COAST FROM THE SEA

Monte Cristo (☎ 04 95 72 01 04; www.croisieres-montecristo.com; ☺ May-Sep) and **Ruscana** (☎ 04 95 71 41 50; www.amour-des-iles.com; ☺ May-Sep) offer *promenades en mer* (boat excursions) to Îles Lavezzi and Bonifacio. The full-day excursion passes the Réserve Naturelle des Îles Cerbicale and beaches south of Porto-Vecchio, including Plage de Rondinara, before reaching Îles Lavezzi, Île Cavallo and Bonifacio (weather permitting); it's an ideal way to gain an overview of the coast's delights. There is a stop for a swim in a lovely little cove.

Both companies have booths at the marina. The trip costs €60/30 for adults/children and includes lunch.

☙ HELICOPTER TOURS // THE BEST WAY TO EXPERIENCE CORSICA'S GRANDEUR

There's something to be said for the bird's-eye view – especially when you're gazing upon a string of idyllic beaches, deep-blue waters and crescent-shaped gulfs. Weather is a factor in how much you'll see, so wait for a crystal-clear day if you can. **Helisud Corse** (☎ 04 95 72 18 63; www.helisudcorse.fr; rte de Bonifacio) has six different tours, starting at €60 per person (10 minutes). For the full monty, you can book a 90-minute flight that takes in the Alta Rocca and the coast down to Bonifacio.

GASTRONOMIC HIGHLIGHTS

☙ A CANTINA DI L'ORRIU €

☎ 04 95 70 26 21; cours Napoléon; mains €13-28; ☺ lunch & dinner Mon-Sat May-Sep
This ever-busy place features a famous produce shop (p138) and a restaurant

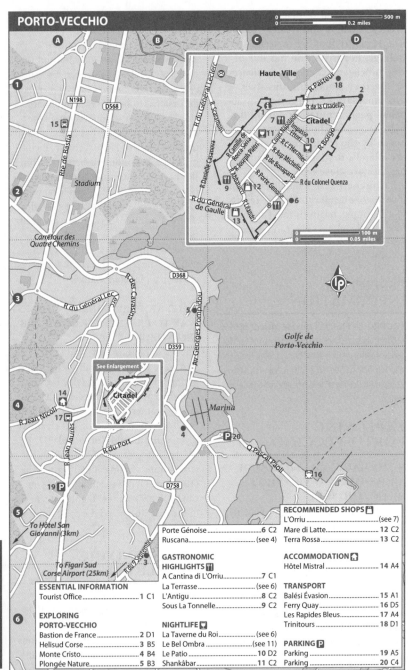

next door. And what a restaurant! This is the gourmet choice in Porto-Vecchio, with excellent meat dishes, cheese and charcuterie platters, homemade ravioli with Brocciu, grilled goat with myrtle, and great salads. Wine enthusiasts will love the selection of local wines; don't worry about having too many to choose from, as many are available by the glass (from €3.50).

☙ LA TERRASSE €€

☎ 04 95 70 47 98; Porte Génoise; mains €15-28, menu €34; ☽ lunch & dinner daily Apr-Jun & Sep-Feb, dinner daily Jul-Aug

Tucked away in the Porte Génoise, La Terrasse is one of Porto-Vecchio's top restaurants. The menu focuses on fish and meat renditions of Corsican staples that sing in the mouth, and desserts are divine. The setting is cosy and, best of all, the views over the gulf are fabulous. Needless to say, the accompanying wine list is top class.

☙ L'ANTIGU €€

☎ 04 95 70 39 33; rue Borgo; mains €19-28, menus €18-23; ☽ lunch Mon-Sat, dinner daily

You can't go wrong at this Porto-Vecchio favourite, where the sun-drenched terrace overlooks the gulf. Sink your teeth into a tender veal fillet or a succulent braised pork tenderloin, but don't miss the desserts – the vanilla-poached Williams pear with gingerbread and Corsican honey ice cream provides a flavour explosion.

☙ SOUS LA TONNELLE €

☎ 04 95 70 02 17; rue Abbatucci; mains €13-25; ☽ lunch & dinner daily Jul-Aug, closed Sun & Mon Sep-Jun

Whether you dine alfresco on a little vine-clad pavement terrace or inside the pretty dining room decorated with earthy tones, this cosy eatery is a treat. In a town where the bar is set high, Sous la Tonnelle still manages to delight diners with a fine selection of fish and meat dishes. If you want a recommendation, try the *petti morti* (veal stew with olives, mushrooms and maize flour sprinkled with grated cheese and browned in the oven).

NIGHTLIFE

The superclub Via Notte (p140) is located to the south of Porto-Vecchio.

☙ LA TAVERNE DU ROI

☎ 04 95 70 41 31; Porte Génoise

This intimate, inviting place tucked into the Porte Génoise features traditional Corsican singing with guitar accompaniment on most nights. The show starts at 10pm.

☙ LE BEL OMBRA

☎ 04 95 70 52 21; place de la République

This busy bar has a wide terrace, great for nursing a beer and watching life go by on the square before you. It's a popular stopoff for the preclubbing crowd in summer.

☙ LE PATIO

☎ 04 95 28 06 99; www.lepatiocorse.com; impasse Ettori

The number-one nocturnal magnet for the hip crowd, this spot sets the tone with lounge music, a sleek bar and a cluster of trendy gazebos on a square. It's the sort of place that has a great atmosphere most nights of the week, but you'll also find it an excellent spot to sip an alfresco cocktail during the day.

☙ SHANKÂBAR

☎ 04 95 70 06 53; place de la République

The Shanka is a typical *avant-boîte* (preclub bar). Very popular and hip.

THE SOUTH

RECOMMENDED SHOPS

♥ L'ORRIU

☎ 04 95 70 26 21; cours Napoléon; ☼ May-Sep

This treasure trove of regional Corsican products is filled with hams hanging enticingly from the ceiling and cheeses sitting on the shelves, plus wines, jams, sweets and terrines.

♥ MARE DI LATTE

☎ 04 95 23 03 34; 4 cours Napoléon

This boutique stocking items by Corsican designer Stephanie de Peretti is a popular haunt for fashion-conscious ladies. Signature items include elegant handbags, colourful scarves, stunning robes in simple shades and sensational too-good-to-get-wet swimming costumes.

♥ TERRA ROSSA

☎ 04 95 70 04 35; www.terrarossa.fr; 18 rue du Général de Gaulle

It's all about olive oil in this elegant boutique. It sells the highest-quality olive oils – from Corsica, of course – as well as olive products in many guises. Go in, have a look and buy something – it's impossible not to.

TRANSPORT

TO/FROM THE AIRPORT

AIR // Figari Sud Corse airport (FSC; www .figari.aeroport.fr) is about 25km from Porto-Vecchio, near the village of Figari. See p266 for details. There's no public transport to/from the airport. A taxi ride costs about €30.

GETTING AROUND

BUS // Les Rapides Bleus (☎ 04 95 70 10 36; rue Jean Jaurès) operates a daily service (Monday to Saturday in winter) to Bastia (three hours) via Solenzara, Ghisonaccia, Aléria and Moriani. It also operates a

shuttle service to Plage de Palombaggia and Plage de Santa Giulia in summer (€9 return, four daily). **Balési Évasion** (☎ 04 95 70 15 55; rte de Bastia) has buses to Ajaccio via the Alta Rocca (L'Ospédale, Zonza, Quenza and Aullène). Buses depart daily in July and August, and on Monday and Friday during the rest of the year. Eurocorse operates two daily services (one on Sunday) to Ajaccio via Sartène and Propriano in July and August. From September to June, it runs one daily service from Monday to Saturday. In the other direction, buses run twice daily to Bonifacio (30 minutes) in July and August (once daily from Monday to Saturday the rest of the year). You can purchase tickets from **Trinitours** (☎ 04 95 71 24 64; rue Pasteur) or on the bus.

CAR // Driving through Porto-Vecchio is a nightmare in summer.

PARKING // Parking in the centre is almost impossible in the high season. Use one of the few car parks dotted around town (from €2 per hour) or find a hotel that provides a parking space.

BOAT // Boats run from the ferry quay to Marseille; see p268 for details.

AROUND PORTO-VECCHIO

· · · · · ·

SOUTH OF PORTO-VECCHIO

From Porto-Vecchio, follow the N198 to the south and turn left onto rte de Palombaggia (it's signposted), which winds around the coast. This is the Corsican paradise you've been daydreaming about: stylish accommodation, fragrant maquis, gin-clear waters, long stretches of sand edged with pine trees, and splendiferous views over the Îles Cerbicale. Prepare yourself for soggy fingers and toes: you'll probably spend as much time in the water here as out of it. Don't expect a

Robinson Crusoe experience in summer, though – this area is chock-full of cars and sun seekers.

Les Rapides Bleus operates a shuttle service to Plage de Palombaggia and Plage de Santa Giulia in summer; see opposite for details.

♥ BEACHES // TAKE YOUR PICK OF HIP, SECRET, SCENIC EXPANSES OF SAND

This is it – that celebrity of all of the beaches of southern Corsica, the **Plage de Palombaggia**. Immense, crystalline and glossy, it doesn't disappoint the bevy of swimmers and snorkellers who dabble in its gorgeous, lucent depths – nor the loads of sun worshippers who lay themselves out like sardines on the ribbon of white sand. South of Plage de Palombaggia, **Plage de la Folacca** (also known as Plage de Tamaricciu) is no less idyllic. South of Plage de la Folacca, **Plage d'Asciaghju**, which is also very popular for swimming and sunbathing, comes into view. Continue a few kilometres further south over a pass called Bocca di L'Oru and you'll come across another gem of a beach, the gently curving **Plage de Santa Giulia**, lapped by shallow, azure waters against an amphitheatre of maquis- (and villa-!) covered hills.

THE SOUTH

Here's a secret: if you're after more seclusion, head to **Plage de Cateraggio**, which is often overlooked by visitors because getting there involves a 20-minute walk through the maquis. The trail head starts near Ranch Campo; you'll need to ask for directions, as the trail isn't signposted.

☙ WATER SPORTS // DIVE UNDER OR FLOAT ON THE DEEP-BLUE MED

If just splashing around in turquoise waters ceases to do it for you, there are excellent diving options near the Îles Cerbicale, a short distance offshore from Plage de Palombaggia. There's also the photogenic wreck of *La Pinella,* close to Porto-Vecchio's harbour, which is suitable for beginners. Dive centres with good credentials include **Kallisté Plongée** (☎ 04 95 70 44 59, 06 09 84 91 51; www .corsicadiving.com; Plage de Palombaggia; ☉ Jun-Sep) and **Plongée Nature** (Map p136; ☎ 06 64 43 26 04, 06 19 26 26 51; www.plongee-nature.com; av Georges Pompidou, Porto-Vecchio; ☉ Apr-Oct). Both charge about €55 for an introductory dive; single dives start at €40.

The Golfe de Santa Giulia is a fantastic playground for windsurfers, sailors and canoeists, especially beginners and children. **Club Nautique Santa Giulia** (☎ 06 22 74 49 53; www.club-nautique.fr; Plage de Santa Giulia; ☉ Jun-Sep), right on the beach at Santa Giulia, offers windsurfer (€16 per hour) and catamaran (from €33 per hour) rentals, as well as windsurfing and sailing lessons. Canoes and pedal boats are also available (from €12 per hour).

☙ HORSE RIDING // GALLOP ALONG A SECLUDED BEACH

What about cantering or galloping along a deserted Plage de Palombaggia in the early morning, or the lesser-known Plage de Cataraggio in the late afternoon? It's a truly unforgettable experience. Contact **Ranch Campo** (☎ 04 95 70 13 27, 06 03 07 08 04; www.ranchcampo.com; rte de Palombaggia), which offers guided rides for about €20 per hour.

☙ COSTA MARINA // SMART EATERY WITH AMPLE VIEWS

Brimming with good cheer, this hip **eatery** (☎ 04 95 70 36 57; rte de Palombaggia; mains €10-24; ☉ dinner Apr–mid-Oct) overlooking the coastal road features excellent grilled meat, fish dishes, pasta (the tortellini with gorgonzola tastes divine) and pizza. Top marks for wooden furniture and a breezy terrace. Smart service too.

☙ TAMARICCIU // THE TRENDIEST PAILLOTE FOR MILES AROUND

This furiously fashionable *paillotte* (beach restaurant) awash with teak fittings is right on the beach. The point here is to see and be seen, and in summer getting a table on the terrace can be a titanic struggle. How about the food? **Tamaricciu** (☎ 04 95 70 49 89; www.tamaricciu .com; rte de Palombaggia; mains €16-32; ☉ lunch daily mid-Apr–Jun & Sep–mid-Oct, lunch & dinner daily Jul & Aug) specialises in the greats of Mediterranean cuisine: grilled fish (sea bass, John Dory), meat dishes (lamb, beef) and pasta, all beautifully presented. The lunchtime menu also includes pizza served bubbling hot. Service is brisk.

☙ VIA NOTTE // CLUBBING ON A GRAND SCALE

This is the hottest **club** (☎ 04 95 72 02 12; www.vianotte.com; rte de Porra) in Corsica, and one of the most famous in the Med. With superstar DJs and up to 5000 revellers most nights in summer, it has to be seen to be believed. It's in the open air and there's even a swimming pool.

THE SOUTH

NORTH OF PORTO-VECCHIO

To the north, the coast has plenty to set your heart aflutter: liberally sprinkled with perfect coves and grandiose bays, turquoise waters and crystalline beaches, it's a powerful fix for any beach addict. There are a few hidden treasures in the hinterland too, including the Vallée du Cavu and some excellent wineries.

♥ BAYS & BEACHES // LOSE TRACK OF TIME ON FABULOUS BEACHES

There's an embarrassment of riches when it comes to choosing a fine stretch of sand. Take the N198 to the north. After a few kilometres, turn east onto the D468 towards the beaches at Punta di Benedettu, Cala Rossa and Baie de San Ciprianu. **Punta di Benedettu** is small and low-key, **Plage de Cala Rossa** has two excellent *paillottes*, and the immense **Plage de San Ciprianu** is a classic beauty. Where else can you swim, snorkel, paddle, windsurf and eat fresh fish all in one day?

Further to the north is the stunning **Golfe de Pinarello** (Pinaraddu), with its **Genoese tower** and yet more beautiful expanses of sand lapped by shallow waters.

♥ NAUTICAL ACTIVITIES // GLIDE ON UNBELIEVABLY AZURE BAYS

There's plenty to do in the Golfe de Pinarello and the Baie de San Cipriani if you want to get wet. Both gulfs are prime areas for all sorts of water sports, including windsurfing, sailing and kayaking. Recommended nautical centres include **École de Voile San Ciprianu** (☎ 04 95 71 00 48, 06 14 67 91 55; Plage de San Ciprianu), 10km north of Porto-Vecchio, and **École de**

Voile de Pinarello (☎ 06 86 85 62 08; Plage de Pinarello; ☻ Apr-Oct). The centres rent windsurfing equipment, catamarans, kayaks and pedal boats. Private and group sailing and windsurfing lessons are also available.

Based at the southern tip of the Golfe de Pinarello, **Sportsica** (☎ 06 24 26 51 83; sport.sica@orange.fr; Plage de Pinarello; ☻ Jun-Sep) offers kayaking with a difference. On excursions around Île de Pinarello (inaccessible on foot), the guide imparts environmental and geological knowledge, and you'll have the opportunity to disembark on the island and make an easy five-minute walk up to the Genoese tower. The half-day tour (€30) includes swimming stops in secluded coves. Good news for families: this outfit has 'tri-yaks' (kayaks built for three), ideal for two parents and a kid.

♥ VALLÉE DU CAVU // PICNIC IN A LITTLE-TRAMPED VALLEY

Outdoor activities, emerald-green rock pools and grandiose scenery are the hallmarks of this little-travelled valley, a few kilometres east of Ste-Lucie de Porto-Vecchio. Walk along the forest track and find a series of languid *vasques* (natural pools) where you can lounge in crystal-clear waters and picnic on perfect stone slabs.

At the entrance of the valley, **A Tyroliana** (☎ 06 18 40 44 39, 06 11 63 06 68; ☻ 9am-5pm mid-Jun–mid-Sep) is an atmospheric *parc aventure* set amid stately maritime pine trees. With four circuits of varying difficulty (from €12), as well as a baby *parc* for children (€6), it's a great way to commune with nature.

Cycling is a good way to explore this scenic valley. **Sportsica** (☎ 06 24 26 51 83; sport.sica@orange.fr) offers relaxed rides on the forest road along the Cavu river, with

THE SOUTH

swimming stops. Kids over eight years are welcome. The meeting point is at the *parc aventure*.

To get to the valley, take the D168a and drive past the village of Tagliu Rossu.

☙ DOMAINE DE TORRACCIA // SAMPLE ONE OF THE BEST CORSICAN WINES

A mandatory stop for wine lovers, the well-established **Domaine de Torraccia** (☎ 04 95 71 43 50; Lecci; ☺ 8am-8pm Mon-Sat & 8am-1pm Sun Jul-Aug, Mon-Sat 8am-noon & 2-6pm Sep-Jun) produces top-quality, organic wines. The Cuvée Oriu (red, rosé and white) is tops. You can also buy the winery's excellent olive oil.

☙ CASTELLU D'ARAGGIO // TAKE A LESSON IN HISTORY

For some cultural sustenance, make a beeline for the prehistoric site of **Castellu d'Araggio** (admission free), about 3km off the N198, high in the hills. This small castle is less visited than the sites of Cucuruzzu and Capula, but it is well preserved and the views from the top of the thick walls over the Golfe de Porto-Vecchio are spectacular. It takes about 30 minutes to get to the castle from the village of Araggio.

The journey also makes for a great two-hour horse-riding excursion – there's something magical about riding up to the ruins on horseback. Contact the friendly **Centre Équestre d'Araggio** (☎ 06 14 58 66 25; rte de Gialla, Arragio; rides per hour €17; ☺ year-round), which has horses suitable for all levels of experience, as well as for children.

☙ 37°2 // FRESH FISH AND PIZZA ON THE BEACH

A thong's throw from the Ranch'o, this **paillotte** (☎ 04 95 71 70 24; Plage de Cala Rossa; mains €8-20; ☺ lunch & dinner May-Sep) is a casual hang-out with a light, satisfying menu: dishes such as pizza and grilled sea bass are flawlessly cooked and beautifully presented. Comfy mattresses just in front of the restaurant are a post-lunch-siesta delight.

☙ LE FIGUIER // MELLOW DINING IN A ROUNDABOUT WAY

The location of this **restaurant** (☎ 04 95 72 08 78; rte de Cala Rossa; mains €10-25; ☺ dinner daily, lunch Tue-Sun May-Sep) – near a roundabout – doesn't scream 'holiday', but the soothing decor (granite walls, vegetation, wooden furniture), mellow atmosphere and food offer ample compensation. The menu explores a range of options, from truly finger-licking pizza (don't miss *Le Figuier,* topped with cured meat and mozzarella) and grilled meats to salads and a dozen carpaccios.

☙ LE ROUF // CREATIVITY AND ULTRAFRESH CLASSICS

Of the row of eateries boasting lovely terraces overlooking the Baie de Pinarello, **Le Rouf** (☎ 04 95 71 50 48; Plage de Pinarello; mains €10-35, lunch menu €14; ☺ lunch & dinner May-Sep) has a hip touch that makes it stand out. The 'gastronomic' menu specialises in ultrafresh *pêche du jour* (catch of the day) and high-quality meat dishes. The standard menu is a great combination of creative dishes (crab with avocado, semibaked red tuna), and timeless classics such as beef or fish tartare, pizza and salads.

☙ RANCH'O // CATCH OF THE DAY BESIDE THE BAY

This upmarket **paillotte** (☎ 04 95 71 62 67; Plage de Cala Rossa; mains €15-26, menus €24-29; ☺ lunch & dinner May-Sep) occupies a privileged spot on the beach – if the wooden terrace was any nearer to the water

THE SOUTH

you'd have to swim to dinner. It has a good reputation for fresh seafood, particularly lobster and *poissons du golfe à la plancha* (grilled local fish), as well as pasta.

L'ALTA ROCCA

• • • • • •

The Alta Rocca pulls out all the stops when it comes to dramatic scenery. A world away from the bling and bustle of the coast, this is a spot where you can really feel a sense of wilderness. Located at the south of the long dorsal spine that traverses the island, it's a bewildering combination of dense forests and granite villages strung over rocky ledges. And there's the pièce de résistance: the iconic Aiguilles de Bavella. These serrated rock towers are staggeringly photogenic.

The region also musters up a handful of well-preserved megalithic remains that are must sees for anyone with an interest in Corsica's ancient civilisations. If you're looking for light adventure, there are plenty of options, from hiking and canyoning to horse riding and climbing.

ESSENTIAL INFORMATION

TOURIST INFORMATION // Tourist office (☎ 04 95 78 56 33; alta-rocca@wanadoo.fr; Zonza; 8.30am-1pm & 2-6.30pm Mon-Sat mid-Jun–mid-Sep) In the centre of Zonza. Has some information and brochures, and a leaflet detailing walking trails in the area.

TRANSPORT

BUS // Alta Rocca Voyages – Ricci (☎ 04 95 78 86 30; www.altarocca-voyages.com) links Ajaccio to Zonza (three hours, daily) via Levie, Ste-Lucie de Tallano, Sartène, Propriano and Olmeto. It also serves the Col de Bavella in July and August. Balési Évasion

(☎ 04 95 70 15 55) serves Porto-Vecchio from Ajaccio, via Aullène, Quenza, Zonza and L'Ospédale; buses run daily from Monday to Saturday in July and August, and on Monday and Friday during the rest of the year. It also serves the Col de Bavella in July and August. **Eurocorse** (☎ 04 95 21 06 30) plies the Ajaccio–Zonza route via Olmeto, Propriano, Sartène, Ste-Lucie de Tallano and Levie (Monday to Saturday).

PARKING // There aren't many designated parking facilities in the villages of the Alta Rocca, so finding parking space might be difficult in summer. The Bavella area is choked with cars and coaches in high season – come early to get a parking space.

L'OSPÉDALE & AROUND

pop 30

If the heat and crowds of Porto-Vecchio get too much for you, escape to the cool, calm surroundings of L'Ospédale, 20km above town via the winding D368. At an altitude of about 1000m, L'Ospédale is blessed with a fabulous location with sweeping views over the Golfe de Porto-Vecchio. It's also close to the Forêt de L'Ospédale, which offers excellent walking opportunities and tranquil picnic spots.

❤ FORÊT DE L'OSPÉDALE //
A GLORIOUS FOREST OF LARICIO PINES

To see the forest's treasures, you'll need to stretch your legs. There's some good walking around the hamlet of **Cartalavonu**, located right in heart of the forest; to get here, take the D368 from L'Ospédale a short way into the forest, then follow the road peeling off to the left. The easy **Sentier des Rochers** (Rocks Path), also known as the Sentier des Tafoni, is an interpretive walk that visits the *tafoni* (cavities) formed in the rocks by erosion. Another superb option is the two-hour hike to the **Punta** di a Vacca Morta (1314m), from where the 360-degree view over the far south is truly sensational.

If you want to see the forest from a Tarzan perspective, **Xtrem Sud** (☎ 04 95 72 12 31; www.xtremsud.com; Forêt de L'Ospédale; adult/child €22/18; ☺ Jun–mid-Sep) has set up a wonderful *parc aventure* in the middle of the forest, just before the Barrage de L'Ospédale when you come from Porto-Vecchio. There are three levels of difficulty and, for the little 'uns (from the age of three), there's a separate baby *parc*. The *parc aventure* also features a lovely *via ferrata* (literally 'iron path'; see p213), which is included in the admission price.

❦ WALKING TO PISCIA DI GALLO // WATERFALLS AND FRESH SENSATIONS

This 90-minute round-trip walk to the Piscia di Gallo waterfall, through pine forests and maquis, begins near a couple of snack bars beside the D368, 1km on from the Barrage de L'Ospédale. The start of the walk is marked by a signpost. You can't descend to the basin itself because it's too steep; you'll have to see the waterfall from a lookout.

❦ U FUNTANONU // WHOLESOME CORSICAN STAPLES IN RUSTIC-CHIC SURROUNDS

On the main drag in the centre of L'Ospédale, **U Funtanonu** (☎ 04 95 70 47 11; mains €15-24, lunch menu €22; ☺ lunch & dinner May-Sep) sits snug in a dining room that combines wooden furniture, beamed ceilings and exposed stone walls with more-contemporary fixtures, such as elegant cutlery and virginal white tablecloths. It's the best place around to try local specialities, such as *terrine de sanglier à la myrte* (wild-boar pâté with myrtle) and ravioli with Brocciu.

❦ LE REFUGE // TRADITIONAL FARE IN REMOTE CARTALAVONU

After a stroll in the majestic Forêt de L'Ospédale or a walk to the Punta di a Vacca Morta, nothing beats digging into a satisfying plate of *petti morti* (veal stew) at this simple yet authentic **inn** (☎ 04 95 70 00 39; mains €15-18; ☺ lunch & dinner May-Oct), bucolically nestled in the forest at Cartalavonu. There are no views to speak of, but the scent of laricio pines will impart an otherworldly quality to your meal.

ZONZA

pop 1800
Somewhere you've seen that stunning photo of a mountain village with the soaring Aiguilles de Bavella as a backdrop. This is Zonza. Truth is, it's hard not to be dazzled by the fabulous backdrop and the uberscenic country lanes that criss-cross the area.

A hub in the Alta Rocca, Zonza is also an excellent place to base yourself, with a good range of accommodation options and eateries.

❦ HORSE RACES // PLACE A BET AT EUROPE'S HIGHEST RACECOURSE

About 2km from Zonza on the road to Bavella, the **Hippodrome de Viseo** (Zonza; www.hippodrome-zonza.fr) is the highest racecourse in Europe (950m), and is very popular among Corsicans from all over the island. The racing season lasts from early July to late August, with meetings held on Sundays. If you're here on a race day, it's well worth joining the throng of betting-crazy locals; the atmosphere is festive and the setting – ensconced in a forest of laricio pines, with the Alta Rocca mountains as a backdrop – is fabulous. For exact dates of meetings, contact the tourist office (p143) in Zonza or check out the website.

🍷 AUBERGE DU SANGLIER // DRINK IN QUINTESSENTIAL ALTA ROCCA VIEWS FROM THE TERRACE

Don't focus on the food in this no-nonsense eatery. What's the pull, then, you may ask? In a word: views. **Auberge du Sanglier** (☎ 04 95 78 67 18; mains €8-15, menus €12-22; ☯ lunch & dinner mid-Mar–Oct) boasts an open-air terrace with pupil-dilating panoramas over the mountain ranges, best appreciated at sunset with a cold Pietra in hand.

🍷 L'AIGLON // PALATE-PLEASING DISHES IN A TIMELESS INTERIOR

Old books, pictures, sturdy tables, a fireplace and low ceilings keep the mood convivial at **L'Aiglon** (☎ 04 95 78 67 79; mains €16-23, menu €23; ☯ lunch & dinner Apr-Oct). The menu here has been thoughtfully and creatively designed: titillate taste buds with, say, the transhumance platter, comprising grilled *figatelli* (liver sausages), chestnut polenta, tomatoes and fresh Brocciu. Do keep space for the homemade sweet treats, though – the *moelleux à la châtaigne et glace aux marrons* (chestnut cake and candied-chestnut ice cream) is a marvel.

QUENZA & AROUND

pop 220

Like nearby Zonza, Quenza has a truly photogenic setting. At an altitude of 813m, the town is cradled by thickly wooded mountains, with the Aiguilles de Bavella looming on the horizon. The air here is intoxicatingly crisp. This little charmer is quieter than Zonza and is popular with walkers.

🍷 CHEZ PIERROT // SOUTHERN CORSICA'S MOST IDIOSYNCRATIC VENTURE

If you're after a typically Corsican atmosphere in the most tranquil location imaginable, look no further than multifaceted **Chez Pierrot** (☎ 04 95 78 63 21; Ghjallicu) run by charismatic Pierrot, a local character who's lived here since childhood. A B&B (see p252), equestrian centre and restaurant, Chez Pierrot is particularly famous for its *table d'hôtes* (evening meals served around a shared table; dinner €23); the unwaveringly authentic menu – including soups, charcuterie, veal or tripe, cheese and homemade cake – is served in a staunchly rustic dining room. Pierrot also offers fantastic horse-riding excursions (about €15 per hour) to rarely visited points around Plateau de Ghjallicu and Plateau du Coscione. It's on Plateau de Ghjallicu, about 5km uphill from Quenza.

🍷 WALKING ON PLATEAU DU COSCIONE // FEEL TRANSPORTED TO THE MONGOLIAN STEPPE

So bucolic. If you've ever fancied tramping on a carpet of cool moss, this is your chance. It's exquisite! The Plateau du Coscione, one of the wildest, eeriest and most tranquil areas in Corsica, comprises undulating, grassy meadows and *pozzines* (small waterholes linked together by rivulets). Reminiscent of Mongolian plateau pastureland, it's home to herds of semiwild horses and cattle in summer. It makes for a fantastic half-day hike.

With your own wheels, start from Chez Pierrot. Follow the road for 6.6km until you reach an abandoned building that used to serve as a ski refuge (it's known as Bucchinera). Leave the car at the car park and just follow the 4WD track – you can't get lost. There's no set itinerary; walk to your heart's content following the tracks that criss-cross the plateau.

LEVIE (LIVIA) & AROUND

pop 720

With an interesting museum and a lovely archaeological site amid superb scenery, Levie is a good place to brush up on your Corsican history. Another reason to linger is A Pignata, possibly the best farm inn in southern Corsica. Culture plus nature plus good food – a perfect equation.

🌱 MUSÉE DE L'ALTA ROCCA // SAY HELLO TO LA DAME DE BONIFACIO

After a long-awaited renovation, the now well-organised **Musée de l'Alta Rocca** (☎ 04 95 78 46 34; admission €4; 🕙 9am-6pm May-Oct, 10am-5pm Tue-Sat Nov-Apr) makes for a perfect introduction to Alta Rocca's (pre)history, geology and culture. The star of the exhibits is La Dame de Bonifacio (Bonifacio Woman), the oldest human remains ever unearthed on Corsica; she is thought to have lived on the island about 8500 years ago.

🌱 PIANU DI LEVIE // EXPERIENCE PREHISTORIC LIFE AT THE CUCURUZZU AND CAPULA ARCHAEOLOGICAL SITES

After a visit to the Musée de l'Alta Rocca, it's time to go out in the field. Even if your interest in ruins is only slight, the enchanting setting and lofty views are reason enough to come to **Pianu di Levie** (☎ 04 95 78 48 21; adult/child €5.50/3; 🕙 9am-6pm Apr, May & Oct, 9am-7pm Jun & Sep, 9am-8pm Jul & Aug), about 7km to the north

of Levie. It comprises two archaeological sites, the *castelli* (castles) of **Cucuruzzu** and **Capula**, connected by an interpretive trail. Both feature well-preserved megalithic remains. The Cucuruzzu site is an interesting example of Bronze Age monumental architecture. Set in a granite wilderness, the ruins indicate that this was the site of an organised community whose activities originally were based on agriculture and animal husbandry, but broadened during the later Bronze Age (1200 to 900 BC) to include milling, pottery and weaving. A 20-minute walk from Cucuruzzu, the Castellu de Capula is somewhat more recent, although it is likely that Cucuruzzu was still in business when it was founded; it is believed that Capula continued to be inhabited into the Middle Ages. The admission price includes the use of an individual audioguide (in English) that brings the castles to life with minilectures on, for example, curiosities of Corsican nature such as *tafoni* and the ubiquitous chestnut tree.

Allow at least a good 1½ hours to tour the site.

🌱 I FRASSEDI // TOP-QUALITY CHEESE AND CHARCUTERIE DIRECT FROM THE PRODUCER

You can't go wrong at this **farm** (☎ 06 12 34 21 71) – this is where locals go when they want to purchase *tomme corse* (semihard ewe's-milk cheese) and goat's cheese (March to September), as well as authentic cured meats (November to April). It's perfect fodder for a DIY meal at nearby Pianu di Levie. If you come in the late afternoon you might see Jacques Viti, the owner, milking the goats. I Frassedi is about 1km before the entrance of the Pianu di Levie archaeological site.

☙ ATELIER DU LOTUS // SEE TRADITIONAL KNIFE MAKERS AT WORK

Don't know what a *curnicciulu* is? It's time to get a hands-on education at the Atelier du Lotus (☎ 04 95 74 05 13; www .couteaulotus.canalblog.com; Levie; ⊙ Mon-Sat year-round). Knife making is a Corsican tradition that had its origins with the shepherds. In this wonderfully authentic workshop, you can see two young Corsican knife makers hot forging, grinding, shaping…. All knives are handmade and incorporate top-quality materials; prices start at €150. Even if you don't buy, it's worth a stop. The workshop is signposted.

☙ A PIGNATA // ENJOY A GARGANTUAN CORSICAN MENU IN LOVELY SURROUNDS

You'll need to fast the day before – lunch and dinner at A Pignata (☎ 04 95 78 41 90; rte du Pianu di Levie; menu €37; ⊙ dinner Fri-Sat & lunch Sat-Sun Mar, lunch & dinner daily Apr-Oct) are fixed seven-course *menus*. From *velouté de potimarron à la châtaigne* (a creamy soup with chestnut and gourd) and oven-baked lamb to cannelloni with Brocciu and cheese platters, this *ferme-auberge* (farm inn) offers a stellar parade of local dishes. Dine in a vast, rustic-style room with a huge fireplace or, in summer, enjoy million-dollar views over the rolling hills of the Alta Rocca from the terrace. A Pignata is also an upmarket B&B (p253).

STE-LUCIE DE TALLANO (SANTA LUCIA DI TALLÀ)

pop 400

Another contender for the title of the prettiest village in the Alta Rocca, Ste-Lucie de Tallano is perched on a ledge above the Vallée du Rizzanese. With its web of quiet streets, its higgledy-piggledy stone houses with reddish-orange tiled roofs, and its main square dominated by *pétanque* players, this immediately likable place couldn't be more *Corse profonde*. Ste-Lucie is also famous for its quality olive oil and, in March, the festival A Festa di l'Oliu Novu, draws crowds from all over Corsica.

☙ THE VILLAGE // MOSEY AROUND A QUINTESSENTIAL ALTA ROCCA VILLAGE

For a village of its size, Ste-Lucie has quite a few monuments worthy of interest, including the well-proportioned Église Ste-Lucie, and the Renaissance-style Couvent St-François, an imposing building scenically positioned at the edge of the village on the road to Levie. Don't miss the Maison Forte, a muscular granite house built to shelter the population in times of danger; it's behind the church.

☙ OLIVE OIL // SHOP FOR THE PERFECT OLIVE OIL

See the green nets that are laid out beneath the olive trees on the outskirts of Ste-Lucie? They catch the falling olives, loosened from the trees with special scissors during the harvest in November. The village's premier sight is the moulin à huile (oil mill).

You'll find a few shops selling olive oil in the village, but they tend to favour quantity rather than quality. Locals recommend buying the oil made by Nepita (☎ 06 87 87 04 28; www.nepita.fr), available either at the *épicerie* (grocery store) on the main square or directly from the producer in the nearby hamlet of Poggio di Tallano. This olive oil (€19 per bottle) really is exceptional, and it's organic to boot.

🌱 A FESTA DI L'OLIU NOVU // MINGLE WITH OLIVE-OIL PRODUCERS AT A COUNTRY FAIR

Every year on the last weekend of March, Ste-Lucie brings together olive-oil producers from all over Corsica. Up to 8000 visitors join in the fun, which includes tastings and craft exhibitions.

🌱 CHEZ DUMÉ // A SLICE OF LOCAL LIFE

This no-nonsense **eatery** (☎ 04 95 78 80 67; mains €6-15; ☽ lunch & dinner May-Oct), about 100m from the main junction, won't provide culinary revelations, but it is high on atmosphere. The terrace is a good vantage point to watch the *pétanque* players on the square.

COL & AIGUILLES DE BAVELLA

For sheer visual pleasure, the Aiguilles de Bavella (Bavella Needles) are unsurpassable. Jabbing the skyline at an altitude of more than 1600m, these granite pinnacles resemble a giant shark's jaw and are, unsurprisingly, an all-time photographic favourite. About 8km northeast of Zonza, they are best observed from the Col de Bavella (1218m).

Within easy reach from the coastal cities of the south, the Col de Bavella is a big-ticket attraction in the high season. Try to come in spring or early autumn; in summer you'll spend your time dodging fellow visitors and struggling for parking. On 5 August, the Pélerinage Notre-Dame-des-Neiges – a pilgrimage to the miracle-working Madonna, whose statue stands at the *col* (pass) – is a hugely popular event.

Bavella and adventure go hand in hand. Walking, swinging through a *parc aventure,* rock climbing, canyoning, or

simply picnicking…it can all be done in the vicinity of the *col.* From the *col,* you can make an astonishing 30km descent to Solenzara following the D268; see p166 for more.

🌱 ADVENTURE SPORTS // GET ACTIVE IN GRANDIOSE SCENERY

Once you've had your fill of gorgeous panoramas of the Bavella Needles, you might want to explore the area in more depth, and there's no better way to do it than canyoning. Of all the stellar spots for canyoning in Corsica, the Bavella area tops the list, with three major canyons: Canyon de la Vacca, Canyon de la Purcaraccia and Canyon de la Pulischella. They're all very atmospheric (and refreshing!); you can expect rappelling, various jumps and leaps into crystal-clear natural pools, with the added thrill of fantastic views. All canyons are accessible to beginners and children, provided they're reasonably fit. Canyoning outings last about half a day and are guided by a qualified instructor. Plan on €50 per person.

Blessed with supreme granite monoliths, sheer spires, near-vertical walls, the Bavella area is also a climbing hot spot, with dozens of mind-boggling ascents graded 3 to 8 (easy to difficult). For novices, there's also a *falaise-école* (training cliff).

There are also excellent hiking options in the vicinity of the Col de Bavella, with well-marked trails suitable for all levels of fitness. The most popular walk goes to the Trou de la Bombe, a hole in a ridge southeast of the *col* (about two hours return).

In search of new sensations? Try the *parc aventure* set up by **Corsica Madness** (☎ 06 13 22 95 06, 04 95 78 61 76; www.corsica madness.com; per person €15-25; ☽ mid-Jun–mid-Sep), about 2km from Col de Bavella in the direction of Zonza; look for the kiosk by the roadside and the sign Corsica Madness. The main draw is the sensational setting, with the Aiguilles de Bavella forming a perfect backdrop. There are three different circuits of varying levels of difficulty, but no baby *parc* for toddlers.

Major outdoor-activity operators include **Corsica Madness** (☎ 06 13 22 95 06, 04 95 78 61 76; www.corsicamadness.com; Zonza), **Corsica Forest** (☎ 06 16 18 00 58; www.corsica-forest.com; Solenzara) and **Xtrem Sud** (☎ 04 95 72 12 31, 06 18 97 03 46; www.xtremsud.com; Forêt de L'Ospédale).

❦ AUBERGE DU COL DE BAVELLA // TRADITIONAL FARE IN A TYPICAL CORSICAN INN

If you need to recharge the batteries after all that exertion, this **inn** (☎ 04 95 72 09 87; www.auberge-bavella.com; mains €9-17, menus €15-22; ☺ lunch & dinner Apr-Oct) might just be the ticket. Carnivores will find nirvana here, with megasized *côte de boeuf à la moelle* (rib of beef with marrowbone) and faultless local charcuterie. It's best to come here for dinner to avoid the coach parties in summer and, if the owners are in the right mood, you might enjoy a festive *soirée corse* with guitar music and Corsican songs.

THE EAST

3 PERFECT DAYS

🌱 DAY 1 // ON HORSEBACK IN THE HILLS
Exploring the Morianincu is like stepping back in time, so the best way to experience it is on horseback (p158). Spend a morning in the saddle enjoying the cool green shade of the region's chestnut forests, then switch to car or bicycle for a jaunt along the Corniche de la Castagniccia (p156) to the pretty little village of Cervione (opposite). Take in the church and museum, or just hang out in one of the village cafes, before having dinner at Aux 3 Fourchettes (p156).

🌱 DAY 2 // HISTORY AND HILLTOP VILLAGES
Take advantage of the cool of the morning to explore the ancient Roman site at Aléria (p163), then enjoy a leisurely lunch at the floating seafood restaurant Aux Coquillages de Diane (p163). In the afternoon, escape the heat with a driving tour around the pretty hilltop villages of the Fiumorbu (p164), perhaps taking a dip in the Abatescu river at Catastaju.

🌱 DAY 3 // MESSING ABOUT ON THE RIVER
Wake up over coffee and croissants at Solenzara's Glacier du Port (p165), then head up the valley for some aerial fun and games at the Corsica Forest Parc Aventure (p166). Spread a picnic lunch on the riverbank and spend the afternoon cooling off in one of the Solenzara river's perfect natural swimming pools (p166), then return to town for a slap-up seafood dinner at La Fonderie (p167).

TRANSPORT

BUS // **Rapides Bleus** (☎ 04 95 31 03 79; www
.kallistour.com) buses, operated by Corsicatours, run
along the east coast between Bastia and Porto Vecchio
(three hours), calling at Moriani-Plage, Cateraggio (for
Aléria), Ghisonaccia, Solenzara and several other destinations; it runs daily in summer, and Monday to Saturday
between mid-September and mid-June. Bikes can be
carried for an extra charge. See p163 for other bus services to/from the Costa Serena and Côte des Nacres.

LA COSTA
VERDE

· · · · · ·

**The Costa Verde, which stretches
south from Folelli to the Phare
d'Alistro, and inland to the hill villages of Cervione and the Morianincu, has a lopsided charm. While the
coastal section of this microregion
is nothing to write home about, the
mountainous hinterland is dazzlingly
beautiful, with a series of *villages
perchés* (perched villages) strung
along forest-clad ridges, a fistful of
religious buildings steeped in history,
and glorious coastal panoramas.**

Although it's less than half an hour's
drive from Bastia, this little-known corner of Corsica falls below the radar for
many travellers – not that we're complaining. Another pull is the smattering
of quality restaurants and cute *chambres
d'hôtes* (B&Bs), plus lots of easy hiking.
Bring a good map and start exploring.

ESSENTIAL INFORMATION

TOURIST INFORMATION // Costa Verde
Tourist Office (☎ 04 95 38 41 73; www.costa
verde-corsica.com; N198, Moriani-Plage; ⏱ 9am-1pm &
3-8pm Mon-Sat, 9am-1pm Sun Jul & Aug, 9am-noon &
2-6pm Mon-Fri Sep-Jun)

CERVIONE

pop 1200
The liveliest of the Costa Verde's inland
villages, Cervione is special: the setting is
enchanting, with neat stone houses hud-
dled around a cathedral, a small maze
of alleys and archways to explore, and a
main street lined with cafes on one side
and stunning views on the other.

EXPLORING CERVIONE

❦ **LOCAL CHURCHES //** **RELIGIOUS
ARCHITECTURE, COLOURFUL
FRESCOS AND TRADITIONAL
MUSIC**
You can't miss the yellow facade and
majestic bell tower of the **Cathédrale
St-Érasme** (place de l'Église), one of Corsica's
earliest baroque churches. Dating from
the first half of the 18th century, it boasts
an impressive black-and-white marble
floor, a magnificent baroque organ and
beautifully carved wooden choir stalls.
From late June to early September the
cathedral hosts regular concerts of choral
music and performances of traditional
Corsican polyphonic chants.

A hidden gem that is well worth a
detour, the Romanesque **Chapelle Ste-
Christine** harbours fabulous frescos
from the 15th century, which adorn the
twin apses inside and show scenes from
the life of Christ. The chapel is about
3km from Cervione; take the road to
Prunete for about 500m, then follow the
signs for Cappella Santa Cristina. The
key should be in the door.

❦ **MUSÉE DE L'ADECEC //** **LEARN
ABOUT THE ISLAND'S RURAL PAST**
Housed in the 16th-century former residence of the bishop of Aléria, the **Musée
de l'ADECEC** (☎ 04 95 38 12 83; place du Musée;

(Continued on page 156)

THE EAST

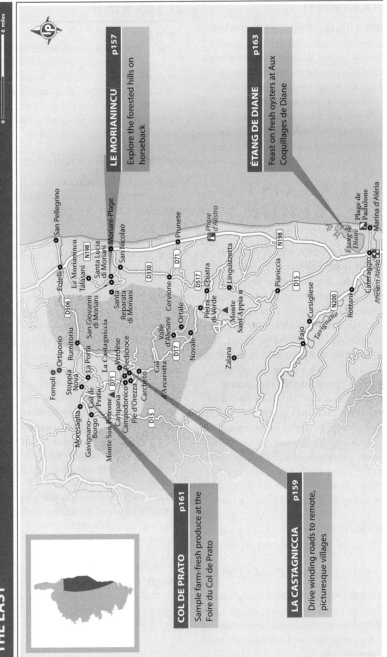

LE MORIANINCU p157

Explore the forested hills on horseback

ÉTANG DE DIANE p163

Feast on fresh oysters at Aux Coquillages de Diane

COL DE PRATO p161

Sample farm-fresh produce at the Foire du Col de Prato

LA CASTAGNICCIA p159

Drive winding roads to remote, picturesque villages

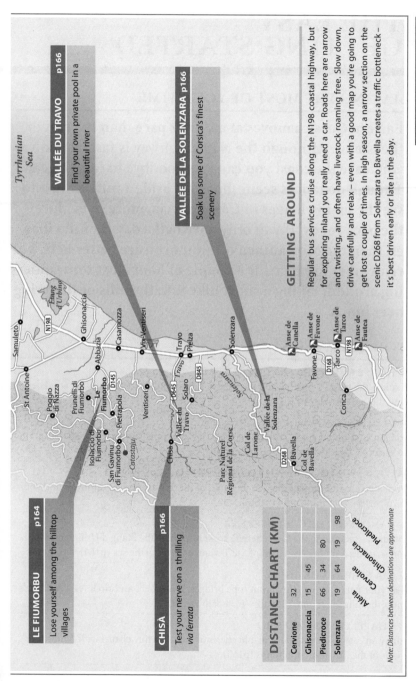

VALLÉE DU TRAVO   p166

Find your own private pool in a beautiful river

VALLÉE DE LA SOLENZARA p166

Soak up some of Corsica's finest scenery

LE FIUMORBU   p164

Lose yourself among the hilltop villages

CHISÀ   p166

Test your nerve on a thrilling *via ferrata*

GETTING AROUND

Regular bus services cruise along the N198 coastal highway, but for exploring inland you really need a car. Roads here are narrow and twisting, and often have livestock roaming free. Slow down, drive carefully and relax – even with a good map you're going to get lost a couple of times. In high season, a narrow section on the scenic D268 from Solenzara to Bavella creates a traffic bottleneck – it's best driven early or late in the day.

DISTANCE CHART (KM)

	Aléria	Cervione	Ghisonaccia	Piedicroce
Cervione	32			
Ghisonaccia	15	45		
Piedicroce	66	34	80	
Solenzara	19	64	19	98

Note: Distances between destinations are approximate

THE EAST

THE EAST
GETTING STARTED

MAKING THE MOST OF YOUR TIME

Eastern Corsica moves at a slower pace than the rest of
the island. Although the N198 highway is fast, as soon as
you leave the coast you can kiss goodbye to fourth gear.
Though distances seem short, set aside a full day just to
see the main villages in Castagniccia, more to explore
the back roads. If you only have half a day for hill villages, then the Morianincu or Fiumorbu are better bets, but
remember to put aside a couple of hours just for wandering around, taking a short hike into the hills or lingering
over lunch.

TOP ACTIVITIES

♥ HORSE RIDING IN THE COSTA VERDE
Explore the Costa Verde hills on horseback, riding cool, shaded trails that wind deep
into the chestnut forests (p158).

♥ CLIMBING MONTE SAN PETRONE
Pull on your hiking boots and head for the hills, for a challenging climb to the summit
of eastern Corsica's favourite mountain (p161).

♥ WILD SWIMMING IN THE SOLENZARA
Pack a picnic and wander the granite banks of the Solenzara river until you find your
own perfect swimming pool (p166).

♥ CANOEING THE COSTA SERENA
Paddle a canoe along the Costa Serena coast to explore the Étang d'Urbino and Pinia
forest, or descend the last 10km of the Tavignano river to the sea (p164).

♥ VIA FERRATA DE CHISÀ
Test your nerve on the Himalayan rope bridges, spiderwebs and zip lines of Corsica's
most thrilling *via ferrata* (literally, 'iron path'; p166).

♥ CHAPELLE SANT'ALESSIO
Enjoy an easy hike past 100-year-old chestnut trees to a tiny chapel with fantastic
views of the Corsican mountains (p160).

GETTING AWAY FROM IT ALL

The coast is the busiest part of eastern Corsica – to escape the crowds, head inland.

★ **Mountain villages** Lose yourself among the winding back roads of the Castagniccia or the Fiumorbu and discover sleepy hilltop villages where time seems to move more slowly (p159, p164)

★ **Country hikes** The hills of eastern Corsica are a hiker's paradise – every village is a starting point for walks both short and long. Pack a picnic and head for the remote Chapelle Sant'Alessio (p160)

★ **River swimming** Discover your own private swimming pool amid the smooth granite slabs of the Travo river (p166)

FESTIVALS & EVENTS

There are a few local events worth thinking about in advance.

★ **A Merendella in Castagniccia** Festival celebrating regional cuisine, held in Piedicroce over the Easter weekend (p159)

★ **Marché d'Arcarotta** Every Sunday in July and August there's a market devoted to local produce at the Col d'Arcarotta (p160)

★ **Foire du Col de Prato** Lively agricultural fair held on the last weekend of July or the first weekend in August (p161)

★ **Fiera di a Nuciola** Hazelnut festival held in Cervione on the fourth weekend in August (p156)

TOP EATING EXPERIENCES

❦ **A MANDRIA DE SÉBASTIEN**
Traditional Corsican cuisine in a rustic cottage (p167)

❦ **LA FONDERIE**
Gourmet dining near the marina (p167)

❦ **AUX COQUILLAGES DE DIANE**
Eat oysters at a floating restaurant (p163)

❦ **AUBERGE DES DEUX VALLÉES**
Try lamb roasted with chestnut honey (p162)

❦ **AUX 3 FOURCHETTES**
Homemade charcuterie in a family-run restaurant (p156)

❦ **SANT' ANDRIA**
Quality food with a quality view (p162)

RESOURCES

★ **Castagniccia** (www.castagniccia.fr) Official tourist office site for La Castagniccia

★ **Costa Serena** (www.corsica-costaserena.com) Tourist information on Costa Serena

★ **Costa Verde** (www.costaverde-corsica.com) Useful guide to the Costa Verde micro-region

★ **Côte des Nacres** (www.cotedesnacres.com, in French) Tourist info for Côte des Nacres

★ **IGN 1:25000 Maps** Map sheets 4349OT and 4351OT are essential for exploring the back roads and hiking trails of Castagniccia and Le Morianincu

(Continued from page 151)

adult/child €4/3; ⊗ 9am-noon & 2-6pm Mon-Sat) is dedicated to traditional Corsican culture, and offers a fascinating insight into the island way of life in the 19th and early 20th centuries. The highlights include an exhibition on winemaking and distilling, and a re-creation of a blacksmith's forge.

❦ CORNICHE DE LA CASTAGNICCIA // SOAK UP THE SCENERY ALONG THIS SPECTACULAR ROAD

The D330 road, known as the Corniche de la Castagniccia, threads for 5km across the mountainside from Cervione to San Nicolao. Whether you walk, cycle or drive, it offers a superb panorama over the coastal plain and the sea before reaching the ribbonlike Cascade de l'Ucelluline, about 1.5km before San Nicolao. Nestled in a gorge between two road tunnels, the falls mark the start of an exciting canyoning descent, and are spectacularly floodlit at night in July and August. The waterfall's name comes from the Corsican word for 'fledgling', a reference to the hundreds of crag martins that build their nests on the surrounding cliffs in early summer.

About 20m past the bridge (heading towards San Nicolao), a steep, narrow path on the left leads up to a shady nook beside the stream, overlooking the bridge down below – the perfect spot for a picnic with a view.

❦ HAZELNUTS // GO NUTS ABOUT THE LOCAL DELICACY

After three successive years of hard frosts wiped out the local citrus orchards in 1905–07, the fruit growers of Cervione turned to *la noisette* (the hazelnut) for salvation, and by the 1940s the plump and flavoursome *noisettes de Cervione*

were much in demand among French pâtissiers, restaurateurs and gourmands.

The industry tailed off after WWII but has been revived in recent years; since 2000 it has been celebrated annually in the Fiera di a Nuciola (Fête de la Noisette, Hazelnut Festival). During the fourth weekend in August the place de l'Église and La Traverse are crowded with stalls displaying the wares of local producers and artisans – roasted hazelnuts, hazelnut oil, hazelnut paste, hazelnut flour, and countless cakes, candies and pastries – and there are tastings in the town hall, concerts in the church, and folk music and kids' events in the streets, all rounded off with a fireworks display on Sunday night.

If you can't make it for the festival, you can buy hazelnut-based goodies (and other local foodstuffs) at Buttega di l'Artisgiani di Cervioni (place de l'Église; ⊗ 10.30am-12.30pm & 4-8pm Mon-Sat).

GASTRONOMIC HIGHLIGHTS

❦ AUX 3 FOURCHETTES €

☎ 04 95 38 14 86; place de l'Église; mains €8-13, menu €15; ⊗ lunch & dinner

Tucked beneath the cathedral (literally – the rustic dining room is in a vault beneath the cathedral floor), this friendly family-run restaurant serves up hearty local fare such as wild boar stew, pork cutlets with butter beans, chestnut fritters, and fruit from the garden, as well as homemade charcuterie, wine and eau-de-vie. Grab a table on the cute little vine-shaded terrace beside the square.

❦ U CASONE €

☎ 04 95 38 10 47; off place de l'Église; mains €5-17, menus €12.50-20; ⊗ lunch & dinner Tue-Sun

Along an alley off the village square, with a terrace shaded by a huge lime tree, this pleasant little restaurant offers a menu that ranges from pizzas (from €5!) expertly cooked in a wood-fired oven to palate-pleasing fish and meat dishes. Tuck into a grilled *côte de bœuf* (beef rib), or enjoy the rich, gamey flavour of traditional Corsican *terrine de sansonnet aux myrtes* (starling pâté with myrtle berries).

LE MORIANINCU

The Morianincu – the hinterland of Plage-Moriani – is a region of verdant forests and muscular mountains studded with a succession of picturesque villages. The villages' austere facades, elegant bell towers and higgledy-piggledy schist-slab rooftops preside over an arresting landscape of dense chestnut groves and rippling hills, with the sapphire-blue sea forming a perfect backdrop.

♥ **MORIANINCU VILLAGES //**
WINDING BACK ROADS AND
PEACEFUL VILLAGES

The sleepy villages of the Morianincu are a perfect place to get off the beaten track, to slow down, wander at will and enjoy the expansive, ever-changing views.

As the D34 zigzags up from Moriani-Plage to **San Nicolao**, it passes through a picturesque village cemetery crammed with templelike family tombs and watched over by a beautiful baroque bell tower. The village itself is dotted with photos dating from the late 19th and early 20th centuries, displayed in the actual locations where they were originally taken, and offers grand views over the coast.

The lower of the two roads leading north from San Nicolao takes you to the scattered hamlets of **Santa Lucia di Mo-**

ACCOMMODATION

The east coast is lined with campsites and holiday villages, but the best of the region's accommodation is inland in the *chambres d'hotes* (B&Bs) and *gîtes* (self-contained cottages) of La Castagniccia and Fiumorbu. See the Accommodation chapter for a list of recommended options. The following are some of our favourites:

★ Go green at the ecofriendly *gîtes* of U **Paesolu a Suvera a u ventu** (p253)

★ Lost in an ocean of greenery, the **Chambres d'Hôtes La Diligence** (p254) is a true get-away-from-it-all destination

★ A Tuscan-style villa perched on a hilltop, the **Villa Clotilde** (p255) offers peace, solitude and panoramic views

---

riani, precariously perched on a ridge, from where a road climbs even more tortuously up to **San Giovanni di Moriani**. The slender 33m-high bell tower of the church of **St-Jean-L'Évangéliste** is one of the tallest in Corsica, towering over a bucolic scene of chestnut trees, scattered tombs and grazing horses; it also marks the starting point for San Giovanni's botanical trail (below).

Continue uphill through the hamlets of Serrale and Cioti then turn right and follow the D34 to its end at **Santa Reparata di Moriani**, where a remote *gîte d'étape* (walkers' lodge) caters to hikers in search of peace and solitude.

♥ **BOTANICAL TRAIL // LEARN**
ABOUT LOCAL PLANT LIFE AS YOU
HIKE

Pick up an information leaflet (available in English) from the tourist office at

TOP **FIVE**

SWIMMING SPOTS

The beaches along the east coast are a little lacking in the charm department, but that doesn't mean missing out on a cool dip on a hot afternoon. The region's rivers tumble from the hills in a cascade of perfect swimming pools.

- ★ **Cascade de l'Ucelluline** (p156) – Waterfall pools for the adventurous
- ★ **Pont de l'Enfer** (below) – Shady picnic spots and shallow water safe for kids to splash about in
- ★ **Catastaju** (p164) – A deep-green rock pool close to good day hikes and an isolated *gîte d'étape* (walkers' lodge)
- ★ **Vallée du Travo** (p166) – Golden granite and sparkling green water in a remote valley where adventurous swimmers can seek out their own secluded spot
- ★ **Vallée de la Solenzara** (p166) – Take your pick of expansive river pools, some with tiny coarse-sand beaches

Moriani-Plage (p151), park the car at San Giovanni di Moriani's church, and set off on this hike (waymarked with red paint and Sentier Botanique signs) lined with little signs that help you to identify more than 50 species of native Corsican trees, shrubs and flowers. The route climbs up through the hamlet of **Cioti**, where you can sample the local goat's-milk cheese, and on to the **Chapelle San Mamilianu**, perched on a ridge, before descending through the woods to **Serrale** and heading back to the church. Take your binoculars – there's a chance of spotting a golden eagle.

The total distance is 4.5km, with a height gain of 300m; allow three hours. You can make the route shorter by turning right along the road when you reach Cioti. Continue to Serrale, the next hamlet, and look out for the Sentier Botanique sign pointing up a stepped alley on the right. From here the path descends a staircase into the woods, where you follow the red paint marks back to your starting point (2km, one hour).

♥ PONT DE L'ENFER // PICNIC BESIDE A SHADED SWIMMING HOLE

Two kilometres north of Santa Lucia di Moriani, the narrow, potholed D330 (signposted Poggio-Mezzana) arrives at the Pont de l'Enfer (Hell's Bridge). Here the little Canapajo river has been dammed with stones to create a long, natural bathing pool, its banks shaded by walnut, chestnut and alder trees. The shallow water and lack of strong current make it a popular picnic spot for local families, and there are deeper pools to be discovered upstream from the bridge.

♥ LES ÉCURIES DE LA COSTA VERDE // CANTER THROUGH THE CHESTNUT FORESTS

Leave the car behind for a bit and try exploring the chestnut forests of the Morianincu at a gentler pace. The riding centre Les Écuries de la Costa Verde (☎ 04 95 30 64 39, 06 14 55 89 01; http://ecuriescostaverde .free.fr, in French), at the northern approach to Moriani-Plage, offers two-hour guided horseback trips through the woods to the village of San Giovanni di Moriani (€30; experienced riders in the mornings, beginners in the afternoons); it also offers exhilarating gallops along the beach at Moriani-Plage. For the little 'uns (aged 3 years and over), pony rides are available (€12 per hour).

LA CASTAGNICCIA

······

La Castagniccia (kas-tan-*yeetch*), derived from the Italian word for chestnut, owes its name to the Genoese, who planted the first chestnut trees here in the 16th century. Since then, chestnuts – whether roasted and made into a sweet paste, or dried and ground into flour – have been at the heart of the region's economy. This is Corsica at its most rural and remote, with majestic mountains and lush valleys, tiny villages and hillsides shaggy with broad-leaved chestnut trees, all linked by a network of narrow, winding roads

But scenery is not the only drawcard. The Castagniccia is also of strong historical and cultural interest – it was the birthplace of Pascal Paoli, father of Corsica – with beautiful baroque churches, historic chapels and convents, and lively fairs and festivals. Here, old traditions die hard, making it a fascinating introduction to the lifestyle of rural Corsica.

ESSENTIAL INFORMATION

TOURIST INFORMATION // **Castagniccia Tourist Office** (☎ 04 95 35 82 54; www.corso rezza.com; Piedicroce; ☻ 9.30am-5pm Mon-Fri) In the alley above the fountain.

EXPLORING LA CASTAGNICCIA

♥ **PIEDICROCE // CHILL OUT IN CASTAGNICCIA'S 'CAPITAL'**
Straddling the crossroads of Castagniccia's principal routes, the charming village of Piedicroce enjoys wonderful panoramas of the surrounding valleys. The **Église Sts Pierre et Paul** – a colourful Baroque confection that's home to Corsica's oldest church organ – is worth a look, but the main attraction is simply hanging out and enjoying scenery.

Stop for a beer – or a hearty lunch – at **Le Refuge** (☎ 04 95 35 82 65; mains €10, menu €17; ☻ lunch & dinner Apr-Oct), whose terrace offers a fine panorama of the village of Carcheto, perched on a neighbouring ridge, with Carpineto poking through the forest in the background.

About 1km to the north on the D71 (towards Campana), the ruins of the **Couvent d'Orezza**, a Franciscan monastery founded in 1453, exude an eerie atmosphere. Once one of the most important religious centres in Corsica, the monastery was the spot where Pascal Paoli met Napoléon Bonaparte in 1790. During WWII it was used as a hiding place by the Resistance, and was blown up by German troops in 1943.

If you're here in Piedicroce on the Easter weekend, you can join in the festivities of **A Merendella in Castagniccia**, when local producers of charcuterie, chestnuts, cheese and other delicacies offer the chance to sample their wares; there are also craft stalls selling hand-carved chestnut wood and horn implements, cafe tables set up around the church, and folk singers performing in the streets. Details are available from the tourist office.

❦ EAUX D'OREZZA // SAMPLE CORSICA'S FAVOURITE MINERAL WATER AT SOURCE

From Piedicroce it's an easy drive downhill along the D506 to **Eaux d'Orezza** (☎ 04 95 39 10 00; www.orezza.com; admission free; ⏱ 8am-8pm Mon-Sat, 9am-8pm Apr–mid-Oct, 8am-6pm Wed-Sun mid-Oct–Mar), a former 19th-century spa where mineral water is still bottled. Known since Roman times, the naturally sparkling spring waters are so rich in iron that some of it has to be removed before bottling – the raw stuff bubbling through the fountain at the gates has a distinct metallic tang. Prebooked guided tours are available for groups of 10 or more, but individuals are free to wander in the lovely landscaped grounds.

❦ CARCHETO // EXPLORE AN ANCIENT CASTAGNICCIA VILLAGE

Carcheto is the pretty *village perché* that dominates the view from Piedicroce. Check out the prominent bell tower marking its **Église Ste-Marguerite**, one of Corsica's most interesting churches. The 17th-century building is adorned with baroque stucco and trompe l'œil, plus a series of frescos painted by local artists in naive style. The village itself includes several fortified **tower houses** that date back to the 13th century, some of which have been restored and converted to holiday *gîtes* (see p254).

Another reason to pause in Carcheto is to pay a visit to the lovely **waterfall** that lies a couple of hundred metres down a path leading from the place de l'Église (it's signposted *Cascade*). The ribbonlike fall ends in a perfect, circular rock pool draped with greenery; it's a simply wonderful place to take a refreshing dip.

❦ COL D'ARCAROTTA // SHOP FOR LOCAL GOODIES AT A SUMMER MARKET

The D146 winds slowly up to the Col d'Arcarotta (819m), which is famous for its market, held every Sunday in July and August. Hundreds of visitors gather to browse stalls selling everything from locally produced charcuterie, cheese, chestnut biscuits and raspberries to items carved from the ornamental green stone known as *vert d'Orezza*. The Auberge des Deux Vallées (p162), which has a terrace that provides a spectacular view across the valley, is also located here.

❦ CHAPELLE SANT'ALESSIO // HIKE AMONG 100-YEAR-OLD CHESTNUT TREES

This isolated little chapel above the village of **Ortale** makes a good objective for an easy hike. The shady path follows a line of ancient, huge-girthed chestnut trees before breaking out into the maquis; at the chapel you can enjoy a picnic with breathtaking views that stretch from the sea on one side to Monte San Petrone on the other.

Start just past the last buildings at the uphill end of the village of **Valle d'Alesani**; there's a small parking place on the left and a fountain on the right. The easy-to-follow path, marked with orange paint splashes, climbs up to the right of the fountain. The round trip is 3.5km, and should take 1½ hours.

❦ LA PORTA // CHURCH ARCHITECTURE AND CHARCUTERIE

Another lovely settlement in the heart of the Castagniccia, La Porta is famed for its 17th-century **Église St-Jean Baptiste**, one of the most beautiful baroque churches in Corsica. The overblown

THE EAST

splendour of its facade and majestic bell tower, 45m in height, is matched inside by a superb church organ and various well-preserved paintings.

If you're feeling peckish, **Chez Élisabeth – L'Ampugnani** (☎ 04 95 39 22 00; mains €10-18, menus €15-25; ☺ lunch & dinner Tue-Sun Mar-Dec, lunch Sep-Jun) is a typically Corsican *restaurant de village* (village eatery). The menu adheres to tried-and-true classics, such as veal stew, lamb, cannelloni, pastas and salads, and the terrace at the back has a lovely view down the valley.

You can stock up on Corsican delicacies, including charcuterie, jams and *canistrelli* (biscuits made with almonds, walnuts, lemon or aniseed) at **Casi di Cornu** (☎ 04 95 39 23 91), a tiny produce shop in Stoppia Nova, about 5km from La Porta on the road to the Col de Prato.

❦ FOIRE DU COL DE PRATO //
MINGLE WITH LOCAL FARMERS AT A COUNTRY FAIR

Every year on the last weekend in July or the first weekend of August, the **Col de Prato**, between La Porta and Morosaglia, is given over to this popular festival, which brings together local farmers ex-

hibiting their prize sheep, goats and pigs; producers offering tastings of charcuterie, cheese and honey; and artisans selling jewellery, books and clothing. Up to 8000 visitors join in the fun, which includes children's games, poetry recitals, and performances of traditional music and dance, plus a boules competition and a race to the summit of Monte San Petrone.

On the Sunday morning a wooden figure of St Peter is carried in procession to the ruined 16th-century **Église de San Petro d'Accia**, perched on a ridge 1.5km south of the *col* (pass).

❦ MONTE SAN PETRONE //
CLIMB TO THE SUMMIT OF CASTAGNICCIA'S FAVOURITE MOUNTAIN

If you want to work off any extra pounds gained in the area's fine restaurants, you can tackle Monte San Petrone (1767m), the highest peak in the Castagniccia. The summit is crowned with a crucifix and a little statue of St Peter, and is one of the finest viewpoints in Corsica, with the whole of the central range of mountains on one horizon, and the islands of the Tuscan archipelago on the other.

∼ WORTH A TRIP ∼

For many Corsicans, the village of **Morosaglia**, on the western edge of the Castagniccia, is almost talismanic: it's revered as the birthplace of the Babbu di a Patria (Father of the Nation), Pascal Paoli (see the boxed text, p193). When his remains were returned to his home village on 3 September 1889 (he died in exile in Britain in 1801), villagers lined the route to pay their respects. The house where he was born, the **Maison Natale de Pascal Paoli** (☎ 04 95 61 04 97; rte Principale; adult/child €2/1; ☺ 9am-5pm) offers an insight into the life of the Corsican hero through paintings, costumes and personal letters.

For lunch, you can't miss **Osteria di U Cunventu** (☎ 04 95 47 11 79; mains €10-22; ☺ lunch & dinner Wed-Mon), a charming eatery on the main street offering a blackboard menu of seasonal delights. Regular dishes to look out for include grilled prawns flambéed in Corsican eau-de-vie, and the generous Corsican salad with a bit of everything. There's a small terrace blessed with lovely views over the hills.

The normal route begins at the Col de Prato, from where a forest road runs south through shady beech woods before a final short, steep climb up to the rocky summit. Alternatively, you can start from the hamlet of **Campodonico**; from here the route is shorter, but it's also steeper and lacks shade. Plan on five to six hours for the 12km round trip on either route. The route is technically easy but fairly long, so you'll need a reasonable level of fitness.

GASTRONOMIC HIGHLIGHTS

❦ AUBERGE DES DEUX VALLÉES // COL D'ARCAROTTA €

☎ 04 95 35 91 20; mains €11-16, menus €17-27; ☽ lunch & dinner mid-Jun–mid-Sep

Perched on the ridge between the valleys of Orezza and Alesani, this rustic country inn, decked out like a hunter's cabin, has a terrace with superb views of the peak of Punta Ventosa. The highlight of the menu is lamb slow roasted in chestnut honey, but other dishes worth trying include *buglidicci* (pancakes with ewe's-milk cheese), and roast pork stuffed with *figatellu* (liver sausage).

❦ RESTAURANT SAN PETRU // VALLE D'ALESANI €€

☎ 04 95 35 94 74; menus €16-22; ☽ lunch & dinner Apr-Dec

This place owes its reputation to a menu based solidly on good-quality local produce. Dishes include a delicious *salade de confit de porc aux châtaignes* (salad of pork, cooked in its own fat, and chestnuts) and, if you want to challenge your palate, *carpaccio de museau* (carpaccio-style pig's snout). The decor in the dining room won't win any prizes, but the outdoor seating is pleasant enough.

❦ SANT' ANDRIA // CAMPANA €€

☎ 04 95 35 82 26; menus €20-24; ☽ lunch & dinner Mon-Sat, lunch Sun May-Sep

Choose a chestnut-wood table in the rustic dining room or take a seat on the terrace, where you can soak up the splendid views over the valley, and treat yourself to a glass of Appellation d'Origine Contrôlée (AOC) Ajaccio while you ponder the menu of Corsican specialities – we went for the *veau Corse mijoté à l'ancienne* (slowly stewed Corsican veal), the *terrine de courgettes* (zucchini terrine) and tiramisu made with chestnut flour, and were not disappointed.

TRANSPORT

CAR // A map of Castagniccia looks like spaghetti spilt on a crumpled green tablecloth – the region's steep, forested hillsides are laced with a tangle of narrow, twisting roads. You'll rarely get above third gear (average speed is around 30km/h), so relax, enjoy the scenery and be prepared to get lost at least once. There are no petrol stations up here, so fill your tank before heading into the hills.

COSTA SERENA & CÔTE DES NACRES

· · · · · ·

The Costa Serena stretches from the inland lighthouse of the Phare d'Alistro, poised above the N198 coastal highway, to the Travo river. The two main towns, Aléria and Ghisonaccia, aren't about to win any awards for tourist destination of the year, but their safe, sandy beaches pull in plenty of visitors. More interesting are the remains of Roman Aléria and the pretty hill villages of the Fiumorbu.

South from here, and centred on the yachting centre of Solenzara, is the Côte des Nacres, named for the seashells that were once abundant on this coast. The beaches around Solenzara are the best on the east coast, but again the real attractions lie inland – the remote valley of the Travo river, and the spectacular scenery on the road to Bavella.

ESSENTIAL INFORMATION

TOURIST INFORMATION // Costa Serena Tourist Office (☎ 04 95 56 12 38; www .corsica-costaserena.com; rte de Ghisoni, Ghisonaccia; ☜ 9am-12.30pm & 2-8pm Mon-Sat, 9am-noon Sun Jul & Aug, 9am-12.30pm & 2-5.30pm Mon-Sat Sep-Jun) Côtes des Nacres Tourist Office (☎ 04 95 57 43 75; www.cotedesnacres.com; N198, Solenzara; ☜ 9am-noon & 3-7pm Jun & Sep, 9am-8pm Jul & Aug, 9am-noon & 2-5pm Mon-Fri Oct-May)

TRANSPORT

BUS // The Rapides Bleus (☎ 04 95 31 03 79) Bastia–Porto-Vecchio bus stops at Cateraggio (for Aléria; 1¼ hours, daily mid-June to mid-September, Monday to Saturday mid-September to mid-June). Autocars Cortenais (☎ 04 95 46 02 12) operates a service to Aléria from Corte (one hour, one daily Tuesday, Thursday and Saturday) in July and August only. Transports Tiberi (☎ 04 95 57 81 73) has buses from Bastia to Solenzara (1¼ hours, one daily Monday to Saturday), via Aléria.

ANCIENT ALÉRIA & AROUND

♥ ANCIENT ALÉRIA // DELVE INTO CORSICA'S GREEK AND ROMAN PAST

Established by ancient Greeks around 550 BC and taken over by the Romans in the 2nd century BC, the prosperous settlement of Aléria (originally known as Alalia) was once the capital of Corsica. Its ruins, occupying a small hill overlooking the Tavignano river, have sup-

plied archaeologists with a treasure trove of impressive finds.

Even if the idea of an archaeology museum usually sends you to sleep, the Musée Archéologique Jérôme-Carcopino (☎ 04 95 57 00 92; Fort de Matra; admission incl archaeological site €2; ☜ 8am-noon & 2-7pm mid-May–Sep, 8am-noon & 2-5pm Oct–mid-May) is well worth a visit. Housed in the impressive Fort de Matra, built by the Genoese in 1484, its four rooms house an impressive collection of Etruscan, Greek and Roman pots, vases, lamps and jewellery. The highlight is the collection of beautifully decorated 5th-century-BC Greek pottery, including drinking vessels in the shape of animal heads.

The archaeological site is a 300m walk southwest from the fort. It boasts the remains of a forum, some temples and parts of the Roman baths, but the largest part of the city is still to be excavated – what you see is only 10% of the city's full extent.

♥ ÉTANG DE DIANE // ENJOY OYSTERS FRESH FROM THE LAGOON

The peaceful Étang de Diane, a large saltwater lagoon about 3km north of Aléria, was once used by the Romans as a harbour and oyster farm. The Roman ships are long gone, but oysters, mussels and clams are still farmed here. Floating on a pontoon moored in the southwest corner of the lagoon, right next to the shellfish farm, Aux Coquillages de Diane (☎ 04 95 57 04 55; mains €13-22; ☜ lunch Sun-Thu, lunch & dinner Fri & Sat Feb-May & Oct-Dec, lunch & dinner Jun-Sep) is a stylish eatery dressed in nautical decor. The obvious choice here is the oysters au naturel, but the menu also includes lots of other seafood delicacies such as fritto misto of prawn, squid and octopus; grilled sea bass; and lobster any way you like (€160 per kilogram).

☙ KAYAK THE COAST // EXPLORE LAGOON AND RIVER UNDER PADDLE POWER

The Tavignano river flows into the sea near the Plage du Padulone, Aléria's main beach. Corsicaventura (☎ 04 95 48 82 06, 06 67 26 52 49; www.ernella.net; Camping Ernella, N200) has a summer outpost on the beach, where you can hire kayaks and Canadian canoes to explore the coast and river. Join a guided four- to five-hour expedition (€45 per boat) along the coast to the Étang d'Urbino, or descend the last 10km of the Tavignano river to the sea, ending at the beach; the latter is a pleasantly laid-back trip over mostly calm water that's suitable for beginners.

☙ DOMAINE MAVELA // STOCK UP ON CORSICAN BOOZE

This boutique distillery (☎ 04 95 56 63 15; ⌚ 9am-noon & 2-6pm Mon-Sat Sep–mid-Jan, Apr & May, 9am-8pm Jun-Aug) produces liqueurs (myrtle, chestnut, plum), Corsican eau-de-vie, and even a Corsican malt whisky (sold under the brand P&M). You can tour the works and buy the booze, but that's not all – you'll also find here one of Corsica's best wine cellars, where you can sample many of the island's finest wines – what about a Gentile Noble, a Clos Canarelli or a Domaine Torraccia to go with that gourmet picnic? – and an impressive selection of locally produced cheese, charcuterie, honey and preserves. It's on the D343; turn right off the N198 about 4km south of ancient Aléria.

LE FIUMORBU

The Fiumorbu microregion to the west of Ghisonaccia doesn't have any major sights, but it's certainly worth exploring its cluster of *villages perchés,* built like eagles' nests on hilltops or snuggled within dense forests. It's not promoted heavily as a tourist destination, so it remains largely overlooked by visitors.

DRIVING TOUR

Distance: 50km
Duration: four hours
From the N198 south of Ghisonaccia take the D244 inland to Pietrapola, once famous for its thermal baths, then make your way to San Gavinu di Fiumorbu, which clings to a hillside in a curve of the valley. Just before the village a left turn leads in 3km to Catastaju, where a *gite d'étape* (p255) on the Mare a Mare Centre trail sits on the banks of the Abatescu river. This is the starting point for lots of excellent hikes, and the white-granite bed of the river here forms a series of beautiful green bathing pools.

Head north to sleepy Isolaccio di Fiumorbu (700m), the highest hamlet in the area, then zigzag down to Prunelli di Fiumorbu, the prettiest *village perché* in the region. From a bench in the shade of an ancient green oak you can soak up the panorama of wooded hills, coastal plain and the Étang d'Urbino, before wandering through picturesque, flower-bedecked lanes to the old church, or browsing the eclectic collection of curiosities in the Musée Mnémosina (Memory Museum; ☎ 04 95 56 74 75; Prunelli di Fiumorbu; adult/child €2/1; ⌚ 3-6pm Sat, or by appointment). If you're tempted to stay the night, check out Villa Clotilde (p255).

Head for lunch at the Caffè Buttéa (☎ 04 95 56 74 75; Prunelli di Fiumorbu; mains €9-15; ⌚ lunch & dinner Tue-Sun), an agreeable bistro with a limited menu but excellent cuisine, before descending the looping hairpin bends of the D345 back to the coastal highway.

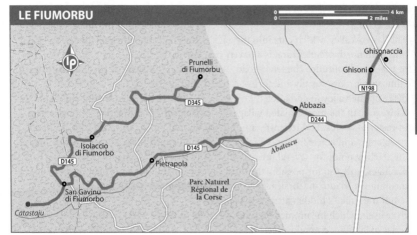

LE FIUMORBU

THE EAST

CASAMOZZA

☙ A TRIBBIERIA – PASQUALE PAOLI // KNOCK BACK SOME CORSICAN ALES

The closest thing eastern Corsica has to a pub, **A Tribbiera** (☎ 04 95 56 37 23; ☉ Tue-Sun) certainly has novelty value. This lively bar with an attached microbrewery gives you the chance to sample a range of unique boutique beers, flavoured with arbutus berry, Corsican honey or clementines and served by the *mezzu* (25cL), *pinta* (50cL), *carafon* (1L) or *funtana* (2L). It's not all about the beer though; socialising is a major activity in the sunny courtyard or inside the big main bar. On Friday you could be entertained by live music. It's about 3km south of Ghisonaccia on the N198.

SOLENZARA & AROUND

☙ SOLENZARA // HANG OUT BY THE HARBOUR

In the charisma stakes, Solenzara's heavily trafficked centre and bland buildings come a poor second to the picture-postcard beauties further south. But the lively marina is a pleasant place to watch the world sail by, and the town is blessed with a hatful of well-regarded restaurants, and some lovely beaches to the south.

Stroll along the main drag, and pop into **A Buttega di A Mandria** (☎ 04 95 31 59 35; rte Principale; ☉ Tue-Sun Apr-Oct), an excellent food shop where you can buy a handmade basket and fill it with local produce. Then head down to the harbour for a homemade ice cream at **Glacier du Port** (☎ 04 95 57 42 21; port de plaisance; ☉ Apr-Sep), where you can relax on the terrace and watch the comings and goings in the marina.

☙ BEACHES // SUNBATHE, SWIM, SIP A BEER IN THE SHADE

Beaches are Solenzara's main raison d'être. The pleasant **town beach** is a short stroll away, across a footbridge at the north side of the harbour, but a series of bays to the south – **Anse de Tarco**, **Anse de Favona** and the much-photographed **Anse de Fautea**, with the bonus of a Genoese watchtower, have a more attractive setting. Best of the lot is the half-moon-shaped **Anse de Canella** 5km south of Solenzara, with fine white sand, turquoise water, shady trees and a couple of bars.

♥ VALLÉE DU TRAVO // ESCAPE TO THE HILLS

The Travo Valley, which cuts into the hills 6km north of Solenzara, is a haven of peace and solitude. The D645 road climbs ever more steeply and tortuously up the valley to end after 17km at Chisà, one of the most isolated villages in eastern Corsica. Hidden away among steep crags and dense forests, Chisà is the starting point for several interesting hikes, and also for possibly the most thrilling *via ferrata* in Corsica.

But the valley's hidden attraction is the river itself, which in summer presents a series of languid, emerald-green *vasques* (natural pools) lined with golden granite slabs perfect for picnicking and sunbathing. You can reach the river via a steep path that descends from a small metal gate beside the road, on the village side of the Pont de Bura. From here it's possible to follow the riverbed downstream to find your own perfect pool.

As far as lunch goes, your only option is the basic **Pension-Restaurant U Chisà** (☎ 04 95 57 31 06; Chisà; menu €15; ☽ lunch & dinner Jul & Aug).

♥ VIA FERRATA DE CHISÁ // SCARE YOURSELF SILLY ON A THRILLING VIA FERRATA

Leading from the village of Chisà up to the summit of U Calanconi and back down again, the **Via Ferrata de Chisà** (☎ 04 95 57 84 24; www.viaferratachisa.fr; per person €15, equipment hire €10) is one of the most challenging in Corsica. It begins with a 17m Himalayan rope bridge across a river, then scales a 100m-high granite cliff using metal ladders and wire ropes; the final scary overhang is surmounted by climbing a spiderweb of steel cable. The descent involves a 50m Himalayan bridge and an adrenaline-pumping 230m

zip line. The route begins at a wooden cabin at the top of the village, open at weekends only; from Monday to Friday, ask at the **Gîte d'Étape Bocca Bè** (☎ 04 95 56 36 61) across the road. Allow three to four hours.

Experienced *via ferrata* climbers can tackle the circuit alone, but beginners should join a group led by a qualified guide; the tourist offices at Ghisonaccia (p163) and Solenzara (p163) have lists of suitable guides. The minimum age is 12 years.

♥ VALLÉE DE LA SOLENZARA // STUNNING SCENERY AND WILD SWIMMING

The D268, which connects Solenzara with the Col de Bavella, 30km to the west, ranks as one of the most dramatic mountain roads in Corsica – and that's saying something! The view of the granite pinnacles of Bavella as you cross the **Col de Larone** (608m) is genuinely breathtaking.

From the coast, the valley of the Solenzara river coils lazily into the mountains. Huge, rounded boulders in the broad riverbed speak of tumultuous winter torrents, but in summer the Solenzara is a series of limpid green *vasques* that look like something out of a shampoo advertisement. There are several places with parking and easy access to the river, notably near the **Pont de Calzatoju**, 12km from Solenzara.

♥ CORSICA FOREST PARC AVENTURE // TEST YOUR NERVE AT A PARC AVENTURE

☎ 06 25 97 27 95, 06 16 18 00 58; www.corsica-forest .com; rte de Bavella; adult/child €17/14; ☽ 9am-6pm May-Sep

This adventure park, just beyond the U Rosmarinu campsite, is a must do for those who want to enjoy the valley from a different perspective. There are 25 challenging obstacles, including a gut-wrenching 65m zip line over the river, but fear not – there's a 10-minute introductory session on what to do, and you'll be safely secured at all times. There's also a 'baby *parc*' for the kids (€6).

If the 1½-hour circuit leaves you craving a further adrenaline rush, there's also a superb *via ferrata*, **A Buccarona** (adult/child €17/14; 9am-6pm May-Sep), which is even more challenging. Corsica Forest Parc Aventure also arranges guided canyoning trips in the Aiguilles de Bavella; see p148 for more information.

☙ A MANDRIA DE SÉBASTIEN // A STEP BACK IN TIME FOR HUNGRY CARNIVORES

Stepping through the doorway of **A Mandria de Sébastien** (☎ 04 95 57 41 95; N198, Solenzara; mains €12-25, menus €22-25; lunch & dinner Tue-Sat, lunch Sun Apr-Dec), a converted *bergerie* (shepherd's hut) at the northern entrance to Solenzara, is like stepping back half a century. The walls are beguilingly adorned with ancient tools and other knick-knacks, and in summer tables are set beneath a pergola in the garden. Bona fide carnivores will find nirvana here: meat is grilled to perfection, and the local charcuterie is faultless. Service could use a little improvement, but once you taste the food you'll forget how long it took to arrive. Credit cards aren't accepted.

☙ LA FONDERIE // FINE DINING NEAR THE HARBOUR

Set in a former blacksmith's forge near the harbour, this fine-dining **establishment** (☎ 04 95 57 42 47; port de plaisance, Solenzara; mains €8-25; lunch & dinner May-Sep) has an attractive terracotta-tiled terrace where you can watch the swallows swoop over the nearby reed beds. The menu includes dishes such as carpaccio of swordfish with lemon and pink peppercorns, bream stuffed with chorizo, and fillet of beef with *pâté de foie gras* (duck- or goose-liver pâté) and figs; other drawcards are the friendly, relaxed service and chill-out tunes in the background.

THE CENTRAL MOUNTAINS

3 PERFECT DAYS

❦ DAY 1 // THE KERNEL OF CORSICA
Start gently in picturesque Corte (opposite), then drive out due north along the N193 to the lightly trafficked Vallée du Niolo. On your way you can stop at Prumitei – Centre des Arts du Feu (p175) to see skilled craftspeople at work. In the Vallée du Niolo, allow a few hours to explore the cluster of villages (p179) near Calacuccia, the 'capital' of the valley. A two-hour horse-riding excursion (p180) in the magnificent Forêt du Valdu Niellu is the perfect finish to a fantastic day.

❦ DAY 2 // ALFRESCO ATTRACTIONS
In Corte, rise early to make it to Vallée de la Restonica (p177) before the crowds arrive. Drive along the river until you find the perfect bathing pool and smooth rocks (p178). Come lunchtime, tuck into an *omelette au Brocciu* (omelette with goat's or ewe's-milk cheese) at Bergeries de Grotelle (p178). Suitably re-energised, you could tackle the ascent to Lac de Melu (p178) or, if you'd like something more gentle, leave the valley and drive to Pont de Noceta (p183) for an afternoon dip in the Vecchio river.

❦ DAY 3 // FORESTS AND FRESH MOUNTAIN AIR
From Corte, make your way to the peaceful mountain hamlet of Vizzavona, surrounded by the majestic Forêt de Vizzavona (p184); be sure to stop at Cantina di Matteu (p184) in Venaco for gourmet picnic supplies on the way. In the forest, take your pick from the gentle walking options on offer: try Cascades des Anglais (p184) or Cascade du Voile de la Mariée (p184). Spend the afternoon at Parc Vizzavona Aventure (p184) for a bout of action amid pine trees. Heading back to Corte, enjoy a hearty Corsican meal at U Stazzu (p176).

TRANSPORT

CAR // The N193, which links Bastia to Ajaccio, cuts through the mountains, and serves Corte, Venaco, Vivario and Vizzavona.

PARKING // It's comparatively easier to park your car in Corte than in the coastal cities, though the streets in the centre are still congested in summer. Corte has a few car parks for €1.50 per hour.

BUS // Eurocorse Voyages (☎ 04 95 21 06 30) runs buses between Ajaccio and Bastia (twice daily, Monday to Saturday), stopping at Vizzavona, Vivario, Venaco and Corte. From July to mid-September, Autocars Mordiconi (☎ 04 95 48 00 04) runs buses from Corte to Porto (one daily, Monday to Saturday) via Calacuccia and Évisa. Autocars Cortenais (☎ 04 95 46 02 12) has one bus to Bastia from Corte via Ponte Leccia on Monday, Wednesday and Friday. It also operates a service to Aléria from Corte (one daily Tuesday, Thursday and Saturday) in July and August only.

TRAIN // Chemins de Fer de la Corse (☎ 04 95 23 11 03; www.train-corse.com) runs four trains daily from Ajaccio, stopping at Vizzavona, Vivario, Venaco, Corte, Ponte Leccia and Bastia. For Calvi and Île Rousse, change at Ponte Leccia.

BICYCLE // Altipiani (☎ 06 86 16 67 91; www.altipiani-corse.com; 5 rue du Professeur Santiaggi, Corte; bicycle per day €18) hires out bikes.

CORTE (CORTI)

· · · · · ·

pop 6350

Corte, roughly midway between Bastia and Ajaccio, feels different to other Corsican cities. This is the heart and soul of Corsica. Caretaker of the island's identity, the town was, so briefly, the capital of an independent Corsica between 1755 and 1769, and remains a symbol of its people's aspirations and longings.

Beautifully positioned at the confluence of several rivers, Corte is blessed with an awesome setting. From the N193, you can view the fairy-tale sight of Corte's citadel atop a craggy mount that bursts forth from the valley. The town's sizeable student population – testified to by the number of bars in the main street– gives the town a special buzz during term time. During the summer, it's mainly tourists who walk the streets and fill the cafes, supplemented by a sun-bronzed bevy of hikers enjoying day walks amid the soul-stirring scenery of the Restonica and Tavignano Valleys, both of which open out at the foot of the town.

ESSENTIAL INFORMATION

TOURIST OFFICES // Tourist office (☎ 04 95 46 26 70; www.centru-corsica.com; ☺ 10am-5pm Mon, Wed & Sat, 9am-7pm Tue, Thu & Fri Jul & Aug, 9am-noon & 2-6pm Mon-Fri Sep-Jun) In the Caserne Padoue at the entrance to the citadel. Has information about Corte and the valleys of the central mountains.

EXPLORING CORTE

❦ CITADEL & MUSÉE DE LA CORSE // GET THE LOW-DOWN ON CORSICA'S PAST AND CULTURE

For a bird's-eye view of Corte and the cobbled alleys of the *haute ville* (upper town), haul your way up to the citadel, which seems to grow organically from the rocky pinnacle to which the town clings. The citadel itself was built in 1419, while the two buildings facing one another past the gate, the Caserne Padoue (Padoue Barracks) and the Caserne Serrurier (Serrurier Barracks), were added in the 19th century. The latter houses the organised Musée de la Corse (Museu di a Corsica; ☎ 04 95 45 25 45; admission €5.50; ☺ 10am-6pm Tue-Sun Apr–mid-Jun & mid-Sep–Oct, 10am-8pm mid-Jun–mid-Sep, 10am-5pm Tue-Sat Nov-Mar), the island's major museum

(Continued on page 174)

THE CENTRAL MOUNTAINS

THE CENTRAL MOUNTAINS

THE CENTRAL MOUNTAINS

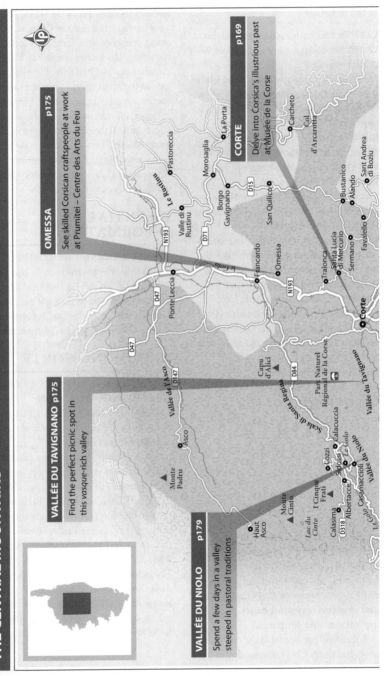

OMESSA   p175

See skilled Corsican craftspeople at work at Prumitei – Centre des Arts du Feu

CORTE   p169

Delve into Corsica's illustrious past at Musée de la Corse

VALLÉE DU TAVIGNANO p175

Find the perfect picnic spot in this *vasque*-rich valley

VALLÉE DU NIOLO p179

Spend a few days in a valley steeped in pastoral traditions

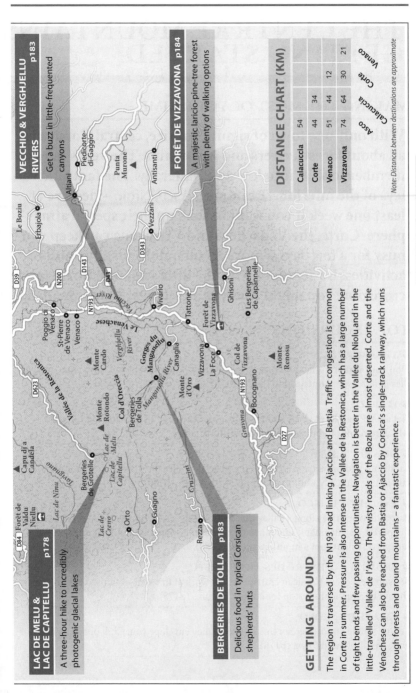

LAC DE MELU & LAC DE CAPITELLU   p178

A three-hour hike to incredibly photogenic glacial lakes

VECCHIO & VERGHJELLU RIVERS   p183

Get a buzz in little-frequented canyons

FORÊT DE VIZZAVONA   p184

A majestic laricio-pine-tree forest with plenty of walking options

BERGERIES DE TOLLA   p183

Delicious food in typical Corsican shepherds' huts

DISTANCE CHART (KM)

	Asco	Calacuccia	Corte	Venaco
Calacuccia	54			
Corte	44	34		
Venaco	51	44	12	
Vizzavona	74	64	30	21

Note: Distances between destinations are approximate

GETTING AROUND

The region is traversed by the N193 road linking Ajaccio and Bastia. Traffic congestion is common in Corte in summer. Pressure is also intense in the Vallée de la Restonica, which has a large number of tight bends and few passing opportunities. Navigation is better in the Vallée du Niolu and in the little-travelled Vallée de l'Asco. The twisty roads of the Boziu are almost deserted. Corte and the Vénachese can also be reached from Bastia or Ajaccio by Corsica's single-track railway, which runs through forests and around mountains – a fantastic experience.

THE CENTRAL MOUNTAINS
GETTING STARTED

MAKING THE MOST OF YOUR TIME

With only one town of significant size, central Corsica is all about forests, rivers and mountains. The key is to remember to shift into low gear – literally. The fantastic valleys of the interior – Restonica, Asco, Niolo – deserve at least one week if you want to soak up their special atmosphere. Corte, the Vénachese and Vizzavona can keep you busy for a few days – more if you indulge in any outdoor activities. Be generous with the little-explored Boziu microregion: you might find you stay longer than intended.

TOP EXCURSIONS

❦ TREASURE HUNTS
Don your explorer's hat and meet the Cortenais – they'll help you solve clues and riddles in a treasure hunt around Corte (p175).

❦ LE BOZIU
Get an MP3 guide at Corte's tourist office and explore this enticing microregion, which remains off the radar for most visitors (p181).

❦ DONKEY RIDES
Saddle up and immerse yourself in the majestic Vallée du Niolo; take a multiday excursion if you really want to commune with nature (p180).

❦ VALLÉE DE L'ASCO
A spectacular drive along a valley that feels like the end of the world – stately forests, the purest air imaginable and fantastic swimming spots await and, if you're really lucky, you might spot a mouflon or two (p180).

❦ PRUMITEI – CENTRE DES ARTS DU FEU
See some excellent Corsican craftspeople at work at this well-organised centre, which should be a mandatory stop for culture vultures (p175).

❦ VALLÉE DU NIOLO
Let the serene atmosphere of this isolated valley envelope you. Chill out in a village or walk amid splendid forest (p179).

GETTING AWAY FROM IT ALL

As central Corsica is much less touristy than the rest of the island, it's fairly easy to find peaceful spots.

★ **Gorges du Manganellu** Leave the N193 road and retreat to this timeless valley that feels like it's in the middle of nowhere (p183)

★ **Asco** The only settlement in the Vallée de l'Asco, the village of Asco is steeped in pastoral traditions (p180)

★ **Le Boziu** For real solitude, Le Boziu, right on Corte's doorstep, beckons – you'll be almost alone on its narrow lanes (p181)

★ **Vallée du Tavignano** Just on the outskirts of Corte yet light years away from city life, this valley has wonderful walks and tantalising natural pools (p175)

TOP ACTIVITIES

★ **Parcs aventure** What about zip lining 180m above the Asco river? Safe, fun, easy…and thrilling (p180).

★ **Horse riding** A ride among the laricio pines of the Forêt du Valdu Niellu or along the Vallée du Tavignano is unforgettable (p180, p175).

★ **Canyoning** Central Corsica offers little-frequented canyons that are just perfect for your initiation into the sport (p180, p183).

★ **Hiking** Wherever you go, you'll find gentle walking paths that lead to fantastic spots ranging from glacial lakes to deep laricio-pine forests.

TOP EATING EXPERIENCES

❦ **PÂTISSERIE CASANOVA**
Killer Corsican sweet treats (p176)

❦ **U STAZZU**
Delightful *storzapretti* (a kind of dumpling with Brocciu cheese), plus farm-raised veal (p176)

❦ **A CANTINA DI MATTEU**
Goods sourced from small-scale producers (p184)

❦ **HÔTEL MONTE D'ORO**
Old-fashioned atmosphere in a venerable institution (p184)

❦ **BERGERIES DE TOLLA**
Charcuterie platters in a shepherd's hut (p183)

❦ **U FRAGNU**
One of central Corsica's top secrets (p181)

RESOURCES

★ **Central Corsica** (www.centru-corsica .com) Comprehensive site on Central Corsica

★ **Centru di Corsica** A leaflet providing information on central Corsica; available at Corte's tourist office (p169)

★ **Parc Naturel Régional de la Corse** (PNRC; www.parc-naturel-corse.com, in French) Website of the body that administers much of inland Corsica

★ **Niolo Tourist Office** (www.office -tourisme-niolu.com) The low-down on the Vallée du Niolo

(Continued from page 169)

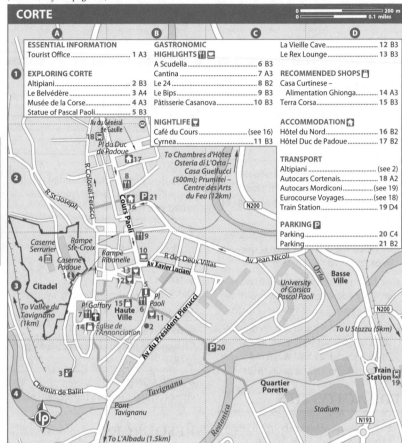

CORTE

ESSENTIAL INFORMATION	
Tourist Office	1 A3

EXPLORING CORTE	
Altipiani	2 B3
Le Belvédère	3 A4
Musée de la Corse	4 A3
Statue of Pascal Paoli	5 B3

GASTRONOMIC HIGHLIGHTS	
A Scudella	6 B3
Cantina	7 A3
Le 24	8 B2
Le Bips	9 B3
Pâtisserie Casanova	10 B3

NIGHTLIFE	
Café du Cours	(see 16)
Cyrnea	11 B3

La Vieille Cave	12 B3
Le Rex Lounge	13 B3

RECOMMENDED SHOPS	
Casa Curtinese –	
Alimentation Ghionga	14 A3
Terra Corsa	15 B3

ACCOMMODATION	
Hôtel du Nord	16 B2
Hôtel Duc de Padoue	17 B2

TRANSPORT	
Altipiani	(see 2)
Autocars Cortenais	18 A2
Autocars Mordiconi	(see 19)
Eurocourse Voyages	(see 18)
Train Station	19 D4

PARKING	
Parking	20 C4
Parking	21 B2

and a definite must see for anyone interested in Corsica's history and culture. The building has two main galleries, with a third space allocated to temporary exhibits. On the 1st floor, the **Galerie Doazan** exhibits a selection of traditional Corsican craft objects illustrating themes including agriculture, pastoral life and cottage industries such as weaving. On the next level, the **Musée en Train de se Faire** (Museum under Construction) deals with contemporary subjects such as industry, tourism and music. It's worth investing an extra €1.50 for the English audioguide.

To reach the upper levels of the citadel, you have to pass through the museum. To enjoy just as impressive a panorama for free, climb the stairs beneath the ramparts to the viewpoint of **Le Belvédère**.

❤ COURS PAOLI // FEEL THE PULSE OF CENTRAL CORTE

The experience of rambling along cours Paoli, Corte's main thoroughfare, and its lateral *rampes* (paved streets), will live long in the memory; at aperitif time, the *cours* looks like it's hosting a miniature version of an Italian *passeggiata*. Start from **place Paoli**, Corte's focal point, which is dominated by a **statue of Pascal Paoli**, and stroll down the *cours*. There are plenty of reasons to linger – the *cours* is lined with a string of pleasant terrace restaurants and bars. See if you can resist the tantalising display of sweet treats at Pâtisserie Casanova…

❤ CITY TREASURE HUNT // SOLVE PUZZLES AND MEET LOCALS

Explore Corte in a fun way, discovering intriguing parts of the capital that are so easily overlooked or missed. **Altipiani** (☎ 06 86 16 67 91; www.altipiani-corse.com; 5 rue du Professeur Santiaggi; treasure hunts €10; ☺ daily Apr-Oct) has set up a treasure hunt that comprises a series of location clues which will guide you around the centre on foot, taking in many of the city's beautiful sights. You'll need the help of knowledgeable locals to solve some riddles – a great way to meet the Cortenais. It takes about two hours to complete.

❤ VALLÉE DU TAVIGNANO // TAKE A SOLITARY WALK THROUGH CORSICA'S DEEPEST GORGE

If you feel overwhelmed by the vehicles in the Vallée du Restonica, you'll love the car-free Vallée du Tavignano. Corsica's deepest gorge is only accessible on foot

and remains well off the beaten track, despite being on Corte's doorstep.

From Corte, the signposted track heads through the maquis and scrubland, hugging the river as it climbs deep into the mountains. About 5km from Corte the gorge walk really kicks in and the scenery becomes increasingly dramatic. Reached after about 2½ hours, the **Passerelle de Rossolino** footbridge is an idyllic spot for a picnic. There's no shortage of transparent green *vasques* (natural pools) in which you can dunk yourself. Just blissful!

The Vallée du Tavignano also lends itself to superb horse-riding excursions from Corte. Contact **L'Albadu** (☎ 04 95 46 24 55; Ancienne rte d'Ajaccio; half-day €40; ☺ Apr-Oct).

There aren't any facilities in the valley, so stock up on food and bring plenty of water.

GASTRONOMIC HIGHLIGHTS

❤ A SCUDELLA €

☎ 04 95 46 25 31; 2 place Paoli; mains €9-15, menus €12-22; ☺ lunch & dinner Mon-Sat, closed mid-Dec–mid-Jan

Although locals say that it used to be better, A Scudella remains one of the highly rated venues on place Paoli for modern Corsican fare. The menu is carefully composed, with such tempting dishes as

THE CENTRAL MOUNTAINS

≈ WORTH A TRIP ≈

Set in a converted brick mill in **Omessa**, about 13km north of Corte (it's conveniently located on your way to Vallée d'Asco or Vallée du Niolo), **Prumitei – Centre des Arts du Feu** (☎ 04 95 36 24 28; www.prumitei.fr; adult/child €6/3; ☺ 9.30am-12.30pm & 4.30-7pm mid-May–mid-Sep, 9am-noon & 2-5pm mid-Sep–mid-May) is well worth a visit. As well as hosting concerts, exhibitions and various cultural events, this multifaceted cultural centre is active in handicraft production, especially bronzeware, glassmaking and pottery. You can see the artisans at work in their workshops, and there's a shop where you can buy the products made on site. Audioguides are available in English.

mignon de porc aux figues et aux raisons –
the English translation of pork with figs
and grapes doesn't do it justice!

♥ CANTINA €

place Gaffory; mains €8-14; lunch & dinner Jun-Sep
This pocket-sized restaurant sits snugly
in a vaulted stone dining room. Consid-
ering its location near place Gaffory, it
could have been a typical tourist trap;
instead, well-prepared classics such as
charcuterie platters or bruschette (try the
Cantina) go down a treat and are served
with a smile.

♥ LE 24 €€

☎ 04 95 46 02 90; 24 cours Paoli; mains €13-24,
menus €18-24; lunch & dinner daily Jul & Aug,
lunch Mon-Sat & dinner daily Sep-Jun
Taste buds are delighted at this ode to de-
sign – the contemporary decor sits prettily
with the exposed stone walls, a pair of
sweeping stone arches and a lovely old
dresser. Run by a young couple, Le 24 has

ACCOMMODATION

Forget about luxurious hotels in the
central mountains. It's all about charming B&Bs and low-key, yet comfortable,
hotels. And they're all reasonably priced.
For a list of recommendations, see the
Accommodation chapter (p240). These
are some of our favourites:

★ The friendly **Chambres d'Hôtes Casa
  Vanella** (p256) is a good base from
  which to explore the Vallée du Niolo

★ Located in the little-explored Boziu,
  the **Chambres d'Hôtes Casa di Lucia**
  (p256) is a true get-away-from-it-all
  destination

★ A huge villa in a quiet village, the
  Maison d'Hôtes Casa Giafferri
  (p257) has bags of character

an innovative menu that uses top-quality
ingredients and changes with the seasons.
The house desserts, chalked up on the
blackboard, hit the right spot. Mmm, tiramisu with *canistrelli* (biscuits made with
almonds, walnuts, lemon or aniseed).

♥ LE BIPS €

☎ 04 95 46 06 26; 14 cours Paoli; mains €5-23;
 lunch & dinner year-round
You'd never guess from outside that
there's an atmospheric dining room with
exposed beams and stone walls downstairs. Le Bips is without a doubt the
best-value restaurant you'll find along
cours Paoli. Generous pasta dishes or
salads for less than €10? Yes, it's possible.

♥ PÂTISSERIE CASANOVA €

☎ 04 95 46 00 79; 6 cours Paoli; pastries from €2;
 7am-7pm Mon-Sat year-round
Expanding waistlines since 1887, this
pastry shop has a tantalising array of sweet
delights, from tarts with herbs to maca-
roons and *falculella*. Everything is confected on the premises from family recipes.
It also doubles as a coffee lounge – perfect
for dessert or a gourmet coffee break after
exploring central Corte.

♥ U STAZZU €

☎ 04 95 46 31 84, 06 23 01 62 08; off N200; menu
€25; lunch & dinner year-round
There may not be many gastronomic
reasons to leave central Corte behind,
but this little-known farm inn is one
of them. Marie-Rose Guglielmi knows
her stuff when it comes to cooking *storzapretti* (a kind of dumpling with Brocciu cheese) or meat dishes made with
lamb from the farm. You'll eat in a rather
bland dining room, but it's the local
specialities that are the pull here. Located
about 5km east of Corte, off the N200, U
Stazzu isn't well signposted; drive past

the junction with the D214 that leads to Bustanico and, after 300m, take the dirt track on the right for another 300m. And you're there. Reservations are necessary.

NIGHTLIFE

The bar scene is kept alive by students in winter, and by a constant influx of thirsty hikers and tourists in summer.

☙ CAFÉ DU COURS

☎ 04 95 46 00 33; 22 cours Paoli
On the ground floor of Hôtel du Nord (p255), this stained-wood bar is Corte's oldest watering hole. The vibe is cool, casual and busy, and there's a huge menu of drinks and snacks.

☙ CYRNEA

rue du Professeur Santiaggi
Many of the bars in central Corte have sold their soul to the god of tourism, but this unfussy place is different. Corsican-speaking locals kick back with a prelunch Dami (Corsican pastis) – the cheapest in Corsica, at €0.80 – and visitors chill out with an ice-cold Pietra in hand.

☙ LA VIEILLE CAVE

☎ 04 95 46 33 79; 2 ruelle de la Fontaine
You'll need to look out for this wine bar, which is set back from the main street. The cosy cavelike interior creates an intimate setting and, as to be expected, there's a good selection of *vins au verre* (wine by the glass; from €1); make it the perfect aperitif with a small charcuterie platter. The cellarman can guide you through some of his 100-plus references.

☙ LE REX LOUNGE

☎ 04 95 46 08 76; 1 cours Paoli
Whether you're after cocktails, liqueurs or wine, Le Rex Lounge should see you right. With its sleek decor and loungey vibes, it's a nice place to revive your spirits with a mojito while watching the world go by.

RECOMMENDED SHOPS

☙ CASA CURTINESE – ALIMENTATION GHIONGA

Bring your camera, as this produce shop near place Gaffory is the most photogenic in Corte; the interior, crammed with all kinds of Corsican goodies, is delightfully timeless. Come here after siesta time and you might see the owner chatting with friends in Corsican. So authentic.

☙ TERRA CORSA

rue Sauveur Casanova; ⊙ Mar-Oct
Marc and Antonia Cesari's delicatessen is a fragrant emporium of homemade cured meats, jams, terrines and liqueurs. It also doubles as a small restaurant in the high season, with a small terrace where you can tuck into a charcuterie platter or sample the delicious veal with preserved chestnuts and honey.

VALLÉE DE LA RESTONICA

· · · · · ·

The Vallée de la Restonica is one of the prettiest spots in all of Corsica. The river, rising in the grey-green mountains, has scoured little basins in the rock, offering sheltered pine-wood settings for swimming, sun-bathing and picnicking. From Corte, the D623 winds its way through the valley for 15km to the Bergeries de Grotelle, where a car park and a huddle of shepherds' huts (three of which offer drinks, local cheeses and

snacks) mark the end of the road. From them, a rugged trail climbs up to a pair of high mountain lakes.

The valley's delights are easily – perhaps too easily – available to anyone with a vehicle. For 10 months of the year, the valley is tranquil and a mildly trafficked delight. In high summer, hordes of visitors throng up the valley.

EXPLORING VALLÉE DE LA RESTONICA

♥ VASQUES // REFRESH YOURSELF IN MINIATURE SWIMMING POOLS
The Vallée de la Restonica's hidden attraction is the river itself, which in summer presents a series of languid, sparkling green *vasques* fringed with granite slabs, ideal for picnicking and sunbathing. Come early and find your own pool, but be prepared for some company in summer – you'll have to share the best spots with other *vasque*-hunting visitors. Not peaceful enough for you? Consider exploring the Vallée d'Asco the next day.

♥ LAC DE MELU & LAC DE CAPITELLU // MOUNTAIN WALK TO PHOTOGENIC GLACIAL LAKES
This is a relatively demanding half-day, but the rewards are well worth the effort. From the Bergeries de Grotelle car park (1375m), a path marked with yellow blobs leads to a pair of picture-pretty glacial lakes, Lac de Melu (1711m) and Lac de Capitellu (1930m).

The path to Lac de Melu follows the left (west) bank of the Restonica for most of the way. With its inky waters fringed by dwarf alder trees and juniper bushes, the lake is a lovely reward for a rather strenuous ascent. There's a short chain section and a couple of iron ladders to help you negotiate the steepest part, just

THE CENTRAL MOUNTAINS

TOP FIVE

PICNIC SPOTS
When it comes to finding the perfect picnic spot nothing can beat jacuzzi-like *vasques* (natural pools) amid a forest. Crystal-clear waters + fresh air + shade = perfection. Just make sure you stock up on local charcuterie and cheese before setting off.

* ⋆ **Gorges du Manganellu** (p183) – Our favourite (shh…)
* ⋆ **Vallée de la Restonica** (left) – Pros: lovely pools; cons: crowded in summer
* ⋆ **Vallée de l'Asco** (p180) – Lovely pools by a Genoese bridge
* ⋆ **Pont de Noceta** (p183) – Excellent spot near Venaco
* ⋆ **Vallée du Tavignano** (p175) – Hush and seclusion

before the lake. Allow a generous hour from the car park. If you still have some energy to burn, consider climbing up to Lac de Capitellu, a further 45 minutes' steep ascent away and even more spectacular. Allow 3½ to four hours, not counting stops, to complete this out-and-back walk. Back to the Bergeries de Grotelle, treat yourself to an *omelette au Brocciu* – you've earned it.

Walking shoes are essential. Start early morning to escape the heat (and the crowds).

♥ AUBERGE DE LA RESTONICA // ENJOY A HEARTY MEAL BY THE RIVER
Located in a rustic building (with a disappointingly modernish dining room) barely 1.5km from Corte, **Auberge de la Restonica** (☎ 04 95 45 25 25; mains €13-24, menus

€16-25; ⊙year-round) is famous for its robust Corsican cuisine (wild-boar terrine, Corsican soup) and trout from the river.

TRANSPORT

BUS // A shuttle bus (adult/child return €4/2) operates from mid-July to mid-August, starting from a small information kiosk located 2km into the valley, and running to the car park at Bergeries de Grotelle. It leaves on the hour from 8am to noon, with return journeys from 2pm until 6pm. Caravans and campervans are halted at Tuani, 7km from Corte.

CAR // Consider leaving your vehicle at the small information kiosk, 2km into the valley, and taking the hourly shuttle bus. The 30km/h speed limit makes sound sense on this narrow road.

PARKING // Parking costs €5 at Bergeries de Grotelle; finding a space in July and August can be nigh on impossible.

BICYCLE // Altipiani (☎ 06 86 16 67 91; www.altipiani-corse.com; 5 rue du Professeur Santiaggi, Corte; bicycle per day €18) hires out bikes. They're an ideal way to avoid the gridlock-traffic purgatory in the valley, but you'll need triathlete's legs.

VALLÉE DU NIOLO

· · · · · ·

Nowhere guards the secrets of traditional Corsica better than this remote and utterly picturesque valley. Relatively isolated from the rest of the island, it is well worth a few days of exploration. From Corte, head north along the N193 as far as Francardo, then turn west onto the D84. The narrow road winds its way for about 20km through a vertiginous ravine known as Scala di Santa Regina, one of the island's most dramatic mountain landscapes. Then the road reaches Calacuccia, the 'capital' of the Niolo and

a great base for getting to know this special area, sometimes known as the kernel of Corsica. Whether you want to get active or kick off your shoes and relax, you'll be spoilt for choice.

ESSENTIAL INFORMATION

TOURIST OFFICES // Association Sportive du Niolu (☎ 04 95 48 05 22, 06 22 50 70 29; www.asniolu.com; rte de Cuccia, Calacuccia) Can organise any activity in the valley. Tourist office (☎ 04 95 47 12 62; www.office-tourisme-niolu.com; Calacuccia; ⊙9am-7pm Jul & Aug, 9am-noon & 2-5pm Sep-Jun) Beside the main road in Calacuccia. Has various brochures about the valley and a hiking pamphlet, *Niolu Les Randonnées* (€1), which outlines five walks varying in length from 1½ hours to a full day.

EXPLORING VALLÉE DU NIOLO

♥ NIOLO VILLAGES // CHILL OUT IN SERENE VILLAGES
After the Scala di Santa Regina, you'll soon hit Calacuccia, blessed with a lovely setting. Above an artificial lake, this quiet village lies in the shadow of the iconic Monte Cinto (2706m), and I Cinque Frati (The Five Monks), five jagged peaks that glower over the rural community below.

The D84 leads west from Calacuccia towards the tiny hamlet of Albertacce. On the way, a couple of attractive detours beckon: follow a sign to the right for Lozzi, the trail head for climbing Monte Cinto; above the village, there's a staggering view of the valley. From Albertacce a stirring 6.5km drive up the D318, with plunging views of the valley to the south, brings you to Calasima (1100m), which lays claim to being Corsica's highest village. To the north, you can make out the peak of Monte Cinto, the cutaway slab of Paglia Orba and the distinctive jagged peaks of I Cinque Frati.

Back in Calacuccia, a drive around the southern side of the lake brings you to the peaceful village of **Casamaccioli**, which hosts the Santa di u Niolo festival.

If you fancy a dip, there are plenty of opportunities for bathing in the mountain streams between Casamaccioli and Albertacce.

❤ SANTA DI U NIOLO //
IMMERSE YOURSELF IN A HIGHLY REVERED FESTIVAL

In early September (usually around 8 September), Casamaccioli attracts thousands of pilgrims and local émigrés for one of Corsica's most venerated religious festivals, the Santa di u Niolo, during which a gaudy statue of the Madonna is proudly paraded through the village. This is your chance to attend competitions of *chiam'e rispondi* (improvised calls and responses).

ADVENTURE SPORTS //
ACTION, FRESH AIR AND BEAUTIFUL SCENERY

The Vallée du Niolo is a fantastic playground for active types and nature lovers, with hiking, rock climbing, canyoning and *parc aventure* (adventure park) all readily available. All activities are accessible to beginners. The most iconic canyon descents include La Ruda and Frascaghju, with leaps and abseiling throughout some splendid gorges (from €45 for a half-day); contact **Association Sportive du Niolu** (☎ 04 95 48 05 22, 06 22 50 70 29; www.asniolu.com; rte de Cuccia, Calacuccia) for canyoning and other adventures.

If you prefer to clip-clop in the majestic Forêt du Valdu Niellu or up to Lac de Ninu, contact the friendly **Ranch u Niolu a Cavallu** (☎ 06 11 05 79 04; www.ranchunioluacavallu.com; rte de Verghio, Albertacce). Donkey rides (from €35) can be arranged with **La Promenâne** (☎ 06 25 70

∼ WORTH A TRIP ∼

Well off the beaten path thanks to its splendid isolation, the easily overlooked **Vallée de l'Asco**, the northernmost of the interior's great valleys, is a dream come true for nature lovers and photographers, with plenty of breathtaking landscapes. This is also one of the few areas in Corsica where you have a reasonable chance of spotting mouflon and eagles.

From Corte, drive north along the N193 via Ponte-Leccia, then take the turning west onto the D47. You can make a first stop at **Asco Vallée Aventure** (☎ 04 95 47 69 48; www.interracorsa.com; ☺ 9am-6pm Jun-Sep), which is a leisure park offering various outdoor activities, including *vie ferrata* (literally, 'iron paths'; see p213), a *parc aventure* (adventure park), a circuit with 12 zip lines, and a treasure hunt for kids; the less energetic can simply dunk themselves in the transparent green Asco river nearby. After a few kilometres, you'll reach **Asco**, the only sizeable settlement in the valley, with a dramatic location and stunning mountain views. A magnificent swimming spot can be found about 1km below the village, at a renovated **Genoese bridge**. Should you fall in love with the area, you'll find a couple of accommodation options (see p256) in the village. Continue further up the valley through a stately forest of laricio pines to **Haut Asco**, a former ski station, and a great base for short and long walks. Haut Asco is the end of the road, but if you get stuck there's a hotel and restaurant.

70 71; www.randonne-ane-corse.com; Albertacce);
the five-day excursion, which takes
in several *bergeries* (shepherds' huts)
throughout the area, comes particularly
recommended.

GASTRONOMIC HIGHLIGHTS

❦ RESTAURANT DU LAC // SIDOSSI €

☎ 04 95 48 02 73; mains €12-20, menus €16-22;
🕙 lunch & dinner May-Sep

Located at Sidossi, 2km west of Calacuccia, this restaurant is situated near
a lake but, despite its name, can't offer
you any lakeside views at all. No mat-
ter: you're here for the food, right? The
chef makes excellent use of fresh local
produce, especially *manzu* (veal) from
the valley, and free-range lamb; connoisseurs also heartily recommend the
charcuterie.

❦ U CINTU – CHEZ JOJO // ALBERTACCE €

☎ 04 95 48 06 87; mains €12-15, menus €17-23;
🕙 lunch & dinner year-round

You aren't spoilt for choice at this modest, warmly recommended *auberge de
village* (village inn), which has just a
handful of classics on the menu. No
prizes for the decor either, with its pastel
walls and floral fabric-covered lamps.
But top marks for friendliness and hon-
est, high-quality Niolo cooking, such as
homemade charcuterie (in winter) and
Brocciu tart.

LE BOZIU

· · · · · ·

**This microregion begins on Corte's
very doorstep, yet sees only a few
visitors per day. As you drive the
narrow, twisting roads, you'll come
across sleepy hamlets, deep wooded**
**valleys, glorious little village churches
and panoramas to make the heart
beat faster.**

DRIVING TOUR

Distance: 120km
Duration: one day

Here's the ultimate in off-the-beaten-
track driving: a route that takes you
into Corsica's heartland yet remains on
well-surfaced back lanes throughout.
An audioguide (in English) covering the
Boziu is available at Corte's tourist office
(p169).

Follow the N193 northward from
Corte, then branch off to the right
along the D41 towards **Tralonca**, which
has a lovely parish church, painted in
yellow and white. Continue towards
Santa Lucia di Mercurio, then **Sermano**. Within Sermano's little Romanesque chapel of San Nicolao are some
poignant 15th-century frescos. Drive
on as far as **Bustanico**, where there's
another lovely stone church, then loop
left and northward to pass through
Carticasi (9km) and Cambia, 2km
beyond.

Here, take the D39, direction San
Lorenzo, and turn right at a sign indicating the 13th-century **church of
San Quilico**. Deep in a little wood,
this Romanesque building contains
some finely carved sculptures on the
outside, and a series of frescos within;
ask for the key at the house near the
car park.

Retrace your steps as far as Bustanico,
and then follow the sign pointing to
Alando, reached after 2.5km, which
features the Convent of San-Francescu-
di-u-Boziu. If you want to make time
for a lunch break, **U Fragnu** (☎ 06 12 23
76 11; Alando; mains €10-15; 🕙 lunch & dinner year-

THE CENTRAL MOUNTAINS

round), set in a former olive-oil mill, is a wonderfully authentic place where you can feast on delicious Corsican staples; reservations are necessary. Continue to **Favallelo** to admire the impressive frescos of the church of Santa-Maria-Assunta. After 1km, turn left onto the D339 to arrive at the village of Sant Andrea di Boziu after about 9km. The hamlet of **Piedilacorte** has another beautiful parish church which lords over the valley.

Head for **Erbajola**, where the lovely church of San-Martinu is a short 15-minute walk away along a stony track. From Erbajola, follow signs for Foccichia (6km) and Altiani (8km) to the N200 Aléria–Corte road (direction Corte), which you'll turn onto at a junction 8km beyond Altiani. At this crossroads, an attractive **Genoese bridge** spans the stream. From here, Corte and the wider world reappear once more some 20km along the N200.

If you're tempted to linger, you'll discover two excellent accommodation options in the area; see p256 for more information.

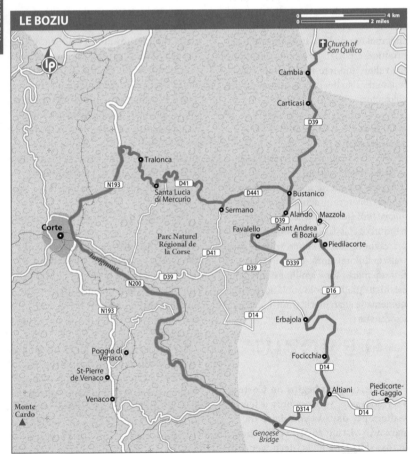

LE BOZIU

CORTE TO VIZZAVONA

· · · · · ·

Here in the mountainous area to the south of Corte you'll find fresh mountain air, deep forests, spectacular scenery, abundant hiking trails and little-explored canyons. Oh, and there's some fabulous cheese, too. The region doesn't have many major sights, but you come here to enjoy the scenery and the laid-back atmosphere.

☙ LE VÉNACHESE // EXPLORE A SERIES OF CHARMING MOUNTAIN HAMLETS

Immediately south of Corte, the Vénachese boasts a few elegant villages offering spectacular mountain views. The N193 squeezes through **St-Pierre de Venaco**, from where you can make a little detour to peaceful **Poggio di Venaco**. A few kilometres further south, **Venaco** is renowned for the quality and variety of its local produce, especially it's ewe's-milk cheese.

For a brief, attractive detour and a break from the N193, take the D143 to the right at the entrance to the village as you approach it from Ajaccio. After 5km, you reach the **Pont de Noceta**, spanning the little Vecchio river and overlooked by towering mountains. There's a great view back to the village at this perfect picnic spot, and you can immerse yourself in the river.

☙ CANYON DESCENTS // FEEL LIKE AN ADVENTURER IN LITTLE-EXPLORED CANYONS

The Vecchio and Verghjellu rivers, between Vivario and Venaco, provide an incredible stage for canyoning outings, with wild scenery and lots of leaps into emerald-green pools. Thrilling sensations aside, another pull is the absolute lack of crowds – here you'll be guaranteed to have the whole place to yourself, which is bliss if you've done a canyon descent in the Bavella area. Canyoning trips can be arranged through **Altipiani** (☎ 06 86 16 67 91; www.altipiani-corse.com; 5 rue du Professeur Santiaggi, Corte). If you want something fun and easy, ask for the '*haut* Verghjellu' trip, which lasts half a day (€38) and involves only a 20-minute walk to get to the start of the canyon. Near Bocognano, the Richiusa is another atmospheric canyon.

☙ WALKING INTO GORGES DU MANGANELLU // EPICUREAN INDULGENCES IN A BUCOLIC SETTING

One of central Corsica's best-kept secrets, the Gorges du Manganellu boast a wonderful bucolic atmosphere. From the hamlet of Canaglia, about 25km south of Corte on the N193, follow the wide track (it's signposted) that runs alongside the Manganellu river. You'll reach the cute-as-can-be **Bergeries de Tolla** (mains €8-14; ☖ lunch mid-Jun–mid-Sep), at an altitude of 1011m, after about two hours. What a reward! Feast on hearty Corsican staples, such as omelette with ewe's-milk cheese and fresh mint, and ease your belt out for the *bergeries'* signature dessert, the tempting *amandes et noisettes grillées au miel de châtaignier* (a mix of chestnut honey, and grilled almonds and hazelnuts).

Along the way, there are plenty of opportunities to take refreshing dips in the Manganellu river, which flows through a succession of gin-clear *vasques,* waterfalls and stands of majestic laricio pines.

THE CENTRAL MOUNTAINS

Allow four hours return from Canaglia. It's a gentle walk on a well-maintained path, with a very mild gradient.

☙ VIVARIO // PICNIC BY THE RIVER

About 9km from Venaco along the N193, Vivario nestles among the mountains. The handsome Pont du Vecchio, designed by Gustave Eiffel, is a viaduct that spans the Vecchio river, precisely 4.5km north of Vivario; carrying the Bastia–Ajaccio railway, it upstages the modern bridge that carries the N193. You'll find some superb freshwater pools at the foot of the bridge.

☙ VIZZAVONA // REJUVENATE MIND AND BODY IN A PRISTINE FOREST

The N193 climbs steeply in the shadow of Monte d'Oro (2389m), the fifth-highest peak on the island, before arriving at the cool mountain hamlet of Vizzavona. A mere cluster of houses and hotels around a train station, Vizzavona is a major hub for a huge number of walkers. There are a few eateries, including Bar-Restaurant de la Gare and Restaurant du Chef de Gare – L'Altagna, which prepare simple meals.

The Forêt de Vizzavona, whose 1633 hectares are covered mainly by beech and laricio pines, is a peaceful haven and a magnet for walkers, with lots of excellent hikes on offer. Look for the signpost indicating a short, gentle path that meanders down through a superb forest of pine and beech to Cascades des Anglais, a sequence of gleaming waterfalls. Continuing southwest along the N193 for a few kilometres brings you to the village of Bocognano. From here the road to the Cascade du Voile de la Mariée (Bridal Veil Falls) is on the left as you leave the village. Impressively fast-flowing in winter, you may find it little more than a dribble in summer.

If you want to take a different approach to viewing the forest, try Parc Vizzavona Aventure (☎ 04 95 10 43 16, 06 85 03 19 90; www.corsicanatura.fr; Col de Vizzavona; admission €15-20; ☸ 9am-5pm mid-Jun–mid-Sep), which has 10 ropeways and clambering nets through the trees. It's beside the N193, just before the Col de Vizzavona.

☙ HÔTEL MONTE D'ORO // TRADITIONAL FARE AND PLENTY OF ATMOSPHERE NEAR VIZZAVONA

At the Col de Vizzavona, this restaurant (☎ 04 95 47 21 06; N193, Col de Vizzavona; mains €15-23; ☸ lunch & dinner May-Sep) is truly special: run by the same family since 1904, it has retained that early-20th-century feel. It's hard not to be overwhelmed by the old-fashioned vibes that emanate from the dining room, which has exposed beams, white tablecloths and vines dangling from the high ceilings. There aren't too many surprises on the menu (veal, wild boar, lamb and Corsican soup), but it's the atmosphere that's the drawcard here.

☙ A CANTINA DI MATTEU // THE BEST PLACE TO STOCK UP ON LOCAL GOODIES IN THE VÉNACHESE

Those who weren't in the know wouldn't give a second glance to this inconspicuous village produce shop (☎ 04 95 47 36 70; N193, Venaco; mains from €4; ☸ 9am-6pm year-round), which doubles as a bistro in summer. But they'd be missing out on stunningly simple, yet delicious, dishes made with the highest-quality ingredients possible, all sourced from the best local producers – the cheese from the Loefgen farm is to die for. Stop here for a drink or a quick bite (such as a sandwich, charcuterie platter or salad) on your Vénachese exploration. It's on the N193.

BACKGROUND

HISTORY

· · · · · · ·

World history is generally told without reference to Corsica, except, in passing, as the place that gave birth to Emperor Napoléon Bonaparte. Even so, Corsica's history is a fascinating and turbulent one. Its strategic position long attracted the attentions of the major Mediterranean and European powers. Armies from Pisa, Genoa, France, Spain and Britain, not to mention the Moors and the forces of the Roman and Holy Roman Empires, have all fought on Corsican soil. This long history of conflict reflects another battle – the islanders' struggle to assert their identity while dominated by a succession of foreign rulers. Indeed, Corsicans have been battling for their independence ever since the Romans occupied their island, beginning in 259 BC.

NEOLITHIC CORSICA

The first inhabitants of the island probably came from what is nowadays Tuscany, the nearest place on the European mainland. They survived by hunting, gathering and fishing. You can still see rock caves of the kind in which they lived at Filitosa in the south.

> *'Corsicans have been battling for their independence ever since the Romans occupied their island'*

Around 4000 BC the islanders, like so many early European societies, became captivated by big stones. At various sites, particularly in the southwestern corner of the island, they erected great standing slabs of stone (menhirs), and shelter-like constructions (dolmens), in which two or more standing stones support a huge, horizontal slab. At some point they began to shape and carve their menhirs, which became simple statues with carved warrior faces.

Examples of these menhirs still stand at various places across the island, including Patrimonio, where a pair flank the stage of the annual Nuits de la Guitare festival.

THE TORRÉENS

In about 1100 BC a new race, possibly originating from the eastern Mediterranean, came to the island. These new islanders have come to be known as Torréens, named after their seemingly indestructible signature edifices, the *torri,* or towers, which stand

» 6570 BC	» 4000–1800 BC	» 565 BC
The skeleton of the 'Dame de Bonifacio' remains the first sure indication of human presence on Corsica	Monoliths and megalithic tombs constructed by the island's inhabitants	Alalia (Aléria) founded by Greeks from Phocaea in Anatolia

BACKGROUND

alongside or on the ruins of menhirs and dolmens. Some of the best examples of these towers dot the coastline of Cap Corse (p46).

Evidence suggests that the Torréens routed their predecessors, the menhir and dolmen builders who, with less-sophisticated weapons, appear to have migrated or fled north. Groups of Torréens then headed south to Sardinia, where they built some of the first conical stone edifices, now called *nuraghi*.

Early *castelli* (castles) are the most significant vestiges of the settled, more organised way of life that the island's inhabitants had begun to lead. You can visit the remains of three of these *castelli* in the mountains between Porto-Vecchio and Propriano.

GREEKS & ROMANS

In the 6th century BC, Greeks from Phocaea, on the coast of Anatolia, founded Alalia at what is today the conurbation of Aléria on Corsica's flat eastern plain. Alalia thrived on trade and Corsica soon rose to relative fame.

For the cosmopolitan, seafaring peoples of the Mediterranean, however, the island was primarily a place for brief port calls. Nobody before the Romans bothered to invest in or take control of the island. When Rome did step in, it was above all for strategic reasons: to prevent Corsica from falling into the hands of its enemy, the Carthaginians.

DON'T MISS...

HISTORIC SITES

- ★ **Pianu di Levie** // Well-preserved megalithic remains (p146)
- ★ **Église de San Michele de Murato** // Glorious example of Pisan church architecture (p57)
- ★ **Citadel of Bonifacio** // Genoa's first military toehold on the island (p129)
- ★ **Genoese towers of Cap Corse** // Typical of over 80 watchtowers around the Corsican coastline (p46)
- ★ **Corte** // Capital of Pascal Paoli's brief-lived Corsican republic (p169)
- ★ **Citadel of Calvi** // Where Admiral Horatio Nelson lost the sight in his right eye (p59)
- ★ **Maison Bonaparte (Ajaccio)** // Napoléon's birthplace, almost a shrine to the Emperor (p102)

» 259 BC	» AD 476	» 774
Rome seizes Corsica and holds on to it for more than five centuries	The Western Roman Empire collapses	Moors from North Africa begin to raid Corsica

Rome conquered Alalia, renaming it Aléria, and set about imposing its way of life and government upon the islanders, exacting tribute, and even selling some of them into slavery. The Romans, though, never went to any great pains to improve the island. In what was to become a recurrent pattern in Corsica, those islanders least willing to bend to invaders retired to the interior and the protection of the unconquerable mountains.

GOTHS, VANDALS & MOORS

After the collapse of the Western Roman Empire in AD 476, the distant Byzantine Empire (the Eastern Roman Empire, based in Constantinople) began to sniff around former Roman territories such as Corsica. The collapse of Rome had left Corsica vulnerable to Rome's own despoilers – the Goths under Totila and the Vandals under Genseric. It's likely that the Vandals, having laid waste to Gaul, took to the water and sacked Aléria too. Byzantium's equally bloody conquest of the island in the first half of the 6th century ended this brief dominion by Germanic tribes.

THE MOOR'S HEAD

A black head swathed in a white bandana; you see it everywhere – on beer-bottle labels, on the Corsican coat of arms that adorns public buildings and fluttering on Corsica's traditional flag. It was Pascal Paoli who made the Moor's head the island's official emblem. Yet no one really knows why. What deepens the mystery is that the Moors, in their incarnation as pirates from the Mediterranean's southern shores, were one of Corsica's traditional enemies. During the Crusades, any crusader who had a victory over the 'infidels' could add the Moor's head to his personal coat of arms, suggesting that the Moor's head was a symbol of Corsica's victory over its enemies.

Why, though, does the Corsican Moor wear his bandana around his forehead, whereas the four Moors on the coat of arms of Sardinia, just to the south, wear theirs as blindfolds? Corsican General Ghjuvan Petru Gaffori, when he attacked the Genoese citadel in Bastia in 1745, was perhaps the first to reposition the cloth. 'Corsica at last has its eyes open,' Gaffori said. And Paoli commented, 'Corsicans want to see clearly. Freedom must walk by the torch of philosophy. Could we say that we seem to fear the light?' Both of these remarks suggest that Corsica had come to identify itself with its Moor's head.

» 1077	» 1133	» 1195
Pope Gregory VII appoints the bishop of Pisa to oversee Corsican affairs	Pope Innocent II places the island under the joint yet separate control of Pisa and Genoa	Genoa conquers Bonifacio

During the 8th century Corsica was also increasingly subject to attack by the Moors, Arabs and Berbers from North Africa. Whether as organised navies or free-booting pirates, the Moors raided for slaves. From time to time they would take possession of a coastal village or a wider coastal region, even venturing deeper inland. From the 8th century right up to the 18th, the islanders lived in perpetual fear of invasion from the Mediterranean's southern shores.

PISA RULES

The 10th century saw the rise to power of the nobility. Important feudal families, often immigrants from Tuscany or Liguria, on the coast of present-day Italy, created fiefdoms on the island and ruled them with a rod of iron. Some historians argue that Corsica's close-knit clan system dates right back to this period.

In 1077 the Pope appointed the bishop of Pisa to oversee his Corsican interests. The then-powerful Italian city of Pisa, continually at odds with its rival, Genoa, set high value on commerce and trade and its bishop effectively served as a front man for Pisan merchants. Corsica too benefited from Pisan overlordship, and this period was one of peace, prosperity and development. Handsome Pisan-style churches were erected in the Balagne, the Nebbio and on and around the northeastern coast. Four prime examples are the Cathédrale du Nebbio in St-Florent, the Église de San Michele de Murato (p57), Aregno's Église de la Trinité (p81), and the Cathédrale de la Canonica in the Réserve Naturelle de Biguglia.

Pisa's good fortune in Corsica aroused the jealousy of Genoa, her perpetual rival. Genoese ambitions took a turn for the better when in 1133 Pope Innocent II divided the island between these two Italian republics. From that time, Genoa set about gaining territory piecemeal, picking off villages and advancing little by little.

First Genoa undermined its rival's supremacy by fortifying the town of Bonifacio in the south. Genoese forces then pushed north, where they turned Calvi into a stronghold. By the 13th century, despite opposition from some island lords who remained loyal to Pisa, Genoa was top dog. Pisa's defeat in 1284 in the sea Battle of Meloria, a small island near Livorno, marked the end of her domination of Corsica.

GENOA TAKES OVER

Before Italian unification in the second half of the 19th century, Genoa was one of the great early modern merchant states and a powerful force in the Mediterranean. Indeed, if it had been more ambitious, Genoa rather than Spain might very well have

BACKGROUND

» 1284	» 1380	» 1553
Genoa defeats Pisa in the naval Battle of Meloria, marking the end of Pisan rule and beginning Genoese occupation	Bastia founded	French troops land and capture Bastia, declaring Corsica French territory

been the first to discover and exploit the Americas; Columbus, after all, was Genoese, whether he was born in Genoa proper or, as some Corsicans would have it, in Calvi, which was controlled by Genoa at the time.

Genoa occupied and dominated Corsica for five centuries, during which time the island was turned into a fortress. However, the Genoese had little sentiment for the Corsicans, who were made to pay taxes and often evicted or excluded from towns and put to work on the land to serve Genoa's commercial and economic interests. Those who disobeyed were punished severely.

Genoa aimed to turn Corsica into its breadbasket. It created towns and set the population to work cultivating olive and chestnut trees (see p234). By the mid-16th century, when the Genoese believed they at last had Corsica under control, the island's strategic importance in the Mediterranean basin was once again a catalyst for major disruption.

> 'Genoa aimed to turn Corsica into its breadbasket'

SAMPIERO CORSO

In 1552 the people of Siena, another powerful city state, like Genoa, on the Italian mainland, rose up against the Spanish garrison that was occupying the city and called on France for protection. The wily Henri II, king of France, saw his chance to gain territory and influence on the shores of the Mediterranean. Corsica, offshore and strategically located, got caught up in a conflict that wasn't her own.

In 1553 a French expeditionary corps reached Bastia under the command of Maréchal de Termes and his second in command, the Turkish privateer Dragut, a French ally. Bastia fell, followed swiftly by other towns, and within only a few days Corsica was declared French territory.

During this campaign, Sampiero Corso, a Corsican colonel in the French army, came to symbolise the fight against the Genoese. However, popular though he was on the island, his unifying presence wasn't enough to safeguard the French victory. Playing off the Mediterranean superpowers, the Genoese appealed to Charles V, king of Spain, for support. Charles, smarting from France's attempt to dislodge his troops from Siena and always eager to thumb his nose at his neighbour north of the Pyrenees, went on the attack and the French, after suffering a series of defeats, signed the Treaty of Cateau-Cambrésis in 1559, recognising Genoese supremacy on the island.

» 1559	» 1567	» 1725
The Treaty of Cateau-Cambrésis recognises Genoese supremacy once more	Death of Sampiero Corso, three years after his failed attempt to assume control of the island of his birth	Pascal Paoli is born in 1725 in Morosaglia, in the Castagniccia region

SAMPIERO CORSO 'THE FIERY'

Born in 1498 near Bastelica, Sampiero Corso became known as 'the most Corsican of Corsicans'. He rose to fame on the mainland as a soldier in the French army. Vehemently anti-Genoese, Sampiero fought with French forces in 1553 in a bid to reconquer his native island. Although the Genoese occupiers dislodged the invading French, he refused to give up hope.

He returned to the island with a band of partisans in 1564, despite having failed to get European backing for his venture. He managed to destabilise the Genoese for a short while but never came near to vanquishing them. Three years later, Sampiero was ambushed and decapitated in a typical Corsican blood feud.

Though a great soldier, Sampiero was short on marital skills. When 47, he married Vannina d'Ornano, 32 years his junior. Some say that while her husband was away campaigning, she fell under the influence of their children's tutor, an attested Genoese spy. More romantically, others have it that she had an affair with Gabriele, a Genoese artist and childhood friend. What's certain is that Sampiero strangled her with his own hands.

Four years later, he was murdered by three Corsican mercenaries, cousins of Vannina, and his head was publicly displayed in Ajaccio. Thus, humiliatingly, ended the life of Corsica's first seeker of an independent existence for the island, murdered by his own compatriots.

After this temporary respite under the French, the Corsicans found themselves once again at the mercy of their familiar oppressor. Sampiero Corso made a brief, independent and abortive attempt to dislodge them in 1564 (see the boxed text, above) but despite a favourable start, his campaign was short-lived and the Genoese consolidated their control.

WARS OF INDEPENDENCE

What is known as Corsica's Forty Years' War began in 1729, when a determined old peasant in a mountain village near Corte refused to pay tax to a Genoese tax collector. Following his example, more and more Corsicans refused to pay their tribute to Genoa. Little by little, the rebels grew bolder, louder and more organised, stealing weapons and, though disparate and uncoordinated, becoming a threat to Genoese rule.

» 1729	» 1755–69	» 1769
First stirrings of the Corsicans' 40-year revolt against Genoese occupation	Pascal Paoli attempts to create an independent state of Corsica	The Battle of Ponte Novo marks the end of Corsica's battle for independence and the beginning of French rule proper

BACKGROUND

Yet again, outsiders were to determine Corsica's destiny, this time in the form of the emperor of Austria and his forces, to whom the Genoese successfully appealed for assistance.

St-Florent and Bastia, briefly held by the rebels, were recovered. After defeat at the Battle of Calenzana (1732), the Genoese forces regrouped and gradually regained control, but it was a transient success. The revolt recovered momentum and, at a meeting in Corte in 1735, the Corsicans drew up a constitution for a sovereign state, free and independent of European interference.

There followed a bizarre episode of the kind that seems to dog Corsican history. In 1736 an eloquent, opportunistic German aristocrat, one Theodore von Neuhoff, disembarked in Aléria. Seeing him as the leader for whom they had been looking, the rebels allowed this eccentric to declare himself king of Corsica. His reign, however, lasted barely nine months.

> *'a bizarre episode of the kind that seems to dog Corsican history'*

Theodore's earlier, undignified flight notwithstanding, the Corsicans, many of them glad to be rid of this exotic interloper, pushed on. The Genoese were so rattled that in 1738 they accepted France's self-interested offer of assistance. The French king, Louis XV, was delighted to be involved once more in the island's affairs, this time with Genoa's blessing instead of in the role of invader. He sent an expeditionary corps to Corsica – paid for by the Genoese – under the command of General de Boissieux.

In 1753, when the last French regiments pulled out, over 1000 Corsicans had gone into exile abroad, the rebellion appeared to be over and Genoese rule seemed again consolidated.

PASCAL PAOLI'S REVOLT

Tranquillity, as tends to happen in Corsica, was brief. In 1755, no more than two years after the last French soldier had sailed away, the charismatic Pascal Paoli (you'll often find the Corsican spelling, Pasquale Paoli) led an insurrection that could so easily have changed the island's fortunes permanently. Educated in Naples, Paoli succeeded where all before him had failed, uniting the factions and rival families as one against Genoa. What's more, he devised a constitutional state – such a novelty in that still dynastic and absolutist age – which, given time, might have ensured Corsica a happy, self-regulating independence. But it was not to be.

» 1769	» 1789	» 1794
Birth in Ajaccio of Napoléon Bonaparte, future emperor of France	Corsica is formally annexed to France	British troops seize St-Florent, Bastia and Calvi; George III, king of England, proclaimed as sovereign in Corsica

BACKGROUND

PASCAL PAOLI – PIONEER

Pascal Paoli, Corsica's revolutionary leader, was at the head of Corsica during its short period of independence between 1755 and 1769. On the island, Pascal, known to Corsicans as the 'father of the nation', is held in the same esteem as Napoléon Bonaparte himself.

Son of Giacinto Paoli, a distinguished rebel leader in the struggle against Genoese occupation, Pascal was born in 1725 in Morosaglia, in the Castagniccia region, where since 1889 his ashes have been buried in the chapel beneath his childhood home (p161). When he was 14, he followed his father, who had gone into exile during the French occupation, to Naples. Here he received his education, reading the works of radical thinkers of the Enlightenment such as Montesquieu and corresponding with Jean-Jacques Rousseau. He was only 30 when he returned to the island and succeeded in uniting the disparate rebel forces. Three months later he was declared General of the Nation.

He managed to winkle out the Genoese from all their strongholds except their six main fortress towns, which they continued to control. But his short-lived military successes aren't his claim to fame. Cultured and intellectually outstanding, as much political and social thinker as military commander, he developed agriculture, began the drainage of malaria-infested coastal marshes – and promulgated a democratic constitution before the French Revolution and over three decades before America's revolutionary thinkers convened to work out something similar in Philadelphia. In just 14 years, he founded Île Rousse as a rival to Genoese Calvi, established the Moor's head (see the boxed text, p188) as Corsica's symbol and set up a mint in the tiny town of Murato. With his power base in Corte, he's also remembered as the founder of Corsica's first university.

His efforts to root out criminality and Corsica's trademark murderous vendettas were heroic. The English writer James Boswell visited Paoli and was a voice for the Corsican cause in Britain. The later religious reformer John Wesley called him, with more than a measure of hyperbole, 'as great a lover of his country as Epaminondas and as great a general as Hannibal'.

In 1769 his outnumbered troops were routed by the superior French forces and Paoli took refuge in England. In 1789 a different post-revolutionary France made its peace with the erstwhile rebel commander and sent him back to France with the title of lieutenant-general. Flattering this was for Paoli but, soon alienated by the excesses of the revolution on the mainland, he summoned a regional assembly in Corte, declared himself president and formally seceded from France, later offering 'his' island to the British.

Retiring to a life of exile in London in 1796, he was granted a pension and died there in February 1807. There's a cenotaph in his honour in Westminster Abbey.

BACKGROUND

» 1794–96	» 1796	» 1807
The brief Anglo-Corsican kingdom	Pascal Paoli retires to London where he lives in exile	Pascal Paoli, hero of the Corsican independence movement, dies in London

Genoa made several desperate, disastrous attempts to regain control of an island that had seemed hers for ever. Then the French seized the opportunity they had been waiting for. In 1764 France, scarcely 30 years after her first intervention at Genoa's request and on the Genoese side, accepted the increasingly enfeebled Genoese city state's offer for her to take over the strongholds of Bastia, Ajaccio, Calvi and St-Florent, thus effectively gaining control of the whole island.

The Treaty of Versailles, four years later, formalised the Genoese cession of Corsica to France, which began acting less like a mediator and more like a ruler.

Pascal Paoli was the victim of decisions taken far away from his island. He mobilised his supporters but they and their resources just couldn't compete. Their defeat at the Battle of Ponte Novo on the River Golo, northeast of Ponte Leccia, on 8 May 1769, marked the beginning of French rule of Corsica and Paoli fled to London.

CORSICA, FRANCE

Yet again Corsica had a military government of outsiders. In re-establishing law and order and taking control of the administration, the French followed the example of the Genoese, but more softly, softly. They promulgated a new set of laws, the Code Corse, relevant to the island and taking into account its peculiarities, and they made earnest efforts to increase the yield of Corsican agriculture. Corsica increasingly adapted itself to a style of French governance – but one that would soon be blown apart, on the island as on the mainland, by the French Revolution.

Many Corsicans initially applauded the revolution. For the impoverished islanders, it gave new voice to popular dissatisfaction. In 1789 a decree proclaimed: 'Corsica belongs to the French Empire and its people shall be governed by the same constitution as the rest of France'. An amnesty was granted and Paoli returned to the island.

But reconciliation between Corsica and France was not total. In 1793 Paoli was blamed for the failure of the French revolutionary government's expedition to Sardinia, just to the south of Corsica. He had, it was alleged, committed fewer troops than the government had expected. In Paris, the extreme Revolutionary Convention that had judged and executed Louis XIV and his queen, Marie-Antoinette, ordered Paoli's arrest for counter-revolutionary behaviour. Paoli, for his part, declared Corsica's secession, and requested help from Britain.

Spain, France, the Austro-Hungarian Empire – and here, invited to feast at the table, was yet another imperial player. For Britain this was an opportunity of the same kind that Genoa's cry for help had been for France.

» 1811	» 1894	» 1914–18
Emperor Napoleon decrees that Corsica will be a single département	Completion of the railway between Ajaccio and Bastia	In WWI 30,000 Corsicans die fighting for France

Ranging the Corsican coast in 1794, the British fleet easily captured St-Florent, Bastia and Calvi (it was during the battle for Calvi that Admiral Horatio Nelson lost the sight in his right eye). George III, king of England, was proclaimed sovereign in Corsica. But Paoli soon became disillusioned with the British. He had believed Britain to be liberal and enlightened but quickly grasped that his new sponsors were no more likely to benefit Corsicans than so many other alien rulers had been. Local hero Paoli was passed over for the vice-royalty and again went into exile in London, where he died in 1807, in receipt of a modest British government pension until his last day.

The Anglo-Corsican kingdom had lasted just over two years. As Jonathan Fenby drily observes in his excellent *On the Brink: The Trouble with France,* 'two years of nominal rule by George III, who was proclaimed "Anglo-Corsican King"… cannot have been much of a consolation for having lost America'.

Following the English departure in 1796, the island's affairs came once again under the jurisdiction of France and its post-revolutionary leader, Napoléon Bonaparte, Corsican by birth but little else.

> *'Napoléon's… single ambition for Corsica was to make it French, once and for all'*

Far from promoting the special interests of the island of his birth, the future emperor's single ambition for Corsica was to make it French, once and for all and completely. Immediately, Napoléon's enforcers came into conflict with the clergy, resulting in an anti-French insurrection in 1798. Mistrustful of Corsica's own political class, Napoléon excluded Corsicans from island administrative posts and broke the island up into the two *départements* that exist to this day.

19TH & 20TH CENTURIES

Corsica periodically asserted its individuality during the 19th and 20th centuries, rejecting on occasion central government decisions from Paris. The clan structure endured and there was an upsurge in banditry. During this period levels of rural poverty endured, and attempts to develop infrastructure and agriculture achieved little.

Under France's second empire (1852–70; at its head, Napoléon III, son of Napoléon I's brother Louis) real investment was made in Corsica's infrastructure (such as the Corsican rail network that continues to trundle along today). Corsicans took

BACKGROUND

» 1940	» 1943	» 1962
Corsica is occupied by more than 90,000 Italian and German troops during WWII	Corsica is the first region of France to be liberated by the Allied forces in WWII	Arrival of first *pieds noirs,* French returnees from newly independent Algeria

NAPOLÉON BONAPARTE: SON OF CORSICA?

Paradoxically, the island's most famous son did more to Frenchify Corsica than any other individual. Despite his early expressions of Corsican patriotic feeling, Napoléon was extremely ambivalent, even hostile, about his native island.

In his final exile on the island of St Helena in the southern Atlantic, someone asked him why he'd never done more to help develop Corsica's economy. His answer: '*Je n'en ai pas eu le temps*' (I never had the time). His policy towards Corsica, once installed as emperor of all France, was chilly, even cynical. Let the Corsicans keep their religion and their priests, he said, but let them love France and serve in her armies. A mere two roads, one between Ajaccio and Bastia, one between Bastia and St-Florent, should suffice, he said, for a people whose principal highway should be the sea. Native Corsicans, he decreed, were to be excluded from the administration of the island since they simply weren't trustworthy.

In 1814, the year of Napoléon's first definitive defeat, the people of Ajaccio threw a bust of the Emperor into the sea, while the citizens of Bastia actually welcomed British troops. Corsican resentment, however, seems to have passed with time and, by the mid-19th century, the house in Ajaccio where Napoléon was born (p102) was almost a place of pilgrimage. Nowadays, Napoléon is still lionised as the homeboy who made good in the wider world and brought the island fame.

advantage of the greater employment opportunities available in mainland France in enormous numbers, and they also filled a disproportionately high number of posts throughout the French colonial empire. On the downside, 30,000 Corsicans, a huge number compared to the island's slender population, died for France on the European battlefields of WWI.

> '30,000 Corsicans... died for France on the European battlefields of WWI'

WWII brought hostilities to the island itself. In 1940 Corsica was occupied by more than 90,000 Italian and German troops. Those who opposed the occupation forces took to the countryside, to the maquis, the tangled cloak of undergrowth that covers much of the island, and the term was coined to describe the whole of the French resistance movement. In 1943, Corsica was the first region of France to be liberated and, like its neighbouring islands in the Mediterranean, served as a forward base for the liberation of mainland Europe.

» 1975	» 1976	» 1981
The island is divided into two départements, Haute Corse and Corse du Sud	Front de Libération Nationale de la Corse (FLNC) formed	Inauguration of the University of Corsica Pascal Paoli in Corte and creation of the Corsican regional assembly

THE CORSICAN MALAISE

Corsica's latter-day difficulties date primarily from the 1960s, when a movement for Corsican autonomy was formed to combat what some perceived as France's 'colonialist' policy towards the island. One particular source of friction was France's use of Corsica for the resettlement of thousands of *pieds noirs,* French citizens living in North Africa who fled Algeria when that country achieved independence.

In 1975 tensions exploded when Corsican separatists, led by the Simeoni brothers, unearthed a scandal in the eastern coastal town of Aléria, involving fraudulent wine-making practices in a winery run by a *pied noir.* The protesters occupied a building used to store wine and an attempt by the police to resolve the situation ended in two deaths.

The Front de Libération Nationale de la Corse (FLNC) was formed in 1976, and talk of autonomy increasingly turned to claims for full independence. That year averaged more than one bombing *per day* and the violence, usually against property and often settling arcane internal scores, continued at a reduced level for well over a decade.

In the early 1980s two measures were adopted to appease the nationalists. Firstly, a university was opened in Corte; for many years, after the French had closed down Pascal Paoli's university, young Corsicans had travelled to mainland France or Italy for their higher education. Secondly, the Assemblée de Corse was created; previously, the island had belonged to the Provence-Alpes-Côte d'Azur region. The détente arising from these measures was short-lived, however, and in 1983 the government tried unsuccessfully to proscribe the FLNC.

By the 1990s the FLNC had broken into multiple splinter groups, all armed and mostly violent, and other independent groups had sprouted. From 1993 to 1996 these groups warred against each other every bit as vigorously as they had previously opposed the perceived coloniser. Long regarded as the caretakers of Corsica's environment against external depredations and indifference, the nationalist movements were increasingly seen by many as gangs of hoods and thugs, who considered Rambo-like armed conflict and protection of their cronies' private interests as more important than political action.

The quarrel continues to this day in various arenas such as policies for economic development, the environment and language. Tourism is a particularly sensitive area. It brings wealth to an island with poor soil for agriculture, few resources and virtually no industry. Yet for the nationalists, tourism is seen as a tool of assimilation. Much of their rage is reserved for concrete holiday developments (second homes are a favourite

» 1983	» 1998	» 2001
The central government outlaws the FLNC	France's top official on the island, Claude Érignac, is assassinated by nationalist extremists	Assassination of François Santoni, former leader of the FLNC

target of the bombers), which tend to be ghost communities, except for the two months of high summer (this said, the separatists have maintained a strict hands-off policy regarding tourists themselves).

CORSICA TODAY

The assassination in 1998 of Claude Érignac, the regional *préfet* (prefect) and as such the most senior representative of the French state on the island, had a huge impact. His death sparked strong expressions of disgust among Corsicans themselves, with as many as 40,000 taking to the streets to demonstrate.

French President Lionel Jospin's government launched a 'Clean Hands' operation, aiming to reinforce law and order on the island, but his tough approach failed to win the hearts and minds of most Corsicans, who felt they had been demonised as terrorists.

The responses of successive French governments both left and right were alternatively muscular police enforcement and open or off-the-record talks with nationalist leaders. The cause of law and order wasn't helped by the torching of an illegal beachside shack by, it was soon revealed, undercover police working to instructions from none other than Bernard Bonnet, the hardline successor to the murdered Érignac as *préfet* (this was no set-up: Bonnet was tried, found guilty and sentenced to three years in prison for his abuse of power).

As a result of negotiations in 1999 within what came to be known as the Matignon Process, a law was passed granting greater autonomy to the island and retaining several of its preferential fiscal privileges. It also stipulated that the Corsican language should be taught as a subject in primary school – and approved a massive program of yet more investment in the island amounting to €2000 million over 15 years.

In July 2003, after 30 years of nationalist violence and 200 years of French rule, Corsicans were invited to vote on their future status in a referendum linked to plans for decentralisation throughout France which would have united Corsica's two *départements* into a single administrative region. The vote was split virtually 50:50 right up to polling day, when those who rejected the proposal, which was supported by nationalist leaders, won by a small margin. The result was seen as a snub to both these local leaders and to Prime Minister Jean Pierre Raffarin's plans to decentralise power while keeping Corsica under French rule.

In December 2007, almost 10 years after the event, Yvan Colonna, one time lifeguard, fireman and trainee teacher who became a goatherd – and whose father was

» 2002	» JULY 2003	» 2003
The Matignon agreement grants additional autonomy to the Assemblée Territoriale, the Corsican regional government	Arrest of Yvan Colonna, accused of the murder of Claude Érignac	The anti-independence lobby narrowly wins a referendum on autonomous rule for Corsica

a member of the French parliament –was convicted of the assassination of Claude Érignac (see the previous section) and sentenced to life imprisonment. After a major manhunt and nearly five years on the run, he had been captured, hiding in a shepherd's hut in southern Corsica, together with a bag containing a grenade, a Luger pistol, a pair of balaclavas and €3700. Still locked up, he has repeatedly claimed his innocence and, especially around Cargèse and Corte, you'll see banners and slogans in his support.

In the 18 months preceding our research on the island, there were 22 clan slayings, mostly a settling of scores in broad daylight and many carried out with powerful hunting guns equipped with telescopic sights. Not one has resulted in a prosecution, principally because witnesses are unwilling or too scared to talk. By contrast, in 2008 the number of bombings, whether for political or gangland motives, was at its lowest since 1973. However, at 89 blasts, it's still a figure that would make most of the rest of the world shudder.

Corsica's long legacy of terrorism, violence, significant graft and insularity to the outside world shows little sign of abating despite the desire of the vast majority of islanders to have a job, relative comfort and be able to get on with their lives as both Corsicans and French citizens.

BACKGROUND

» 2004	» DECEMBER 2007	» 2008
A right-wing coalition wins regional elections, thanks to a pact with the Corsican nationalists	Yvan Colonna is found guilty and sentenced to life imprisonment	Part of the Assemblée de Corse building burns following a nationalist demonstration

ALL ABOUT CORSICA

· · · · · · ·

BEING CORSICAN

Corsicans are conservative, stoical, tradition-loving people with an integrity that doesn't suffer fools gladly. While their reputation for being hostile and unwelcoming is unjustified, there's a grain of truth in the stereotype. Don't expect to find arms wide open to greet you, particularly in some of the more remote mountain villages. That said, once you've earned the trust and respect of a Corsican, you won't find a more hospitable, generous host.

If asked, an overwhelming proportion of the population will say that it feels Corsican first of all and only secondly French. Centuries of invasion and occupation have created a kind of siege mentality. Just look at the island's military and defensive architecture – muscular citadels and bastions guard strategic coastal towns like Bastia, Calvi and Bonifacio, while a necklace of 67 Genoese watchtowers girdle the coast, originally intended as an advance warning system for pirate attacks.

Hardly surprising then is the insular, inward-looking mentality of the islanders. While few Corsicans are blatantly xenophobic, a deep-seated desire to protect their cultural identity can sometimes lead to an island-first mindset and an acceptance of outsiders that on occasion borders on mere tolerance. The message behind the bullet-ridden road signs, with the French place name spray-painted out will be lost on very few.

The tourist industry, by far the island's largest provider of employment, is, for some, a mixed blessing. According to more than a few nationalists, the steady stream of tourists (more than two million annually, bringing in a minimum of €1 billion) only serves to exploit the environment and denude the region's cultural fabric. Compare the homogenous coastal development and the ostentatious *maisons d'Américains* (sumptuous homes financed by returnee Corsicans who want to make a statement of wealth and success) with the modest, fortress-like native architecture constructed from local materials like granite and slate and you'll instantly be aware of the contradictory forces at play. Add to this a love-hate relationship with mainland France and what are perceived as its self-interested policies for the region, and you may begin to understand the Corsican psyche.

ROAD SIGNS

Road signs in Corsica express much more than an indication of the next village or town. With the French version of the name spray-painted out by more-ardent nationalists, they represent a modest, high-profile political statement. They're also targets in a more literal sense. You're bound to come across signs peppered with bullet holes to the point where some are illegible. Far from being the work of B-grade movie hoods, they're an expression of the jubilation of a group of hunters at the day's bag, or the result of a little sharpshooting practice in preparation for the next prowl through the maquis in search of warm-blooded prey.

THE FAMILY & THE CLAN

Corsicans have long learned to rely on no one but themselves, and the family remains central to island society. Attitudes are changing, but many families still live according to the traditional family model, with women staying at home and men going out to earn a crust. These clearly defined gender roles were originally dictated by the practical division of labour – with the men away from home pasturing their flocks, women were left running the house and raising the children – although nowadays they're as much about tradition and social convention as practical necessity. Still, 29 out of 51 representatives in the Corsican assembly are female, demonstrating the growing sea change in attitudes.

Family ties are strong in Corsica. Children often live in the family home until well into their 30s or until marriage, when they may then move out but remain within shuffling distance of the family roof. This is largely an economic decision as young people, particularly if unemployed, simply cannot afford to leave home. Unless, of course, it's to emigrate.

Outside the main towns life can be desperately quiet – especially in the mountain villages in winter, when there's a mass exodus of Corsica's young people to Marseille, Nice and Paris until the tourist season rolls around again. For many village families who have moved to Ajaccio, Bastia or other coastal towns, the original home still retains a powerful pull. Closed and shuttered for most of the year, it comes to life each major holiday, when family members return to their village and their roots.

Certain rules of inheritance have served to preserve Corsican family unity and continuity. The affiliation to a clan automatically provides an extended family, which also includes members of a village community in a structure that is protective of its influence and authority. However, Corsica isn't one big happy family; ties within families, clans and villages are matched by wariness of those on the outside – other families, clans and villages.

HONOUR & VENDETTA

A sense of honour is a particularly important legacy of the island's turbulent past. A bloody vendetta might result from a land dispute, amorous rivalry or nothing more than injured pride. Blow and counterblow, such tit-for-tat killings might continue for generations unless the parish priest managed to broker an accord that both families would accept.

The island has spawned a number of 'bandits of honour', outlawed and seeking refuge in the maquis, sometimes for years, after having avenged an offence by violent means. Even today, such cases rarely come to trial because of the silence of potential witnesses, even from the families of those gunned down, and the police's inability to assemble enough evidence to secure a conviction.

> *'A bloody vendetta might result from… nothing more than injured pride'*

Weapons have always been an important part of Corsican culture – and not only for hunting. Today, though, visitors need not fear getting caught in the crossfire of feuding families or protectionist mafia rackets; apart from the odd burnt-out shell of a building, you probably won't even be aware of the internal machinations of the island's myriad factions.

Corsica's traditions, marked by a code of obligatory hospitality and often wildly disproportionate rough justice, have never been universal on the island nor without dissenters. However the response to the violent traditions has often itself been of equal violence. Pascal Paoli, during the brief lifespan of independent republican Corsica in the mid-18th century, perhaps meant to help his countrymen rethink their antique and chilling concept of honour, when he razed the homes of vendetta murderers and put up signposts to publicise the occupants' crimes. Napoléon was even more extreme: if a murderer could not be arrested, he had four of the offender's close kinsmen arrested and executed instantly.

IMMIGRANTS & ÉMIGRÉS

Armenians, Parsees, Jews and Corsicans too; the 260,000 inhabitants of the island are way outnumbered by the number of émigré Corsicans. How many have left the island and sunk roots elsewhere can only be guessed at, especially since many have intermarried, choosing partners from their new society. Guestimates vary wildly between 800,000 and 1.5 million, worldwide. What's more verifiable are official statistics indicating that in mainland France there are around 600,000 Corsicans – a number that swells considerably each autumn, once the tourist season is over and the island's hotels and restaurants put up their shutters and dismiss their staff. Most Corsican residents on the mainland, whether seasonal or permanent, live in Marseille and around Provence.

'Corsica's best and brightest left the island to study and often did not return'

This is no new phenomenon. In the 19th century as the French Empire expanded, particularly in Africa and Southeast Asia, Corsicans, escaping from an island with no industry to speak of and few prospects for employment, sought their fortune in faraway lands. From privates to senior officers, they were active in the army and were to be found – out of all proportion to the island's population –behind administrative desks as customs officers, governors, administrators and many more occupations that called for a suit or uniform. Two presidents of Venezuela can claim Corsican ancestry and it's estimated that around 4% of the population of Puerto Rico has a predominance of Corsican blood in its veins.

In early modern times, privileged Corsicans would head for Italy for their education from school to university. Pascal Paoli (see the boxed text, p193) opened the first university in Corsica in 1765, but when the French took over soon after, they closed it down. For the next two centuries, Corsicans seeking higher education were obliged once again to leave the island for Italy or, as was increasingly the case, for the French mainland. The result was an epidemic brain drain. Corsica's best and brightest left the island to study and often did not return. This negative flow was only remedied in 1981, when the University of Corsica Pascal Paoli in Corte opened for business in response to nationalist demand.

Of Corsica's total population of 281,000, roughly 100,000 live in the two major towns of Ajaccio and Bastia. Although this island-wide figure represents an overall increase of 1% in the last decade (and a healthy figure compared with the all-time low of 170,000 inhabitants in 1955), depopulation remains a serious concern in the mountain hamlets and villages. A high 84% of Corsica's population lives in the 87 *communes* around the coast, while in as many as 137 *communes* of the interior, more than half of the villagers are aged over 60.

Inversely, one in 10 people living on Corsica is non-French. Moroccans account for just over a half of these, ahead of Portuguese, Italians and Tunisians. In fact, outside Île de France, Corsica is the region with the highest proportion of foreigners in France. Of those who come to Corsica, most are young men seeking work in the agricultural, building and, to a lesser degree, tourism sectors. They are easily absorbed during 'the season' but with significant unemployment in the more spartan months and the annual brain drain of Corsica's youth to mainland France, resentments can run rife.

FAITH, FEASTING & FOLKLORE

Conservative and for much of the year politely reserved, Corsicans let go with a bang during their great festivals. These boisterous occasions reveal much about the islanders' long-held beliefs, mixing myth with faith and folklore.

Although the island is overwhelmingly Catholic, Catholicism in Corsica coexists with vestiges of mystical and superstitious practices such as the *spiritu* (the dead who return from beyond to revisit their terrestrial homes) and the malign power

BACKGROUND

RELIGIOUS FLOURISHES

Corsica's greatest architectural treasures are ecclesiastical; products of Pisan and Genoese influences that brought new and more sophisticated architectural styles to the island. The most notable and numerous of these are the Pisan Romanesque churches of the 11th century and the northern Italian baroque of the 17th and 18th centuries.

At the end of the 11th century the Pope appointed the bishop of Pisa to oversee papal interests on the island and as a result there are some delightful examples of Pisan Romanesque churches and cathedrals. They are distinctive by the chequered polychrome walls and engagingly naive sculptures and friezes. Among the most impressive are the Cathédrale de la Canonica, south of Bastia, and the Église de San Michele de Murato (p57) in the mountains south of St-Florent. You'll come across others in the Nebbio, Castagniccia and Balagne regions, where Pisan influence was strongest.

In contrast to the restrained Pisan style is the extravagance of the baroque style that the Genoese introduced to the island six centuries later. Rather than the simple, graphic facades favoured by the Pisans, the island's baroque churches are notable for their sculptural triangular or curvilinear pediments and sumptuously decorated interiors, which make extensive use of trompe l'œil, stucco and polychrome marbles. Many churches in the Balagne and Castagniccia were built in this style, often with freestanding bell towers. Out of a total inventory of about 150, good examples include the churches and oratories of Bastia and La Porta's church of St-Jean Baptiste (p160) in Castagniccia.

of the *occhju,* the evil eye. Other popular and fearful forces are the *strega,* a witch who slips through the keyhole at night to prey upon young children and suck their blood, and the *lagramanti,* spirits of the mist who hover near lakes and rivers, their laments enticing passers-by to a watery doom. More positively, the *signatoru* is a medium with the power to cure illness and parry the force of the evil eye by incantations.

Beliefs shaped by centuries of rural life are evident in many of the more memorable festivals, especially the elaborate Easter week processions in, for example, La Cerca and the Catenacciu, plus Bonifacio's unique procession of the Five Orders. And there's certainly no lack of religious fervour in each town's saint's day celebrations and during the lavish Holy Week processions of towns such as Bonifacio, Sartène, Cargèse, Calvi and Erbalunga.

For the visitor, observing a Corsican festival holds the key to a deeper understanding of the people themselves. The striking costumes and jewellery of the women show a profound appreciation of skilled handicraft, while traditional pastimes like polyphonic singing, horse- and boat-racing allow men to display their courage, nerve and skill. Rural fairs celebrating local produce are also hugely popular and allow the visitor to immerse themselves in local culture and buy top-quality regional specialities.

THE CORSICAN VOICE

BACKGROUND

'A voice from the depths of the earth, a song from the dawn of time.' So wrote Dorothy Carrington on first hearing Corsica's unique polyphonic singing. You're bound to hear it, wafting out of cafes and restaurants or played over the speakers sotto voce as you inspect supermarket shelves or sit waiting at a bus station. But for uninterrupted pleasure and time to appreciate its melodic intricacies and haunting refrains, you need to attend a recital, often as not held in the local parish church. In summer, several ensembles tour the island and any tourist office can give you details of upcoming events.

As emotional as flamenco, recalling ancient Gregorian chants and with strains that seem to have wafted over from the southern, Arab and Berber side of the Mediterranean, it speaks to the soul. It's singing for solidarity, typically in a trio or small chorus, where each male participant takes a different melody, and it's sung a cappella, without musical accompaniment. The Corsican anthem, *Diu vi Salvi Regina,* at once hymn and both battle and rallying cry, is often sung a cappella on public occasions.

'paghjella speak of powerful emotions – separation and parting, lament, loss and unrequited love'

The *paghjella,* for three or four male voices, is the form that you're most likely to hear. The men, usually dressed in black, stand with a hand over one ear so as to hear their own 'inner voice' without being distracted by the sounds of their neighbours. Often, they will put an arm around each other's shoulders, emphasising the collaborative, mutually supportive nature of what they are creating. Each voice contributes a different harmonic element: one provides the melody, another the bass, while the third, more high-pitched, improvises on the theme. The themes of the *paghjella* are usually secular and speak of powerful emotions – separation and parting, lament, loss and love, more often than not unrequited.

Corsican vocal music is not always performed a cappella. It might sometimes be accompanied by wooden or horn flutes, percussion or the *cetera,* a 16-stringed instrument. Most Corsican folk instruments are typically wind-based, as you'd expect from a primarily pastoral society. Fifes and flutes such as a *caramusa, u liscarolu* and a *ciallamella* are fashioned from wood or bone. Rhythm is often provided by *chjoche* (castanets), while violins, the *cetera* or guitars will supply the string accompaniment.

Groups that have recorded traditional Corsican forms (and whose recordings you will find on the island) include the seminal Canta U Populu Corsu, now fragmented and dispersed in different musical directions, the Celtic-inspired and hugely successful I Muvrini, the professional choir A Filetta and I Chjami Aghjalesi.

A new breed of musicians has evolved a hybrid sound that blends both traditional Corsican music and wider influences. Cinqui So, from Ajaccio, mixes polyphonic music with earthy world music beats, while Isula, with its dance beats, and more rock-oriented groups such as Ghostone, Triok and Blague à Part also pay tribute to their musical roots.

> ### TINO ROSSI
>
> In the field of popular music and in his prime, Ajaccio-born Tino Rossi simply *was* Corsica to mainland France and much of the world beyond. With his dapper suits, slicked-back hair and Latin lover persona, he managed in the course of his crooning career, from his first recordings in the 1930s through to his death in 1983, to record precisely 1014 songs and sell over 300 million records.

SACRED SONG & THE CUNFRATERNITA

Sacred song, often to this day sung in Latin, tends to be more formal, though infused with elements of the *paghjella*. This is the genre of the Mass and accompanies religious festivals such as local saint's days or the elaborate Holy Week processions. Often the singing at such public celebrations is undertaken by members of the local *cunfraternita,* or lay brotherhood.

At funerals too, the *cunfraternita* normally sings. The *voceru,* a women's art, is sung, mournfully, at the wake that usually follows. The women sob and rock to and fro as if in a trance, and their singing is halting and usually improvised. In the old days, during vendettas, the *voceri* were typically accompanied by cries for vengeance. In the *lamentu,* a gentler expression of the same general genre, a woman bemoans the absence of a loved one.

The *chjam'e rispondi* have a call and response form that recalls the conventions of some spiritual and blues music. As *chjam'e rispondi* are improvisational, they lend themselves to competitions.

OUTDOORS

· · · · · · ·

If you want it, Corsica's got it. The extraordinarily varied terrain of this sparsely populated island and the fretted coastline lapped by azure waters provide an incredible stage for the action seeker in search of anything from canyoning and *parcs aventure* (adventure parks) to multiday horse-riding trips – not to mention superb Via Ferrata circuits and fantastic hiking trails. Seafaring types will appreciate the good kayaking and diving opportunities that abound on Corsica's coasts.

If you're not *that* sporty, take heart. There's no need to be an extreme athlete to enjoy the outdoors in Corsica. There's something for everybody; all outfits welcome beginners and provide initiation circuits and courses that are tailor-made for those who want to experience the island's wild side without the strain. High standards of professionalism are pretty uniform whatever the activity you choose. This is your chance to stimulate your senses in grandiose scenery.

DIVING

When it comes to providing enthralling diving for the experienced and novices alike, Corsica is without peer in the Mediterranean. Its appeal is due primarily to its unbeatable repertoire of diving adventures. Shipwrecks, planewrecks, fish life in abundance and a dramatic seascape (as dramatic as on land, which is saying a lot), with needles, drop-offs and arches, are the reality of diving here. You'll come across big groupers, barracudas, dentex and rays, as well as a host of technicolour critters that flutter around rock formations. Those riches are accessible to beginners, and there are sites for all levels. It's also a great place to learn to dive. Added bonuses include low pollution and warm waters in summer.

The best season for diving is from May to October. The water temperature peaks at a warm 25°C in August. A 5mm wetsuit is recommended. Visibility varies a lot, from a low of 10m at certain sites to a maximum of 40m. The *libeccio* (southwesterly wind) can roil the waters in some of the less protected gulfs.

DIVE CENTRES

There are about 35 dive centres in Corsica. Most are open from April to October. All of them are affiliated to one or more professional certifying agencies (usually CMAS and, less frequently, PADI). You can expect well-maintained equipment and qualified instructors who speak English. But like a hotel or a restaurant, each dive centre has its own style. Do your research and opt for the one that best suits your expectations. They offer a whole range of services and products, such as introductory dives *(baptêmes)*, night dives, exploratory dives, speciality dives (eg Nitrox dives) and certification programs (usually CMAS or PADI). The price of an introductory dive includes equipment hire, while the price of an exploratory dive varies according to how much equipment you need to rent. You'll be looking at €40 to €55 for an introductory dive and €35 to €45 for a single dive. There are usually five- and 10-dive packages, which are much cheaper than single dives. An Open Water Certification program costs from €300.

If you're a certified diver, don't forget to bring your C-card and your logbook with you. Dive centres welcome divers regardless of their training background, provided they can produce a certificate from an internationally recognised agency, such as CMAS or PADI.

A medical certificate is also mandatory if you take a course or several dives. You can get one from your doctor in your home country or have it emailed to the dive centre. Otherwise, you can get one from any doctor in Corsica (€23 – the price of a consultancy).

DIVE SITES

THE SOUTH

Porto-Vecchio is consistently billed as a great diving destination. A dozen or so dives can be taken in this area, mainly in the vicinity of the Îles Cerbicale. These islets act as a magnet for a wealth of species. Porto-Vecchio also boasts one excellent wreck, at the harbour's entrance.

Bonifacio's main claim to fame is the concentration of groupers (big ones!) near the Îles Lavezzi – sightings are guaranteed. The quiet awe of a dive with these thick-lipped creatures is unforgettable. Mérouville is an iconic spot, although it tends to be pretty congested in summer.

The Tizzano area is a real gem, with a host of untouched sites for those willing to venture away from the tourist areas. Diving here is focused on the *secs* (seamounts) that lie off Cap Senetosa. It's got plenty of fish and it's atmospheric. The hitch? Most sites are exposed to the prevailing winds – expect agitated seas.

Around the Golfe du Valinco it's the dramatic underwater terrain that impresses more than anything, making for unique profiles. You'll be rewarded with a profusion of seamounts, giant arches, boulders and faults – it's very scenic – as well as large numbers of species, including barracudas. Red coral can also be found at depths exceeding 30m.

BACKGROUND

INTERVIEW: GEORGES ANTONI

Why is diving in Corsica so special? Corsica is a like an oasis in the Mediterranean. Conditions are optimal: there's no pollution, no industries, no sewage, no fertilisers. Another key factor is the topography: there's no continental shelf here, so you get fantastic drop-offs and a dramatic seascape that you won't find anywhere else in the Med.

What about fish life? We also have two big marine parks, Scandola and Lavezzi, and marine life is abundant. We get lots of barracudas and rays, which you would normally only encounter in tropical seas. And groupers are so prolific!

What's your favourite area? Each area in Corsica has its own riches. Take Porto-Vecchio: you'll feel like you're diving in the Seychelles. In the Cap Corse, the ambience is totally different. And near Bastia, you've got excellent wrecks. All the divers I've met in Corsica rave about the diving here, whatever the location.

Georges Antoni is a Corsican underwater photographer, film-maker and writer.

THE WEST COAST

The Golfe d'Ajaccio is a diver's treat, with a good balance of scenic seascapes and dense marine life. The most spectacular dives in this area are found mainly in the southern section of the gulf, between the Tour de l'Isolella (also known as the Punta di Sette Nave) and Capo di Muro. There's also a handful of sites scattered along the Îles Sanguinaires in the north.

Golfe de Lava and Golfe de Sagone boast a vibrant assemblage of dramatic rock formations that shelter a stunning variety of species. And there's the iconic Banc Provençal, which ranks as one of the best dives in the Mediterranean. In the Golfe de Sagone, the wreck of an airplane that crashed in 1971 adds a touch of variety.

Golfe de Porto is consistently billed as one of Corsica's best diving areas. Do you see the exceptional coastal wilderness of the gulf and the crags and cliffs of Les Calanques that fret the skyline? It's more or less the same story below the waterline. This gulf boasts a rich diversity of underwater wonders, with a jaw-dropping topography – just as on land – and masses of fish due to the proximity of the Réserve Naturelle de Scandola. Don't miss it. One proviso: it's very exposed to the *libeccio,* the prevailing wind.

CALVI & LA BALAGNE

The many contrasts in the area around Calvi make it attractive to divers. While the southern part of the bay is nothing to write home about, the shoreline around the Pointe de la Revellata, to the west, is extraordinary. The wreck of a B-17 bomber in the Baie de Calvi is another draw.

There's nothing to boggle the mind in the Baie de L'Île Rousse, but at least it offers relaxed diving, and the handful of sites that are available – rocks rising from a sandy seabed and cloaked with magnificent sea fans – are truly beautiful. The Golfe de St-Florent has a couple of good surprises up its sleeve too.

DON'T MISS...

DIVE SITES

- ★ La Pinella (Porto-Vecchio) // A photogenic shipwreck, close to the harbour
- ★ Le B-17 (Calvi) // Wreck of a well-preserved B-17 bomber
- ★ La Canonnière (Bastia) // This 45m-long wreck shelters groupers, lobster, corbs and conger eels
- ★ Mérouville (Bonifacio) // Bonifacio's signature dive; groupers galore!
- ★ Les Cathédrales & Les Aiguilles (Golfe du Valinco) // Dubbed 'an underwater Bavella', these long-standing favourites boast a contoured terrain
- ★ Sette Nave (Golfe d'Ajaccio) // Lots of nooks and crannies in the rock formations and a profusion of marine life
- ★ Le Banc Provençal (Golfe de Lava) // A phenomenal seamount that brushes the surface and a magnet for all kinds of species
- ★ Punta Mucchilina (Golfe de Porto) // Tons of fish, a small shipwreck and an awesome terrain, just outside Réserve Naturelle de Scandola

BASTIA & THE EAST

Corsica's eastern coast is usually overlooked by most divers, which is a shame. True, this side of the island lacks the dramatic seamounts and contoured terrain that are so commonly encountered on the west coast, but the gently sloping sand-and-silt sea bed is strewn with rocky outcrops that provide shelter for a whole range of critters. And wreck fans will find nirvana here too, along the eastern coast of Cap Corse, with a number of well-preserved ship- and planewrecks in less than 30m of water.

SNORKELLING

If the idea of total immersion doesn't exactly appeal to you, snorkelling is possible in most areas. It is a fantastic opportunity to explore the underwater world with minimal equipment and without the hefty costs associated with diving. Corsica's rocky shoreline is a magnet for all kinds of species, and the sheltered bays provide safe havens for snorkelling. Bring your equipment, because rental gear is not widely available. A few dive centres operate dedicated snorkelling trips. Top tip: combine sea kayaking and snorkelling – paddling to more-fertile grounds expands your possibilities.

KITESURFING, WINDSURFING & SURFING

Given the constant winds that bluster around the island, windsurfing and kitesurfing are popular pastimes here.

Windsurfer rentals and lessons are available at virtually all *centres nautiques* (nautical centres) but the best spots are on the south coast, near Bonifacio, which has the best winds year-round. For those of us whose windsurfing dreams are more modest, lots of fun can be had in the main gulfs on the west coast, including Golfe du Valinco and Golfe d'Ajaccio.

Looking for a new high? Kitesurfing is one of the fastest-growing sports in Corsica and should be on every adrenaline junkie's 'must-do' list. Kitesurfing takes the best of board sports and combines it with incredible airborne action. While it may be impressive to watch, it's harder to master. Aficionados of surfing, skateboarding and windsurfing will recognise the moves – that'll help, but you'll need some lessons before hitting the water. First you learn how to fly the kite, then you practise body dragging (letting the kite pull you across the water) and finally you step on board.

The Corsican kitesurfing epicentre is on the southern coast at Bonifacio. Plage de la Tonnara, Plage de Piantarella, Plage de Balistra and Golfe de Sant' Amanza are the best spots, where you'll find major schools offering lessons and rental gear. In the north, Calvi and Algajola are good places to head to.

Hawaii it ain't, but Corsica has a thriving local surfing scene, especially in the Ajaccio area. *The* Corsican surf spot is Capo di Feno, with good breaks year-round. Algajola, east of Calvi, is also a prime surf spot.

If you want to learn to surf, there's a surfing school in Ajaccio.

WHITE-WATER RAFTING

Corsica's best white water is found along the Golo Valley (near Ponte Leccia) and in the Tavignano Valley (near Corte). Both offer magical white-water experiences for both first-time runners and seasoned enthusiasts.

SEA KAYAKING

With its craggy coast and generally good conditions, Corsica is now garnering fame as a sea kayaking hot spot. Aside from being an ecofriendly approach to environment – paddling leaves minimal imprint – sea kayaking is a great way to explore the pristine coast at a gentle pace. The sheltered coves provide magnificent kayaking (and bathing) opportunities, and paddlers get to savour secluded bays and beaches seldom visited by others. And kayaks can nudge into some of the tiny islets that are denied to larger boats and that are not accessible by road.

> *'Sea kayaking is a great way to explore the pristine coast at a gentle pace'*

Most outfits also offer guided kayaking trips, with a focus on the environment, geology and marine life – a wonderful way to get more out of your holiday.

Guide and rental companies are clustered around Propriano, Porto-Vecchio, Tizzano, Porto, Île Rousse and Bonifacio. Most *centres nautiques* have one- or two-person kayaks for hire. Some outfits also have 'tri-yak' (kayak built for three), ideal for two parents with a kid.

Some recommended spots include the Golfe de Pinarello near Porto-Vecchio, Campomoro, Tizzano, Porto Pollo, Calvi and Île Rousse. See the destination chapters for contacts.

CANYONING

A must-do for thrill seekers and nature lovers, canyoning is a mix of climbing, hiking, abseiling *(rappel),* swimming and some serious jumping or plunging down water-polished chutes *(toboggans)* in natural pools, down a river gorge and waterfalls. In recent years Corsica has seen an explosion of interest in canyoning, and it's no wonder – it's an exhilarating way to explore the most scenic and least accessible areas of the rugged interior.

The Massif de Bavella is the mother of all canyoning experiences on the island, with three iconic (though now heavily commercialised) canyons: La Vacca, La Purcaraccia and Le Pulischello, which are set in some of the island's most memorable scenery. They are suitable for all levels. Another classic venue is the Canyon du Baracci near Propriano. In the Vallée du Niolo, the Canyon de la Ruda and the Canyon de Frascaghju are the main hot spots and are accessible to beginners, while Canyon de Falcunaghja, a very aerial circuit with no less than 17 rappels, is best suited for sporty types. Near L'Ospédale, the Canyon de Piscia di Gallo is a must, with a series of impressive rappels. If you want to escape the crowds, the canyons located in the Corte area are a good choice, as they are much less hyped – the Canyon du Vecchio and the Canyon du Verghjellu come recommended. In the Vizzavona area, near Bocognano, the Canyon de la Richiusa ranks as one of the most atmospheric spots in central Corsica.

Experience is not necessary. Water confidence and reasonable fitness are an advantage. Adventure centres that offer canyoning (see the destination chapters) provide wetsuits, helmets and harnesses. All canyoning trips are led by qualified instructors who intimately know every pool, slide, boulder and waterfall in any particular canyon. A half-day's canyoning will set you back around €50. Bring a picnic and spare clothes.

CYCLING & MOUNTAIN BIKING

Ready to sweat it out? There's no better way to immerse yourself in the vibrant colours, heady scents and rugged scenery of Corsica than cycle touring – as long as you're fit enough to handle the island's mountainous topography, that is. Corsica has diverse terrain, tough ascents and swooping descents, an abundance of camping grounds and *gîtes d'étapes* (walkers' lodges) and countless country roads, most of which are gloriously free of traffic. The Castagniccia, the Casinca, the Cap Corse, the Central Mountains, the Alta Rocca, the Balagne and the West Coast (especially between Porto and Calvi, and between Ajaccio and Propriano) are excellent cycling areas, all blessed with exceptionally scenic backroads.

The biggest bonus of all might be the opportunities to discover the 'real' Corsica, with its secretive villages and traditional culture, far from the madding crowds and the glitz of the coastal cities.

If this gets your legs twitching, try to avoid July and August, which are unpleasant, for the heat and the enormous influx of tourists. Spring and autumn, with their moderate temperatures, are the best seasons.

Bike hire is available in the main seaside cities, but if you're going to be doing extensive cycling, consider bringing your own wheels. Bike shops are thin on the ground, so it's essential to carry spare parts. Most outlets require a deposit (cash, signed travellers cheques or credit card) of anything from €30 to €250. Several places arrange guides, plan itineraries and run biking tours.

Mixing cycling with public transport works pretty well. Bikes can be carried on the train and some bus services carry bikes too. Cyclists keen to see Corsica's mountainous interior usually begin by taking the train to Corte, Vizzavona or some other starting point high in the mountains. (See p274 for information on travelling by train with your bike.)

BACKGROUND

DON'T MISS...

CANYON DESCENTS

★ **Baracci** // Near Propriano; easy (p121)

★ **La Ruda** // Vallée du Niolo; easy and very scenic (p180)

★ **La Vacca** // Bavella area; fantastic scenery but crowded in summer (p148)

★ **Verghjellu** // Near Corte; easy and uncrowded. Lots of small leaps (p183)

★ **La Richiusa** // Near Vizzona; lots of fun for all levels (p183)

HORSE RIDING

Feel like seeing the island from horseback instead of a car seat? Saddling up is a fun and ecofriendly way to commune with the Corsican wilderness and enjoy the long sandy beaches, glorious hinterlands and lush forests. Horse riding is commonplace on the island and opportunities can be found just about everywhere, within reach of the main tourist areas. You don't need any riding experience, as riding schools *(centres équestres)* cater to all levels of proficiency. Unlike many parts of the world where beginners only get led by the nose around a paddock, here you really can get out into the countryside on maquis, forest and beach rides.

> '*Saddling up is a fun and ecofriendly way to commune with the Corsican wilderness*'

Rides range from one-hour jaunts (from around €17) to week-long, fully catered treks. The best thing about horse riding in Corsica is that you can access terrain you can't get to otherwise – a wise way to escape the crowds. The best time to trek is in spring or autumn, when it's a bit cooler, though summer excursions usually explore the cooler mountain areas. Particularly good areas include the Alta Rocca, the Castagniccia, Sartène, Solenzara, Corte (especially the Vallée du Tavignano), the Vallée du Niolo and the Porto-Vecchio area. Choose a ride based on the particular landscape you'd like to see, since all of the operators are friendly, reputable outfitters.

Donkey rides are also available near Propriano, in the Vallée du Niolo and in the Balagne – children (and adults) love it!

See the destination chapters for more details of individual riding centres.

PARAPENTING

On the north coast, the St-Florent and Calvi areas rank as the best paragliding spots in Corsica, with consistently excellent upliftings throughout the year. If you're new to dangling yourself in the air, you can tandem paraglide. The descent from the mountain is amazing, with pupil-dilating views over the coast. Landing is on the beach. Children are welcome.

PARCS AVENTURE

Parcs aventure (adventure parks) are very popular in Corsica, and we recommend that you to try it at least once during your stay. The experience of swinging through the forest à la *George of the Jungle* is one that few nature lovers should pass up. Don't be confused, though: it's *not* a theme park.

Various companies have built a network of fixtures into the trees, at heights varying from a few metres to about 25m above ground. They usually include aerial platforms, walkways, 'Tarzan' swings, suspension bridges, cable bridges, vertical nets and zip lines (also known as Tyrolean slides), which are all connected. Visitors are strapped into harnesses and hooked onto a cable-and-pulley system that allows them to move safely from tree to tree.

It's another great and thrilling way to see nature, and it's amazingly safe. Children are welcome provided they are over 1m in height. For kiddies, special 'baby *parcs*' have been installed. Depending on the circuit, the tour lasts anything from 30 minutes to two hours. All you need is shorts or long pants, a T-shirt and trainers. You are provided with a harness and helmet, and the circuit usually begins with a crash course on how to use the equipment. Qualified instructors are positioned at designated areas throughout the circuit and can provide tips or assistance.

> ## ZIP LINING
>
> Corsica's zip lines (also known as Tyrolean slides) let you soar freestyle along cables over gulches, woods and rivers while strapped into a harness. The hardest part is stepping off the platform for the first zip – the rest is pure exhilaration!
>
> All *parcs aventure* include zip lines in their circuits but for the full monty, head to Vallée de l'Asco, where you'll find a dedicated circuit, with a succession of 12 zip lines, the longest of which spans over 250m!

The most reputable *parcs aventure* are concentrated in southern Corsica. The best ones are located in Bavella, L'Ospédale, Propriano, Solenzara, Vallée du Cavu (near Porto-Vecchio) and Vizzavona. Other good playgrounds include Vallée de l'Asco and Vallée du Niolu in central Corsica.

ROCK CLIMBING

As the most mountainous of the Mediterranean islands, Corsica is something of a Holy Grail for any would-be Spiderman or Spiderwoman. The majority of climbing options are concentrated in central or southern Corsica. The most famous spot is around Aiguilles de Bavella, with superb cliffs and granite spires. Other hot spots include the Vallée du Niolu, the Vallée de la Restonica, the Vallée de l'Asco and the Gorges du Prunelli. For super-climbers, the Paglia Orba is the ultimate face.

Adventure centres around the island run courses and organise climbing trips.

SKIING

Strange as it may seem, Corsica has three winter ski resorts: Bastelica-Ese in the Vallée du Prunelli, about 30km east of Ajaccio, Ghisoni and Verghio. The season normally runs from December to March. They have limited infrastructure: a few *refuges* (mountain huts) that rent out equipment, a couple of ski lifts and a few downhill runs. Frankly, it's nothing thrilling, but where else in Europe can you ski with the azure waters of the Mediterranean in the background?

Cross-country skiing is also popular in the Forêt de Valdu Niellu, high in the Vallée du Niolu, and on the Coscione plateau in the Alta Rocca.

VIA FERRATA

Another fun and dizzying approach to Corsica's mountains, *via ferrata* (literally, 'iron path' in Italian) is increasingly popular on the island. It uses intriguing and often ingenious combinations of ladders, metal brackets, chiselled footholds and

WALKING & THE GR20

∙∙∙∙∙∙∙

Corsica is necklaced with an excellent network of walking paths, mountain huts and *gîtes d'étape* (walkers' lodges), allowing walkers the opportunity to explore the island's deeper recesses and its convoluted hinterland of enigmatic valleys.

Walking options range from the most challenging two- or three-week hike, such as the 200km-long GR20, to an easy afternoon stroll along the coast; there is something for all tastes and all abilities. There are also countless options for shorter walks.

The best source of information for walkers is the Parc Naturel Régional de la Corse (PNRC). The PNRC includes more than 1500km of hiking and walking pathways. The **Maison d'Information Randonnée du PNRC** (PNRC walking information office; ☎ 04 95 51 79 10; www.parc-naturel-corse.com; 2 rue Major Lambroschini, Ajaccio) publishes a wealth of information about the park in English, Spanish and French, along with a number of walking guides (mostly in French).

For more information on walking, contact the **Comité Régional de la Randonnée Pédestre de Corse** (☎ 04 95 77 18 21; 6 rue du Capitaine Benedetti, Sartène).

The GR20 has its own website (www.le-gr20.com).

THE GR20

Linking Calenzana, in the Balagne, with Conca, north of Porto-Vecchio, this fantastic high-level walk stretches diagonally from northwest to southeast, following the island's continental divide.

The diversity of landscapes makes this a memorable adventure, with forests, granite moonscapes, windswept craters, glacial lakes, torrents, peat bogs, maquis, snowcapped peaks and plains.

Although the mythical GR20 is a genuine mountain route that requires physical commitment, it can be undertaken by anyone reasonably fit and with a good deal of motivation. It's usually covered in 15 *étapes* (stages) but you can tailor it to your own expectations and make it shorter if you wish, thanks to various access points along the way.

The obvious way to divide the GR20 is into two sections: from Calenzana to Vizzavona (over nine days), and south from Vizzavona to Conca (in six days). Vizzavona is the most convenient midway point, with train and road links to Ajaccio and Bastia. Between Calenzana and Vizzavona, it's possible to join the trail at several villages along the way: Haut Asco (at the end of Day 3), Castel di Verghio (at the end of Day 5) and Tattone, a short side trip from the main trail (on Day 8). For just a small taste of the GR20, Days 4 and 5 take in some of the most spectacular scenery of the whole walk, across the Cirque de la Solitude.

In the southern section of the GR20, Zicavo (Day 13), and Quenza and Bavella (Day 14) are all popular access points for walkers. Reaching Zicavo and Quenza involves a detour from the GR20, but these traditional villages, tucked away in remote valleys, are well worth exploring in their own right.

Hint: it's possible to do *demi-étapes* (half-stages): Days 5, 13 and 14 can be broken down into two days each.

WALKING & THE GR®20

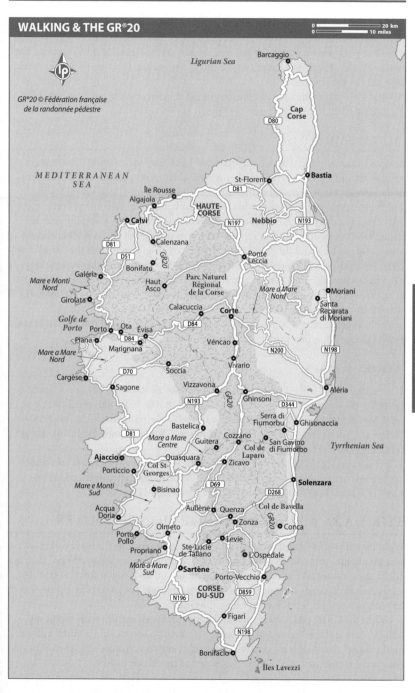

GR®20 © Fédération française
de la randonnée pédestre

0 _____ 20 km
0 _____ 10 miles

Ligurian Sea

Barcaggio

Cap Corse

D80

MEDITERRANEAN SEA

St-Florent
D81

Bastia

Île Rousse

Algajola

HAUTE-CORSE

N197   **Nebbio**   N193

Calvi

Calenzana

D81

D51

GR20

Bonifatu

Ponte Leccia

Galéria

Parc Naturel Régional de la Corse

Mare e Monti Nord

Haut Asco

Mare a Mare Nord

Moriani

Santa Reparata di Moriani

Girolata

Calacuccia

Corte

Golfe de Porto

Porto   Ota   Évisa

D84

Plana

D84

Marignana

Véncao

Mare a Mare Nord

N200   N198

D70

Soccia

Vivario

Cargèse

Sagone

Vizzavona

GR20

Aléria

N193   Ghinsoni

D344

Serra di Fiumorbu

Ghisonaccia

Bastelica

Mare a Mare Centre

Guitera   Cozzano

San Gavino di Fiumorbo

Tyrrhenian Sea

Ajaccio

Quasquara

Col de Laparo

Zicavo

Porticcio

Col St-Georges

Mare e Monti Sud

Bisinao

D69

Solenzara

Aullène   Quenza

Col de Bavella

D268

Acqua Doria

Zonza

GR20   Conca

Porto Pollo

Olmeto

Levie

Propriano

Ste-Lucie de Tallano

L'Ospedale

Mare a Mare Sud

Sartène

Porto-Vecchio

CORSE-DU-SUD

D859

N196

Figari

N198

Bonifacio

Îles Lavezzi

The GR20 can be comfortably walked any time between May and October, although some parts of the route remain snow-covered until June, making them tricky to negotiate. The peak-season months of July and August are best avoided if you have an aversion to crowds. From mid-August to the end of September, there are frequent storms, especially in the afternoon.

Weather in the mountains can fluctuate quickly between extremes. You can call ☎ 08 92 68 02 20 for the latest weather reports (in French).

ACCOMMODATION

Refuges (mountain huts) are usually manned from May to September. Some stay open until mid-October if the weather is fine. Most *refuges* on the GR20 offer *petit ravitaillement* (supplies), soft drinks, alcohol (beer and wine) and simple meals, which can save several kilograms in the backpack. Water is available at every *refuge,* but between stops there are very few sources of drinking water. Camping gear is strongly recommended, as there is only a limited number of places available in *refuges* along the way, and they tend to fill up quickly in summer. Note that, as of May 2009, reservations can be made online at the PNRC-run *refuges* (check out www. parc-naturel-corse.com). When camping you have access to equipment inside the huts. Note that there are also a few hotels along the way – at Haut Asco, Castel di Verghio and Vizzavona.

Don't forget to carry a good supply of cash, as there are no ATMs on the GR20 and credit cards are only accepted in a few places.

BOOKS & MAPS

The excellent Fédération Française de la Randonnée Pédestre (FFRP) Topo-Guide *À Travers la Montagne Corse* (No 67) details the GR20. The FFRP also publishes *Corse entre Mer et Montagne.* Albiana's *GR20 Le Grand Chemin* (in French) is also comprehensive. Cicerone's *Corsican High Level Route: GR20* is a handy English-language companion for the trail.

Waymarking *(balisage)* and signposting of the path is usually excellent (red and white paint stripes) but topographical IGN 1:25,000 maps are recommended (Nos 4149OT, 4250OT, 4251OT, 4252OT, 4253OT and 4253ET).

THE MARE A MARE & MARE E MONTI ROUTES

Well-known and much-enjoyed walks across the island include the Mare e Monti (Sea and Mountains) and Mare a Mare (Sea to Sea) trails. Although less overhyped than the GR20, these routes take in some spectacular mountain and coastal scenery, with the added bonus of ending each day comfortably in a village. They also offer a shorter and less intimidating physical challenge than the GR20.

Unlike the GR20, which stays high in the mountains away from settlements, the Mare a Mare and the Mare e Monti routes pass through some of the prettiest villages on the island. The routes are generally less taxing and less crowded than the GR20 and offer considerable comfort, with *gîtes d'étape* and hotels every night.

THE MARE A MARE ROUTES

Three Mare a Mare paths link the west and east coasts via the central mountains.

MARE A MARE NORD

The Mare a Mare Nord is said to be the prettiest of the Mare a Mare trails. It links Moriani on the east coast to Cargèse on the west and passes through vastly different areas. It is split into 10 days, each lasting from four to six hours and reaching altitudes of up to 1600m. For the final section of the walk, between Évisa and Cargèse, the route merges with that of the Mare e Monti Nord. It is better to avoid walking during the period between November and April, when parts of the route may be buried under snow.

MARE A MARE CENTRE

The Mare a Mare Centre provides an excellent opportunity if you want to explore the more traditional, inland areas of Corsica. The route can be completed in seven days, each with three to seven hours' walking. Starting in Ghisonaccia on the east coast, and finishing in Porticcio on the west coast, it passes through the little-known microregions of the Fiumorbu and the Taravo before crossing the hinterland of Ajaccio.

The maximum altitude is 1525m at Col de Laparo (Bocca di Laparu), so the best time to do the walk is between April and November. Take a detailed map, as the markings are not very regular.

MARE A MARE SUD

This famous, easy walk links Porto-Vecchio in the southeast to Propriano in the southwest. The walk is divided into five days, each of which lasts an average of five hours, and reaches a maximum altitude of 1171m. With fine views to the Aiguilles de Bavella and Monte Incudine, it crosses through the magnificent region of Alta Rocca and many of the island's most beautiful villages. The third day of the trail offers three options: a short version that skips the Plateau de Jallicu, a detour through the village of Aullène or a long version via Zonza, which adds a day to the itinerary. This route is passable year-round.

THE MARE E MONTI ROUTES

As the name suggests, these are paths between the sea *(mare)* and the mountains *(monti)*. Accommodation is offered by *gîtes d'étape* in villages along the way.

MARE E MONTI NORD

The Mare e Monti Nord (literally 'Sea to the Northern Mountains') is a superb (and not very demanding) walk linking Calenzana in the Balagne to Cargèse, south of the Golfe de Porto. It is divided into 10 days of four to seven hours each, and its highest point is 1153m. It passes through several exceptional natural sites, such as the Forêt de Bonifatu, the Réserve Naturelle de Scandola and the Gorges de Spelunca, and stops in some gorgeous villages, notably Galéria, Ota and Évisa.

BACKGROUND

THE GR20

Day	From	To	Duration (hr)	Distance (km)	Difficulty
1	Calenzana (275m)	Refuge d'Ortu di u Piobbu (1570m)	7	10	Demanding
2	Refuge d'Ortu di u Piobbu (1570m)	Refuge de Carozzu (1270m)	6½	8	Demanding
3	Refuge de Carozzu (1270m)	Haut Asco (1422m)	4½-5	6	Moderate
4	Refuge d'Asco Stagnu (1422m)	Bergeries de Ballone (1440m)	7	8	Demanding
5	Bergeries de Ballone (1440m)	Castel di Verghio (1404m)	6½-7	13	Moderate
6	Castel di Verghio (1404m)	Refuge de Manganu (1601m)	5½	14	Moderate
7	Refuge de Manganu (1601m)	Refuge de Petra Piana (1842m)	6	10	Demanding
8	Refuge de Petra Piana (1842m)	Refuge de l'Onda (1430m)	5	10	Easy
9	Refuge de l'Onda (1430m)	Vizzavona (910m)	5½	10	Moderate
10	Vizzavona (910m)	Bergeries de Capannelle (1586m)	5-5½	13.5	Moderate
11	Bergeries de Capannelle (1586m)	Refuge de Prati (1820m)	6-7	16	Moderate
12	Refuge de Prati (1820m)	Refuge d'Usciolu (1750m)	5-5½	9.5	Demanding
13	Refuge d'Usciolu (1750m)	Refuge d'Asinao (1530m)	7½-8	14.5	Moderate
14	Refuge d'Asinao (1530m)	Refuge de Paliri (1055m) via the Alpine Route	5¾-6¼	13	Moderate
15	Refuge de Paliri (1055m)	Conca (252m)	4½-5	12	Moderate

The route is passable year-round, but the periods before and after the main season (May to June and September to October) are preferable to avoid the worst of the heat. The path crosses the Mare a Mare Nord in two places: Évisa and nearby Marignana.

MARE E MONTI SUD

This path runs between the bays of two well-known seaside resorts in southwest Corsica – Porticcio and Propriano. It's divided into five days of five to six hours and ascends to a maximum height of 870m. There are stops in Bisinao, Coti-Chiavari, Porto Pollo and Olmeto. The walk ends in Burgo (7km north of Propriano).

The highlights are the incredible views over the bays, the historic Genoese towers and superb beaches (the Baie de Cupabia and Porto Pollo). Like its northern counterpart, this path is passable year-round and is not particularly difficult. Spring and autumn are the best times. The path meets the Mare a Mare Sud in Burgo.

There are only two *gîtes d'étape* on the route, one in Bisinao and one in Burgo. In the other villages you can stay in a hotel or at a campsite.

OTHER WALKS

Walking in Corsica is by no means limited to the GR20 and the Mare a Mare and Mare e Monti walks. There's every bit as much, and perhaps more, for those who prefer an easy walk of a single day, half a day or less. Details of some of the best short walks are in the regional chapters of this guide.

The PNRC can provide brochures on easy 'country walks' it has designed around the villages of Alta Rocca, Boziu, Fiumorbu, Niolo, Taravo, Vénachese and Giussani – all in interior parts of the island that visitors don't often see. These walks, all three to seven hours in length for the round trip, are perfectly suited to casual walkers and even to families.

FLORA & FAUNA OF CORSICA

· · · · · · ·

A rich variety of flora and fauna, much of it protected, thrives on Corsica. Set so much as a little toe into the island's interior and you'll come across a menagerie of free-roaming pigs, cows, goats, sheep, mules and other domesticated and feral land animals. Delve deeper into the mountainous terrain (pack patience and a pair of binoculars in your rucksack) and you'll be well rewarded.

FAUNA

♥ WILD BOAR (SANGLIER)

Boar hunting is a centuries-old Corsican tradition. All the same, wild boar, tough, doughty cousins of the domestic pig, continue to thrive. Omnivorous and prowling Corsica's extensive and little-trodden maquis and forest, they snout out acorns, chestnuts, roots, fruit, insects and worms. If you see the forest floor scuffed and uprooted, a wild boar's probably been at work; they're the bane of the farmer, to whose lands they can cause extensive damage. Females and piglets stick together. If you see a lone one, it's probably a male (take care – he can put on a surprising show of speed and those tusks are sharp!)

> 'If you see the forest floor scuffed and uprooted, a wild boar's probably been at work'

♥ RED DEER (CERF DE CORSE)

The last indigenous Corsican red deer, a native of Corsica ever since antiquity, died on the island in the 1960s, but was reintroduced in 1985 from Sardinian stock. Initially confined to protective enclosures in Quenza, Casabianca and Ania di Fiumorbu, the first deer were released into the wild in the late 1990s and are now breeding modestly. These gentle creatures live on brambles, strawberry trees, acorns and chestnuts, and now number over 100. Wild boars, foxes, stray dogs and poachers continue to threaten their existence.

♥ MOUFLON

Corsica's mountain king, the mouflon, reigns in the Bavella and Asco protected areas. These hardy herbivores, a type of short-fleeced sheep, roamed in their thousands at the beginning of the 20th century but now number between 400 and 600. Hanging out in lower valleys between December and February, they retreat to higher altitudes to avoid the

BACKGROUND

DON'T MISS...

BIRDWATCHING SPOTS

★ Réserve Naturelle de Scandola // View osprey from an offshore boat (p83)

★ Barcaggio // At the tip of Cap Corse looking over to the protected Îles Finocchiarola (p46)

★ Étang & Réserve Naturelle de Biguglia // Where migrating birds take a break (p228)

★ Vallée de la Restonica // Raptors wheeling overhead (p177)

worst of the summer heat. If the one you spot (look for distinctive white facial markings) has huge 80cm-long coiled horns, it's a male.

HERMANN'S TORTOISE

Once widespread around the northern Mediterranean littoral, this slow mover, easily identified by its orange and black stripes, is nowadays extremely rare in mainland France. Between mid-November and February it hibernates in the maquis, tucked away under piles of leaves. Averaging about 20cm in length, it can live for up to 80 years. In the face of declining numbers, it's being specially bred in semicaptivity at the Village des Tortues, near Ponte Leccia, in the Parc Naturel Régional de la Corse.

CORSICAN SNAIL

This tiny little fellow, officially classified as critically endangered, merits a mention. Endemic to Corsica and generally tucked inside a black and brown striped shell, the green-bodied Corsican snail *(helix ceratina)* only just hangs on. Having not been seen since 1902, a group were discovered near Ajaccio in 1995. Assailed by the airport, a military base, a large car park and a busy beach, these plucky molluscs had chosen a tough spot to make their last stand. The six hectares of coastal land they inhabit is now protected, and a captive breeding program is underway.

OTHER CREATURES

The maquis can bristle with animal activity on a smaller scale. Weasels and foxes slink, dark-green snakes slither (don't worry if you come across one; they're not poisonous and won't attack unless threatened) and shiny back *malmignatte* spiders scuttle (look for red stripes on the abdomen); they're venomous but mercifully rare.

BIRDS

The island's a delight for birdwatchers. Along Corsica's central spine and more accessibly in places such as the Vallée de la Restonica near Corte, birds of prey such as the golden eagle and red kite soar up high above the treeline. Within the forests, the Corsican finch, wren and spotted flycatcher live their lives.

But it's the Corsican coastline that has the richest pickings for twitchers. Everywhere, gulls wheel and cormorants in plenty hang their wings out to dry. The shag, a web-footed bird with black-green plumage, nests on the protected Îles Finocchiarola off Cap Corse and in the Réserve Naturelle de Scandola, where the peregrine falcon is another known nester.

The edge-of-the-world hamlet of Barcaggio on Cap Corse is prime birdwatching territory. Spring sees storks, herons, spotted crakes and dozens of other migratory birds drop by.

BEARDED VULTURE (GYPAÈTE BARBU)

You'll need to keep your eyes well peeled to spot a bearded vulture or lammergeier with its soaring wingspan of up to 3m. Look for the distinctive black 'beard' under its beak, and white or yellowish plumage covering the lower part of its body. The rarest of Europe's four vulture species, the bearded vulture nests in rocky niches at high altitude (around 1500m) but descends to lower altitudes in winter. You won't find this solitary bird joining the vultures' feeding frenzy at a carcass. It waits for its moment, seizes a sizeable bone then drops it from a height onto a rocky surface to shatter the bone and release the marrow at its heart. Your best chance of seeing it is in the Monte Cinto massif. With barely 250 breeding pairs left in Europe, it's on the endangered species list. Starvation is one of the biggest threats to its survival. In the Parc Naturel Régional de la Corse, park authorities monitor the dozen or so pairs that live within its bounds and supplement their natural diet with additional food in the form of goat and sheep carcasses at sites in Ascu and the Forêt de Tartagine.

❦ OSPREY (BALBUZARD PÊCHEUR)

The osprey is a formidable fisher, thanks to its sharp eyesight and talons that can sink into the slipperiest of fish. With a white body and brown wings, it can be spotted around Cap Corse and on the rocky coasts and headlands of the Réserve Naturelle de Scandola, where it nests. Having dropped to only three couples in the 1970s, it's now very slowly recovering numbers.

❦ CORSICAN NUTHATCH (SITELLE)

The Corsican nuthatch, one of the few species endemic to the island, flutters in the Vallée de la Restonica. Discovered at the end of the 19th century, this ground-dwelling bird is recognisable by the white 'brow' across its head. Rarely exceeding 12cm in length, it flits around conifer forests, dining on insects and pine seeds.

❦ AUDOUIN'S GULL (GOÉLAND D' AUDOUIN)

Very rarely found on mainland Europe Audouin's gull clings on in (or rather, just off) Corsica, nesting among rocks on the protected Îles Finocchiarola off Cap Corse. Its main point of identification is the dark-red, black-striped, yellow-tipped beak.

FLORA

A mere 15% of Corsican land is cultivated, while forest and maquis carpet more than half of the island. The habitat of its trees and flora splits neatly into three zones:

Mediterranean (up to 1000m) Cloaked at ground level by the extensive maquis. Oak, olive and chestnut trees thrive, according to area.

Mountain (1000m to 1800m) Clad with pine and beech forest.

Alpine (above 1800m) Ground--hugging, sparse grasses and small mountain plants cling on above the treeline.

THE ASPHODEL

This hardy plant with its white or delicate pinkish flowers grows at all altitudes and can survive in just about any kind of soil. Flowering in the springtime, it has three distinct names in Corsican (and several dialectal variants too), depending upon whether the speaker is referring to the living plant, its dried form or when it's burnt to give light. Traditionally, its stalks would be twisted to make torches, while the leaves would be used for stuffing mattresses and saddles. More symbolically, they would be woven into crosses which villagers believed would protect or enhance their harvests.

TREES

Common varieties of tree that you're certain to see include the following.

Olive (olivier) Thrives on low, dry, sunny coastal slopes, particularly in the Balagne on the northwest coast. Its pollen-rich yellow flowers bloom in June. The bitter fruit is pressed to extract the prized AOC Corsican olive oil.

Chestnut (châtaignier) Introduced to the island in the 16th century, the chestnut quickly lent its name – La Castagniccia – to the eastern plains on which it was cultivated. Its husks open in October to expose a flavourful brown fruit, which is used in local cuisine or ground into flour. See also p234.

Holm oak/holly oak (chêne vert) Recognisable by its deep-hued bark and dark, oval, spine-tipped leaves. Traditionally, its wood was processed into charcoal. Its acorns impart a very special flavour to pigs that gobble them.

> ### PRICKLY FRUIT
>
> The prickly pear (*figue de barbarie* in French, or Barbary fig) is a member of the *Cactaceae* family that thrives anywhere between 800m and 1800m. Originating in Central America and brought back by Christopher Columbus, it resembles a cactus, with bristly, pulpy, oval-shaped pads and yellow flowers. Its sweet, juicy red fruits are thirst-quenching, but don't be tempted to grasp one with your bare hands; the soft skin is coated with myriad near-invisible, hair-like prickles that irritate the skin and are the very devil to extract from your fingers.

Cork oak (chêne liège) More common in the south of the island, around Porto-Vecchio, its bark is peeled off every 10 years or so to fashion stoppers for wine bottles – a long-standing Corsican tradition that suffers these days from the increasing use of plastic corks.

Laricio pine In the higher mountain areas, the tough Corsican or laricio pine dominates and can grow up to 100m high. As it ages, this long-living tree spreads its grey-green foliage horizontally like a parasol. Some island specimens (you'll come across some venerable examples in the Forêt de Vizzavona) are reckoned to be up to 800 years old.

Maritime pine (pin maritime) Recognisable by its orange-red, deeply fissured bark and needles that come in pairs, it's less hardy than the laricio pine and thrives, as the name implies, in coastal and lower-lying areas.

SHRUBS & OTHER PLANTS

Nearly 3000 species of flora have been identified on Corsica. Since the island has been physically separated from the European mainland for millennia, a good number of plants have evolved separately from their cousins on the mainland and are unique to Corsica. There are 130 endemic plants, while a further 75 exist only here and on its neighbour, Sardinia. In the more remote Alpine zones, nearly half of the species that survive the harsh winters at this height are endemic.

THE MAQUIS

The maquis positively bursts with sweet-smelling plants and herbs, most of which flower in spring and early summer. Extending over around 2000 sq km, it's made up of dense thickets of often thorny plants whose tough, leathery leaves preserve moisture. Here, tree heather can grow 2m tall, its white flowers exuding a honey-like perfume.

Typically scrubby and short, the maquis is tough enough to survive summer's intense heat, burns quickly, but grows rapidly too. It provides a safe haven for most of Corsica's 40 kinds of orchid and pungent herbs such as rosemary, thyme, lavender, myrtle and the tiny blue-violet flowering Corsican mint with its heady summertime aroma. Drier hillsides and the lower flanks of mountains flame with bright yellow broom throughout the summer.

TYPICAL CORSICAN FLORA

Other common species that you're likely to come across:

Autumn crocus This late bloomer lives up high. The distinctive pink to lilac flower with its spear-shaped petals appears well before the scarcely visible leaves, which grasp it around its base.

Corsican hellebore This poisonous plant, a variant found only in Corsica and Sardinia, has frondy, toothed leaves (in which shepherds used to wrap their fresh cheeses) and a profusion of lovely, light-green flowers.

Corsican peony Once profuse, this local variant of peony has papery pink or red flowers with yellow stamens and likes to live beneath beech trees. A victim of its very prettiness, it's becoming rarer, mainly as a consequence of overpicking.

Corsican thyme Here's another variant upon a popular theme, found only in Corsica and Sardinia. Low growing, bushy, with delicate pink and white flowers and a powerful aroma, it thrives anywhere between 500m and 2000m.

Cyclamen The tiny wild cyclamen, an early flowerer, peeks out from rocks and crannies in pink clusters.

Mastic A tall shrub whose red fruits turn black and exude a resin-like fragrance.

Myrtle A bushy evergreen shrub with aromatic leaves and lovely, fragrant white flowers that bloom in spring. Its blue-black berries make a wonderful flavouring for liqueurs.

Rock rose/cistus The most common maquis shrub, it thrives up to around 1200m. You'll recognise it by its five-petalled flowers, which are either white or pinkish-mauve with yellow stamens. Among several varieties of rock rose is the more diminutive Montpellier cistus with its dainty white flowers.

Strawberry tree Known in French as the *arbousier* and nothing to do with strawberries, this shrub thrives in thickets and woods and can grow to over 10m. It has small, white bell-shaped flowers that dangle in clusters. The fruit is small, crinkly surfaced orange or red balls.

UNDERWATER PLANTS

Don a snorkel and mask, and be dazzled by the Corsican coastline's extravaganza of flora – as rich and as brilliant underwater as any on dry land. Two forms of special interest are:

Poseidonion Endemic to the Mediterranean, this green plant (named after Poseidon, the Greek god of the sea), forms vast grassy meadows on the sand creating a choice biotope, home to numerous species of fish seeking shelter or spawning in the foliage.

Seaweed There are several forms: brown, green or red, hard or soft. Calcified varieties can have superb mineral formations. Certain species of red algae are recorded nowhere else in France.

A FRAGILE ENVIRONMENT
· · · · · · ·

'Le soleil a tant fait l'amour à la mer qu'ils ont fini par enfanter la Corse' (The sun made love to the sea so often that they finally gave birth to Corsica). So eloquently and fancifully, Antoine de St-Exupéry, author of *Le Petit Prince* (The Little Prince), described the origins of the island.

Around 30 million years ago a lump of land broke away from mainland Europe, slowly spun around an axis somewhere in the middle of the Gulf of Genoa, and eventually came to a standstill 170km southeast of Nice on mainland France. Corsica was born.

With an area of 8722 sq km, the island spans 183km from top to bottom and 85km at its widest point. At its northern end the long 40km-long peninsula of Cap Corse points towards Italy like a giant's finger. Inland, mountains run riot. No sooner does the land rise above sea level than it soars into the clouds, climaxing with Monte Cinto (2706m). Plenty of other peaks – Monte Ritondu (2622m), Paglia Orba (2525m), Monte Pedru (2393m) and Monte d'Oro (2389m) – beat the 2000m barrier.

Corsica's constantly fretted shoreline wriggles its way for more than 1000km, if you were to religiously make your way around every bay, cove and inlet. The two coasts, west and east, differ. Into the more fragmented west coast, buffeted by the dominant wind from the west, four deep gulfs – of Porto, Sagone, Ajaccio and Valinco – have been scoured and crags rear from the sea. Alongside the more gentle, less dramatic eastern coast runs the lowland agricultural plain of Aléria.

> ## DON'T MISS...
>
> ### PROTECTED AREAS
>
> ★ **Réserve de Biosphère de la Vallée du Fangu** // Paddle a canoe along its quiet length (p71)
>
> ★ **Réserve Naturelle de Biguglia** // A treasure for walkers and birdwatchers (p228)
>
> ★ **Réserve Naturelle de Scandola** // Approached only by boat for fabulous seascapes (p83)
>
> ★ **Parc Naturel Régional de la Corse** // Huge protected swath of high, inland Corsica (p227)

BACKGROUND

THE ISSUES

FIRE

Fires are by far the biggest threat to the island's sun-sizzled environment. The scrubland of the Corsican maquis, which flares at the strike of a match, is assailed from many sides. Of the thousands of fires reported each year, it's calculated that some 90% are started by campers, cigarette smokers, arsonists or irresponsible visitors on picnics. Other culprits include hunters (setting fire to forests to drive out wild boar), property developers (who sometimes start fires wilfully), shepherds (who burn expanses of land to make meadows for grazing) and farmers (burning stubble to produce potash, which is used to improve soil quality).

BACKGROUND

TREADING LIGHTLY

We've no wish to play nanny and much of this is common sense. That said, you too, as a visitor, can play a modest role in helping to preserve Corsica's unique natural environment. By sticking to a few simple, unencumbering precepts, your impact will be all the less heavy.

★ Buy a sturdy, heavy-duty plastic bag for all your purchases (they're great for lugging gear to the beach or tidying away camping equipment, too).

★ Pack all your litter and dump it in an official container. Wildlife will grub it up in the hope of dinner if you bury it. While it can be messy, it's socially responsible to pack out the detritus of others who are less responsible.

★ Don't use detergents or toothpaste, even if they claim to be biodegradeable, anywhere near streams. The same rule applies to natural functions, it goes without saying…

★ When out walking, stay on designated trails. Every footstep is a threat to the coastal foreshore and fragile, high-mountain plants, which use the brief summer to reproduce.

★ Obey the 'no camping' restrictions if you're trekking.

★ Never light a fire in the open air anywhere on the island, except in the rare places where it's allowed. Barbecues and campfire coffee are fun but forest and maquis fires are the scourge of Corsica.

★ Be content to simply look at flowers and plants. Many struggle to survive.

As many as 20 fires are reported on a single summer's day – an alarming trend that Mediterranean Europe's increasingly drier and hotter climate exacerbates. In the summer of 2003, unrelenting temperatures cost Corsica almost €11 million in firefighting expenses, as fire swept across 270 sq km of land in the worst conflagrations for 30-odd years. The summer of 2009 again saw fires rage across much of Corsica.

'Fires are…the biggest threat to the island's sun-sizzled environment'

Preventive measures include a summertime island-wide ban (until 30 September) on all campfires, barbecues and other outdoor fires, and prohibiting smoking in forests and the maquis year-round. Lighting up (anything) warrants a €750 fine.

INFRASTRUCTURE & OVERDEVELOPMENT

As all along the northern Mediterranean littoral, there are huge pressures to open up the coast to urban development. Counterbalancing this, many environmental and Corsican nationalist forces, conscious of the concrete excesses of the island of Mallorca to the west, and northwards, on the Côte d'Azur, oppose all but the most stringently controlled expansion; *Vergogna à tè chí vendi a terra* (Shame upon you, who sell your land) is the title of a popular nationalist rallying song. Both sides in this long-standing debate wish to avoid such blight. The issue is how and to what extent. In the

Bonifacio region – mercifully not yet typical of the rest of Corsica but an indication of what might be – more than half of all residences nowadays are second homes, empty for the majority of the year.

Metaphorical mountains of garbage are by no means peculiar to Corsica but the problem is accentuated when tiny coastal communities such as Porto see their population increase more than tenfold during the brief, hectic holiday period, with all the accompanying demands upon the urban infrastructure.

In places such as Barcaggio and Roccapina, the trampling of visitors has killed off the fragile plants whose roots serve to anchor the sand dunes.

Most Corsicans are keen to promote the ecological wellbeing of their island and environmental issues figure large in the demands of many nationalist factions. The latter aren't averse to showing muscle too, if they believe the issue to be important enough. In 1973, for example, there was what almost amounted to a popular uprising against offshore toxic-waste disposal by an Italian multinational in what was termed the so-called *boues rouges* (literally 'red slicks') affair. Corsican econationalism, as it is called (which, on that occasion, manifested itself as Corsican terrorists bombing the waste-dumping Italian ships), still persists.

This said, in the opinion of many Corsicans, the nationalist movement (if it's indeed possible to speak in terms of a single movement), has forfeited most of its ecological credentials as it splintered into factions.

PROTECTION & PRESERVATION

UNESCO-RECOGNISED NATURAL AREAS

The **Réserve Naturelle de Scandola**, on the island's northwest coast, inscribed on the Unesco World Heritage list for the richness of its marine and bird life. To its south, the **Golfe de Porto, Golfe de Girolata** and the plunging red cliffs of **Les Calanques** that stagger south along the coastline between Porto and Piana are similarly Unesco recognised. The coastline around Galéria, immediately north of the Scandola reserve, also enjoys international recognition as the **Réserve de Biosphère de la Vallée du Fangu**, 234 sq km dedicated to scientific research.

PARC NATUREL RÉGIONAL DE LA CORSE (PNRC)

The single most decisive step in the preservation of Corsica's unique wildlife was the creation of the Parc Naturel Régional de la Corse (PNRC) in 1972. Protecting more than two-thirds (specifically, 3505 sq km) of the island, the reserve is the island's biggest promoter of environmental consciousness. Unlike national parks in France, which can only protect uninhabited areas, the PNRC, within whose boundaries more than 25,000 people live, 'protects and stimulates the survival of the natural, cultural and human heritage'.

Positive measures include the creation of some 2000km of marked trails, not to mention costly measures taken to preserve endangered species and to educate and sensitise locals and visitors through, for example, guided nature walks and information centres.

BACKGROUND

NATURE RESERVES

Corsica has six Réserves Naturelles that give a measure of protection to particularly vulnerable natural sites.

RÉSERVE NATURELLE DE SCANDOLA

Established in 1975 and the first to be created, it's also the most stringently protected. The reserve extends over a 919-hectare pocket of dramatic coastal land, plus 1000 hectares of sea that swims with 125 fish species and 450 types of seaweed. Although you can't step ashore, it's a hugely popular venue for boat trips from west-coast ports.

RÉSERVE NATURELLE DES BOUCHES DE BONIFACIO

In the far south, more islands are protected by the Réserve Naturelle des Bouches de Bonifacio, which covers a full 800 sq km of the straits between Corsica and Sardinia. Here, the marine life is particularly rich and enjoys special protection; a full 120 sq km of water are strictly off limits to scuba-divers. The reserve is best known for its revived brown grouper population – protected since 1993 after decades of unregulated fishing had practically wiped them out from the western shores of the Mediterranean.

RÉSERVE NATURELLE DES ÎLES FINOCCHIAROLA

Off the northernmost tip of Cap Corse lie these three pin-prick islands (four hectares in all), off limits to visitors between 1 March and 31 October to allow several rare and protected birds (such as the Audouin's gull, cory shearwater and Scopoli's shearwater) to breed in peace.

RÉSERVE NATURELLE DE BIGUGLIA

South of Bastia, the Réserve Naturelle de Biguglia provides a safe haven for more than 100 bird species and serves as a vital stopover between Europe and Africa for migrating birds. Up to 20,000 birds winter in the reed-beds around the shallow, 1450-hectare lagoon that forms Corsica's largest and most important wetland. With luck and bin-

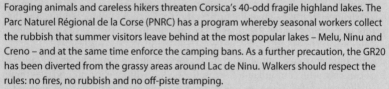

WATCH YOUR STEP

Foraging animals and careless hikers threaten Corsica's 40-odd fragile highland lakes. The Parc Naturel Régional de la Corse (PNRC) has a program whereby seasonal workers collect the rubbish that summer visitors leave behind at the most popular lakes – Melu, Ninu and Creno – and at the same time enforce the camping bans. As a further precaution, the GR20 has been diverted from the grassy areas around Lac de Ninu. Walkers should respect the rules: no fires, no rubbish and no off-piste tramping.

Summer grazing threatens *pozzines* (from the Corsican *pozzi,* meaning 'pits'). These small waterholes are linked together by rivulets that flow over an impermeable substratum (like peat bogs). Lush, green and often squelchy, they're like little green oases amid more-desiccated grasses. They feel like a carpet of cool moss – and do just feel them rather than walk over them. Most are fairly inaccessible. If you're walking the GR20, you'll come across them around Lac de Ninu and on the Plateau de Coscione.

oculars, you'll spot warblers of all types, herons, the red-footed falcon, black- and white-winged terns and maybe an osprey.

RÉSERVE NATURELLE DES ÎLES CERBICALE

At the lower end of the east coast, the Réserve Naturelle des Îles Cerbicale – a cluster of five islets northeast of Porto-Vecchio – also protects marine birdlife and manages to pack 136 distinct species of flora into its 36 hectares.

'Up to 20,000 birds winter in the reed beds around the shallow…lagoon'

RÉSERVE NATURELLE DES TRE PADULE DE SUARTONE

Newest of the Corsican reserves, it was created to protect these three unique seasonal, wet-weather ponds and their unique amphibian life in an area traditionally used for animal grazing. It's around 10km north of Bonifacio, set back from the sea by around 1.75km.

CONSERVATOIRE DU LITTORAL

On the coast, environment protection is tackled head-on by the **Conservatoire du Littoral** (www.conservatoire-du-littoral.fr, in French). This public body engages actively by, for example, building protective barriers around the Roccapina and Barcaggio dunes to prevent further erosion by tourists and over-grazing livestock trampling across the fragile sands, and so crushing the plants that help to stabilise them.

Of much greater significance, the Conservatoire buys up choice and threatened coastal sites – a massive 25% of Corsica's roughly 1000km of coastline – in order to protect them. These include the 5300-hectare Désert des Agriates (which was being considered as a potential nuclear-testing site until the Conservatoire intervened back in 1989); southern Corsica's dune-rich Sartenais coastline (2500 hectares); the Bouches de Bonifacio; and the tip of Cap Corse.

OFFICE NATIONAL DES FORÊTS

The **Office National des Forêts** (ONF; www.onf.fr/corse, in French) manages the island's national forests. Activities include educating the public through forest visits and fire prevention measures such as cutting out more firebreaks and planting more fire-tolerant ground foliage.

BACKGROUND

CORSICAN FLAVOURS

· · · · · · ·

First things first: don't mistake Corsica for, say, Provence, over the water. Sophisticated haute cuisine prepared by superstar chefs? Rare as summer snowballs. If you're in search of uberchic restaurants, silver cutlery and unflappable service, you've come to the wrong place. The *cucina corsa* (Corsican cuisine) is what the French call a *cuisine du terroir* – country cuisine, literally 'of the land'. It's more traditional family cooking than creative concoctions, typically hearty and wholesome fare made using tried-and-true recipes and fresh, local produce. And what produce!

HOME GROWN & BORROWED

Many Corsican dishes have evolved historically from the agrarian peasant diet of the mountains. In the 18th century most Corsicans, under threat from would-be colonisers, retreated to the safety of the high interior, a terrain that lent itself well to pig-, sheep- and goat-rearing. The carpet of maquis covering the peaks yielded an abundance of aromatic herbs – wild mint, fennel, catmint, rosemary and laurel – and natural produce such as honey and the versatile chestnut.

Only one thing has changed in the intervening years; despite Corsica's stretched-out coastline, it wasn't until the 20th century, when its people began reclaiming their shores, that the island's wealth of fish and seafood began to find its way to the table.

'Many Corsican dishes have evolved historically from the agrarian peasant diet of the mountains'

Corsican cuisine owes its distinct characteristics to a host of factors. In particular, its Mediterranean location offers a wealth of raw materials: fragrant olive oils, sun-loving fruits and vegetables, and mouth-watering cured meats, easily and economically preserved in the Mediterranean heat.

Of course, several classic elements of French gastronomy are evident in Corsican cuisine, notably the cooking methods, such as the stewing of meat *en daube,* in red wine and garlic. Some staples from the Italian kitchen have crossed the short passage of water to the island as well. Especially on the east coast, it's common to find on the menu a regional variation of polenta (often using chestnut flour), cannelloni and lasagne.

Despite the influence of Italian and French cuisine, however, Corsican cuisine remains relatively untouched by exterior trends, so while you won't see a chip shop or McDonald's on its streets, you're equally unlikely to come across a juice bar or sushi restaurant.

The endurance of this wonderful earthy style of cooking that takes full advantage of the fruits of the land is refreshing.

All we can say is *buon appititu*!

STAPLES & SPECIALITIES

The ingredients that make Corsican cuisine so distinctive are above all the regional charcuterie (cured meats), the chestnut, the local seafood and Brocciu (fresh sheep- or goat-milk cheese, also spelled Bruccio and Brucciu)

CHARCUTERIE & OTHER MEATS

Carnivores will have found their spiritual home in Corsica. Meat of every species, shape and genesis dominates the local diet. Corsicans are renowned for their appetite for charcuterie, especially their sausages and hams, whose particular flavour is derived from *cochons coureurs* (free-ranging pigs), which traditionally feed on chestnuts, acorns, and plants imbued with the fragrance of the maquis. From these herb-saturated porcines comes the *figatellu*, a thin liver sausage and Corsica's pride (it's produced from December to February), and also the prosciutto-like *lonzu* and *coppa*, as well as *salciccia* and *prisuttu*.

As you travel, look out too for regional specialities such as:

Fittonu di Bastelica A variant of *figatellu* that's particularly rich in liver.

Salamu di Quenza A sausage that's cured and dried at high altitude for longer than the norm.

Jambon du Niolo Especially tasty ham from this deep, inland retreat.

Tripes cuisinées de Castagniccia Tripe slowly simmered with parsley, mint and cabbage.

The *assiette de charcuterie* (charcuterie platter) you will see as a starter on many a *menu Corse* will consist of a sampling of thin slices of four or five of these meats. If you want to know which is which, ask your server. Most pork-based charcuterie is made during winter. Unlike some other meats, which may cure over anything from six months to a couple of years, *figatelli* are generally eaten soon after production. If *figatelli* feature on the menu in summer, they're probably the frozen variety, which may have less flavour.

Main courses, generally speaking, will conform to your idea of French cookery, but look out for local specialities such as these:

Sanglier (Wild boar) Especially in long-simmering stews called *civets* or *daubes* in French or *tiani* (*tianu* in the singular) in *menu Corse*. *Sanglier* is best eaten during the hunting seasons of autumn and winter.

Stuffatu Slow-braised mutton stew, especially popular in winter.

Ghialadicciu An equivalent, gently simmered stew of pig's stomach.

Premonata Beef stewed with juniper berries.

Cabri Goat kid, typically roasted with rosemary and garlic.

Veal with olives A more frequent presence on menus, though rarely made with veal from calves raised on the island.

BACKGROUND

DON'T MISS...

FAVOURITE CORSICAN FLAVOURS

- ★ **Fiadone** // Lemon-flavoured Corsican cheesecake
- ★ **Sanglier** // Wild boar, at its best simmered in a stew
- ★ **Patrimonio AOC wine** // A fine red, ideally bought from the vineyard
- ★ **Lonzu** // Salted, cured, tender fillet of pork
- ★ **Brocciu** // Crumbly white cheese, almost an emblem of Corsica
- ★ **Pietra beer** // Refreshing, chestnut-flavoured lager type beer
- ★ **Assiette de charcuterie corse** // A mixed platter hors d'œuvre

Most of these rich meat dishes will be served with *pulenta,* a Corsican version of the maize-based Italian polenta, here made from chestnut flour.

Recipes for blackbird and other wild birds, roasted with sage or cooked as a *salmis* (partially roasted, then gently simmered in wine, shallots and onions) or prepared in terrines, also attest to the ingenuity of an isolated people.

FISH & SEAFOOD

Is your stomach starting to rebel at so much artery-clogging cured meat? It's time to give your taste buds something different. The warm waters of the Mediterranean provide an ample and varied net of produce: sea bream, sea bass, squid, sardines, scorpion fish, lobster and red mullet. Oysters and mussels are a speciality around the east coast. *Langoustes* (lobster) appear on menus all around the coast, usually served with pasta, simply cooked in a little olive oil and garlic, or in *ziminu* (or *aziminu*), the Corsican version of Provençal *bouillabaisse* (normally served for a minimum of two people). Sardines stuffed with Brocciu are generally delicious, while inland you'll come across plenty of farmed trout, stuffed with either almonds or a selection of herbs from the maquis. *Rougets à la bonifacienne* is a southern speciality featuring red mullet cooked with anchovies, tomatoes and garlic. Once you (or even better, your chef) manage to penetrate the spiky shell of the *oursin* (sea urchin), it reveals its delicate, star-shaped flesh.

> 'Brocciu, a cheese so noble, so highly regarded that it merits its own AOC'

SAY CHEESE!

Ah Brocciu, a cheese so noble, so highly regarded that it merits its own AOC (Appellation d'Origine Contrôlée)! It pops up on practically every single menu, in a variety of guises.

'CORSICAN' CHARCUTERIE?

*Prisuttu, lonzu, coppa, figatellu, salsiccia...*Corsican charcuterie has achieved cult status among connoisseurs. But standards do vary a lot. Some unscrupulous producers in Corsica import (legally) pigs from the Netherlands, Sardinia, Brittany or Spain, let them feed only a week or two on chestnuts, slaughter them, transform the meat into charcuterie, label it *'charcuterie corse traditionnelle'* (traditional Corsican charcuterie) and sell it to gullible visitors.

One oddity is *saucisson d'âne,* a rich sausage made from donkey meat that you'll find in many a delicatessen. Yet the flesh of the donkey, before mechanisation a respected beast of burden, has never been consumed in Corsica. 'What to do, m'sieur?', one *traiteur* asked us rhetorically. 'The clients expect it, I provide it.' In reality, Corsica has never minced its donkeys and what's on sale comes from either Italy or Provence, on the mainland.

As long as there's no official certification label (there's talk about establishing an Appellation d'Origine Contrôlée (AOC) for charcuterie, similar to the one used for Corsican wines, honey, olive oil and Brocciu cheese), your best bet is to stock up in reputable produce shops.

Mild, crumbly and white, not a million miles from ricotta, it's made from the *petit-lait* (whey) of either goat's or ewe's milk. True Brocciu (as opposed to the inferior-tasting *brousse,* which is made from imported or powdered milk), is available only between December and June, when the lactating goats and sheep provide their characteristic milk. Corsicans take this distinction seriously; a restaurant caught passing off *brousse* as Brocciu can be closed down.

Brocciu can be eaten fresh, as a creamy *fromage frais,* baked with the zest of oranges or *cédrat* (a sweeter type of lemon) in a *fiadone* cheesecake, or drained, salted and aged for use in savoury dishes. Be sure to try an omelette of Brocciu. The cheese combines particularly harmoniously with mint, with which it will almost always be paired in an omelette. You can also enjoy Brocciu in pasta dishes, such as cannelloni and lasagne, or stuffed into vegetables.

Brocciu may be the diva of Corsican cheeses but there are plenty of others to excite your palate. *Brebis* and *chèvre* are the generic names given to a range of ewe's and goat's milk cheeses (the latter produced from January to August). Some, despite Brussels legislation, are still made with unpasteurised milk – and taste all the better for it. Favourites that you're likely to find include:

Bastelicaccia A soft, creamy ewe's-milk cheese with a natural crust.

Sartinesi A raw, hard-pressed, sharper-tasting ewe's-milk cheese.

Tomme Corse A semi-hard, granular, raw, ewe's-milk cheese.

Niolincu A popular soft cheese from the south.

Vénacu Also soft and hailing from the Alta-Rocca .

Another famous – or rather infamous – Corsican dairy product is *casgiu merzu* (literally and descriptively 'rotten cheese'). Starting life as a fresh young goat's cheese, it's left and left (for up to 10 years in extreme cases) until it crawls with little white maggots. It's variously described as crumbly with a sharp tang and having the texture of peanut butter (we can't speak with authority; there are limits to how far we'll go in the cause of research!).

Restaurants – where you'll never find *casgiu merzu* – often serve hard cheeses as a starter or as an alternative to dessert (you'll also find them on offer as a bar snack). They come accompanied by a basket of crusty bread, plus a dollop of sweet fig jam, which acts as a delicious relish, counteracting the sharp flavour of the cheese. If they feature on your menu, do try *buglidicci* (pancakes with ewe's-milk cheese).

> *'Amazingly for such a relatively small island, six distinct varieties of olive flourish'*

OLIVE OIL

Corsican olive oil *(oliu di Corsica),* a staple of the Corsican kitchen, is extremely aromatic. An AOC was introduced in 2004. It controls quality and at the same time recognises and gives further impetus to Corsican farmers' endeavours to revive long-abandoned olive groves. Amazingly for such a relatively small island, six distinct varieties of olive flourish. The principal olive oil–producing regions are the Balagne, the Alta Rocca and the Casinca, and production takes place from February to June.

BACKGROUND

BACKGROUND

CHESTNUTS

Since the 16th century, Corsicans have planted *châtaigniers* (chestnut trees), known as *l'arbre à pain* (the bread tree) because it was a staple of so many Corsicans' diet.

Nothing was wasted. The wood was fashioned into furniture and whittled into stakes for fencing. The leaves and branches were fed to the goats and what remained would be used for winter heating.

Tasty dishes made with chestnuts include *beignets au Brocciu à la farine de châtaigne* (Brocciu cheese frittered in chestnut flour), *gâteau à la farine de châtaigne* (chestnut cake), *castagnacciu* (a moister chestnut cake) and *falculelli* (pressed, frittered Brocciu served on a chestnut leaf). And let's not forget Pietra, Corsica's wonderfully rich amber ale flavoured with chestnuts, or the delightful ham from free-range pigs raised on chestnuts with its distinctive flavour.

HONEY

Beekeeping on the island is a long-established tradition, evolved over centuries. You may raise your eyebrows at the dubious cause-and-effect argument of the 17th-century French philosopher Jacques Bossuet, who claimed, 'Because of the high quality of the honey that they consume, Corsicans are taller than the common man.' What's incontrovertible is that Corsican honey *(mele di Corsica)*, also meriting an AOC label, is very special. It's produced from bees that feed exclusively on the wildflowers of the maquis (plant your hives near cultivated land and you'll lose your AOC status). There are six recognised varieties of honey, differing according to terrain and time of year and elaborately described in terminology appropriate to a wine-tasting ('Amber, lingering on the palate with a residual bitterness' is how a spoonful of chestnut honey is sensuously evoked). As the weeks pass and summer advances, beekeepers transport their hives ever higher, following the flower line.

INTERVIEW: PAUL-ANTOINE LANFRANCHI

Paul-Antoine Lanfranchi owns a *gîte d'étape* and a well-regarded restaurant in the Haut Taravo Valley (see p110), which is famous for its home-cured meats. 'We are the fourth generation of butchers, and our cured meats are 100% organic and natural. I use secret, family recipes passed on by my grandmother. We rear our own Corsican pigs and let them roam, free-range. They feed only on chestnuts and acorns, which gives the meat a distinct flavour.' Does homemade charcuterie taste really different from industrial charcuterie, Monsieur Lanfranchi? 'The texture and the flavours are totally different. Try the two kinds of charcuterie, and you'll see what I mean. But *charcuterie artisanale* has a cost: you'll be looking at €30 for a kilogram of *coppa*.' For charcuterie lovers, what's the best way to buy genuine, and the best? 'Go in the mountain villages, and buy charcuterie direct from the producer. And follow the seasons: an authentic *figatellu* is never made in summer. If you find *figatellu* at a market or in a restaurant in summer, just skip it!' For an idea of Paul-Antoine's products, check out his website www.chez-paul-antoine.com (in French).

SNACKS

The 'sandwich Corse' seen on many cafe menus is a *panino* (grilled sandwich, Italian style) filled with charcuterie and cheeses. Varieties include the Libecciu, the Stellu (according to the menu, 'the most Corsican of *panini*'), the Velacu and the Astu. Equally handy if you're on the hoof is the *bastelle,* a little rectangular wallet of pastry or dough, filled with onion, Brocciu cheese, or pumpkin.

Traditional Corsican soups, typically served in winter, are a meal in themselves. Strict vegetarians beware. What's billed as a vegetable soup, made with butter beans and garden vegetables, will often be simmered in meat stock, or even contain *lardons,* small hunks of pork or sausage. Check before you order.

DESSERTS

For dessert, try the wonderful *fiadone* (a light flan made with Brocciu, lemon and eggs), the calorie-loaded *beignets au Brocciu* (Brocciu fritters), the toothsome *ambrucciata* (tart with Brocciu) or the high-energy *canistrelli* (biscuits made with almonds, walnuts, lemon or aniseed). Corsican homemade jams (made with clementines, figs, chestnuts and so on) are also delicious.

Especially inland, you'll see a variety of cakes, tarts, biscuits and *beignets,* made from the subtle-tasting chestnut flour.

DRINKS

ALCOHOLIC DRINKS

BEER

Two breweries on the island produce four different beers. Pietra is an amber beer whose ingredients include chestnut flour from the Castagniccia. Enthusiasts contend that even though the beer doesn't taste of chestnuts, its presence is nevertheless largely responsible for the beer's unique characteristics. Serena is a lighter product of the same brewery; the label bears a Corsican Moor's head. The pale Colomba beer, launched in 1999, is flavoured with maquis herbs, principally myrtle. In 2002 Torra, called *bière du maquis* (maquis beer), was launched by another brewery based near Ajaccio. The pale Torra is flavoured with arbutus while the amber Torra is flavoured with myrtle.

WINE

We have to thank the ancient Greeks for introducing the vine to Corsica in pre-Christian times. Nowadays the third-largest wine-producing island in the Mediterranean after Sicily and Sardinia, Corsica has nine AOC-labelled wines. These are produced mainly from the original rootstocks of the country, using varieties of grape such as Vermentinu (white), Sciaccarellu (favoured in granite areas) and Niellucciu (related to the Italian Sangiovese, unique to Corsica and the most popular variety).

Around 7000 hectares of vine are under cultivation on the island, notably in the Nebbio and on the eastern coast, and most vineyards can be visited. Corsican wines (red, white and rosé) can be bought in produce shops for as little as €5 a bottle and

CORSICAN WINES – HEAVEN IN A GLASS

Appellation d'Origine Contrôlée (AOC) wines have met stringent regulations governing where, how and under what conditions they are grown, fermented and bottled. Red wines account roughly for 40% of the total production of AOC wines in Corsica; white wines 11%; and rosés 49%.

AOC Ajaccio (Golfe de Porto to Golfe d'Ajaccio) Most famous domaines: Comte Peraldi, Clos Ornasca, Domaine Abbatucci, Clos Capitoro

AOC Coteaux du Cap Corse & AOC Muscat du Cap Corse (Cap Corse) Most famous domaines: Clos Nicrosi, Domaine Pieretti, Domaine Gioielli, Domaine de Pietri

AOC Sartène (Vallée de l'Ortolo, Propriano area, Tizzano area) Most famous domaines: Domaine Fiumiccicoli, Domaine Saparale, Domaine Sant' Armettu, Domaine Mosconi

AOC Calvi (Area: the Balagne interior) Most famous domaines: Clos Landry, Domaine Alzipratu, Domaine Renucci

AOC Figari (Area: around Figari and Pianottoli-Caldarello) Most famous domaines: Clos Canarelli, Domaine de la Murta

AOC Porto-Vecchio (Area: around Porto-Vecchio) Most famous domaines: Domaine de Torraccia, Domaine de Granajolo

AOC Patrimonio (Area: around Patrimonio and St-Florent) Most famous domaines: Domaine Gentile, Domaine Orenga de Gaffory, Clos de Bernardi, Domaine Leccia, Domaine Lazzarini

AOC Vin de Corse (Area: eastern plain, from Bastia to Solenzara) Most famous domaines: Domaine de Muso-leu, Clos d'Orléa, Clos Fornelli, Clos Poggiale

the mark-up in restaurants is not scandalous. These are not necessarily the most distinguished of wines but they're increasing in quality and some of them have gained national recognition.

In both value and volume, wine is Corsica's principal export. It's a drop in the Med compared with overall French output but still brings in some €120 million annually. Around 45% of any year's production is consumed on the island and drunk while still young. The remainder makes its way to France and other European countries in roughly equal proportions. This said, you'll need to know a specialist vintner if you're to experience a Proustian recollection of your holiday anywhere outside *la métropole*. Wine production takes place between September and October.

BRANDIES & LIQUEURS

Cap Corse Mattei, invented by Louis Napoléon Mattei in 1872, is a local wine-based aperitif, comparable to red martini and made from muscat wine. Casanis is a *pastis*. Although not strictly from Corsica (it's from Marseille), it was developed by a Corsican with the good island name of Casabianca, and the label has the Moor's head symbol on it. You won't be shot for asking for a Ricard or Pernod, but ask for a Casa anyway and pronounce it ca-*zah*. Other excellent aperitifs include liqueurs, usually flavoured with myrtle (*liqueur de myrte*) or chestnut (*liqueur de châtaigne*), and sweet *muscat du Cap Corse*.

'Acquavita is generally home-made and, at 45% alcohol by volume, is like rocket fuel'

Eau-de-vie (*acquavita* in Corsican), originally a medicinal tipple, is best enjoyed as a digestif after dinner. It's particularly good when based on a citrus fruit the Corsicans call *cédrat* (for all practical purposes, a lemon) or on myrtle or other maquis plants. *Acquavita* is generally homemade and, at 45% alcohol by volume, is like rocket fuel. If at the end of dinner your server puts down a little plate with a couple of sugar cubes on it and an unlabelled bottle, pour a few drops from the bottle over the sugar cubes and suck them. This is a very old custom and a very good one.

Whisky lovers might want to try P&M, which is the only Corsican whisky, blended and distilled in Corsica.

NONALCOHOLIC DRINKS

WATER

Although tap water is drinkable throughout the island, most locals prefer bottled mineral water. Corsican mineral waters are excellent.

Orezza High-quality sparkling water from the Castagniccia (see p160). Very carbonated and rich in iron, it's even served in the chicest restaurants of Paris. Check out the website www.orezza.fr.

St-Georges Well-known still water from Col St-Georges, near Ajaccio. The bottles were designed by famous French designer Philippe Starck – but they're plastic bottles for all that and pollute just as much. You can see them on www.eauxstgeorges.fr and maybe wonder if he earned his fee.

Zilia Spring water from the Balagne.

SODAS

There's a Corsican variation of Coca-Cola, called Corsica Cola, with a Corsican Moor's head on the label. Let's face it: it's too sweet and, the name apart, bears not too much resemblance to Coke.

BACKGROUND

FOOD GLOSSARY

· · · · · · ·

THE BASICS

boulangerie boo·lon·zhree bakery
climatisation klee·ma·tee·za·syon air-conditioning
déjeuner day·zher·nay lunch
dîner dee·nay dinner
(non-)fumeur (non·)few·mer (non)smoking
l'addition la·dee·syon the bill
menu mer·new set menu
petit déjeuner per·tee day·zher·nay breakfast
épicerie ay·pee·sree grocery store

STAPLES

bière byair beer
café ka·fay coffee
eau o water
lait lay milk
sel sel salt
thé tay tea
riz ree rice

MEAT, CHICKEN & POULTRY

agneau a·nyo lamb
bifteck/steak beef·tek/stek steak
bœuf berf beef
bœuf haché berf ha·shay minced beef
cervelle ser·vel brains
charcuterie shar·kew·tree cured or prepared meats (usually pork)
chèvre she·vrer goat (can also refer to goat's cheese)
civet see·vay game stew
coppa ko·pa spare rib (pork)
côte kot chop (of pork, lamb or mutton)
côtelette kot·let cutlet
dinde dund turkey
figatellu fee·ga·te·loo liver sausage
foie fwa liver
ghialadicciu gya·la·dee·choo braised pig's stomach
grillade gree·yad mixed grill
jambon zhom·bon ham

lapin la·pun rabbit
lard lar bacon
lonzu lon·dzoo pork fillet
marcassin mar·ka·sun young wild boar
mouton moo·ton mutton
oie wa goose
pieds de porc pyay der por pigs' trotters
porc por pork
poulet poo·lay chicken
prizuttu pree·tsoo·too cured ham
rognons ron·yon kidneys
sanglier song·glee·yay wild boar
saucisson so·see·son large sausage
saucisson fumé so·see·son foo·may smoked sausage
tripes treep tripe
viande vyond meat
volaille vo·lai poultry

FISH & SEAFOOD

bouillabaisse boo·ya·bes Mediterranean-style fish soup, made with several kinds of fish
calmar kal·mar squid
crabe krab crab
chaudrée sho·dray fish stew
coquille St-Jacques ko·keey san·zhak scallop
crevette grise krer·vet grees shrimp
crevette rose krer·vet ros prawn
fruits de mer frwee der mair seafood
gambas gom·ba king prawns
huîtres wee·trer oysters
langouste lang·goost lobster
moules mool mussels
palourde pa·loord clam
poisson pwa·son fish
sardine sar·deen sardine
saumon so·mon salmon
soupe de poisson soop der pwa·son fish soup
thon ton tuna
truite trweet trout

VEGETABLES, HERBS & SPICES

ail ai garlic
anis a·nees aniseed
artichaut ar·tee·sho artichoke
asperge a·spairzh asparagus
aubergine o·bair·zheen aubergine/eggplant
avocat a·vo·ka avocado
betterave be·trav beetroot
carotte ka·rot carrot
champignon shom·pee·nyon mushroom
courgette koor·zhet courgette/zucchini
concombre kon·kom·brer cucumber
crudités krew·dee·tay chopped raw vegetables
épice ay·pees spice
haricots a·ree·ko beans
haricots blancs a·ree·ko blong white beans
haricots verts a·ree·ko vair French (string) beans
herbe airb herb
legumes lay·gewm vegetables
maïs ma·ees sweetcorn
poivron pwa·vron green pepper
poireau pwa·ro leek
laitue lay·tew lettuce
lentilles lon·tee·yer lentils
oignon on·yon onion
olive o·leev olive
petits pois per·tee pwa peas
persil payr·see parsley
pomme de terre pom der tair potato
salade sa·lad salad or lettuce
tomate to·mat tomato

DESSERTS & SWEETS

beignet be·nye doughnut
canistrelli ka·nee·stre·lee dry biscuits
figatone fee·ga·to·nay chestnut flan
flan flon egg-custard dessert
gateau ga·to cake

ACCOMMODATION

FINDING ACCOMMODATION

From great-value *gîtes d'étape* (walkers' lodges) and *gîtes ruraux* (self-catering cottages in the country) to atmospheric B&Bs and stylish hotels, there's a wide array of accommodation options in Corsica.

The smarter hotels tend to be concentrated around the coast and in a few hinterland towns; the Ajaccio, Calvi, Bonifacio and Porto-Vecchio areas have the widest choice. There are also a great deal of small-scale, often family-run, establishments – not really the period hotel you were dreaming of, but they blend in pretty well with the environment, and are comfortable and intimate.

Chambres d'hôtes, the French equivalent of B&Bs, offer a pleasant alternative to hotels. They can be found all over Corsica, but are normally tucked away in the hills or in scenic locations; options include everything from restored village houses, modern buildings or country villas to rooms in family houses. On the whole, standards are high and rooms are generally excellent value. Many *chambres d'hôtes* also offer *table d'hôtes* (evening meals served around shared tables), but these must be reserved in advance.

Maisons d'hôtes (boutique-style B&Bs) are the latest trend. At the time of writing there were about two dozen in Corsica, but new places should have opened by the time you read this. They are normally found in the hinterland and boast wonderful locations.

Although *gîtes d'étape* are primarily set up for walkers, they are better equipped and much more comfortable than refuges; some have impeccable facilities that would put many a hotel to shame. They

BOOK YOUR STAY ONLINE

For more accommodation reviews and recommendations by Lonely Planet authors, check out the online booking service at www.lonelyplanet.com/hotels. You'll find the true, insider low-down on the best places to stay. Reviews are thorough and independent. Best of all, you can book online.

PRICE GUIDE

The following is a guide to the pricing system used in this chapter. Unless otherwise stated, prices quoted are for a double room with private bathroom.

€	up to €60
€€	€60 to €140
€€€	over €140

also welcome nonwalkers, space permitting, and usually offer doubles (with shared bathrooms). Most *gîtes d'étape* are dotted around the island's hinterland, and are accessible by car. They boast wonderful settings – think secluded hamlets and breathtaking views.

Gîtes ruraux are private houses and lodges that can be rented (normally by the week) for self-catering holidays. They are scattered all over the island, but are usually in the hinterland.

Résidences de tourisme (condominium-style accommodation) are dotted all around the coast. Most are bungalow-type self-catering options, which you can rent on a weekly basis. They are often located near the beach.

PRICES & BOOKING

The peak season is July and August, when Corsica is chock-a-block with visitors. Coastal accommodation rates hurtle through the ceiling during these two months, and can be up to triple the prices charged in the low season. Note that half board is mandatory in many hotels in Corsica at this time. It's imperative to make reservations well in advance if you're planning to visit the island in July and August, as most reasonably priced accommodation gets snapped up fast.

For the rest of the year, tariffs can be very reasonable. You'll find excellent

deals, and fewer people, in the shoulder months: April, May, June, September and October. Many resort hotels function only between April and October, but some B&Bs are open year-round, as are certain hotels in the main cities. Seasonal opening and closing dates tend to vary so, if you're planning an early or late break, do check in advance.

BASTIA & THE FAR NORTH

BASTIA

❦ HÔTEL LES VOYAGEURS // BASTIA €€

☎ 04 95 34 90 80; www.hotel-lesvoyageurs.com; 9 av Maréchal Sébastiani; s €60-95, d €75-105; Ⓟ ⚒ ▫ ☞

Run by the same family for over a century, yet thoroughly modern and comprehensively renovated, Hôtel Les Voyageurs is justifiably popular with tourists and business visitors alike. The attractive lounge and reception area streams with light, and the 24 rooms have soothing pale-yellow walls, glass-and-wrought-iron furniture and sparkling bathrooms. The best of the doubles are cavernous, and come with a cosy sofa and a bath-tub.

CAP CORSE

❦ MAISON ST HYACINTHE // SANTA MARIA DI LOTA €

☎ 04 95 33 28 29; www.maison-saint-hyacinthe.com; Santa Maria di Lota; s with shared bathroom €25-30, d €40-50; Ⓟ

You don't need to be religious to enjoy a stay at this peaceful convent, which lies deep in the hills behind Bastia. Run by Polish nuns, it offers 45 basic but impeccably maintained single and double rooms (13 doubles have their own bathroom) in a modern, motel-like building set in spacious gardens. There's even a terrace bar overlooking the valley. It's well signed from the D80; at Miomo, take the D31 westward for 2.5km.

❤ HÔTEL DEMEURE CASTEL BRANDO // ERBALUNGA €€€

☎ 04 95 30 10 30; www.castelbrando.com; rte Principale, Erablunga; d €105-210; ⊙ mid-Mar–Sep; ⓟ ⌧ ⌨ ⧉ ⌱

This stylish and welcoming boutique hotel is set in a mid-19th-century mansion surrounded by palm-shaded gardens and three modern annexes that house even more luxurious accommodation. Its 45 rooms are tastefully decorated in cream and peach, and are furnished with elegant antiques. There are also two swimming pools, a jacuzzi and a private library.

❤ U SANT'AGNELLU // ROGLIANO €€

☎ 04 95 35 40 59; www.hotel-usantagnellu.com; d incl breakfast €90-150, incl half board €120-170; ⊙ Apr-Sep

You'll sleep cosseted and comfortable in this beautifully restored pink villa, located opposite the church in the centre of the village. Choose one of the seven rooms that face the sea, retire early and set your alarm to enjoy the sunrise as it streaks across the bay. Your cheerful hosts, the Albertinis, have a particular affinity with the place – hardly surprising, since they were married in room 8 when the hotel still functioned as public offices. The hotel is 4km from Macinag-

gio; take the D80 westward and turn left onto the D53, signed Rogliano.

❤ CHAMBRES D'HÔTES CASA MARIA // NONZA €€

☎ 04 95 37 80 95; www.casamaria-corse.com; d incl breakfast €70-90, f incl breakfast €120-160; ⌧ ⌨ ⧉

This tastefully restored, warmly recommended 18th-century mansion sits beside the lane that leads up to Nonza's tower. Four of its five rooms have sea views, and three sit harmoniously beneath the sloping roof; the family suite consists of two adjoining rooms that share a bathroom. Breakfast is served in a large vine-shaded garden, into which banks of purple bougainvillea cascade.

❤ CHAMBRES D'HÔTES LE RELAIS DU CAP // NONZA €€

☎ 04 95 37 86 52; www.relaisducap.com; Marine de Negru; d with shared bathroom €50-75, apt per week €400-820; ⊙ Apr-Oct; ⌨

Tucked improbably between a towering cliff and a shingle beach, this family-run B&B offers four country-style doubles with shared bathroom and staggering sunset-facing sea views. The terrace has a spectacular vista, plus a barbecue, self-catering facilities, and tables where you can enjoy the copious buffet breakfast (€7). There's also one self-contained apartment that can accommodate up to four people. This place is 4km south of Nonza; a track leads off the D80 down to the shoreline.

LE NEBBIO

❤ MAISON LE RORQUAL // ST-FLORENT €€€

☎ 04 95 37 05 37; www.maison-rorqual.com; rte Plage de la Roya; d €230-450; ⓟ ⌧ ⌨ ⌱

Hidden from view among wooded private gardens at the far end of the Plage de Roya, this luxury villa boast five fan-

RESOURCES

Check out the websites listed here for help booking rental accommodation.
Aller en Corse (www.allerencorse.com)
Gîtes de France Corse (www.gites-corsica.com)

TOP FIVE

ATMOSPHERIC B&BS

Find heaven in one of these lovely B&Bs:

★ **Chambres d'Hôtes La Diligence** (p254) – A former coach inn in La Castagniccia

★ **Chambres d'Hôtes Bergeries de Piscia** (p250) – Converted *bergeries* (shepherd's huts) in Piscia

★ **Maison d'Hôtes Châtelet de Campo** (p248) – A renovated granite mansion in the Haut Taravu

★ **Maison d'Hôtes Casa Giafferri** (p257) – Artists' vibes in the central mountains

★ **Chambres d'Hôtes U Castellu Piattu** (below) – Views of Patrimonio's vineyards and limestone peaks

tastic rooms, each individually designed, and decorated with flair and originality using driftwood, slabs of rock, river pebbles, stained glass, mosaics and designer fabrics. From the infinity pool in the garden there's a stunning view over the gulf.

♥ CHAMBRES D'HÔTES U CASTELLU PIATTU // **BRIETTA** €€

☎ 04 95 37 28 64; www.castellu-piattu.fr.st; d incl breakfast €70-92; Ⓟ 🐕

Located deep in the heart of the Patrimonio wine-growing region (the name means 'Hidden Castle'), this idyllic B&B is a superb example of how modern architecture can blend perfectly with a rural setting. Built from local stone and fitted with chestnut-wood furniture, the five rooms are set around a gorgeous pool with views of craggy limestone hills and serried rows of vines. It's 2km south of Patrimonio on

the back road to Brietta – it's best to follow the directions on the website.

♥ LA DIMORA // OLETTA €€€

☎ 04 95 35 22 51; www.ladimora.fr; rte de St-Florent; d €145-330; Ⓟ 🐕 🖥 🖳

Only a few minutes' drive from the bustle of St-Florent, this gorgeous boutique hotel has been created from the ruins of an 18th-century farmhouse. From the vaulted chambers of the lobby to the thick stone walls of the bedrooms, original features have been skilfully blended – think chunky retro furniture, old timber and thick rugs on stone floors, all in cool and sober shades of biscuit, taupe and burnt umber. The garden – complete with ancient olive tree, pool, Turkish bath and massage room – is a delight.

♥ CHAMBRES D'HÔTES GAUCHER // **VALLECALLE** €€

☎ 04 95 37 60 60; http://hotescorses.free.fr; s incl breakfast €50-55, d incl breakfast €60-65; Ⓟ

This delightful rambling 18th-century mansion has been comprehensively and tastefully renovated by the Gaucher family. There are only three bedrooms, each vast and minimally furnished, with crisp sheets and cream bedspreads. Outside, you can enjoy the lovely garden and terrace with striking views. If you'd like dinner (a bargain €20, including wine and coffee), order in advance. Monsieur Gaucher speaks excellent English.

CALVI & LA BALAGNE

CALVI

♥ HÔTEL BELVÉDÈRE €€

Map p65; ☎ 04 95 65 01 25; www.resa-hotels-calvi .com; place Christophe Colomb; d €47-100; 🐕 📶

In the shadow of the citadel and overlooking place Christophe Colomb, the Belvédère has 24 smallish but comfortable

ACCOMMODATION

rooms, some with magnificent views of the bay, plus a pleasant panoramic breakfast room. It's a particular bargain out of season. Credit cards aren't accepted.

❦ HÔTEL LE ROCHER €€

Map p65; ☎ 04 95 65 20 04; www.hotel-le-rocher .com, in French; bd Wilson; r €90-185; ⊙ mid-Apr–mid-Oct; ⊠

The 20 spacious rooms of this central hotel all have fresh furniture, attractive fabrics, marble bathrooms, flat-screen TV and balconies. Its three mezzanine rooms (€134 to €185) have views of the Golfe de Calvi and can accommodate up to four people.

❦ HÔTEL LA VILLA €€€

off Map p65; ☎ 04 95 65 10 10; www.hotel-lavilla .com; chemin de Notre Dame de la Serra; 2-person villas €310-720; ⓟ ⊠ ▯ ▩

Tucked away in the hills overlooking Calvi and set in gorgeous gardens with stunning views of the bay (not least over the brim of its fabulous infinity pool), La Villa brims with boutique trappings. Clean lines, cappuccino-and-chocolate colour schemes, designer fabrics and minimalist motifs distinguish the rooms, while other facilities include a two-star Michelin restaurant, a fitness centre, spas, tennis courts and access to a private beach down on the coast. Why, there's even a helipad, should you prefer to leave the car at home.

❦ HÔTEL RESTAURANT LE MAGNOLIA €€

Map p65; ☎ 04 95 65 19 16; www.hotel-le-magnolia .com; rue Alsace Lorraine; d €60-140; ⊙ Apr-Nov; ⓟ ⊠

Occupying a 19th-century belle époque mansion, Le Magnolia is an oasis at the heart of Calvi's old quarter. The 11 rooms, substantially renovated in 2008,

are each named after a French literary figure and are individually decorated in a tasteful manner – you can sleep, for example, with Madame Bovary, bedecked in cherry tones. The hotel overlooks a delightful garden restaurant (p68) with the eponymous magnolia tree at its heart.

AROUND CALVI

❦ HÔTEL-RESTAURANT STELLA MARE // ALGAJOLA €€

☎ 04 95 60 71 18; www.stellamarehotel.com, in French; chemin Santa Lucia; r €65-120; ⊙ mid-Apr–mid-Oct; ⓟ ⊠ ⊛

Each of the Stella Mare's 16 trim and tidy rooms has a splendid panorama of either the mountains or the coast. Ask for No 10, which has views of both, and a balcony too. There are great sea views from the terrace, where a buffet breakfast (€10) and evening sundowners are served. The friendly staff can advise on local activities and walking trails.

ÎLE ROUSSE

❦ HÔTEL CALA DI L'ORU €€

off Map p73; ☎ 04 95 60 14 75; www.hotel-caladiloru .com; bd Pierre Pasquini; r €64-133; ⊙ Apr-Oct; ⓟ ⊠ ▩

Here's a friendly, family-run hotel with loads of character. The very creditable paintings and photos in public areas are by the owner's sons, and even Mum has a canvas or two on display. A large terrace and most of the 26 rooms overlook a tranquil garden that features plants and shrubs of the island. The pool's much more than a puddle in a corner.

❦ HÔTEL ISULA ROSSA €€

Map p73; ☎ 04 95 60 01 32; www.isularossa.com; rte du Port; d €45-115; ⊙ mid-Apr–mid-Oct; ⊛

Lucien and his wife, aided or encumbered by their charming toddler Avelina, run a particularly welcoming spick and span operation within a well-cast anchor of the ferry jetty. The 21 rooms, half with sea views, are freshly decorated in attractive pastel shades, and are equipped with flat-screen TV and particularly large bathroom mirrors. Except in high summer, the rooms represent exceptional value.

❦ HÔTEL-RESTAURANT LE GRILLON €

Map p73; ☎ 04 95 60 00 49; www.hotel-grillon.net, in French; 10 av Paul Doumer; d €38-60, incl breakfast & dinner €77-100; ☷ Mar-Oct; Ⓟ ⌧ ☍

With simple, well-maintained rooms (bathrooms have been recently renovated) and a popular ground-floor restaurant (*menus* €13.50 to €16.50) serving lunch and dinner daily, this friendly place offers real value. The hotel is at the rear, and its informal reception is in the public bar.

LA BALAGNE INTERIOR

❦ GÎTE D'ÉTAPE MAISON FORESTIÈRE DE TARTAGINE // FORÊT DE TARTAGINE MELAJA €

☎ 04 95 35 68 73; mairie-olmi-cappella@wanadoo.fr; D963; s/d €25/40, r per person incl half board €40; ☷ mid-Apr–mid-Oct; Ⓟ

At the road's end, this former forestry-commission house offers simple accommodation. Overlooking the river Tartagine, with its tempting rock pools and shaded riverside walks, the lodge makes a great base for hikes both simple and demanding (the warden can advise you).

❦ CHAMBRES D'HÔTES A FLATTA // AROUND CALENZANA €€

☎ 04 95 62 80 38; www.aflatta.com; d €85-115, ste €125-205, r per person incl half board €50; ☷ Apr-Oct; Ⓟ ⌧ ☍ ▤

Here's the ultimate getaway, located a gorgeous 3km solitary drive beyond Calenzana, from where it's signed. At the head of a tight valley, it snuggles beneath sheer, jagged peaks, while in front the valley widens towards the open sea. Though on the smallish side, the five rooms are a delight, with beamed ceilings and tiled bathrooms with kidney-shaped baths. For even greater comfort, opt for the suite, which has a huge four-poster bed, a bathroom with double washbasins and a separate toilet. There's a cosy bar bedecked with cycling photos – notably of Jacques Anquetil, legendary French racing cyclist and father of A Flatta's owner – and an excellent restaurant. Dine on the terrace for unparalleled views down the valley.

❦ CASA MUSICALE // PIGNA €€

☎ 04 95 61 77 31; www.casa-musicale.org, in French; r €59-100

This warmly recommended place has oodles of character and a charming restaurant (p79). Its seven rooms (ask for La Solana, which has a particularly large balcony) have wall frescos and magnificent views. The hotel promotes regular music concerts and recitals; at these times, and indeed throughout the summer season, reservations are all but essential.

❦ HÔTEL U PALAZZU // PIGNA €€€

☎ 04 95 47 32 78; www.hotel-corse-palazzu.com; d €130-150, ste €220-270; ☷ Apr-Oct

A palace indeed! Returning to Pigna after three decades on the French mainland, Dominique Franceschini and his wife Vivianne have refurbished and redecorated this magnificent 18th-century mansion. Its three superplush doubles and two regal suites are all decorated with rich fabrics, antique furniture, original carpentry and appealing period features; the suites each have a private terrace as well.

❤ HÔTEL-RESTAURANT LE NIOBEL // **BELGODÈRE €€**

☎ 04 95 61 34 00; www.hotel-niobel-corse.com, in French; d €60-75; ⌚ Easter–mid-Sep; Ⓟ

Run by a cheerful young couple with roots in La Balagne, Le Niobel, located 200m from the village square, was originally the boarding house for Belgodère's school. Part of the Logis de France small-hotel network, the hotel has 11 well-maintained rooms, three with balconies overlooking the valley. At the tempting restaurant (*menu €20*), open to all for lunch and dinner from Easter through to mid-September, you can dine inside or, for a splendid panorama, on the terrace.

❤ CHAMBRES D'HÔTES U CHYOSU DI A PETRA // **OLMI-CAPPELLA €€**

☎ 04 95 61 91 01; www.locations-corses.com, in French; s/d incl breakfast €50/70; ▨

At first sight, you'd swear that this delightful *chambres d'hôte*, signed on the main road above the village, had been there for centuries. In fact, the owner created it himself, hauling up over 50 tonnes of stone and scouring the region for old doors, window frames, beams – anything abandoned yet recyclable. Each of its four rooms has a distinct character, the welcome couldn't be warmer (you'll enjoy a free aperitif on arrival and a copious buffet breakfast with 12 varieties of homemade jam), and there's a lovely shared living room. The open-air guest self-catering area has both a fridge and a cooking range.

❤ HÔTEL A SPELUNCA // **SPELONCATO €€**

☎ 04 95 61 50 38; www.hotel-a-spelunca.com, in French; d €60-80; ⌚ Apr-Oct; Ⓟ

This handsome building beside the village church was constructed in 1850 by Cardinal Savelli, director-general of police in Rome and a native son of Speloncato. Reception is friendly, and the hotel's 18 comfortable rooms, built around a central staircase, are furnished with pieces of the era. Those beneath the eaves have been recently renovated and offer the best views.

❤ HÔTEL MARE E MONTI // **FELICETO €€**

☎ 04 95 63 02 00; www.hotel-maremonti.com; d €84-132; ⌚ Apr-Oct; Ⓟ ▨ ▨

This trim hotel was originally constructed by a Corsican family who made good in South America and returned home with their riches. A noble stone staircase sweeps upward to its 16 trim rooms, each paved with terracotta tiles; most have great mountain views. There's a mosaic-lined swimming pool, a pretty rear garden and an agreeable restaurant, Sol e Luna, which serves lunch and dinner daily and is furnished in antique style.

THE WEST COAST

GOLFE DE PORTO

❤ HÔTEL COLOMBO // **PORTO €€**

Map p88; ☎ 04 95 26 10 14; www.hotel-colombo-porto.com, in French; rte de Calvi; d incl breakfast €55-110; ⌚ mid-Apr–mid-Oct; ▨

Built on three levels following the steep slope of the hillside (it's odd to go downstairs to bed), this delightful boutique-style hotel comes warmly recommended. Corridors are wide, bright and white, and are adorned with striking images by local photographer Robert Candela; rooms are mostly a soothing sky blue, with views of garden, sea and mountain. The lovely small garden, shaded by a giant palm, is surrounded by a riot of bougainvillea.

❦ HÔTEL RESTAURANT BELLA VISTA // PORTO €€

Map p88; ☎ 04 95 26 11 08; www.hotel-corse.com, in French; rte de Calvi; d €65-93, r per person incl half board €35; ☼ Apr–mid-Oct; ℗ ⌘

An easy walk from the summertime hubbub of the port area, this welcoming hotel is built in attractive granite and has a high-quality restaurant (p90). Rooms are bright and trim, and all have a balcony overlooking either the rear garden or Capu d'Ortu. Half board is compulsory in August.

❦ M'HOTEL CORSICA // PORTO €€

Map p88; ☎ 04 95 26 10 89; www.hotel-corsica-porto .com; d €55-85; ☼ Apr–mid-Oct; ℗ ⌘ ⌂

The unmissable pink M'Hotel Corsica is unspectacular, but it provides excellent value. It's also quiet, sitting at the edge of a eucalyptus wood, well apart from the bustle of the marina – gaze from the pool and all is greenness before you. Its 30 simply furnished rooms all have a balcony, and the toilet cubicle is separate to the bathroom. Some bedrooms have air-con (€10 supplement), while others, for that extra degree of independence, have a kitchenette (€6 supplement, minimum three nights).

❦ LA CHÂTAIGNERAIE // ÉVISA €

☎ 04 95 26 24 47; www.hotel-la-chataigneraie.com, in French; d €40-53; ☼ mid-Apr–mid-Oct; ℗

A stout building of grey granite on the western side of the village, La Châtaigneraie (Chestnut Grove) is run by a friendly Corsican and his Californian wife. It's a welcoming, homely place with 12 no-frills, impeccably clean bedrooms and a restaurant (p93) that merits a visit in its own right.

❦ HÔTEL LES ROCHES ROUGES // PIANA €€

☎ 04 95 27 81 81; www.lesrochesrouges.com, in French; d €114-129; ☼ mid-Mar–mid-Nov; ℗ ⌂

At the entrance to Piana on the Porto side, Les Roches Rouges first opened as a prestige hotel in 1912, and little seems to have changed since this time, apart from the addition of a telephone or two and wi-fi access; indeed, one of the hotel's many charms is its lived-in, just-slightly-dog-eared condition. Though far from the bargain it once was, the place continues to ooze faded, turn-of-the-century elegance with its magnificent dining room and sweeping foyer, where guests play chess and backgammon. Rooms are huge and sparsely furnished; ask for one with a sea view – and what a view! – for an extra €7.50 per person.

❦ MAISON D'HÔTE GIARGALO // PIANA €€

☎ 04 95 27 82 05; www.giargalo.com; ancien chemin Piana à Ota; r incl breakfast €50-77, r per person incl half board €47-58; ℗

Located 300m up the road behind the tourist office, this most attractive option has five charmingly decorated rooms. The cuisine draws upon Corsican specialities and organic produce (including home-grown vegetables), and Madame's bread, pasta and an impressive assortment of jams are all homemade. Drinking water is drawn from the hotel's own well, and solar panels power your lighting.

GOLFE DE SAGONE

❦ HÔTEL THALASSA // CARGÈSE €€

☎ 04 95 26 40 08; www.thalassalura.com; d €95, r per person incl half board €140-150; ☼ May-Sep; ℗

You half expect Monsieur Hulot to come loping round the corner at this hugely friendly family-run place, constructed

ACCOMMODATION

by the Garidaccis half a century ago. The garden leads onto the beach, and the 26 airy rooms are neat and simply furnished; all except four have a balcony, and three have wheelchair access. Regulars – some are third-generation visitors – come back year after year, so book early. Half board is obligatory in July and August.

GOLFE D'AJACCIO & AROUND

🌱 HÔTEL KALLISTÉ // AJACCIO €€

Map p101; ☎ 04 95 51 34 45; www.hotel-kalliste -ajaccio.com; 51 cours Napoléon; d incl breakfast €78-103; 🅿 🔀 🤶

A typical 19th-century Ajaccio town house from the outside, the Hôtel Kallisté has had its insides ripped out to convert it into an attractive boutique-style hotel. The 30 rooms, with their exposed brick- and stonework and terracotta tiles, gleam bright and white (even if some are on the small side), while the vaulted corridors have an almost-monastic feel. There's nothing self-denying, however, about the copious buffet breakfast, served in a spacious room with attractive wooden tables and chairs; there's even a large flat-screen TV in case you can't live without the morning news. Reception also serves, incongruously, as a car-rental outlet.

🌱 HÔTEL LES MOUETTES // AJACCIO €€€

off Map p101; ☎ 04 95 50 40 40; www.hotelles mouettes.fr; 9 cours Lucien Bonaparte; r €100-290; 🕙 mid-Mar–mid-Nov; 🅿 🔀 🖥 🤶 🖳

Les Mouettes occupies a lovely 19th-century mansion that in its time has served as both convent and cinema studios. Laze on the shaded terrace, lounge by the pool beneath a pair of century-old palms, or step down to the secluded beach just below. Of the 28 rooms, 21 have sea views; the superior-grade

rooms have particularly large balconies. You'll sleep in illustrious company – among the hotel's celebrity guests feature a couple of ex–prime ministers, the near–prime minister Ségolène Royal, Eric Cantona and Michael Schumacher.

🌱 HÔTEL MARENGO // AJACCIO €€

off Map p101; ☎ 04 95 21 43 66; www.hotel-marengo .com; 2 rue Marengo; d with shower €59-63, with private bathroom €75-85; 🕙 Apr-Oct; 🔀

This charmingly eccentric hotel is down a cul-de-sac off bd Madame Mère. Once a private villa, the hotel has 17 delightfully and individually decorated rooms with balconies overlooking a flowery garden terrace, while reception is an agreeable clutter of tasteful prints and personal objects. 'Cet hôtel a une âme,' (This hotel has a soul), the manageress told us with panache – and we knew what she meant.

🌱 LE MAQUIS // PORTICCIO €€€

☎ 04 95 25 05 55; www.lemaquis.com; d €180-550; 🕙 closed 6 weeks Jan & Feb; 🅿 🔀 🖥 🤶 🖳

This delightful hideaway (a favourite of Nicolas Sarkozy) sits amid beautifully maintained grounds, 2km south of Porticcio. In addition to its private beach, it has two pools, one of which is indoors, heated and open year-round. The 27 bedrooms are spacious and, like the public areas, individually and exquisitely furnished with antique pieces. Its restaurant, L'Arbousier, offers gourmet cuisine in an equally tasteful environment.

🌱 MAISON D'HÔTES CHÂTELET DE CAMPO // CAMPO €€

☎ 04 95 53 74 18; www.chatelet-de-campo.com; d incl breakfast €95-120, ste incl breakfast €130-150; 🅿 🖳

Nearly a decade ago, Elisabeth and Dominique Herzet (both excellent speakers of English) abandoned careers in Belgium to renovate this delightful granite mansion, constructed by a Corsican who had made his fortune in Panama. The mansion's three doubles are light, airy and furnished with great taste, while the suite has its own terrace. The views from the 2nd-floor balcony, open to all, are inspiring, and there's a gorgeous pool and garden, complete with shady gazebo. The sole impediment: there's a minimum of two nights' stay (three between June and September). Be sure to reserve ahead.

THE SOUTH

PORTO POLLO & AROUND

❦ HÔTEL LE GOLFE // PORTO POLLO €€€

☎ 04 95 74 01 66; www.hotel-corse-porto-pollo .com; d €160-450; ☺ Mar-Dec; Ⓟ ✉ 🖵 📶
This temple of luxury overlooking the harbour revels in minimalist lines and soothing colour accents. The sweeping views from the balconies make a sundowner taste all the sweeter.

PROPRIANO

❦ HÔTEL BELLEVUE €

Map p119; ☎ 04 95 76 01 86; www.hotels-propriano .com; av Napoléon; s €42-83, d €49-99; Ⓟ 📶
Propriano's most affordable option, the Bellevue is right on the heaving waterfront. Rest assured, however, the rooms are soundproofed and, even if they're fairly standard in appearance, they're fresh and well tended. Those facing the sea have enticing views that are well worth the extra fiscal outlay.

❦ LE LIDO €€€

Map p119; ☎ 04 95 76 06 37; www.le-lido.com; av Napoléon; r €120-225; ☺ May-Sep; Ⓟ ✉ 📶
Though the decor is ageing a bit, this small-scale venture boasts an irresistible

> ◤ **TOP FIVE**
>
> **ROOM WITH A (SEA) VIEW**
> Competition is fierce in this department:
>
> ★ **Hôtel Alivi** (p251) – Perched in the hills overlooking the Golfe de Santa Giulia
>
> ★ **Hôtel Les Roches Rouges** (p247) – Turn-of-the-century elegance and views over the Golfe de Porto
>
> ★ **Chambres d'Hôtes A Littariccia** (p251) – Stunning views of Plage de Palombaggia
>
> ★ **Hôtel Le Pinarello** (p252) – Stylish decor and unforgettable views over the Golfe de Pinarello
>
> ★ **Hôtel Les Mouettes** (opposite) – A 19th-century mansion overlooking the Golfe d'Ajaccio

location at the western edge of town, between two beaches. The 14 haciendalike rooms are situated around a leafdappled courtyard and have rear terraces that open onto the beach. The attached restaurant rates as one of the best in the region.

LE SARTENAIS

❦ CHAMBRES D'HÔTES DOMAINE DE CROCCANO // SARTÈNE €€

☎ 04 95 77 11 37; www.corsenature.com; rte de Granace; d incl breakfast €76-87; ☺ Jan-Nov; 📶
The three rooms, with exposed stone walls and period furniture, occupy a granite cottage nestled within a 10-acre property. The breezy terrace offers eagle's-eye panoramas, and there's also a small equestrian centre. In July and August, the owners prefer to rent the rooms by the week (€700). Located about 3.5km from Sartène, this is an excellent bucolic retreat.

☙ HÔTEL SAN DAMIANU // SARTÈNE €€

☎ 04 95 70 55 41; www.sandamianu.fr; d €105-190; ⏰ Apr-Oct; Ⓟ Ⓧ ▯ 🛜 ☵

The San Damianu has a perfect location just staggering distance from the *vieille ville* (old town), sleek rooms with all the mod cons, a soothing yellow colour scheme, million-dollar views over the Vallée du Rizzanese, and a sparkling swimming pool.

☙ HÔTEL LILIUM MARIS // TIZZANO €€

☎ 04 95 77 12 20; www.lilium-maris.com; Plage de Tizzano; d €75-165; ⏰ Apr-Sep; Ⓟ Ⓧ 🛜 ☵

Lilium Maris' main drawcard? Its sensational position right on the beach. Rooms are stylishly furnished and have plenty of natural light. Book a sea-facing room, as the other ones overlook the car park.

LE SARTENAIS TO BONIFACIO

☙ CHAMBRES D'HÔTES BERGERIES DE PISCIA // PISCIA €€

☎ 04 95 71 06 71; http://corse-chambres-hotes.com, in French; d incl breakfast €90-150; ⏰ Apr-Oct; ☵

Find bucolic bliss at these converted *bergeries* (shepherds' huts) that boast a *faaabulous* location. The panoramic pool comes high on the list of best swims ever: the views of the coast are simply out of this world. Rooms are a bit on the poky side, but are quirkily decorated with a combination of wood and other natural materials. The property includes a *parc animalier* (animal park) as well as an equestrian centre. The food (*menu €38*) is a definite plus – you'll feast on hearty Corsican fare in an atmospheric room. This is a delight

for urbanites searching for a rustic-chic getaway.

BONIFACIO & AROUND

☙ DOMAINE DE LICETTO // BONIFACIO €

off Map p130; ☎ 04 95 73 03 59, 04 95 73 19 48; www.licetto.com; rte du Phare; d €45-90; Ⓟ

Located just a couple of kilometres east of Bonifacio yet light years away from the hustle and bustle of the coast, this is a very nice surprise. Look at the rates! The seven rooms sport well-chosen tiles and modern furnishings, and feel fresh and comfortable. The eight self-catering apartments are more ordinary. There's a well-regarded on-site restaurant (p133).

☙ HÔTEL DES ÉTRANGERS // BONIFACIO €

Map p130; ☎ 04 95 73 01 09; fax 04 95 73 16 97; av Sylvère Bohn; d €38-73; ⏰ Apr–mid-Oct; Ⓟ Ⓧ 🛜

The Foreigners Hotel deserves a pat on the back for quoting very reasonable rates even in high season. Rooms are clean, modern and, if not especially aesthetically appealing, comfortable. Of course, this value-for-money place is no secret – bookings are essential in high season. It's on the main road, north of the harbour.

☙ HÔTEL GENOVESE // BONIFACIO €€€

Map p130; ☎ 04 95 73 12 34; www.hotel-genovese .com; rte de Bonifacio; d €130-285; ⏰ Oct-Mar; Ⓟ Ⓧ 🛜 ☵

This nearly-but-not-quite boutique hotel will appeal to design-savvy travellers, with its stylish furniture, soothing tones and lovely swimming pool built on the ramparts. Try to score an outside-facing room, rather than a darker courtyard-facing one.

✿ HÔTEL LE COLOMBA // BONIFACIO €€

Map p130; ☎ 04 95 73 73 44; www.hotel-bonifacio -corse.fr; rue Simon Varsi; d €80-160; 🌑 Mar-Nov; P ✖ 🛜

Supercentral Le Colomba is excellent value for money. It occupies a renovated 14th-century building and features clean rooms with all the necessary comforts; some are embellished with period furniture. Breakfast (at an extra cost) is served in a welcoming vaulted room.

PORTO-VECCHIO

✿ HÔTEL MISTRAL €€

Map p136; ☎ 04 95 70 08 53; www.lemistral.eu; rue Jean Nicoli; d €55-145; 🌑 Mar-Oct; P ✖ 🛜

This reliable pile wins no prizes for character but it's centrally located and has well-equipped (if smallish) rooms with clean bathrooms. Some have balconies and are nicer than others, so ask to see a few. Rejoice: parking is free.

✿ HÔTEL SAN GIOVANNI €€

Map p136; ☎ 04 95 70 22 25; www.hotel-san -giovanni.com, in French; rte d'Arca; s €65-110, d €70-130; 🌑 Mar-Oct; 🛜 🖳

The San Giovanni makes you feel you've stepped into a Garden of Eden – the 1.25-hectare landscaped gardens are a treat, with lots of flowers, ponds and palm trees, not to mention a lovely pool. Other perks include bike hire, jacuzzi and tennis court. By comparison, the rooms lack wow factor. It's on the southwestern outskirts.

AROUND PORTO-VECCHIO

✿ HÔTEL ALIVI // GOLFE DE SANTA GIULIA €€€

Map p139; ☎ 04 95 52 01 68; www.santa-giulia.fr; d €135-360; 🌑 Apr-Oct; P ✖ 🖳 🛜 🖳

This sleek, intimate hotel perched in the hills overlooking the Golfe de Santa Giulia hits all the right charm buttons, with 10 handsomely designed rooms; angle for a room with a sea view. The icing on the cake is the lovely swimming pool.

✿ CHAMBRES D'HÔTES A LITTARICCIA // PALOMBAGGIA €€

Map p139; ☎ 04 95 70 41 33; www.littariccia.com; rte de Palombaggia; d incl breakfast €60-200; 🖳

This well-tended property has six cocoonlike rooms in two neat houses, plus a small pool, adjective-defying views of Plage de Palombaggia and an affable welcome. Simply turn up, absorb and enjoy.

✿ LES BERGERIES DE PALOMBAGGIA // PALOMBAGGIA €€€

Map p139; ☎ 04 95 70 03 23; www.hotel-bergeries -palombaggia.com; rte de Palombaggia; d €165-560; 🌑 Apr-Nov; P ✖ 🛜 🖳

Set in the hills overlooking the Plage de Palombaggia, this boutique-style hotel offers a mix of comfort, style and ambience, with 13 tastefully decorated rooms, some with a sea view. The coup de grâce is the pool, which looks like the location for a photo shoot from *Vogue*.

✿ CHAMBRES D'HÔTES L'HÔTE ANTIQUE // PETRALONGA SALVINI €€

off Map p139; ☎ 04 95 71 20 17, 06 22 24 85 73; www.lhote-antique.com; d incl breakfast €75-95; ✖ 🛜

From this B&B you can easily reach Porto-Vecchio, Plage de Santa Giulia, Plage de Rondinara and Bonifacio, making it an ideal base. The five rooms are very spacious and well appointed; some rooms have exposed beams and balconies. *Table d'hôtes* (€27) are available twice a week. Petralonga Salvini is about 14km south of Porto-Vecchio, off the N198; take the D459 to the right and follow the signs.

ACCOMMODATION

♥ HÔTEL LE PINARELLO // PLAGE DE PINARELLO €€€

Map p139; ☎ 04 95 71 44 39; www.lepinarello.com; d €270-455; ⌚ mid-Apr–Oct; Ⓟ ⚒ 🛜

Right on Plage de Pinarello, this modern abode combines location, service and sleekness. Rooms have all been stylishly decorated with rich designer fabrics, and are colour coordinated in cooling creams and earthy hues. The views over the sea are unforgettable.

♥ MOTEL DES AMANDIERS // PLAGE DE PINARELLO €

Map p139; ☎ 04 95 71 43 64; d €46-62; ⌚ May-Oct

It's no misprint – the rates are correct. The Motel des Amandiers is the best-value hotel for miles around, with seven adjoining rooms set in verdant gardens. Sure, the layout of the rooms screams '70s, but at these prices, and with such a location, nobody's complaining.

L'ALTA ROCCA

♥ CHAMBRES D'HÔTES U SPITAGHJU // L'OSPÉDALE €€

☎ 04 95 26 77 53, 06 12 51 01 25; d incl breakfast €60-80; 🛜

A home away from home, this perky little B&B occupies a lovingly restored stone house on the main drag. The three rooms are muted and tasteful, with crisp linen and glistening bathrooms. The garden at the back offers mind-boggling views over the Golfe de Porto-Vecchio.

♥ CHAMBRES D'HÔTES DE CAVANELLO // ZONZA €€

☎ 04 95 78 66 82; www.locationzonza.com; hameau de Cavanello; d €60-70; 🛜 🖭

This is a pretty pocket of Corsica, rural and pleasing on the eye. It features nine well-proportioned, functional rooms, and several hectares of meadows and forests that hide you from all but the

wildlife. There's also a lovely half-moon-shaped pool, so you may be reluctant to leave this place of easy bliss. Breakfast costs €7. The B&B is about 2km from Zonza.

♥ HÔTEL LE TOURISME // ZONZA €€

☎ 04 95 78 67 72; www.hoteldutourisme.fr; rte de Quenza; s €80-110, d €90-160; ⌚ Apr-Oct; Ⓟ ⚒ 🖥 🛜 🖭

This reliable number is nothing glam, but the 18 rooms are light filled and well organised. Be sure to ask for a valley-facing room – the views are splendid! There are also five colourful rooms in an annexe across the street. The pièce de résistance is the small pool at the back, with inspirational views of the Alta Rocca.

♥ LE PRÉ AUX BICHES // ZONZA €

☎ 06 27 52 48 03; www.lepreauxbiches.com; d with shared bathroom €50; ⌚ May-Oct

Revive your childhood fantasies of camping out at this trippy venue. L'Alta Rocca's quirkiest accommodation option, its offers splendid isolation in a field surround by laricio pines, 10 minutes' walk down from Zonza. Digs are in six Mongolian-style yurts that can sleep up to six people. They're comfortable, with parquet flooring and colourful furnishings, and the ablution block is in top nick. Meals (from €15) are available on request. A refreshing dash of originality.

♥ CHEZ PIERROT // QUENZA €

☎ 04 95 78 63 21; Ghjallicu; d incl half board €105

It's hard not to be impressed by the end-of-the-world feeling that emanates from this place, on Plateau de Ghjallicu, about 5km uphill from Quenza. Rest your head in one of the five well-kept rooms in a granite building, then sign up for a horse-riding excursion (about €15 per hour) with Pierrot, the charismatic owner, or head to the eerie Plateau du Coscione for a picnic or a short walk.

♥ GÎTE CORSE ODYSSÉE // QUENZA €

☎ 04 95 78 64 05; www.gite-corse-odyssee.com; r per person incl half board €50-60; ☼ Apr–Sep

This *gîte d'étape* in a modern building boasts a superquiet location on a forested site about 1km from Quenza. Beds are in two- to seven-person dorms. It's not your average *gîte* – rooms here are all individually decorated in warm tones. Your hosts are very helpful (Nathalie speaks good English), and the meals are copious and wholesome.

♥ A PIGNATA // LEVIE €€

☎ 04 95 78 41 90; www.apignata.com; rte du Pianu; d incl half board €80-155; ☼ Mar–Oct; 🖥 🛜 🖳

Hidden in the foothills of the Alta Rocca, this boutique-style inn is a peach of a place, with superb rooms and splendid suites that are decorated with a contemporary twist. And yes, there's a (heated) swimming pool. The restaurant (p147) rates as one of the best in southern Corsica. The perfect marriage of authenticity and modernity.

♥ CHAMBRES D'HÔTES U PALAZZU // STE-LUCIE DE TALLANO €€

☎ 04 95 78 82 40, 06 79 07 93 77; upalazzu@orange .fr; d incl breakfast €75; ☼ mid-Apr–Oct

This place, set in a characterful town house, has charm in spades. The three rooms are decorated with period furniture, four-poster beds (in two rooms), ancient tiles and pastel-coloured walls. The sunny garden is the perfect remedy to a day spent on twisty roads.

♥ GÎTE D'ÉTAPE U FRAGNONU // STE-LUCIE DE TALLANO €

☎ 04 95 78 82 56; www.alta-roc.fr; dm per person incl half board €40; ☼ Apr–mid-Oct

A far cry from your usual *gîte d'étape*, U Fragnonu occupies a converted oil mill about 300m from the main square. The four-bed dorms are impeccable, as are the communal areas. Meals are copious and tasty. The owner is a canyoning and climbing guide, and organises day trips to Bavella.

THE EAST

LA COSTA VERDE

♥ U PAESOLU A SUVERA A U VENTU // CERVIONE €

☎ 06 83 43 57 07; www.ecotourismecorse.com; rte d'Anghione; 4-person gîtes per week €350-620

A hamlet of five *gîtes* in the style of traditional Castagniccia village houses and shepherds' huts, U Paesolu is part of an ecotourism centre utilising environmentally friendly processes such as cork and hemp insulation, solar-heated water, and reed beds for the treatment of waste water. The *gîtes* are simply but attractively furnished (to encourage socialising there are no TVs), and sleep four to eight people; the owners offer courses in painting, basketwork and ethnobotany, among other things. You will find it situated 1km east of Cervione on the D71.

♥ CASA CORSA – CHAMBRES D'HÔTES DOUMENS // PRUNETE €€

☎ /fax 04 95 38 01 40; www.casa-corsa.net; Acqua Nera; s/d incl breakfast €59/66; Ⓟ

This modern ochre-coloured house has a stylish Provençal feel, with six cosy rooms embellished with lots of decorative touches such as terracotta tiles, chestnut beams, colour-washed walls and colourful bedspreads. Hearty breakfasts are served under a lovely vine-covered pergola. It's 6km south of Moriani-Plage and 5km east of Cervione, about 100m off the N198 via a dirt track.

♥ HÔTEL-RESTAURANT LE BELVÉDÈRE D'E CATARELLE // SAN GIOVANNI DI MORIANI €€

☎ 04 95 38 51 64; www.corsica-catarelle.com; s €60-70, d €70-135, ste €104-135, r per person incl half board €68-100; ☺ Mar-Nov; ℗

This intimate 10-room hotel has a pleasantly rustic atmosphere, with pine furniture, white walls and colourful bedspreads. Best of the lot is the suite called Anne, which features sloping beamed ceilings, warm fabrics and a private roof terrace. Another draw is the garden dining area, which has ravishing views over the Morianincu and the sea. It's gay- and biker-friendly. Half board is compulsory in July and August.

LA CASTAGNICCIA

♥ CHAMBRES D'HÔTES LA DILIGENCE // VERDÈSE €

☎ 04 95 34 26 33; sophie.le-villain@wanadoo.fr; s/d incl breakfast €45/59; ☺ Apr-Oct; ▣

Situated in the heart of the peaceful village of Verdèse (a few kilometres north of Piedicroce), this bijou *chambres d'hôtes* is located in a former coach inn that has been tastefully restored. The five rooms radiate charm, and contain beamed ceilings, original fireplaces, period furnishings and parquet floors. At the end of the day, make sure you treat yourself to a copious *table d'hôtes* (dinner €23; available five days a week) on the terrace; the delicious Corsican specialities are made using the finest local produce.

♥ TOUR DE TEVOLA // CARCHETO €

☎ 04 95 31 29 89; www.tevola.com; 4-person gîtes per week €250-410; ▣

Best-selling Corsican author Jean-Claude Rogliano has restored a medieval tower house in the picture-postcard village of Carcheto to create six charismatic *gîtes* that share a common garden, terrace and pool, complete with barbecue and a functioning traditional bread oven. The rooms are snug (the old building has thick stone walls and narrow windows), but the setting and atmosphere could not be more authentic.

♥ CHAMBRE D'HÔTES PETRI // GAVIGNANO-BORGO €

☎ 04 95 48 43 27; psantori@aol.com; s/d incl breakfast €52/60

No English is spoken at this welcoming B&B in the hamlet of Borgo, a few kilometres south of Morosaglia. Never mind – it's snug and has a likeably old-fashioned feel, with wood-panelled ceilings, parquet flooring and walls carpeted with country-style floral patterns. Killer views are thrown in for good measure. The terrace at the rear is a treat, and Monsieur Petri will be happy to explain everything you ever wanted to know about Corsican charcuterie (but were too afraid to ask). There's only one room, so book ahead.

♥ U VECCHJU MULINU // FORNOLI €€

☎ 04 95 28 91 87; http://monsite.wanadoo.fr/vecchju -mulinu; d per week €230-410; ℗ ▣

This ancient water mill nestled within lush green gardens has been converted into three attractive *gîtes* (two doubles, one for four people) that have equal parts traditional and modern appeal. Mix in a warm welcome, a beautiful garden with barbecue, a cool pool and a great location (about 4km from Ortiporio), and you've got a recipe for a restful retreat. The owner is fluent in English.

COSTA SERENA & CÔTE DES NACRES

❦ TAGLIO DI SACRAMENTO // VIX-VENTISERI €€

☎/fax 04 95 57 43 83; www.taglio-di-sacramento .com; Villa le Cèdre Bleu; d incl breakfast €70-110; Ⓟ ⚡ ⚑

This adorable and peaceful B&B seduces all who stay – there's a fresh, modern feel and the attention to detail is impressive. The three rooms are coolly tiled, and are decorated in soothing pastels and fluttering voiles, with nice prints on fresh walls and pale exposed beams. Beaches are a short drive away. It's about 6km south of Ghisonaccia, about 700m off the N198 (look for the small signpost), along a twisting road.

❦ GÎTE D'ÉTAPE DE CATASTAJU // CATASTAJU €

☎ 04 95 56 70 14, 06 79 74 81 58; dm €15, dm per person incl half board €33; ☾ Apr-Oct; Ⓟ

Set in a converted hydroelectric power station (don't be put off, this is a French hydroelectric power station: small, cute and even rather pretty), this *gîte d'étape* on the Mare a Mare Centre hiking trail (p217) is tucked away amid glowingly verdant forest. It features well-kept four- to 10-bed dorms, with the beautiful *vasques* (natural pools) of the Abatescu river just outside the door.

❦ VILLA CLOTILDE // PRUNELLI DI FIUMORBU €€

☎ 04 95 57 93 92, 06 79 49 00 44; d incl breakfast €55-70, apt per week €450-600

Swap stress for bliss at this Tuscan-style palazzo. The two gleaming rooms offer unremitting comfort – oak parquet floors, period furnishings and excellent bedding – not to mention ravishing views over the valley from private balconies. Breakfast is served in an atmospheric dining room or on the terrace. There's also an apartment that can sleep four to six people, available by the week only.

❦ HÔTEL LA SOLENZARA // SOLENZARA €€

☎ 04 95 57 42 18; www.lasolenzara.com; rte Principale; r incl breakfast €75-110; ☾ mid-Mar–Oct; Ⓟ ⚡ ▣ � ⚑

Deservedly three-star, this stately Genoese villa overlooking the harbour mixes modern and traditional decor in a feast of high ceilings, ancient tiled floors, exposed beams and antique mirrors. The swimming pool sits in a beautiful garden with sea views, and is complemented by a minispa that includes a jacuzzi, Turkish bath and massage room.

THE CENTRAL MOUNTAINS

CORTE

❦ CHAMBRES D'HÔTES OSTERIA DI L'ORTA – CASA GUELFUCCI €€

off Map p174; ☎ 04 95 61 06 41; www.osteria-di-l -orta.com; d €85, d incl half board €140; Ⓟ � ⚑

Restored with great taste and restraint, this large powder-blue *maison de famille* (family house) is run by a welcoming young couple. The four rooms and single suite are airy and spacious, with parquet flooring, and power showers. Half board is required in July and August. Dinners (€25) come in for warm praise.

❦ HÔTEL DU NORD €

Map p174; ☎ 04 95 46 00 68; www.hoteldunord -corte.com; 22 cours Paoli; r €95; Ⓟ ⚡ �

Never mind the busy thoroughfare in summer and the somewhat-peeling exterior – the grande dame of Corte's sleeping scene is kept in top nick. It features a fine selection of cheerful and spacious rooms with all the creature comforts.

☙ HÔTEL DUC DE PADOUE €€

Map p174; ☎ 04 95 46 01 37; www.ducdepadoue .com; place Padoue; s €92, d €100-111; 🅿 🟦 🛜
Don't be deterred by the scruffy facade of this professionally run abode. Renovated throughout in 2007, the hotel has an inviting interior that offers well-equipped rooms, flat-screen TVs, plump bedding, muted tones and squeaky-clean bathrooms. Ask for a room with a balcony.

VALLÉE DE LA RESTONICA

☙ LES JARDINS DE LA GLACIÈRE €€

☎ 04 95 45 27 00; www.lesjardinsdelaglaciere.com; s €60-85, d €65-95; 🕓 Apr–mid-Nov; 🅿 🟦 🛜 🏊
At the entrance of the valley, this well-run hotel is the perfect place to relax after a day touring the central mountains. It has clean, fresh rooms, impeccable communal areas and a fantastic location by the river, but you should steer clear of the rooms facing the road. There's a lovely pool, but the real clincher is the sprawling garden overlooking the river – you can dunk yourself in the natural pools just below.

VALLÉE DU NIOLO

☙ HÔTEL DES TOURISTES // CALACUCCIA €

☎ 04 95 48 00 04; www.hotel-des-touristes.com; d with shared bathroom €21, s/d with shower €42/50, with private bathroom €50/60; 🕓 Apr–Oct
Rooms are modest but prices are sweet at this venerable old pile, built in 1928. The interior is tidy and serviceable, with three types of room; ask to see a few before settling in. The cheapest ones

(known as *gîte d'étape hôtel*) are unbeatable value, with parquet flooring and an enticing retro feel.

☙ CHAMBRES D'HÔTES CASA VANELLA // CASAMACCIOLI €€

☎ 04 95 48 69 33; www.casavanella.com; d incl breakfast €75-90; 🅿 🛜
This adorable B&B seduces all who stay here. It has a fresh, modern feel, and the five rooms are coolly tiled and decorated in soothing pastels. Your charming hosts, Jean-François and Pascale, are very knowledgable about the valley, and can advise on local activities and walking trails. They also do a *table d'hôte* (€27.50), with local, seasonal products. Pascale speaks good English.

VALLÉE D'ASCO

☙ E CIME €€

☎ 04 95 47 81 84; www.e-cime.com; Asco; d incl half board €115; 🕓 Mar-Oct; 🅿 🛜
Though the modernish rooms are a bit lacking in the charm department, they're comfy enough to receive a tired body after a full day of exploring the valley. No, you're not hallucinating – the view over the valley is real. The attached restaurant (mains €9 to €15) is held in high esteem.

LE BOZIU

☙ CHAMBRES D'HÔTES CASA DI LUCIA // MAZZOLA €€

☎ 04 95 48 69 93; www.casa-di-lucia.com; d incl breakfast €85-95; 🛜
In Mazzola, a hamlet near Alando, this delightful two-suite boutique-style place is run by Jean-Charles Fabiani. He's a painter, and it shows: there's a gallery, the spotless rooms with period furnishings ooze charm, and the terrace is the perfect place to soak up fab views over the Boziu. Monsieur can arrange paint-

ing classes by reservation, and meals are available on request (€15 to €35). A stylish and brilliant-value hideaway.

❤ CHAMBRES D'HÔTES CASA CAPELLINI // SANT' ANDREA DI BOZIU €€

☎ 04 95 48 69 33; www.casacapellini.com; d €80-95; 🖥 📶

This lovely, clean B&B has four restful rooms in a tastefully renovated village house. Top that off with an affable welcome, killer views and hearty dinners (€28), and you have a *chambres d'hôtes* that beckons you to stay for a few extra days.

CORTE TO VIZZAVONA

❤ MAISON D'HÔTES CASA GIAFFERRI // POGGIO DI VENACO €€

☎ 04 95 46 04 33: www.casagiafferri.fr; d incl breakfast €80; 📶

Looking for a night at a place that's extra special? Make a beeline for this splendid *maison d'hôtes* with an artist's vibe. A true find for peace seekers and those in search of offbeat accommodation, it has 14 rooms that all feel like cosy nests; no two are the same. There's even an art gallery. You can count on Annette, your well-travelled, English-speaking host, to make you feel at home. She prepares delicious meals (€15) and can organise cooking classes.

❤ HÔTEL RESTAURANT I LARICCI // VIZZAVONA €

☎ 04 95 47 21 22; www.ilaricci.com; s/d with shared bathroom incl half board €62/84; 🌣 May-Sep; Ⓟ

This large chalet-style building just above the station has 12 cosy rooms, six with mountain views. All have creaky parquet floors and soft beds into which many a weary trekker has sunk. The few with private bathroom cost €6 extra.

ACCOMMODATION

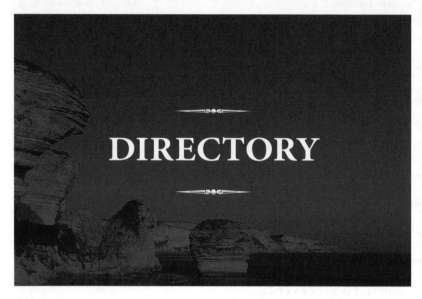

DIRECTORY

BUSINESS HOURS

Businesses tend to open between 9am and noon, and from 2pm or 3pm to 6pm or 7pm, Monday to Friday or Saturday. Many food concerns, such as pastry shops, bakeries, butchers and greengrocers, close at noon too. In July and August, many shops and businesses stay open between 8am and 8pm – and sometimes even later – every day. Others, despite the once-a-year opportunity to replenish the till, continue to close for a couple of hours in the early afternoon.

Banks are open from 8am or 9am to 11.30am or 1pm, then 1.30pm to 4.30pm or 5pm, Monday to Friday or Tuesday to Saturday. Exchange services may end half an hour before closing time.

Post offices are generally open from 8.30am or 9am to 5pm or 6pm on weekdays (perhaps with a midday break); on Saturdays they open from 8am to noon. Opening hours (and days) may be much less at village post offices.

Tourist offices are generally open from at least 9am to noon or 1pm, then 2pm or 3pm to 5pm, Monday to Friday. Hours are more generous in summer, when most offices open seven days a week and many don't observe the midday break.

Sadly, many churches, especially in rural areas, are closed except when Mass is held. Ask for the key at a nearby bar or at the *mairie* (town hall). Urban churches that are also major sights are usually open all day.

Restaurants serve lunch between noon and 2pm or 3pm; dinner is served any time between 6.30pm and 11pm. In the low season, restaurants usually close one day a week; however, in tourist-populated areas many restaurants shut for several months. Between June and September, most restaurants open daily for both lunch and dinner. Paradoxically, in some seaside towns such as Ajaccio, some restaurants close at midday at this time, reasoning that everyone's picnicking on the beach.

Cafes are open from early morning until around 10pm, usually every day of the week. Bars and clubs open daily from 7pm to 2am or 3am, although some bars are open from mid-morning onwards.

CHILDREN

Although purpose-made kids' attractions are scarce, Corsica is an eminently suitable destination if you're travelling with children. With its abundance of beaches and opportunities for outdoor activities, there's plenty to do in a generally hazard-free setting. Most Corsicans are welcoming to children.

The summer sun in Corsica can strike hard, and you should make sure that children are not overexposed to its rays: use a high-protection sunscreen, reapply it several times daily, and ensure they wear a hat. Make sure that they drink lots of liquid as well. There are excellent medical facilities in the main cities.

Lonely Planet's *Travel with Children* by Brigitte Barta et al is crammed with tips for keeping children and parents happy on the road. See also p24 for more on family travel in Corsica.

CUSTOMS REGULATIONS

If you're coming from another EU country, there are no additional taxes on duty-paid items for personal consumption. Duty-free shopping and VAT refunds don't apply to visitors returning to an EU country.

The following items can be brought into France duty-free from non-EU countries: 200 cigarettes or 50 cigars; 1L of strong liquor or 2L of liquor that is less than 22% alcohol by volume; 4L of still table wine; 16L of beer; and other goods up to the value of €183.

DANGERS & ANNOYANCES

When Corsica makes the headlines, it's often because nationalist militants have engaged in an act of violence, such as bombing a public building or robbing a bank. But the violence, if you exclude the occasional torching of someone's holiday home, has never been targeted at tourists, and there's no reason for visitors to fear for their safety. Muggings are unheard of, and your stay should be trouble-free. Still, you should observe the usual precautions; in particular, don't leave any valuables in your car, even in the most innocuous rural idyll.

The main hazards in Corsica are the winding roads that follow narrow

PRACTICALITIES

* Corsica uses the metric system for weights and measures.

* Electric current is 220V, 50Hz AC; plugs have two round pins.

* If your French is up to it, keep your finger on the pulse by reading the daily regional newspaper *Corse Matin*. Or pick up *Arriti* or *O Ribombu* (in French and in Corsican) if you want to get an idea of some nationalist prose. The monthly magazine *Corsica* (in French) is good for the latest on Corsica's current issues.

* For French TV, try the commercial stations Tf1 and M6, or the state-owned channels France 2 and France 3.

* Tune in to the radio stations France Bleu Frequenza Mora (www.bleurcfm.com) or Alta Frequenza (www.alta-frequenza.com) for local news (in French and Corsican) and polyphonic singing.

DIRECTORY

DRIVING TIP

Driving? Let's just say that Corsica is close to Italy geographically, culturally – and in the way its citizens drive. Check in your mirror for a number plate ending in 2A or 2B (the *départements* of Corse-du-Sud and Haute-Corse); too many locals at the wheel have a tendency to drive halfway up your backside before pulling out abruptly, then overtaking in situations where responsible drivers would hold back.

precipices (which are often bereft of any guardrail), and the fairly frequent blind turnings. Add to this the impatience of Corsican drivers and the tendency for livestock to loom before you without warning, and you'll appreciate the need for caution. Indeed, count on an average speed of less than 60km per hour. In general, keep your eyes on the road; if you want to admire the scenery, stop at a lay-by.

If you happen to pass a bunch of stray wild pigs, don't try to feed them or allow children to pet them. They may be cute, but they're also unpredictable and may mistake you for a tasty morsel.

Bring repellent and antihistamine cream with you if you're prone to insect bites, particularly mosquitoes, though both are available from pharmacies here.

It's also worth pointing out that Corsica is far less multiracial in its ethnic make-up than most of the mainland, and travellers may encounter racist attitudes towards Arabs or Africans.

DISCOUNT CARDS

Senior cards entitling those aged over 60 to 50% discount on train travel are available from Chemins de Fer de la Corse (p274), which runs the Corsican train lines.

An International Student Identity Card (ISIC; €13) and its equivalent for teachers, the International Teacher Identity Card (ITIC; €18), can get you discounts on items such as air tickets, sports events, concerts and movies. Many places stipulate a maximum age for the student card, usually 25.

EMBASSIES & CONSULATES

All foreign embassies are in Paris, although some countries also have consulates in other major French cities, such as Marseille and Lyon.

FOOD & DRINK

For most eating options, we indicate the price range of mains, followed by the price of *menus* (two- or three-course set menus, often served only at lunchtime). *Menus* usually don't include wine, although some *fermes-auberges* (farm inns) sometimes include a bottle or carafe of wine.

See p16 and p230 for juicy information about Corsica's rich gastronomy. See p258 for restaurant opening hours.

GAY & LESBIAN TRAVELLERS

Despite the fact that homosexuality does not seem to pose a problem to this conservative and traditional society – in theory at least – there is practically no open gay scene in Corsica. When it comes to being 'out' in public, the adage 'out of sight, out of mind' applies, especially in smaller villages. What you do behind closed doors may be perfectly acceptable to most Corsicans, but open displays of affection, especially between men, will be frowned upon at the very least. Discretion is advisable. That said, few hoteliers will bat an eyelid if a same-sex couple checks into a room together.

Online, check out **Gayscape** (www.gayscape.com) and **Le Guide Gay** (www.leguide gay.com, in French), though information on Corsica is very limited.

HOLIDAYS

Most French people take their annual holiday in July or August, deserting the cities for the coastal or mountain resorts. A fair proportion of these summertime holidaymakers head for Corsica, along with a healthy contingent of foreigners. Corsicans need their holidays too, and tend to head away in winter for skiing on the mainland.

Corsicans observe the following *jours fériés* (public holidays):

New Year's Day (Jour de l'An) 1 January
Easter Sunday & Monday (Pâques & lundi de Pâques) Late March/April
Labour Day (Fête du Travail) 1 May
Victory 1945 (Fête de la Victoire 1945) 8 May
Ascension Thursday (L'Ascension) May
Pentecost & Whit Monday (Pentecôte & lundi de Pentecôte) Mid-May/mid-June
Bastille Day/National Day (Fête Nationale) 14 July
Assumption Day (L'Assomption) 15 August
All Saints' Day (La Toussaint) 1 November
Remembrance Day (Armistice) 11 November
Christmas (Noël) 25 December

INSURANCE

A travel-insurance policy to cover theft, loss and, especially, serious medical problems is a wise precaution. Some policies specifically exclude dangerous activities, which can include scuba div-

PRICE GUIDE

The following is a guide to the pricing system used for eating options in this book. Prices quoted are for an average main course.

€	under €15
€€	€15 to €30
€€€	over €30

ing, motorcycling and even trekking, so read the fine print.

You may prefer a policy that pays doctors or hospitals directly rather than having you pay on the spot and claim later. If you have to claim later ensure you keep all documentation. Check that the policy covers ambulances or an emergency flight home. Paying for your airline ticket with a credit card often provides limited travel accident insurance.

INTERNET ACCESS

Corsica is not the most internet-friendly place; you'll only find internet cafes in bigger towns and resort areas, such as Ajaccio, Bastia, Bonifacio, Calvi, Corte, Porto-Vecchio and Propriano. The connection is generally good and rates are fairly standard at around €5 per hour.

However, wi-fi has spread across the island like a forest fire. Many midrange and all top-end hotels offer wi-fi access, although they usually impose a charge; coverage either extends throughout the hotel or may be restricted to public areas.

LEGAL MATTERS

In principle, the police can search pretty much anyone at any time – whether or not there is probable cause. Foreigners must be able to prove their legal status in France (eg with their passport, visa and/or residency permit) without delay.

DIRECTORY

As elsewhere in the EU, the laws are very tough when it comes to drinking and driving. The legal blood-alcohol limit is 0.05%, and drivers exceeding this face heavy fines, plus several years in jail. Licences can also be immediately suspended. The import or export of drugs can lead to a jail sentence of up to 30 years. The penalty for possession of drugs for personal use (including cannabis, amphetamines, ecstasy etc) can be a fine as high as €3750 and a one-year jail sentence. The fine for littering starts at €150, and the penalties for drunkenness and smoking in public areas are equally severe.

Eighteen is the legal age for voting and driving.

MAPS

The maps available from local tourist offices are usually fine for towns, but are insufficient for navigating more widely. The Michelin map *Corse du Sud, Haute-Corse* (No 345) at a scale of 1:150,000 and the two IGN *Carte de Promenade* maps (No 73 for the north and No 74 for the south) at a scale of 1:100,000 are excellent for driving.

The IGN *Top 25* map has a scale of 1:25,000 and is ideal for walking.

MONEY

Corsica uses the euro (€). For exchange rates, see the inside front cover of this guidebook.

ATMS

Known in French as *distributeurs automatiques de billets* (DABs) or *points argent,* ATMs normally accept Visa, MasterCard and Cirrus, and are the most convenient way to access euros. However, ATMs are not as widespread in Corsica as they are

> ## WARNING
>
> Be warned: many restaurants, hotels and even petrol stations in Corsica don't accept credit cards, and it's very rare for *chambres d'hôtes* (B&Bs) and *gîtes d'étape* (walkers' lodges) to do so. Some places will refuse cards for small amounts (typically under €15), and it's fairly common to come across a reputable restaurant where the credit-card machine happens to have been *en panne* (out of order) for several weeks. Make sure you always enquire first.

in mainland France; most larger Corsican towns have an ATM, but they are scarce in rural areas – Cap Corse, the Alta Rocca and the Haut Taravo have only one or two ATMs each. If you're heading off into the heart of the island, it's wise to stock up with euros beforehand.

CREDIT CARDS

In places where credit cards are accepted (see the boxed text, above), they are the simplest way to pay for major purchases. Visa (Carte Bleue) and MasterCard (Eurocard) are the cards most widely accepted by hotels, supermarkets, major petrol stations and stores on the island, and both can be used to pay for air, train and ferry travel. Credit cards are mandatory if you want to rent a car, as they'll be used as a form of *caution* (deposit).

It's a good idea to check with your credit-card company before leaving home about charges on international transactions.

TIPPING

By law, restaurants and bar prices all include the service charge, so there's no expectation of a *pourboire* (tip). That said, many locals will leave a few coins after a drink, or will round up the restaurant bill by a euro or two. Similarly, if you're happy with your hotel stay, the decent thing to do is leave a couple of euros or so.

POST

Post offices are widespread across the island. In some rural hamlets, they provide a community focus, as they are housed alongside the *mairie* and the local administrative offices. Some larger branches also perform modest banking services.

Send your postcards early in your holiday, since mail takes a little longer to arrive than from mainland France.

TELEPHONE

For mobile phones, Corsica uses the GSM 900/1800 system, which is compatible with the rest of Europe and Australia (though not the USA). The network covers most towns and villages throughout the island, even in the interior. However, you may find yourself without coverage if you're hiking in more-remote areas.

You'll usually find a public telephone in or near the post office. Many in Corsica are in a dilapidated state, and often simply do not function. You can buy a France Télécom *télécarte* (phonecard) at post offices, *tabacs* (tobacconists), supermarket check-out counters and anywhere you see a blue sticker reading *télécarte en vente ici*. The phonecard units positively race by, however, for calls beyond Corsica and mainland France; scratch cards with a number, available at kiosks and some *tabacs,* give you much more talking time if you're calling abroad.

USEFUL NUMBERS & CODES

All telephone numbers throughout Corsica consist of 10 digits; landline numbers start with ☎ 04, and mobile-phone numbers start with ☎ 06. If calling a Corsican number (landline or mobile) from overseas, drop the first 0.

International Direct Dial (IDD) calls to almost anywhere in the world can be made from Corsica's public telephones, but for most you will need to have a *télécarte*.

Some useful numbers and codes:
France country code ☎ 33
International access code ☎ 00
Local directory enquiries ☎ 118 008
International directory enquiries ☎ 118 700

Online, go to **PagesJaunes** (www.pages jaunes.fr) for business numbers or click on the PagesBlanches link on its home page for individuals' numbers.

TIME

Corsica uses the 24-hour clock, with hours separated from minutes by a lower-case *h*. Thus, 3.30pm is 15h30, 9.50pm is 21h50, 12.30am is 00h30, and so on.

Corsica, like the rest of France, is on Central European Time, which is one hour ahead of GMT/UTC. When it's noon in Paris, it's 3am in San Francisco, 6am in New York, 11am in London, 9pm in Sydney and 11pm in Auckland. During daylight saving time, which runs from the last Sunday in March to the last Sunday in October, France is two hours ahead of GMT/UTC.

TOILETS

Public toilets, signposted *toilettes* or WC, are rare on the island. Most people tend to stop by a cafe, down a quick coffee, then

WASHBASINS

Not least of the many Italianate influences on and imports to Corsica is the washbasin bereft of any tap, which you sometimes find in cafes and restaurants. Just press your foot on the knob below the basin or pull the lever at the side and, as for Moses, the water will flow.

use the toilets on the premises (it's generally considered rude or stingy to just use the facilities and walk out). Simply ask, *'Est-ce que je peux utiliser les toilettes, s'il vous plaît?'*

There are few, if any, toilet or washing facilities at beaches. Hikers will find a few chemical toilets near Parc Naturel Régional de la Corse (PNRC; Corsican Nature Reserve) refuges but none along the walking trails. Be prepared to go back to nature at times.

TOURIST INFORMATION

Main towns generally have well-informed, welcoming tourist offices where at least one member of staff speaks English. Increasingly more-rural areas also have some sort of small tourist-information kiosk or centre.

L'Agence du Tourisme de la Corse (☎ 04 95 51 00 00; www.visit-corsica.com) is Corsica's regional tourist office.

The principal tourist offices with a regional remit are Ajaccio (Map p101; ☎ 04 95 51 53 03; 3 bd du Roi Jérôme; www.ajaccio-tourisme. com; ☼ 8am-8pm Mon-Sat, 9am-1pm & 4-7pm Sun Jul & Aug, 8am-7pm Mon-Sat, 9am-1pm Sun Apr-Jun, Sep & Oct, 8am-12.30pm Mon-Fri, 8.30am-12.30pm & 2-5pm Sat Nov-Mar) and Bastia (Map p39; ☎ 04 95 54 20 40; www.bastia-tourisme.com; place St-Nicolas; ☼ 8am-8pm Apr-Sep, 9am-noon & 2-5pm Mon-Sat Oct-Mar).

Overseas French government tourist offices, usually called Maisons de la France, can provide every imaginable sort of tourist information. The general website FranceGuide (www.franceguide.com) lets you access the site for your home country (click on the small Change Website tab at the bottom of the home page).

TRAVELLERS WITH DISABILITIES

France, and especially Corsica, could not be considered progressive in terms of its facilities for people with disabilities. However, the situation is changing, albeit slowly. Hotels and restaurants are modernising, and are adding wheelchair-accessible rooms and toilet facilities (indeed, the provision of at least one disabled-access room is now a requirement of the law for new or modernising hotels). The Ajaccio branch of the Association des Paralysés de France (☎ /fax 04 95 20 75 33; 19 bis Rue du Docteur del Pellegrino) publishes details of places in Corsica (hotels, restaurants, cultural sites and so on) that are accessible to people with disabilities. These details can also be obtained from Ajaccio's tourist office (Map p101; ☎ 04 95 51 53 03; 3 bd du Roi Jérôme; www.ajaccio-tourisme.com; ☼ 8am-8pm Mon-Sat, 9am-1pm & 4-7pm Sun Jul & Aug, 8am-7pm Mon-Sat, 9am-1pm Sun Apr-Jun, Sep & Oct, 8am-12.30pm Mon-Fri, 8.30am-12.30pm & 2-5pm Sat Nov-Mar).

Many ferries have some cabins that are accessible to wheelchair users; see p267 for contact details of major ferry companies.

VISAS

By law, everyone in France, including tourists, must carry some sort of ID on them at all times. For foreign visitors, this means a passport (a photocopy should do if you don't want to carry your passport for security reasons, although you may be required to verify your identity later) or, for citizens of those EU countries that issue them, a national ID card.

There are no entry requirements for EU nationals, and citizens of Australia, the USA, Canada, New Zealand and Israel can visit France as tourists for up to three months without a visa.

For up-to-date information on visa requirements, see the website of the **French Ministry of Foreign Affairs** (www.diplomatie.gouv.fr) and click on 'Going to France'.

WOMEN TRAVELLERS

Women travelling solo should experience no problems in Corsica. Corsicans are almost universally polite to women, and it is very unlikely that you will be subjected to the catcalls you may encounter in big cities on the mainland. Physical attack is rare but, as in any country, women should use their common sense and remain conscious of their surroundings. If you find yourself the recipient of unwanted male attention, it's best to ignore it.

It's wise to dress modestly in the towns of inland Corsica, where communities are more conservative than in coastal cities. Skimpy clothing in such a context is both shocking and inconsiderate.

France's national **rape-crisis hotline** (☎ 0800 05 95 95), run by a women's organisation, can be reached toll-free from any telephone without using a phonecard. In an emergency, call the **police** (☎ 17) or the **Europe-wide emergency number** (☎ 112).

TRANSPORT

ARRIVAL & DEPARTURE

AIR

High season for air travel to Corsica is May to September. Indeed, that's the only time you'll be able to find direct international flights to the island. Outside those months, you'll have to look at flying via a French mainland airport, such as Paris, Lyon, Nice or Marseille.

AIRPORTS

Corsica has four airports: Ajaccio, Bastia, Calvi and Figari. The main hub is Ajaccio's **Campo dell'Oro airport** (AJA; www.ajaccio.aeroport.fr), which is where the bulk of European scheduled and charter flights land. There are frequent flights to/from mainland France operated by Air France and the Corsican home-grown CCM Airlines (Compagnie Corse Méditerranée), also known as Air Corsica, but direct international flights are few and far between – EasyJet flies from London Gatwick once a week (Sundays) from May to September only.

EasyJet also flies weekly in summer from Gatwick to **Bastia Poretta airport** (BIA; www.bastia.aeroport.fr), convenient for Cap Corse, St-Florent and eastern Corsica. **Figari Sud Corse airport** (FSC; www.figari.aeroport.fr), the handiest landing point for access to Porto-Vecchio, Bonifacio and Propriano in southern Corsica, has daily flights from mainland France, plus charter flights in summer from other European countries. **Calvi Ste-Catherine airport** (CLY; www.calvi.aeroport.fr) is served mainly by charter flights, as well

THINGS CHANGE...

The information in this chapter is particularly vulnerable to change. Check directly with the airline or a travel agent to make sure you understand how a fare (and ticket you may buy) works and be aware of the security requirements for international travel. Shop carefully. The details given in this chapter should be regarded as pointers and are not a substitute for your own careful, up-to-date research.

ONLINE TICKETS

Cheap Flights (www.cheapflights.com)

Ebookers (www.ebookers.com)

Expedia (www.expedia.com)

Kayak (www.kayak.com)

Last Minute (www.lastminute.com)

Orbitz (www.orbitz.com)

Priceline (wwwpriceline.com) With this US-based site you can bid for a ticket online.

Skyscanner (www.skyscanner.net)

Travelocity (www.travelocity.com)

as domestic flights from French mainland airports (Paris, Marseille, Lyon and Nice).

CAR & MOTORCYCLE

Driving from the UK, the most direct route to Corsica begins via the Channel Tunnel on **Eurotunnel** (☎ 08705 35 35 35; www.eurotunnel.com), which has at least 10 crossings a day between Folkestone and Calais (from £53 one way, 35 minutes), then across France on the autoroutes to Nice, where you can catch a ferry to Ajaccio, Calvi or Bastia (total 1650km, 19 hours of driving).

BRINGING YOUR OWN VEHICLE

A right-hand drive vehicle brought to France from the UK or Ireland is supposed to have deflectors fixed to the headlights to avoid dazzling oncoming traffic. By law, all vehicles in France must carry a reflective warning triangle and hi-visibility waistcoats, to be used in the event of a breakdown or accident. Recommended accessories include a first-aid kit, spare bulb kit and fire extinguisher. If your vehicle does not have modern EU-style number plates, it must have a GB sticker clearly displayed at the rear.

DRIVING LICENCES & DOCUMENTATION

By law, motorists (driving their own car or a rented vehicle) need to carry a national ID card or passport; a valid driving permit or licence *(permis de conduire)*; car ownership papers, known as a *carte grise* (grey card); and proof of insurance (the *carte verte* or green card). If you're stopped by the police and don't have one or more of these documents, you risk a hefty on-the-spot fine. Never leave your car ownership or insurance papers in the vehicle.

If you're involved in a minor traffic incident with no injuries, the easiest way for drivers to sort things out with their insurance companies is to fill out a Constat Amiable d'Accident Automobile (jointly agreed accident report), known in English as a European Accident Statement. Make sure the report includes any details that will help you prove that the accident was not your fault, if you feel that the other party was in the wrong. If problems arise, alert the police.

In the UK, the **RAC** (☎ 08705 722 722; www.rac.co.uk) or the **AA** (☎ 0870 600 0371; www.theaa.com) can give you more advice.

SEA

Corsica has six ferry ports serving the French and Italian mainland: Bastia, Île Rousse, Calvi, Ajaccio, Propriano and Porto-Vecchio. The island can be reached from the ports of Nice, Marseille and Toulon in France; and from Genoa, Livorno and Savona in Italy. Ferries also link Bonifacio in Corsica with the Italian island of Sardinia.

Advance reservations are essential in high season, especially for motorists planning to take a vehicle. Students under 27, seniors aged over 60 and families get reduced rates with most ferry companies; children aged four to 12 years usually pay

TRANSPORT

50% or two-thirds of an adult fare, and children aged under four sail for free. Most companies also offers packages of, for example, car plus two adults or car plus two adults and two children. Taking a bicycle on board costs around €10 return.

FROM MAINLAND FRANCE

In high season, **Société Nationale Corse Méditerranée** (SNCM; ☎ in France 08 91 70 18 01, in Italy 02 66 117 104, in the UK 020 7491 49 68; www .sncm.fr) operates speedy *navires à grande vitesse* (NGVs) from Nice to Île Rousse (three hours) and Ajaccio (four hours). Normal ferries run from Marseille to Ajaccio (8¾ hours), Bastia (10 hours), Île Rousse (10 hours), Porto-Vecchio (13 hours) and Propriano (9¼ hours). In winter, services are reduced to just a handful of weekly sailings to/from Nice and Marseille.

Corsica Ferries (☎ 08 25 09 50 95; www .corsicaferries.com) runs normal ferries from Nice to Ajaccio (6¼ hours), Bastia (5½ hours), Calvi (5½ hours) and Île Rousse (5½ hours), and from Toulon to Ajaccio (5¾ hours), Bastia and, less frequently, Île Rousse.

La Méridionale (☎ 08 10 20 13 20; www .lameridionale.fr) has overnight sailings from Marseille to Ajaccio, Bastia and Propriano (all 12 hours).

Expect to pay around €380 return for a car and two passengers via NGV from Nice to Ajaccio in July or August.

FROM MAINLAND ITALY

Between April and September, ferries operated by Corsica Ferries and Moby Lines link Corsica with the Italian mainland ports of Genoa, Livorno, Savona and Piombino.

CLIMATE CHANGE & TRAVEL

Climate change is a serious threat to the ecosystems that humans rely upon, and air travel is the fastest-growing contributor to the problem. Lonely Planet regards travel, overall, as a global benefit, but believes we all have a responsibility to limit our personal impact on global warming.

FLYING & CLIMATE CHANGE

Pretty much every form of motor travel generates CO_2 (the main cause of human-induced climate change) but planes are far and away the worst offenders, not just because of the sheer distances they allow us to travel, but because they release greenhouse gases high into the atmosphere. The statistics are frightening: two people taking a return flight between Europe and the US will contribute as much to climate change as an average household's gas and electricity consumption over a whole year.

CARBON OFFSET SCHEMES

Climatecare.org and other websites use 'carbon calculators' that allow jetsetters to offset the greenhouse gases they are responsible for with contributions to energy-saving projects and other climate-friendly initiatives in the developing world – including projects in India, Honduras, Kazakhstan and Uganda.

Lonely Planet, together with Rough Guides and other concerned partners in the travel industry, supports the carbon offset scheme run by climatecare.org. Lonely Planet offsets all of its staff and author travel.

For more information check out our website: lonelyplanet.com.

Between April and October, **Corsica Ferries** (☎ in France 08 25 09 50 95, in Livorno, Italy 0586 88 13 80, in Savona, Italy 019 215 62 47; www .corsicaferries.com) runs to Bastia from Livorno (four hours, or 2¼ hours by high-speed ferry), Savona (six hours) and Piombino (1¾ hours by high-speed ferry). In high summer, it also has a less-frequent service from Savona to Île Rousse (six hours, June to mid-August) and Calvi (six hours, mid-June to August).

Moby Lines (☎ in Corsica 04 95 34 84 94, in Genoa, Italy 010 254 15 13, in Livorno, Italy 0565 93 61; www.moby.it) runs seasonal ferry services (mid-April to September) to Bastia from Genoa (4¾ hours) and Livorno (four hours).

Fares from mainland Italy are lower than from mainland France. For a small car and two passengers travelling from Genoa to Bastia in July and August, the return fare is around €175.

FROM SARDINIA

Many holidaymakers, especially from Italy, combine a driving holiday with a visit to the neighbouring Italian island of Sardinia.

The crossing between Bonifacio and Sardinia's Santa Teresa di Gallura takes about one hour. **Saremar** (Sardegna Regionale Marittima; ☎ in Corsica 04 95 73 00 96, in Sardinia 0565 90 89 33; www.saremar.it, in Italian), Sardinia's public ferry line, makes three sailings daily, in conjunction with Corsica Ferries, from April to September. Fares are around €70 return for two adults and a small car in high season. **Moby Lines** (☎ 04 95 34 84 94; www.moby.it) also serves this route.

La Méridionale (☎ 08 10 20 13 20; www .lameridionale.fr) runs ferries year-round between Porto Torres (Sardinia) and Propriano (four hours).

GETTING AROUND

By far the best way to get around Corsica is by car, whether hired or brought from home. Bus services, especially and paradoxically during the tourist season, are lean (most are geared to getting children and workers between home and school or the nearest town). The train is an attractive, though limited, option, running through stunning countryside between Bastia and Ajaccio, with a branch route to Calvi. For the superfit, Corsica's little-travelled, twisting, climbing roads make for hugely satisfying, if gruelling, cycling.

BICYCLE

Corsica, with its dramatic mountain passes and stunning coast, is superb cycling terrain for experienced cyclists, though the summer heat makes cycling in July and August out of bonds for all except true masochists.

By law, bicycles must have two functioning brakes, a bell, a red reflector on the back and yellow reflectors on the pedals. After sunset and when visibility is poor, road cyclists must turn on a white light in front and a red one at the rear. Marked cycling lanes (on roads) or trails (for mountain bikers) are practically nonexistent, except for a kilometre or two in Bastia and Ajaccio. Cycling in the Parc Régional Naturel de la Corse is not forbidden, but there are few trails suitable for cyclists and you'll need a sturdy mountain bike.

For information on travelling by train with your bike, see p274.

HIRE

Bike hire is available in the main seaside cities, but if you're going to be doing extensive cycling, consider bringing your own wheels. Bike shops are thin on the

TRANSPORT

ground, so it's essential to carry spare parts. Mountain-bike (*vélo tout-terrain*; VTT) hire is widespread and costs around €15 to €20 per day. Most outlets require a deposit (cash, signed travellers cheques or credit card) of anything from €50 to €300.

BUS

Corsica's major towns and many of the little ones in between are linked by bus, as are the airports of Ajaccio and Bastia with town centres. In more-remote areas services are scarce or nonexistent. The unofficial **Corsica Bus** (www.corsicabus.org) website aggregates timetable information for most of the bus services on the island.

Bus services are geared to local inhabitants rather than tourists, meaning that many services are less frequent during the height of the tourist season when schoolchildren are on holiday. In July and August there is often only one departure a day and no departure at all on Sunday and public holidays. Secondary routes often only have service on alternate days or once or twice a week. Many passenger routes year-round are combined with school and/or postal services.

By contrast, there is a trio of summer-only bus services that manage to sustain themselves precisely because of the tourist trade. Between July and mid-September Autocars Mordiconi runs one bus daily along the spectacular route between Porto and Corte, via Évisa and Calacuccia. Similarly, in July and August Transports Santini has a twice-daily run, Monday to Saturday, from Île Rousse and Bastia to St-Florent, while Corsicar runs between Calvi and the fascinating coastal hamlet of Galéria.

Autocars (regional buses) are operated by a range of different bus companies, some of whom might have an office at

the bus station (*gare routière*) of the towns they serve. Often one company sells tickets for all the bus companies operating from the same station, although passengers, as a rule, do not need to worry about buying tickets in advance. You can buy your ticket on any particular route, or leg of a route, from the driver – fares average around €15 per 100km.

The island's two main towns, Ajaccio and Bastia, have the largest bus stations. In smaller places, where a bus stop can constitute a 'station', bus schedules are invariably pinned up in the window of the local tourist office or in the nearest bar to the bus stop (if there's no printed schedule, just ask the bar owner). Bus stations do not have left-luggage facilities.

Primary bus routes and bus-travel companies include the following:
Alta Rocca Voyages – Ricci (☎ 04 95 51 08 19) Ajaccio–Propriano–Sartène–Levie–Zonza–Bavella
Autocars Ceccaldi (☎ 04 95 21 38 06) Ajaccio–Sagone–Évisa
Autocars Cortenais (☎ 04 95 46 02 12) Bastia–Corte; Corte–Aléria
Autocars Mordiconi (☎ 04 95 48 00 04; www .hotel-des-touristes.com) Corte–Calacuccia–Évisa–Porto
Corsicar (☎ 04 95 65 11 35; www.corsicar.com, in French) Bastia–Île Rousse–Ponte Leccia–Calvi
Eurocorse Voyages (☎ 04 95 21 06 30; www .eurocorse.com) Ajaccio–Corte–Bastia; Ajaccio–Propriano–Sartène–Porto-Vecchio and Ajaccio–Propriano–Sartène–Bonifacio; Porto-Vecchio–Bonifacio; Ajaccio–Sartène–Zonza
Rapides Bleus (☎ 04 95 31 03 79; www.kallis tour.com) Bastia–Porto-Vecchio
Transports Santini (☎ 04 95 37 04 01) Bastia–St-Florent, Île Rousse–St-Florent

See the Transport sections of the respective regional chapters for more information.

DISTANCE CHART (KM)

Note: Distances between destinations are approximate

	Ajaccio	Bastia	Bonifacio	Calvi	Corte	Figari	Île Rousse	Macinaggio	Porticcio	Porto	Porto-Vecchio	Propriano	Sartène	St-Florent
Bastia	154													
Bonifacio	136	170												
Calvi	176	92	240											
Corte	84	70	148	92										
Figari	132	166	22	240	144									
Île Rousse	183	69	199	24	72	216								
Macinaggio	192	39	209	132	109	205	108							
Porticcio	17	155	134	161	85	126	185	194						
Porto	82	134	220	81	86	199	100	174	85					
Porto-Vecchio	164	142	28	212	121	23	193	182	125	220				
Propriano	73	191	67	236	138	59	223	230	67	140	76			
Sartène	84	178	54	262	141	46	210	217	80	154	64	13		
St-Florent	176	23	190	70	93	186	46	62	178	146	154	202	189	
Solenzara	131	103	67	156	80	64	152	142	125	174	41	83	82	114

CAR & MOTORCYCLE

To really enjoy Corsica, we strongly recommend that you hire a vehicle. No other form of transport allows you to explore the island's secret backwaters and enjoy as much freedom as a set of motorised wheels. There are some gorgeous runs, cruising along the island's beautiful, dramatic roads – the D81 linking Calvi and Porto, the D84 between Porto and Francardo (via Évisa, the Forêt d'Aïtone and the Scala di Santa Regina), the D69 from just below Vivario to Ghisoni, and the D80 along the dramatic Cap Corse coast between Centuri and Nonza are but a sample of the memorable drives you can undertake.

Exhilarating views aside, motoring around Corsica can be fairly hair-raising on occasion. Roads are narrow; hairpin bends (lacets) are tortuous and often blind; and rocky outcrops often prevent you spotting oncoming traffic (or the menagerie of livestock that wanders freely over mountain roads) until it's bang on top of you, or you're on top of it. Use your horn to announce your presence. Drops at the side of the road may be sheer and barriers are a luxury. Visitors tend to drive timidly; the locals with a panache that verges on the irresponsible.

Corsica has no motorway (autoroute). The main roads are called routes nationales, such as the N198, which skirts the flat eastern coast from Bastia to Bonifacio, or the N193, running through the dramatic relief between Bastia, Corte and Ajaccio. Routes départementales, whose names begin with the letter D, are tertiary local roads, many of them potholed and far from silky smooth. Routes communales, whose names begin with the letter C (or nothing at all), are rural roads best suited to off-road vehicles and mountain bikes.

TRANSPORT

Michelin's *Corse-du-Sud, Haute-Corse* map 345 (scale 1:150,000) is reliable and invaluable for getting around.

FUEL

Petrol *(essence)*, also called *carburant* (fuel), costs around €1.30 per litre (unleaded, 95 or 98 octane). Outside main towns, petrol stations are few and far between so keep an eye on the fuel gauge.

HIRE

You can rent a car when you arrive in Corsica, be it at an airport or in town. Most companies require the driver to be at least 21 years old (23 for some categories of car) and to have had a driving licence for at least one year.

Although multinational rental agencies such as Avis, Budget, Hertz and Europcar (Europe's largest) can be expensive for on-the-spot rental, their prepaid promotional rates are usually more reasonable. Fly-drive deals offered by Avis and Europcar are also worth looking into. All major firms have a desk at the airports in Corsica.

Aggregator websites such as **Holiday Autos** (www.holidayautos.co.uk) and **Autoescape** (www.autoescape.com) compare prices from a range of companies to help you find the cheapest deal. Expect to pay around €230 to €340 per week for a small car.

Most companies require a credit card, primarily so that you can leave a deposit *(caution)*. They'll probably ask you to leave a signed credit card slip without a sum written on it as a deposit. If you don't like this arrangement, ask them to make out two credit-card slips: one for the sum of the rental, the other for the sum of the excess. Make sure to have the latter destroyed when you return the car.

Insurance *(assurance)* for damage or injury you cause to other people is mandatory, but collision damage waivers vary. If you're in an accident where you are at fault, or the car is damaged and the party at fault is unknown (as, for example, if someone dents your car while it's parked), or the car is stolen, the *franchise* (excess/deductible) is the amount you are liable for before the policy kicks in. When signing the rental agreement, you can agree to pay an extra daily fee (anything from to €11 to €16 per day) to reduce the excess (usually €600 to €800 depending on the vehicle size) to either zero or a minimal amount.

The packet of documents you get when hiring a car includes a 24-hour number to call in case of breakdown, and a European Accident Statement. Check how many 'free' kilometres are in the deal you're offered; *kilométrage illimité* (unlimited mileage) means you can drive to your heart's content.

To rent a scooter or *moto* (motorcycle), you will probably also have to leave a deposit (of several hundred euro), which you forfeit (up to the value of the damage) if you're in an accident and it's your fault. Since insurance companies won't cover theft, you'll also lose the deposit if the bike is stolen. Expect to pay about €60/350 per day/week for a 125cc motorcycle. Rates usually include helmet hire.

Some of the major operators in Corsica:

ADA (www.ada.fr, in French)
Avis (www.avis.co.uk)
Budget (www.budget.co.uk)
Europcar (www.europcar.co.uk)
Hertz (www.hertz-en-corse.com)
National-Citer (www.corse-auto-rent.fr)
Rent a Car (www.rent-car-corsica.com, in French)
Sixt (www.sixt.co.uk/holiaycars)

PARKING

Corsican towns are small by any standard and were not designed with cars in mind, so parking can be frustrating. On town maps within destination chapters, we indicate public parking, usually paying, with a small 'P'. *Défense de stationner* means 'No Parking' and you'd be wise to respect the injunction; fines can be harsh.

ROAD RULES

In Corsica, as throughout Continental Europe, people drive on the right side of the road and overtake on the left. Unless otherwise indicated, you must give way to cars coming from the right. North American drivers should remember that turning right on a red light is illegal.

The speed limit in built-up areas is 50km/h. On intercity roads you must slow to 50km/h the moment you pass a white sign with red borders on which a place-name is written in black or blue letters. This limit remains in force until you arrive at the other side of the town or village, where you'll pass an identical sign with a red diagonal bar across the name, indicating that you're leaving the built-up area.

Outside towns and villages, speed limits are 90km/h (80km/h if it's raining) on single-carriageway N and D roads and 110km/h (100km/h if it's raining) on the few stretches of four-lane highway. This said, you're more likely in Corsica to fall short of the speed limit than to exceed it.

French law is tough on drunk drivers and police conduct random breathalyser tests to weed out drivers whose blood-alcohol concentration (BAC) is over 0.05% (0.50g per litre of blood) – two glasses of wine for a 75kg adult. Licences can be suspended.

Helmets *(casques)* are compulsory for motorcyclists and moped riders. Bikes of more than 125cc must have their headlights on during the day. No special

SPEED LIMITS	
Urban areas	50km/h
Single	90km/h
carriageway	(80km/h in rain)
Dual	110km/h
carriageway	(100km/h in rain)

licence is required to ride a scooter with an engine capacity of 50cc or less.

TAXI

All Corsican towns are small enough to get around on foot. Ajaccio and Bastia both have local bus services. Elsewhere, you may find yourself dependent to some degree on taxis.

Taxis in Corsica have a 'Taxi' sign on the roof; the cars can be any colour. Look for phone numbers of taxi companies in the Transport sections of individual towns.

TRAIN

Travelling by train in Corsica – a fun experience in its own right – is much more than simply a means of getting from A to B. Dubbed *U trinighellu* (literally 'the rattler'), the 110-seat railcars (also known as *michelines*) trundle along a remarkable railway line constructed in the 1880s and 1890s. With 38 tunnels (the longest is 4km), 12 bridges and 34 viaducts (one designed by Gustave Eiffel, no less), it represents one of the great triumphs of human ingenuity over topography and ranks among the world's great scenic railways. In 2007 the old *michelines* began to be replaced on the Ajaccio–Corte–Bastia route by modern AMG 800 diesel units with improved wheelchair access and much greater speed and comfort, which, along with track improvements, will eventually reduce the Ajaccio–Bastia journey time from four hours to less than three hours.

TRANSPORT

Corsica's two lines are operated by **Chemins de Fer de la Corse** (CFC; ☎ in Bastia 04 95 32 80 61, in Corte 04 95 46 00 97, in Ajaccio 04 95 23 11 03, in Calvi 04 95 65 00 61, in Île Rousse 04 95 60 00 50; www.ter-sncf.com/corse).

The main, north–south line runs between Bastia and Ajaccio. From the Ponte Leccia junction between Bastia and Corte, a spur runs to the Balagne towns of Île Rousse and Calvi. There was once a third line, connecting Bastia and Porto-Vecchio along the flat east coast of the island but it was badly damaged by German bombing raids in 1943. There's talk of restoring it but no one has yet lifted a hammer.

Except on the Ajaccio–Bastia route, travelling by train is often slower than a bus ride – a factor not helped by the occasional wild goat that wanders on the track. At the train station (gare), you can get updated train timetables and information, which also feature on the website (www.ter-sncf.com/corse). There are no left-luggage facilities at any station.

The train routes are:

Bastia–Ponte Leccia–Corte–Ajaccio Corsica's primary north–south rail route, with dozens of stops in smaller stations, including Furiani, Biguglia, Casamozza, Ponte Novu, Francardo, Venaco, Vivario, Vizzavona and Bocognano. Trains run year-round in each direction four times daily. It takes almost four hours to travel the length of the line from Bastia to Ajaccio.

Bastia–Casamozza Up to 13 trains daily make the short 30-minute journey from Bastia to Casamozza, Monday to Saturday, stopping approximately every two minutes at every local station along the way.

Bastia–Ponte Leccia–Calvi Corsica's east–west link, this line follows the Bastia–Ajaccio line south to Ponte Leccia, then curves west towards the coast, stopping en route in Île Rousse. There are two trains daily, both requiring a change in Ponte Leccia (around three hours Bastia to Calvi).

Île Rousse–Calvi Tramway de la Balagne (p59) – little two-car trains that shuttle back and forth up to nine times daily from mid-April to mid-October along the spectacular coastline between Calvi and Île Rousse. With 15 intermediate stops, including Lumio, Sant'Ambrogio, Algajola and Davia, the full journey takes around 45 minutes. Wherever you happen to be situated along the line, a train will pass in each direction approximately once an hour.

CLASSES & COSTS

Train fares are reasonable, averaging around €16 per 100km; a one-way ticket from Ajaccio to Bastia costs around €22. Children aged under four travel for free and those aged four to 12 years pay 50% of the adult fare.

Cyclists can take their bicycles aboard for a €18 fee, but there is only space for four or five bikes on each train, and places cannot be reserved in advance.

There's only one class and there's no system of advance reservations.

TRAIN PASSES

Senior travellers with a one-year Carte Sénior issued by the French national rail line, the SNCF, can use it on CFC trains to get a 50% reduction. SNCF's Carte Famille Nombreuse, which gives families with three or four children aged under 18 discounts of at least 30%, is likewise valid in Corsica. More information on both annual travel passes is online at www.sncf.com.

The CFC also sells its own rail pass, the Carte Zoom, valid for seven consecutive days of unlimited travel throughout the CFC network. It costs €48 and is sold at all staffed CFC stations. None of the major European rail passes – InterRail, Eurail, Eurorail or even the France Railpass – provides unlimited free travel on the CFC system. The major rail passes do, however, yield a 50% discount on CFC fares between Bastia and Ajaccio (but not on the Tramway de Balagne between Calvi and Île Rousse).

LANGUAGE

French is Corsica's official and working language and the language that Corsicans use most of the time. Corsica is nevertheless impressively bilingual and even trilingual. Many older Corsicans, and even some younger ones, express themselves quite eloquently in Corsican (called *corsu* in Corsican) and even in Italian – not that the differences between the two are all that vast.

Spontaneous use of Corsican by the native inhabitants has been on the decline, but it has benefited from various forms of life support. It's now even part of the curriculum for the primary and secondary schools on the island. This is a significant turnaround from the days when signs posted in Corsican village schools read *'Il est interdit de cracher par terre et de parler corse'* (Spitting on the floor and talking in Corsican are forbidden). Moreover, young people can now study Corsican at the university in Corte. Politicians have seen to it that Corsican enjoys equal status with French on road signs, although you'll see that the French

will often have been edited out with a spray of paint or bullets.

For more information on Corsican, see the 'Corsican' boxed text on the following page. For a more comprehensive guide to the French language (understood and spoken around the island), pick up a copy of Lonely Planet's *French Phrasebook*.

PRONUNCIATION

The pronunciation guides included with each French phrase should help you get your message across. Here are a few of the letters in written French that may cause confusion:

j	as the 's' in 'leisure', eg *jour* (day)
c	before e and i, as the 's' in 'sit'; before a, o and u it's pronounced as English 'k'
ç	as the 's' in 'sit'
r	pronounced from the back of the throat while constricting the muscles to restrict the flow of air

CORSICAN

'Hello' in the Corsican language is *bunghjornu* (literally 'good day'); 'thank you' is *grazie*; 'bread' is *pane*; 'dog' is *cane*; 'Best wishes!' is *Pace i salute!* If this all sounds suspiciously like Italian to you, you're not off the mark. The Corsican language – *corsu* in Corsican – descended from (and is therefore related to) the Tuscan language that formed the basis of standard Italian. If you think Corsican is a dialect of Italian, however, you might neverthe less do well to keep this view to yourself. Though Corsicans are too good-natured to want to punish innocent foreigners for the hasty conclusions they draw, many Corsicans are committed to the view that Corsican is not a dialect, and still less Italian itself, but a distinct language.

Despite this, it's not recommended that you make any effort to communicate with Corsicans in Corsican. As Alexandra Jaffe says in her excellent *Ideologies in Action: Language Politics in Corsica*, Corsican is the language of the Corsican heart and hearth. French 'commands the domain of the formal, the authoritative, the instrumental and intellectual'. You may think you are being ingratiating if you attempt a few words of Corsican. More likely, however, you'll be perceived as patronising or condescending, as if the person you are addressing didn't speak French perfectly well. You may be perceived to be baiting the person you are addressing on what is in Corsica a heavily charged political issue. Finally, again Corsican being the language of the Corsican heart and hearth, you may be perceived as intruding on personal and private space – as if, invited into a stranger's living room, you proceeded immediately into their bedroom. Another way to put it is that presuming to address a stranger in Corsican is akin to the liberty you take in addressing a stranger in the familiar pan-Mediterranean 'tu' form rather than in the more respectful *'vous'*, *'Lei'* or *'usted'* form.

If you speak French or Italian, stick with that. Dedicated Corsophiles can enrol in language courses at the Università di Corsica Pasqual Paoli in Corte or those offered by the association Esse (☎ 04 95 33 12 00) in Bastia.

n, m   where a syllable ends in a single n or m, these letters are not pronounced, but the vowel is given a nasal pronunciation

BE POLITE

An important distinction is made in French between *tu* and *vous*, which both mean 'you'; *tu* is only used when addressing people you know well, children or animals. If you're addressing an adult who isn't a personal friend, *vous* should be used unless the person invites you to use *tu*. In general, younger people insist less on this distinction between polite and informal (indicated here by 'inf'), and you will find that in many cases they use *tu* from the beginning of an acquaintance.

GRAMMAR

All nouns in French are either masculine or feminine and adjectives reflect the gender of the noun they modify. The feminine form of some nouns and adjectives is indicated by a silent e added to the masculine form, as in *ami* and *amie* (the masculine and feminine for 'friend'); other nouns undergo more complex changes.

In the following phrases both masculine and feminine forms have been indicated where necessary (by 'm' and 'f' respectively). The gender of a noun is often reflected by a preceding article, eg *le/un* (m) and *la/une* (f), meaning 'the/a'; or one of the possessive adjectives, eg *mon/ton/son* (m) and *ma/ta/sa* (f), meaning 'my/your/his, her'. French is unlike English in that the possessive adjective agrees in number and gender with the thing in question, eg 'his mother' and 'her mother' are both translated as *sa mère*.

ACCOMMODATION

I'm looking for a ...	Je cherche ...	zher shersh ...
camping ground	un camping	un kom·peeng
guest house	une pension (de famille)	ewn pon·syon (der fa·mee·yer)
hotel	un hôtel	un o·tel
youth hostel	une auberge de jeunesse	ewn o·berzh der zher·nes

Where is a cheap hotel?
Où est-ce qu'on peut trouver un hôtel pas cher?   oo es kon per troo·vay un o·tel pa shair
What is the address?
Quelle est l'adresse?   kel ay la·dres
Could you write it down, please?
Est-ce que vous pourriez l'écrire, s'il vous plaît?   es ker voo poo·ryay lay·kreer seel voo play
Do you have any rooms available?
Est-ce que vous avez des chambres libres?   es ker voo za·vay day shom·brer lee·brer
May I see it?
Est-ce que je peux voir la chambre?   es ker zher per vwa la shom·brer
Where is the bathroom?
Où est la salle de bain?   oo ay la sal der bun
Where is the toilet?
Où sont les toilettes?   oo son lay twa·let

How much is it ...?	Quel est le prix ...?	kel ay ler pree ...
per night	par nuit	par nwee
per person	par personne	par per·son

For phone or written requests:

To ...	A l'attention de ...
From ...	De la part de ...
Date	Date
I'd like to book ...	Je voudrais réserver ...
in the name of ...	au nom de ...
from ... to ...	du ... au ...
credit card (...)	(...) carte de crédit
number	numéro de
expiry date	date d'expiration de la
Please confirm availability and price.	Veuillez confirmer la disponibilité et le prix.

I'd like (a) ...	Je voudrais ...	zher voo·dray ...
single room	une chambre à un lit	ewn shom·brer a un lee
double-bed room	une chambre avec un grand lit	ewn shom·brer a·vek un gron lee
twin room (with two beds)	une chambre avec des lits jumeaux	ewn shom·brer a·vek day lee zhew·mo
room with a bathroom	une chambre avec une salle de bain	ewn shom·brer a·vek ewn sal der bun
to share a dorm	coucher dans un dortoir	koo·sher don zun dor·twa

I'm leaving today.
Je pars aujourd'hui.   zher par o·zhoor·dwee
We're leaving today.
Nous partons aujourd'hui.   noo par·ton o·zhoor·dwee

CONVERSATION & ESSENTIALS

Hello.	Bonjour.	bon·zhoor
Goodbye.	Au revoir.	o rer·vwa
Yes.	Oui.	wee
No.	Non.	non
Please.	S'il vous plaît.	seel voo play
Thank you.	Merci.	mair·see
You're welcome.	Je vous en prie. De rien. (inf)	zher voo zon pree der ree·en

SIGNS

Chambres Libres	Rooms Available
Police	Police Station
Complet	Full/No Vacancies
Entrée/Sortie	Entrance/Exit
Interdit	Prohibited
Ouvert/Fermé	Open/Closed
Renseignements	Information
Toilettes/WC	Toilets
Femmes	Women
Hommes	Men

Excuse me.
Excuse-moi. ek·skew·zay·mwa
Sorry. (forgive me)
Pardon. par·don
What's your name?
Comment vous kom·mon voo
appelez-vous? (pol) za·pay·lay voo
Comment tu kom·mon tew
t'appelles? (inf) ta·pel
My name is …
Je m'appelle … zher ma·pel …
Where are you from?
De quel pays êtes-vous? der kel pay·ee et·voo
De quel pays es-tu? (inf) der kel pay·ee ay·tew
I'm from …
Je viens de … zher vyen der …
I like …
J'aime … zhem …
I don't like …
Je n'aime pas … zher nem pa …
Just a minute.
Une minute. ewn mee·newt

DIRECTIONS

Where is …?
Où est …? oo ay …
Go straight ahead.
Continuez tout droit. kon·teen·way too drwa
Turn left.
Tournez à gauche. toor·nay a gosh
Turn right.
Tournez à droite. toor·nay a drwat

at the corner
au coin o kwun
at the traffic lights
aux feux o fer

behind	*derrière*	dair·ryair
in front of	*devant*	der·von
far (from)	*loin (de)*	lwun (der)
near (to)	*près (de)*	pray (der)
opposite	*en face de*	on fas der

beach	*la plage*	la plazh
castle	*le château*	ler sha·to
church	*l'église*	lay·gleez
island	*l'île*	leel
main square	*la place centrale*	la plas son·tral
museum	*le musée*	ler mew·zay
old city	*la vieille ville*	la vyay veel
quay	*le quai*	ler kay
ruins	*les ruines*	lay rween
sea	*la mer*	la mair
tourist office	*l'office de*	lo·fees der
	tourisme	too·rees·mer
tower	*la tour*	la toor

EATING OUT

I'd like …, please.
Je voudrais …, zher voo·dray …
s'il vous plaît seel voo play
That was delicious!
C'était délicieux! say·tay day·lee·syer
Please bring the bill.
Apportez-moi l'addition, a·por·tay·mwa la·dee·syon
s'il vous plaît. seel voo play
I'm vegetarian.
Je suis zher swee
végétarien(ne). (m/f) vay·zhay·ta·ryun/ryen

I'm allergic	*Je suis*	zher swee
to …	*allergique …*	za·lair·zheek …
dairy produce	*aux produits*	o pro·dwee
	laitiers	lay·tyay
eggs	*aux œufs*	o zer
nuts	*aux noix*	o nwa
seafood	*aux fruits de mer*	o frwee der mair

HEALTH

I'm ill.

Je suis malade.   zher swee ma·lad

It hurts here.

J'ai une douleur ici.   zhay ewn doo·ler ee·see

I'm ...	*Je suis ...*	zher swee ...
asthmatic	*asthmatique*	as·ma·teek
diabetic	*diabétique*	dee·a·bay·teek
epileptic	*épileptique*	ay·pee·lep·teek

I'm allergic	*Je suis*	zher swee
to ...	*allergique ...*	za·lair·zheek ...
antibiotics	*aux antibiotiques*	o zon·tee·byo·teek
aspirin	*à l'aspirine*	a las·pee·reen
bees	*aux abeilles*	o za·bay·yer
penicillin	*à la*	a la
	pénicilline	pay·nee·see·leen

antiseptic	*l'antiseptique*	lon·tee·sep·teek
aspirin	*l'aspirine*	las·pee·reen
condoms	*des préservatifs*	day pray·zair·va·teef
contraceptive	*le contraceptif*	ler kon·tra·sep·teef
diarrhoea	*la diarrhée*	la dya·ray
medicine	*le médicament*	ler may·dee·ka·mon
nausea	*la nausée*	la no·zay
sunblock cream	*la crème solaire*	la krem so·lair
tampons	*des tampons*	day tom·pon
	hygiéniques	ee·zhen·eek

LANGUAGE DIFFICULTIES

Do you speak English?

Parlez-vous anglais?   par·lay·voo ong·glay

Does anyone here speak English?

Y a-t-il quelqu'un qui   ee a·teel kel·kung kee
parle anglais?   parl ong·glay

What does ... mean?

Que veut dire ...?   ker ver deer ...

I understand.

Je comprends.   zher kom·pron

I don't understand.

Je ne comprends pas.   zher ner kom·pron pa

How do you say ... in French?

Comment est-ce qu'on   kom·mon es kon
dit ... en français?   dee ... on fron·say

Could you write it down, please?

Est-ce que vous pouvez   es·ker voo poo·vay
l'écrire?   lay·kreer

Can you show me (on the map)?

Pouvez-vous m'indiquer   poo·vay·voo mun·dee·kay
(sur la carte)?   (sewr la kart)

NUMBERS

0	*zéro*	zay·ro
1	*un*	un
2	*deux*	der
3	*trois*	trwa
4	*quatre*	ka·trer
5	*cinq*	sungk
6	*six*	sees
7	*sept*	set
8	*huit*	weet
9	*neuf*	nerf
10	*dix*	dees
11	*onze*	onz
12	*douze*	dooz
13	*treize*	trez
14	*quatorze*	ka·torz
15	*quinze*	kunz
16	*seize*	sez
17	*dix-sept*	dee·set
18	*dix-huit*	dee·zweet
19	*dix-neuf*	deez·nerf
20	*vingt*	vung
21	*vingt et un*	vung tay un
22	*vingt-deux*	vung·der
30	*trente*	tront
40	*quarante*	ka·ront
50	*cinquante*	sung·kont
60	*soixante*	swa·sont
70	*soixante-dix*	swa·son·dees
80	*quatre-vingts*	ka·trer·vung
90	*quatre-vingt-dix*	ka·trer·vung·dees
100	*cent*	son
1000	*mille*	meel

PAPERWORK

name	*nom*	nom
nationality	*nationalité*	na·syo·na·lee·tay
date/place	*date/place*	dat/plas
of birth	*de naissance*	der nay·sons
sex/gender	*sexe*	seks
passport	*passeport*	pas·por
visa	*visa*	vee·za

QUESTION WORDS

Who?	*Qui?*	kee
What?	*Quoi?*	kwa
What is it?	*Qu'est-ce que c'est?*	kes ker say
When?	*Quand?*	kon
Where?	*Où?*	oo
Which?	*Quel(le)?* (m/f)	kel
Why?	*Pourquoi?*	poor·kwa
How?	*Comment?*	kom·mon

SHOPPING & SERVICES

I'd like to buy …
Je voudrais acheter …   zher voo·dray ash·tay …
How much is it?
C'est combien?   say kom·byun
I don't like it.
Cela ne me plaît pas.   ser·la ner mer play pa
May I look at it?
Est-ce que je peux   es ker zher per
le/la voir? (m/f)   ler/la vwar
I'm just looking.
Je regarde.   zher rer·gard
It's not expensive.
Ce n'est pas cher.   ser nay pa shair
It's too expensive.
C'est trop cher.   say tro shair
I'll take it.
Je le/la prends. (m/f)   zher ler/la pron

Can I pay by …?	*Est-ce que je peux*	es ker zher per
	payer avec …?	pay·yay a·vek …
credit card	*ma carte de*	ma kart der
	crédit	kray·dee
travellers	*des chèques*	day shek
cheques	*de voyage*	der vwa·yazh

Help!
Au secours!   o skoor
There's been an accident!
Il y a eu un accident!   eel ee a ew un ak·see·don
I'm lost.
Je me suis égaré/e. (m/f)   zhe me swee zay·ga·ray
Leave me alone!
Fichez-moi la paix!   fee·shay·mwa la pay

Call …!	*Appelez …!*	a·play …
a doctor	*un médecin*	un mayd·sun
the police	*la police*	la po·lees

more	*plus*	plews
less	*moins*	mwun
smaller	*plus petit*	plew per·tee
bigger	*plus grand*	plew gron

I'm looking for …	*Je cherche …*	zhe shersh …
a bank	*une banque*	ewn bonk
the (…) embassy	*l'ambassade (de …)*	lam·ba·sahd (der …)
the hospital	*l'hôpital*	lo·pee·tal
the market	*le marché*	ler mar·shay
the police	*la police*	la po·lees
the post office	*le bureau de poste*	ler bew·ro der post
a public phone	*une cabine téléphonique*	ewn ka·been tay·lay·fo·neek
a public toilet	*les toilettes*	lay twa·let

TIME & DATES

today	*aujourd'hui*	o·zhoor·dwee
tomorrow	*demain*	der·mun
yesterday	*hier*	yair

What time is it?
Quelle heure est-il?   kel er ay til
It's (eight) o'clock.
Il est (huit) heures.   il ay (weet) er
It's half past (…)
Il est (…) heures   il ay (…) er
et demie.   ay der·mee

in the morning	du matin	dew ma·tun
in the afternoon	de l'après-midi	der la·pray·mee·dee
in the evening	du soir	dew swar

Monday	lundi	lun·dee
Tuesday	mardi	mar·dee
Wednesday	mercredi	mair·krer·dee
Thursday	jeudi	zher·dee
Friday	vendredi	von·drer·dee
Saturday	samedi	sam·dee
Sunday	dimanche	dee·monsh

January	janvier	zhon·vyay
February	février	fayv·ryay
March	mars	mars
April	avril	a·vreel
May	mai	may
June	juin	zhwun
July	juillet	zhwee·yay
August	août	oot
September	septembre	sep·tom·brer
October	octobre	ok·to·brer
November	novembre	no·vom·brer
December	décembre	day·som·brer

TRANSPORT

PUBLIC TRANSPORT

What time does	À quelle heure	a kel er
... leave/arrive?	part/arrive ...?	par/a·reev ...
boat	le bateau	ler ba·to
bus	le bus	ler bews
plane	l'avion	la·vyon
train	le train	ler trun

I'd like a ...	Je voudrais	zher voo·dray
ticket.	un billet ...	un bee·yay ...
1st class	de première classe	der prem·yair klas
2nd class	de deuxième classe	der der·zyem klas
one-way	simple	sum·pler
return	aller et retour	a·lay ay rer·toor

I want to go to ...
Je voudrais aller à ...   zher voo·dray a·lay a ...
The train has been delayed.
Le train est en retard.   ler trun ay ton rer·tar
The train has been cancelled.
Le train a été annulé.   ler trun a ay·tay a·new·lay

ROAD SIGNS

Cédez la Priorité	Give Way
Danger	Danger
Défense de Stationner	No Parking
Entrée	Entrance
Interdiction de Doubler	No Overtaking
Péage	Toll
Ralentissez	Slow Down
Sens Interdit	No Entry
Sens Unique	One-Way
Sortie	Exit

the first	le premier (m)	ler prer·myay
	la première (f)	la prer·myair
the last	le dernier (m)	ler dair·nyay
	la dernière (f)	la dair·nyair
platform	le numéro	ler new·may·ro
number	de quai	der kay
ticket office	le guichet	ler gee·shay
timetable	l'horaire	lo·rair
train station	la gare	la gar

PRIVATE TRANSPORT

I'd like to hire	Je voudrais	zher voo·dray
a/an...	louer ...	loo·way ...
4WD	un quatre-quatre	un kat·kat
bicycle	un vélo	un vay·lo
car	une voiture	ewn vwa·tewr
motorbike	une moto	ewn mo·to

Is this the road to ...?
C'est la route pour ...?   say la root poor ...
Where's a service station?
Où est-ce qu'il y a   oo es keel ee a
une station-service?   ewn sta·syon·ser·vees
Please fill it up.
Le plein, s'il vous plaît.   ler plun seel voo play
I'd like ... litres.
Je voudrais ... litres.   zher voo·dray ... lee·trer
(How long) Can I park here?
(Combien de temps)   (kom·byun der ton)
Est-ce que je peux   es ker zher per
stationner ici?   sta·syo·nay ee·see?

| petrol/gas | essence | ay·sons |
| diesel | diesel | dyay·zel |

LANGUAGE

I need a mechanic.

  J'ai besoin d'un   zhay ber·zwun dun
  mécanicien.   may·ka·nee·syun

The car/motorbike has broken down (at …)

  La voiture/moto est   la vwa·tewr/mo·to ay
  tombée en panne (à …) tom·bay on pan (a …)

The car/motorbike won't start.

  La voiture/moto ne veut la vwa·tewr/mo·to ner ver
  pas démarrer.   pa day·ma·ray

I have a flat tyre.

  Mon pneu est à plat.   mom pner ay ta pla

I've run out of petrol.

  Je suis en panne d'essence. zher swee zon pan day·sons

I had an accident.

  J'ai eu un accident.   zhay ew un ak·see·don

TRAVEL WITH CHILDREN

Is there …?

  Y a-t-il …?   ee a·teel …

I need …

  J'ai besoin de…   zhay ber·zwun der…

a car baby seat	*un siège-enfant*	un syezh·on·fon
a child-minding service	*une garderie*	ewn gar·dree
a children's menu	*un menu pour enfant*	un mer·new poor on·fon
disposable nappies/diapers	*couches-culottes*	koosh·kew·lot
an (English-speaking) babysitter	*une baby-sitter (qui parle anglais)*	ewn ba·bee·see·ter (kee parl ong·glay)
infant milk formula	*lait maternisé*	lay ma·ter·nee·zay
a highchair	*une chaise haute*	ewn shayz ot
a potty	*un pot de bébé*	un po der bay·bay
a stroller	*une poussette*	ewn poo·set

Do you mind if I breastfeed here?

  Je peux allaiter mon zher per a·lay·tay mon
  bébé ici?   bay·bay ee·see

Are children allowed?

  Les enfants sont permis? lay zon·fon son pair·mee

French

with 3500 word two-way dictionary

Also available from Lonely Planet:
French Phrasebook

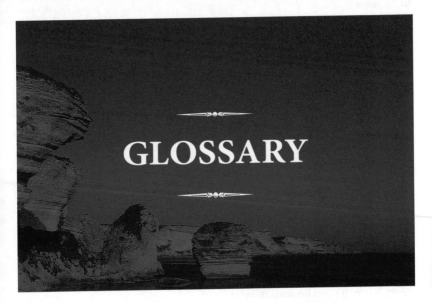

GLOSSARY

This glossary is a list of Corsican (C) and French (F) terms you may come across in Corsica. For terms for food and drinks, and other culinary vocabulary, see p238.

aiguille (F) – rock mass or mountain peak shaped like a needle
anse (F) – cove
AOC – Appellation d'Origine Contrôlée; mark of quality for food and wines
auberge (F) – inn

baie (F) – bay
barrage (F) – dam
bergerie (F) – shepherd's hut
bocca (C) – mountain pass
bouches (F) – straits
buvettes – drinks stands

calanque (F) – rocky inlet
cap (F)– cape
capu (C) – see *cap*; also spelt *capo*
cascade (F) – waterfall
castellu (C) – castle
cave (F) – cellar

chambres d'hôtes (F) – B&B
chapelle (F) – chapel
clos (F) – vineyard
cochon coureur (F) – free-ranging pig
col (F) – mountain pass
commune (F) – smallest unit of local government in rural areas

défilé (F) – gorge, narrow pass
département (F) – administration division of France
désert (F) – desert

église (F) – church
étang (F) – lake, pond

fiera (C) – fair, festival
foire (F) – see *fiera*
forêt (F) – forest
FLNC – Front de Libération Nationale de la Corse; Corsican National Liberation Front

gîte (F) – see *gîte rural*
gîte d'étape (F) – walkers' lodge
gîte rural (F) – self-contained cottage

golfe (F) – bay, gulf
goulet (F) – narrows; bottleneck at entrance to a harbour

île (F) – isle, island

lac (F) – lake

mairie (F) – town hall
maison (F) – office, house
maquis (F) – scrub vegetation
marché (F) – market

pétanque (F) – form of boules
phare (F) – lighthouse
place (F) – square
plage (F) – beach
PNRC – Parc Naturel Régional de la Corse; Corsican Nature Reserve
port de plaisance (F) – marina
pozzi (C) – pits
pozzines (C) – small waterholes linked together by rivulets
préfecture (F) – departmental capital
pointe (F) – point, headland
punta (C) – see *pointe*

randonnée (F) – walk

sanglier (C) – wild boar

tafoni (C) – cavities
torre (C) – circular monument
tour (F) – tower

vallée (F) – valley
vasque (F) – natural pool

BEHIND THE SCENES

THIS BOOK

This is the 5th edition of *Corsica*. Jean-Bernard Carillet and Miles Roddis wrote the previous edition. This guidebook was commissioned in Lonely Planet's London office, and produced by the following:

Commissioning Editors Paula Hardy, Caroline Sieg
Coordinating Editors Justin Flynn, Susan Paterson, Laura Stansfeld
Coordinating Cartographer Amanda Sierp
Coordinating Layout Designer Aomi Hongo
Managing Editor Imogen Bannister
Managing Cartographers Adrian Persoglia, Herman So
Managing Layout Designer Sally Darmody
Assisting Editors Kim Hutchins, Sally O'Brien, Martine Power, Jeanette Wall
Assisting Cartographer Tadhgh Knaggs
Cover Research Marika Mercer, lonely planetimages.com
Internal Image Research Sabrina Dalbesio, lonelyplanetimages.com
Language Content Robyn Loughnane
Project Managers Rachel Imeson, Glenn van der Knijff
Thanks to Mark Adams, Lucy Birchley, Yvonne Bischofberger, Janine Eberle, Owen Eszeki, Mark Germanchis, Michelle Glynn, Imogen Hall, Lauren

THE LONELY PLANET STORY

Fresh from an epic journey across Europe, Asia and Australia in 1972, Tony and Maureen Wheeler sat at their kitchen table stapling together notes. The first Lonely Planet guidebook, *Across Asia on the Cheap*, was born.

Travellers snapped up the guides. Inspired by their success, the Wheelers began publishing books to Southeast Asia, India and beyond. Demand was prodigious, and the Wheelers expanded the business rapidly to keep up. Over the years, Lonely Planet extended its coverage to every country and into the virtual world via lonelyplanet.com and the Thorn Tree message board.

As Lonely Planet became a globally loved brand, Tony and Maureen received several offers for the company. But it wasn't until 2007 that they found a partner whom they trusted to remain true to the company's principles of travelling widely, treading lightly and giving sustainably. In October of that year, BBC Worldwide acquired a 75% share in the company, pledging to uphold Lonely Planet's commitment to independent travel, trustworthy advice and editorial independence.

Today, Lonely Planet has offices in Melbourne, London and Oakland, with over 500 staff members and 300 authors. Tony and Maureen are still actively involved with Lonely Planet. They're travelling more often than ever, and they're devoting their spare time to charitable projects. And the company is still driven by the philosophy of *Across Asia on the Cheap*: 'All you've got to do is decide to go and the hardest part is over. So go!'

Hunt, Laura Jane, Nic Lehman, Ali Lemer, John Mazzocchi, Annelies Mertens, Lucy Monie, Wayne Murphy, Darren O'Connell, Trent Paton, Julie Sheridan, Saralinda Turner

THANKS

JEAN-BERNARD CARILLET

A huge thanks to everyone who helped out and made this trip an enlightenment, including Marie, Emilie, Paul-André, François and Emmanuelle, as well as all the wonderful Corsican people who helped along the way.

Miles and Neil deserve a pat on their back for having borne with me and my numerous queries – thanks guys for your sense of humour and the meal we had in Bastia.

Laura, editor extraordinaire, deserves huge thanks for her top-notch editing and invaluable insight. The carto team, including Mandy Sierp, also helped shape a great guide. I'm also grateful to Caroline, Paula and Imogen for their constant support throughout this challenging adventure.

At home, a phenomenal *gros bisou* to my daughter Eva, who gives meaning and direction to my otherwise roving life.

MILES RODDIS

Ingrid was, as always, great company and hugely supportive – not least with her impressive Lewis Hamilton impersonations around Corsica's tight bends and ribbon-narrow country roads. Sue and Brian Swift were fun travelling companions and shared some great walks with us. Claire Hall of Direct Corsica (www.directcorsica.com) shared some of her insider knowledge of the island, while reader and fellow cyclist Stephen Reynolds sent an exceptionally helpful updating email (always trust a man on a bike!). The lunch Jean-Bernard, Neil and I shared on a terrace in Bastia stays with me as a reminder of two congenial, experienced, enthusiastic, virtual travelling companions. Tourist-office staff were almost without exception a joy to deal with and well informed. Thank you, once again, to Anne-Marie Piazzoli (Calvi), Davia Boutillat (Île Rousse), Nathalie (Piana), Céline Bonzom and Tiina (Porto), Claire Zajpt (Cargèse), and both Pierre-André and Michèle (Ajaccio). My chap-

SEND US YOUR FEEDBACK

We love to hear from travellers – your comments keep us on our toes and help make our books better. Our well-travelled team reads every word on what you loved or loathed about this book. Although we cannot reply individually to postal submissions, we always guarantee that your feedback goes straight to the appropriate authors, in time for the next edition. Each person who sends us information is thanked in the next edition – and the most useful submissions are rewarded with a free book.

To send us your updates – and find out about Lonely Planet events, newsletters and travel news – visit our award-winning website: **www.lonelyplanet.com/contact**.

Note: We may edit, reproduce and incorporate your comments in Lonely Planet products such as guidebooks, websites and digital products, so let us know if you don't want your comments reproduced or your name acknowledged. For a copy of our privacy policy visit www.lonelyplanet.com/privacy.

ters are all for Laila, hoping that she'll come to love nature's grandeur and wildness as much as her Yayo does.

NEIL WILSON
Many thanks to the helpful and enthusiastic staff at tourist offices throughout Corsica, to Carol Downie for company during the restaurant research, and to Ian Jones for his wealth of knowledge about the island. Also, many thanks to coauthors JB and Miles.

OUR READERS

Many thanks to the travellers who used the last edition and wrote to us with helpful hints, useful advice and interesting anecdotes:
Rahul Butta, Alain Chaumont, Jakob Eder, Katrin Flatscher, Neil Fox, Naomi Fox, Mélina Mailhot, Francesca Manta, Margaret McPhate, Tomas Moehler, Christian Oberdanner, Lidia Pavlin, Motel Ta Kladia, Rachel Tucker

ACKNOWLEDGMENTS

Many thanks to the following for the use of their content:

GR®, GRP®, their waymarkings (white/red and yellow/red), and PR® are the Fédération Française de la Randonnée Pédestre's registered trademarks. All rights reserved – www.ffrandonnee.fr

All images are the copyright of the photographers unless otherwise indicated. Many of the images in this guide are available for licensing from Lonely Planet Images: www.lonelyplanetimages.com.

INDEX

INDEX

INDEX

INDEX

MAP LEGEND

Note Not all symbols displayed below appear in this guide.

ROUTES

Tollway
Freeway
Primary Road
Secondary Road
Tertiary Road
Lane
Unsealed Road
Under Construction

Tunnel
Pedestrian Mall
Steps
Walking Track
Walking Path
Walking Tour
Walking Tour Detour
Pedestrian Overpass

TRANSPORT

Ferry Route & Terminal
Metro Line & Station
Monorail & Stop
Bus Route & Stop

Train Line & Station
Underground Rail Line
Tram Line & Stop
Cable Car, Funicular

AREA FEATURES

Airport
Beach
Building
Campus
Cemetery, Christian
Cemetery, Other

Land
Mall, Plaza
Market
Park
Sportsground
Urban

HYDROGRAPHY

River, Creek
Canal
Water
Swamp
Lake (Dry)

BOUNDARIES

International
State, Provincial
Suburb
City Wall
Cliff

SYMBOLS IN THE KEY

Essential Information
Tourist Office
Police Station

Exploring
Beach
Buddhist
Castle, Fort
Christian
Diving, Snorkelling
Garden
Hindu
Islamic
Jewish
Monument
Museum, Gallery
Place of Interest
Snow Skiing
Swimming Pool
Ruin
Tomb
Winery, Vineyard
Zoo, Bird Sanctuary

Gastronomic Highlights
Eating
Cafe

Nightlife
Drinking
Entertainment

Recommended Shops
Shopping

Accommodation
Sleeping
Camping

Transport
Airport, Airfield
Cycling, Bicycle Path
Border Crossing
Bus Station
Ferry
General Transport
Train Station
Taxi Rank

Parking
Parking

OTHER MAP SYMBOLS

Information
Bank, ATM
Embassy, Consulate
Hospital, Medical
Internet Facilities
Post Office
Telephone

Geographic
Cave
Lighthouse
Lookout
Mountain, Volcano
National Park
Picnic Area

LONELY PLANET OFFICES

AUSTRALIA
Head Office
Locked Bag 1, Footscray, Victoria 3011
☎ 03 8379 8000, fax 03 8379 8111
talk2us@lonelyplanet.com.au

USA
150 Linden St, Oakland, CA 94607
☎ 510 250 6400, toll free 800 275 8555
fax 510 893 8572
info@lonelyplanet.com

UK
2nd fl, 186 City Road, London EC1V 2NT
☎ 020 7106 2100, fax 020 7106 2101
go@lonelyplanet.co.uk

Published by Lonely Planet Publications Pty Ltd
ABN 36 005 607 983
© Lonely Planet 2010
© photographers as indicated 2010
Cover photograph Parata tower and Îles
Sanguinaires, Jean-Pierre Lescourret/Corbis.
Internal title-page photograph Bonifacio, Jean-
Bernard Carillet. Many of the images in this guide
are available for licensing from Lonely Planet Images:

Mixed Sources
Product group from well-managed
forests and other controlled sources
www.fsc.org Cert no. SGS-COC-005002
© 1996 Forest Stewardship Council
FSC